The Political Economy of Syria
under Asad

The Political Economy of Syria under Asad

VOLKER PERTHES

I.B.TAURIS
LONDON · NEW YORK

Published in 1995 by
I.B.Tauris & Co Ltd
Victoria House, Bloomsbury Square
London WC1B 4DZ
175 Fifth Avenue
New York NY10010

This paperback edition published in 1997

In the United States of America
and Canada distributed by
St Martin's Press
175 Fifth Avenue
New York NY10010

A CIP record for this book is available from the British Library

A full CIP record is available from the Library of Congress

ISBN 1 86064 192 X

Typeset in Monotype Ehrhardt
by Lucy Morton, London SE12

Printed and bound in Great Britain by WBC Ltd,
Bridgend, Mid Glamorgan

Contents

Acknowledgements

Many people have encouraged and helped me to write this book. I am particularly indebted to those friends and colleagues from Syria who have contributed information and hints, critical discussion and advice, and, not least, their practical assistance, friendship and hospitality. Even though they are in no way responsible for the contents of this book, or for any of the errors and misinterpretations that it might contain, I refrain from mentioning them by name. Such public acknowledgement could still be disadvantageous under the present circumstances. The book, of course, also owes much to discussions with, and to suggestions and comments from, friends and colleagues outside Syria among whom I would like to mention, exemplary not exclusively, Hanna Batatu, Steven Heydemann, Eberhard Kienle, Franz Nuscheler, Sylvia Pölling, Robert Springborg, and Steven Tamari.

There are other people too, whose help can and should be publicly acknowledged. Among them are Udo Steinbach, Director of the German Orient-Institut, whose encouragement and practical support was very important during an early phase of the work on this book; Rania Kanj, then a student of sociology and my research assistant at the American University of Beirut (AUB); and Susanne Fries, documentalist and assistant to the Middle East section at the Stiftung Wissenschaft und Politik in Ebenhausen, whose support in finalizing the book I very much appreciate. Particular thanks are due to Helen Tuschling, a colleague at the AUB and now a professor of English literature at the University of Alexandria, who assiduously took on the unrewarding task of making my English more readable. Material support has been extended, in different phases of the work, by the Stiftung Volkswagenwerk, and by my current employer, the Stiftung Wissenschaft und Politik.

This book has a history, and not everything is said for the first time. Research in Syria has been done, on and off, from 1986 to the spring of 1994 and I have cannibalized some of my earlier publications in order to provide a book. Chapter III is basically an updated and summarized version of a chapter from my *Staat und Gesellschaft in Syrien*. Other chapters include passages from earlier publications of mine in the *Middle East Report*, the *International Journal of Middle East Studies*, and in edited volumes.

The book is dedicated to my father who first brought me to the Middle East.

Note on Transliteration

For the transliteration of Arabic titles and names, I have used the system applied by the *International Journal of Middle East Studies*. Diacritical marks have been omitted, except for ' for `ayn and ' for *hamza*. To make things easier for readers, the titles of conference volumes from party or trade-union conferences, from the annual symposia of the Economic Sciences Association, or similar events in Syria, have been translated into English. It goes without saying that these volumes are all in Arabic. Other Arabic books and articles are referred to by their original titles; English translations are given in the bibliography.

List of Tables and Figure

List of Abbreviations

ASBP	Arab Socialist Ba'th Party
ASU	Arab Socialist Union
CBS	Central Bureau of Statistics
IMF	International Monetary Fund
LS	Syrian Pound
MEED	Middle East Economic Digest
MEFT	Ministry of Economy and Foreign Trade
NC	National Command
PNF	Progressive National Front
RC	Regional Command
SAR	Syrian Arab Republic
SCP	Syrian Communist Party
SWB	Summary of World Broadcast/BBC

To my father

CHAPTER ONE

Introduction

This book deals with the political economy of contemporary Syria. Syria's political structures and regional position, its economy, and its social structure have undergone enormous changes since 1963, when a military coup brought the Ba'th, the main Arab nationalist party of the Arab world, to power, and in particular since the assumption of power by Hafiz al-Asad in 1970. There exists today a body of scholarly literature on Syria whose changing contents and approaches reflect the country's socio-economic and political developments. The reality of the Syria of the 1990s can hardly be grasped through the categories and concepts appropriate for the pre-Ba'thist and even the early Ba'thist era. Syria is no longer the basically rural country and agricultural economy, ruled by the representatives of 100 or so wealthy landed families, which it was after independence. It is no longer the weak and vulnerable player of the regional and international "struggle for Syria" in the 1950s; nor is it the unstable political system which, even during the first period of Ba'th rule until 1970, was characterized by one of the world's highest records for military putsches and coup attempts.[1] There is no need, in this study, for an extensive narrative of events;[2] however, a brief outline of Syria's recent historical development will be given in the following section.

1. Historical Developments and Literature on Contemporary Syria

A French mandate since 1920, Syrian gained formal independence in 1943 and full sovereignty in 1946, when the last French soldiers left the country. According to its constitution, independent Syria was a parliamentary democracy. *De facto* power was concentrated in the hands of the landlord and merchant class, and, increasingly, of the military establishment. The ruling elite was responsible for Syria stumbling into the first Arab–Israeli war, and it largely failed to solve the country's domestic political and social problems. From 1949 the country experienced a series of military takeovers and coup attempts. In the mid-1950s Syria became the focus of a regional conflict concerning the establishment of a Western-oriented military alliance, the Baghdad Pact. Syria's neutralistic stance made it subject to strong Western pressures. While failing to push Syria into the Pact, these pressures destabilized the country and contributed to its hasty and ill-prepared unification with Egypt in 1958. When the leadership of the thus-established United Arab Republic (UAR) embarked on an outspokenly socialist course in 1961, launching a wave of nationalizations that included some of the largest Syrian establishments, a group of conservative Syrian officers assumed power in Damascus and terminated this first unification experiment in contemporary Arab history. Syria re-emerged as a sovereign state, with the political elite of the 1950s back in power for another year and a half.

With the coup, or "revolution" as it was thenceforward referred to, of 8 March 1963, a new power elite took over. The political system of the Ancien Régime, formally at least a parliamentary democracy, was replaced by an internally fragile regime composed of competing forces, namely the civilian leaders of the Ba'th party and young military officers of strong nationalist and, for the most part, socialist convictions, who eventually got the upper hand.[3]

Syria's new rulers moved to set the country on a socialist or, at least, egalitarian path of development in an attempt to liquidate the economic basis of the old ruling class which they had already removed from political power. They speeded up a land reform already initiated under the UAR and, in 1964/65, they nationalized a large number of industrial and commercial establishments. Their radical social policies and a no less radical rhetoric which confronted both the West and the conservative Arab states, left the regime regionally and internationally widely isolated; only relations with the Soviet Union and the other socialist states were expanded. At the same time the political leadership was internally divided into different factions and *jama'at*,[4] each of which had its own basis in the army and the party. Frictions occurred along both political and sectarian lines. In February 1966, a radical wing of the party, led by officers of mainly middle class, rural and minority, particularly Alawi origin, gained the upper hand by military force.[5] Caught in its internal struggles, the regime had to face the 1967 war unprepared; Israeli forces were able to occupy the Golan heights without major resistance.

In November 1970, after some two years of open conflict within the power elite about both internal and foreign policy directions, General Hafiz al-Asad took power in a new military coup. Like his main rival for power, Salah Jadid, Asad was an Alawi military officer from the Latakia region and a convinced Ba'thist since his days as a high-school student. A member of the Ba'thist military committee, which since 1963 had largely controlled Syrian politics, in 1964 Asad became the commander of Syria's air force, and in 1966, following an inner-party and inner-regime coup of leftist forces which he had supported, Minister of Defence. Asad's influence within the regime grew after the spring of 1969 when he staged a first, partial coup of his own that enabled him to put some of his loyalists into important government positions.

With his coup or "Correctionist Movement" as it has since been officially called, socialism, though maintained as a tenet in the rhetoric of the ruling party, was turned into etatism or state capitalism. Restrictions on the private sector were relaxed and rapid economic growth, largely through public expenditure, became the main objective of economic and development policies.[6] The new regime improved its relations with the conservative Arab states and strengthened its ties with Egypt. The October War of 1973 was, partly at least, an efficiently coordinated Syrian–Egyptian–Saudi affair. Though not a military victory, it was certainly a political one. The combination of such national success and tangible economic growth allowed Asad to enjoy a high degree of popularity and legitimacy for several years.

Only after Asad's takeover did stable political structures emerge. In 1971, a parliament was established; in 1972, the Progressive National Front (PNF), an institutionalized coalition of the Ba'th party with a group of tolerated, smaller parties, was set up; and in 1973 a new constitution was promulgated.[7] With government control over a substantial part of agricultural and industrial production and distribution, a rapidly growing public sector and public administration, and with public expenditure being the main determinant of the course of economic development, the state, so it seemed, had developed into an active interventionist and largely autonomous player, creating, rather than being dominated by, social forces and socio-economic relations.[8]

That the state was not completely autonomous became clear during the 1979–82 period as popular unrest and, in parts of Syria, a situation of civil war shook the country and threatened to bring down the regime. The confrontation between the regime and an Islamist-led opposition represented a complex social conflict. A general disenchantment with the regime's regional policies, particularly its open military involvement in Lebanon, begun in 1976, widespread corruption and nepotism, the unrestrained behaviour of the security forces, and the sectarian composition of the regime's core, along with growing social inequalities, and, perhaps, the disappointment and relative economic losses of parts of the independent middle classes of Syria's north-central cities, all played a role.[9] The opposition was only crushed after a brutal and bloody climax in Hama, where government troops put down a rebellion by military force, destroying most of the city. Under pressure, the state had fully displayed its oppressive character; its ruthlessness in dealing with the conflict led Syria's probably best informed scholarly observer at the time to describe its state simply as barbaric.[10]

However, the state as it emerged after 1970 was more than an instrument of brute force. Over the Asad years, regime institutions were developed, the bureaucracy expanded, and corporatist structures bringing large parts of the society under the organizing umbrella of the state were set up and consolidated. Though flawed in some respects, a comparatively stable authoritarian, or authoritarian-bureaucratic state came into being.[11] In 1983/84, with Asad being hospitalized, an open conflict for his possible succession emerged among his barons. The conflict was quickly contained as soon as the President regained his health.[12] General internal stability helped make it possible for Syria to become, for the first time, a serious and active player in regional politics rather than an object of other powers' strategies and intrigues.[13] Syria's importance on the regional scene grew with Egypt's signing its peace treaty with Israel and its subsequent ouster from the Arab League in 1979. Remaining the only confrontation state Israel had to take seriously, Syria began to develop a doctrine of national security which stipulated that it alone build up a "strategic parity with the enemy".

The failure of the then US administration to integrate Syria in its endeavours for a settlement in the Middle East, as well as growing internal pressures, helped to make the Syrian leadership once again lean more heavily on the Soviet Union. Soviet arms shipments increased, and, in 1980, a Soviet–Syrian Treaty of Friendship and

Cooperation was signed. However, Syria failed to become a Soviet proxy in the Middle East, and Soviet obligations towards Syria remained limited. In 1982, Moscow watched silently as the Syrian army was defeated and around a third of her air force was destroyed by Israeli forces in Lebanon, in a war Syria had sought to escape.[14] This blow destroyed whatever illusions Syria might have held about the possibility of actually achieving strategic parity with Israel.[15] In the following years, due to its perennial conflict with the PLO mainstream, its sometimes intransigent policies in Lebanon, its support of Iran in the first Gulf War and its alleged involvement in international terrorism, the Syrian regime manoeuvred itself into a somewhat isolated position both regionally and internationally. Only in the late 1980s did a series of decisive moves to improve its regional position meet with considerable success. Shortly after consenting to the Arab League's 1989 decision to readmit Egypt, Damascus reestablished diplomatic relations with Cairo and a rapid Syrian–Egyptian rapprochement took place. By 1990 a strong working relationship between the two countries had emerged which became clearly visible during the Gulf Crisis and War of 1990/91. Syria's participation in the anti-Iraqi coalition reflected its generally pragmatic policy approach and its strong relations with Saudi Arabia. So did Syria's decision to take part in the US-sponsored Middle East peace negotiations that started with the Madrid conference of October 1991. Since its acceptance of UN resolutions 242 and 338 in 1973, Syria had considered a negotiated settlement of the Arab–Israeli conflict a possibility, a military solution clearly being out of the question.

Analytical approaches and judgements concerning Syria's regional policies differ widely. On the question of the Arab–Israeli conflict, its sources and implications, for instance, some authors have tried to prove Syria's basic unwillingness to accept a peaceful settlement and its expansionist ambitions,[16] while others – notably scholars with a greater knowledge of Syria's internal dynamics – have emphasized not only Syria's importance as an active player in a Middle Eastern peace process, but also the necessity of taking its wish for a settlement and its national security considerations as seriously as those of other regional powers.[17] The fact that there is a discussion over Syria's foreign policies is noteworthy in the first place. Thirty, even 20 years earlier, there was hardly any foreign policy of Syria's own making to deal with.

Over the 1980s, parallel to its relative regional isolation, the country was hit by a deep economic crisis revealing the flaws of its etatist pattern of development based on import substitution.[18] A gradual process of economic policy change began, eventually bringing about a reversal of the overall development strategy, giving form to a more market-oriented economy and increasing the importance of the private sector.[19] Since the late 1980s, perestroika in the Soviet Union and the eventual breakdown of Eastern Europe's socialist regimes as well as Syria's internal economic adjustment have given rise to questions as to whether changes in the international environment and the economic system will in the end have to be followed by a similarly far-reaching restructuring of the political system.[20]

2. Research Interest and Basic Assumptions

Syria's ongoing process of economic transformation is the main focus of attention of this book. Economic transformation and structural adjustment, however narrow or far-reaching, should basically be understood as political rather than purely economic processes. They are matters of policy reform and of political choices that involve winners and losers.[21] The study of Syria, in this respect, could be of special importance for a general understanding of the internal dynamics of transformation processes in other countries, particularly in the Middle East, since Syria can serve, in a sense, as a laboratory case in which external influence has been excluded to a large, if not to the largest possible extent. Political and policy changes in Syria, in other words, have to be viewed as being mainly the outcome of the interplay of internal forces. Syria's changing political environment has, of course, to be taken into consideration. There can be no doubt that the Arab–Israeli peace process or the disappearance of the Soviet bloc has some influence on the economic reform process. In general, however, their impact should not be overstated, and oversimplifications which directly relate Syria's economic opening up to a changing international and regional environment[22] should be warned against.

This is not to say that Syria is autonomous vis-à-vis the regional or the world economy or immune to the political and economic impact of the world system. Syria certainly is dependent on world economic developments outside its control. It is evident, however, that Syria's ongoing transformation process has been characterized by a far higher degree of independence, that is, by far less foreign interference, than has been the case in other, comparable, countries. The relative independence from external forces of Syria's transformation process has even led one scholar to doubt the validity of explanations of Egypt's *infitah* policies mainly in terms of external pressure.[23] Such doubts represent, perhaps, an overgeneralization of evidence from the Syrian case, in much the same way as other scholars may have overgeneralized the Egyptian case. The pressure that international actors, particularly the World Bank, the IMF and development aid agencies of industrialized countries, have exerted on Egyptian policy-makers to adjust their economy according to the former's neo-liberal orientations, thus directly obtaining a role in the formulation of Egyptian development strategies, is well documented.[24] The absence of a similar degree of pressure on Syrian policy-makers does not so much belie the evidence of the Egyptian case, as point to structural differences between Syria and Egypt or other countries of the region, which otherwise share with Syria quite a number of socio-economic and political-structural traits and have undergone similar or at least partially comparable development experiences.[25]

A relatively high level of independence in political decision-making applies not only to Syria's economic policies, but also to other policy fields, and may, in hindsight, be the most important developmental achievement of Ba'thist rule. The absence, to a large extent, of foreign interference, is likely to have enabled the regime to follow a particularly cautious approach in executing economic reform and adjustments, allowing these processes to go ahead comparatively smoothly, i.e. without disturbances. Syria's high level of independence from external forces may thus have contributed to the striking stability of its regime which, to the surprise of a number of international and domestic observers, has survived and indeed remained almost unaffected by dramatic changes in the international environment, including the loss of its main international ally, the Soviet Union, periods of far-reaching regional isolation, a severe economic crisis, and, at the same time, a dangerous loss of internal legitimacy.

In the light of such a comparatively high degree of independence, we assume that the transformation process Syria has experienced since the 1980s represents a domestically engineered response to economic needs. Specific interest will therefore be attached to the question of how such economic needs were translated into reform – or non-reform – policies, that is, to the decision-making process. Decisions, here, are understood, not as a cognitive process of rational choice, but as a

complex collective process of action determined by institutional structures, and by conflicts and collusion of interests.[26] There exist a
number of detailed studies on specific decision-making processes in
Arab states. Most of them deal with foreign policy issues. As a rule,
the point of departure of these studies is the assumption that the
head of state is the prime, or final, decision-maker in each of the
countries in question. They then move on to analyse the international,
regional and domestic constraints influencing particular decisions, the
informational inputs, and the structure and role of the decision-
maker's advisory bodies.[27]

Where economic policy decisions are at stake, even in highly centralized authoritarian systems, things are somewhat more complicated
and, at the same time, more indicative of how such systems function.[28]
Economic and development policies are rarely seen as the dominion of
the head of state, even though he (or she) may have a final word to say;
they are supposed to involve a much larger spectrum of participants
and societal forces, and they are more open to debate and bargaining
than are the state's "high policies". Furthermore, economic policy-
making, however much it represents a response to economic needs, is
not simply determined by economic factors – resources or constraints,
including those from the regional and international environment – or
by the depth of a crisis. The decision for reform itself is a matter of
choice, as are its direction or goals, scope, limits, speed, and the style
in which it is pursued or pushed through. Being a political process,
economic-policy reform has to be interpreted in the light of political
and institutional structures, political and social alliances, the particular
social and economic interests and orientations of societal forces and
their respective political and economic leverage and state of organization, or bargaining power.

Focusing on economic-policy reform, we will therefore try to
examine in some detail how reform policies, or parts thereof, passed
through Syria's political-institutional structure; how different political
and social forces exerted influence, or tried to do so, on the reform
process; how socio-political alliances changed in the course of the
process; and how much the political decision-making process and the
incorporation into it of different social forces have been subject to
change during the process of economic transformation. As a result,
this study should help to develop a more detailed understanding both
of Syria's political economy and the functioning of the authoritarian-
bureaucratic type of Middle Eastern states.

The study will centre on a structural analysis of the economic, social and political subsystems of Syria, and examine, on that basis, the mechanisms of policy decisions, focusing its attention on the *infitah* of the 1980s and 1990s. This approach reflects the basic notion that the three subsystems – the economic, the social, and the political – are mutually interdependent and, in principle, of equal importance for the socio-economic and political dynamics of Syria or any other country. Reductionist analyses, whether tending to view Syrian regime policies as a direct expression of the orientations of the country's comprador or "parasitic" bourgeoisie, or describing the regime elite as semi- or even totally autonomous from socio-economic forces, are hardly acceptable. Although it is true that the regime, by virtue of its absolute hold over the means of coercion and large parts of the country's internal and external resources, has been able to determine the development of class structures to a great extent, if not to create particular social forces, it is not completely independent of these forces. At the least, it has to secure for itself a stable basis of support whose composition may undergo changes over time.

Class, Sect and State

For quite some time now, it has been almost unanimously accepted that the concept of social classes is not only permissible, but necessary, for the study of social structures in the Arab world.[29] Speaking for many of his colleagues, the Egyptian social scientist Mahmud 'Abd al-Fadil has stressed that to examine the class structure of Arab societies neither falsifies their structure, nor does it contradict the traditions of Arab philosophical or social science thought.[30] Models that deny or understate the existence of classes and the importance of class conflict as a motive power of historical development would be unsuitable for understanding the societal realities of Arab states and misinterpret their internal dynamics.[31] Nevertheless, the development of Arab societies need not follow European patterns, and terms stemming from the sociology of 19th- or 20th-century Europe may have to be redefined.[32]

As essentially economically based formations, classes are primarily defined by property relations. Regarding Syria and Arab societies in general, the particular importance of forms of ownership other than legal property, such as usufruct rights, has to be taken into due consideration. Above that, the shape of class structures in Arab countries is influenced by non-economic or not directly economic variables.[33] These include family status and the independence of one's occupational position, as well as regional, tribal, or confessional affiliations which may determine whether, or how and to what extent, someone can obtain access to political power, whether and how he has or is able to deliver *wasta*.[34] These latter factors are playing a role in the distribution of resources not so much as a relic of pre-capitalist relations of production, but rather as an adaptable feature of a specific form of Third World capitalist development and its distortions.

The analysis of class structures in Arab societies is complicated by several facts. Different relations of production exist beside one another, and it is far from clear that remaining traditional or pre-capitalist structures such as subsistence agriculture, rent capitalism, and small goods production would all, and necessarily, give way to capitalist forms.[35] Social change is rapid, social mobility extremely high. Members of one family may fall into different class categories, and dividing lines between classes are easily blurred – not only as a result of mobility, but also because people work in more than one occupational category. Industrial workers and public servants may at the same time be active in agriculture, be petty employers, moonlight in the private sector or enjoy a rent from some plot of land. This particular high permeability of class structures will therefore have to be taken into account.

A particular problem for scholars analysing Syria or comparable states such as Egypt, Algeria, and Iraq which all at some point have been put on a would-be socialist, actually etatist or state capitalist development path by new elites of mainly rural and middle or lower middle class origin, has been to define, in class terms, the ruling stratum. In the 1960s and 1970s, the concept of a revolutionary (salaried) middle class or petty bourgeoisie stood in the forefront.[36] After some theoretical and practical euphoria, particularly in the 1960s and 1970s, with the concept of petty-bourgeois rule and the new ruling elites, students of Syria and other states in the region started to realize, and analyse, the emergence and existence of what came to be named the 'state class', 'bureaucratic bourgeoisie', or 'state bourgeoisie'. This concept, although somewhat vague and debatable,[37] reflects the development of a non-entrepreneurial, self-recruiting ruling stratum which controls the means of coercion as well as a major part of the means of production in highly interventionist or state capitalist Third World countries. This elite cannot be sufficiently understood in terms of its social class or alternatively regional or ethnic origin, as had been implied by concepts of middle class or minority rule, nor can it be convincingly interpreted as an agent or managing committee of sorts acting on behalf of a nascent bourgeoisie which, on its own, is too weak to develop a capitalist economy. This stratum, having imposed itself on existing state and bureaucratic structures and then developing them – rather than emanating from the state apparatus – does not simply represent the upper echelon of the bureaucracy, and it is certainly not a basically disinterested military–bureaucratic elite led by *raison d'état*.[38] It has been shown how much state bourgeoisies tend to destroy the economic and administrative rationality of their original plans and projects by subjecting it to their private social interest and to a rationality of control and regime stabilization.[39] Whatever the character of the state bourgeoisie, it seems obvious that, in Syria and other countries, its specific political and socio-economic interests have largely been influencing the course of transformation processes. To analyse the motives and mechanisms behind economic transformation, therefore, attention has to be paid to the coalitions and conflicts between this ruling stratum and other social strata of importance. It is reasonable to assume that such coalitions are reflected in the attempts of the regime to mobilize and incorporate into regime structures, or demobilize and disenfranchise, particular societal groups and strata, thereby changing, to some extent, the architecture of the political system.

The concentration, in the course of this study, on horizontal, i.e. class-based, lines of social stratification and the interrelations between class interests, political structures, and policies, is not to deny the importance for the political life of Syria and its social structure of vertical, that is regional, tribal, or confessional ties and loyalties. Both such primordial or pre-capitalist as well as more recently developed class lines, in the broad sense outlined above, play a role as elements of social differentiation, stratification and organization in Syria. The continued existence of primordial ties which, as a result of rapid social change and differentiation affecting all communities, have come increasingly to cut across rather than to parallel horizontal lines of stratification, has left a large part of the population with dual, i.e. class versus ethnic, loyalties. In historical situations of political and social tension in particular, confessional or other ethnic loyalties and bounds can certainly outweigh loyalties of class.[40]

In Syria, this has become particularly evident, as mentioned above, in the factional struggles which erupted within the power elite during the first phase of Ba'thist rule (1966–70). The danger lies in over-stressing the minority paradigm that has emerged, largely in response to these events, in scholarship on Syria, that is, increasingly in regarding the relationship between Syria's Sunni majority and its Alawi minority, and the relations between sectarian affiliation and power, as the timeless and central questions of Syria's socio-political or even socio-economic development.[41] A comparative perspective would help to relativize what might appear as confessionalist determinants of Syrian politics and policies.[42] Consider the largely parallel experiences with nationalizations, statist development approaches, economic liberalization, and generally of political authoritarianism and the use of clientelism in Syria, and countries like Egypt or Tunisia, whose regimes are certainly not minority-dominated. While ethnic or confessional bonds are no doubt primordial, their primordiality does not necessarily determine sectarian or ethnicist consciousness and behaviour which are neither primordial nor stable, and which are only realized in connection with specific interests.[43] Both "primordial" and "modern" ties can be made politically effective. It can be assumed that individuals and groups define their identity alternatively on the basis of the former, the latter, or both – according to what they regard as serving their best interests in a particular social context.[44]

As regards policy decisions in general and economic-policy decisions which this study is to focus upon in particular, we can assume economic needs, political considerations related to stability, security, and the state's regional and international position, class interest and, to a lesser extent, orientations at economic schools of thought to be the major determinants. Economic reform policies affect social groups corresponding to their socio-economic rather than their socio-cultural position; gains and losses, in other words, accrue to and are inflicted upon classes, not ethnic groups. By the same token, policy-oriented coalitions and alliances as well as conflicts over such reforms are brought about or fought by different, more or less organized, representatives of socio-economic, corporate, and institutional interests. Moreover, economic transformation involves a decision-making process that is much more institutionalized and far less personalized than, for instance, the appointment of regional governors or the commanders of key military units, or even the allocation of public monies.

Confessional, regional and tribal loyalties no doubt play a role, particularly in the establishment of patronage networks. Asad has deliberately utilized clientelism to secure his personal control over the authoritarian power system that has emerged under his rule; and his regime has thus developed some distinct patrimonial features. In view of the political benefits the regime could draw from the use and spread of patronage, it has regarded the economic costs, or mis-allocations of resources, which clientelism has engendered, as bear-able. On the whole, as will be shown, Syria has, since Asad's takeover, developed into a fairly strong authoritarian state; political and social control have been firmly established. This has been proven not least by the style, manner, and relative independence in which the eco-nomic reform process has been pursued.

There is another analytical risk to be warned against. The extreme concentration of power in the hands of Hafiz al-Asad, and his un-precedented longevity as Syria's president, have made scholarly – and even more so journalistic – interest focus on the person of the President. Though the importance of Asad for the development of Syrian policies and of its polity cannot be ignored, the concentration on the President in academic as well as semi-academic and simply hagiographic literature[45] has somehow reflected the personality cult that has been celebrated in Syria since Asad's takeover, and has fur-thered the impression of Syria being Asad and Asad being Syria. Too strong a concentration on the President's person may induce observers to overstate the importance of what generally is called the "succession question" and underestimate structural and institutional developments.

3. Sources and Data

This study relies both on scholarly literature on Syria and, as much as possible, on primary sources from the country. These include newspapers and pamphlets, grey literature and laws, published and unpublished statistical material, and a series of interviews with poli-ticians, functionaries, officials, unionists, entrepreneurs and others, conducted over the period 1987–94.

A number of scholars, both Syrians and foreigners, have pointed to the fact that Syrian data, as published by Syria's Central Bureau of Statistics (CBS) or various ministries and government agencies, are often inaccurate, sometimes contradicting each other, or incomplete, or may be retroactively changed.[46] Partly, of course, the lack of data reflects the nature of things. For instance, there can be no official and exact data on smuggling, and where smuggling is considerable, there will be no correct data on the real extent of foreign trade. Lack of data would in such cases reflect a problem rather than constitute one.

Data on socio-structural developments are particularly problematic, and meagre. In not a few cases, available data are of only limited help. Neither agricultural census data nor official statistics on employment give an accurate picture of the rural and urban relations of production and class.[47] There are no data on the distribution of income and wealth. Statistical publications sometimes give contradictory information, not only from different authorities. The data from the Ministry of Industry on private industrial establishments, for instance, differ considerably from those of the CBS,[48] and there are enormous differences between the data of labour-force samples and the respective data of the general censuses of 1970 and 1981, all collected and prepared by the CBS.[49] This is not the place to examine where such deficiencies result from technical problems and where they are due to political interest in disguising particular facts or developments. In some cases, the answer is obvious.[50]

The problematic of lacking accurate data should not lead to the assumption that no relevant statements on Syria's socio-economic development can be made. The implication that more data would necessarily lead to a deeper understanding of the country and the processes to be analysed, represents too deep a faith in figures. Statistical data can help us to grasp socio-economic realities, but they can never fully represent societal processes. It has to be emphasized, banal as it may sound, that all available data have to be handled with care. This includes the World Bank and other international organizations whose data are not neccessarily better or more accurate than those of the Syrian authorities. As a rule, therefore, the statistics compiled and the data used in this study should be regarded as representing only approximate values, as reflecting tendencies rather than accurate figures. In a number of cases, official figures have been cross-checked, corrected or complemented by unofficial and unpublished ones, or judged in the light of qualitative evidence from non-statistical sources and participant observation.

4. Plan of the Study

The following chapter will analyse the economic development of Syria under the Ba'th party, particularly under the rule of Hafiz al-Asad, that is, from 1970 to the present. Special interest will be paid to the change of development strategies and the changing relationship between public and private sectors. Our thesis is that it was Syria's economic crisis in the 1980s more than anything else – that is, more than international pressure or reform demands from the bourgeoisie – that made adjustments necessary. The crisis did not, however, force upon the regime a particular reform strategy and agenda. Rather, the reform process should be viewed as a function of economic needs, social change, and political structures.

Chapter III therefore, attempts a brief structural analysis of Syria's rapidly changing social fabric. Based on a stratification model in which the control over means of production is seen as essential, but status and living conditions are taken into account, classes, or more precisely social strata, will be operationally defined, and the development of their conditions, strength, and their relationship with other strata and with the regime will be examined.

Chapter IV analyses the political structure. Though patrimonial elements play a role, the Syrian regime is conceptualized as authoritarian with a strong tendency to develop corporatist structures. The analyses of the functions of president and government, the apparatuses of coercion and control, the party, parliament, the Progressive National Front and the mass organizations should provide the key to then examine, in chapter V, the mechanisms and dynamics of political decision-making by focusing on the economic transformation process of the late 1980s. The examination concentrates on policy formulation rather than questions of policy implementation or alternative policy options. The main interest is not with bureaucratic action, but with the structural background of political decision processes and its development.

The final chapter will deal with the interrelations of economic transformation and political change in Syria, particularly with the question of whether economic adjustments will eventually imply substantial shifts or even fundamental changes in the power structure. The assumption here is that this will not be the case under the present regime, that this regime, however, has created the institutions which may allow a not too disruptive succession process and the establishment of a less personalized and more participatory successor regime.

Notes

1. On the political history of pre-Ba'thi Syria and its international relations cf. Patrick Seale, *The Struggle for Syria. A Study of Post-War Arab Politics* (New Haven/London: Yale University Press, 2nd ed. 1987); Tabitha Petran, *Syria* (London: Ernest Benn, 1972); Douglas Little, "Cold War and Covert Action. The United States and Syria, 1945–1958", *Middle East Journal*, Vol 44 (1990), pp 51–75. On its economic structure cf. Eugen Wirth, *Syrien. Eine geographische Landeskunde* (Darmstadt: Wissenschaftliche Buchgesellschaft, 1971); on its political economy Badr al-Din Siba'i, *Adwa' 'ala al-rasmal al-ajnabi fi suriya, 1850–1958* [Spotlights on Foreign Capital in Syria 1850–1958] (Damascus: Dar al-Jamahir, 1968); idem, *al-Marhala al-intiqaliyya fi Suriya. 'Ahd al-wahda 1958–1961* [The Transition Phase in Syria. The Union Period 1958–1961] (Beirut: Dar Ibn Khaldun, 1975); Raymond A. Hinnebusch, *Authoritarian Power and State Formation in Ba'thist Syria. Army, Party, and Peasant* (Boulder: Westview, 1990), pp 20–119.

2. For a general record of Syria's political history from the takover of the Ba'th party till the present, cf. e.g. Elizabeth Picard, "La Syrie de 1946 à 1979", in André Raymond (ed), *La Syrie d'aujourd'hui* (Paris: CNRS, 1980); David Roberts, *The Ba'th and the Creation of Modern Syria* (New York: St. Martin's Press, 1987); Patrick Seale, *Asad of Syria: The Struggle for the Middle East* (London: I.B.Tauris, 1988); Volker Perthes, *Staat und Gesellschaft in Syrien, 1970–1989* (Hamburg: Deutsches Orient-Institut, 1990), pp 59–81.

3. Itamar Rabinovich, *Syria under the Ba'th 1963–66. The Army-Party Symbiosis* (Jerusalem: Israel Universities Press, 1972).

4. A *jama'a* or *shilla* is a clique of friends or cronies related by common interest or other ties, frequently also, though not necessarily, by common sectarian, tribal or family background.

5. Cf. Nikolaos van Dam, "Sectarian and Regional Factionalism in the Syrian Political Elite", *Middle East Journal*, Vol 32 (1979), pp 191–209; idem, *The Struggle for Power in Syria. Sectarianism, Regionalism and Tribalism in Politics. 1961–1978* (London: Croom Helm, 1979); Alasdair Drysdale, "The Syrian Political Elite, 1966–1976: A Spatial and Social Analysis", *Middle Eastern Studies*, Vol 17 (1981), pp 3–30; Hanna Batatu, "Some Observations on the Social Roots of Syria's Ruling, Military Group and the Causes for its Dominance", *Middle East Journal*, Vol 35 (1981), pp 331–344; idem, *The Egyptian, Syrian, and Iraqi Revolutions. Some Observations on Their Underlying Causes and Social Character* (Inaugural Lecture, Georgetown University, Center for Contemporary Arab Studies) (Washington: CCAS, 1983).

6. Cf. e.g. Michel Chatelus, "La croissance économique: mutation des structures et dynamisme du déséquilibre", in André Raymond (ed), *La Syrie d'aujourd'hui* (Paris: CNRS, 1980); Rizqallah Hilan, *al-Thaqafa wa-l-tanmiya al-iqtisadiyya fi Suriya wa-l-buldan al-mukhallafa* [Culture and Economic Development in Countries Left Behind] (Damascus: Dar Maysalun, 1981); Munir al-Hamash; *Tatawwur al-iqtisad al-suri al-hadith* [The Development of

the Modern Syrian Economy] (Damascus: Dar al-Jalil, 1983).

7. Cf. Jens Thomas, "Zur Staats- und Gesellschaftsstruktur Syriens", in *Blätter für deutsche und internationale Politik*, Vol 19 (May 1974), pp 461–470; Siegfried Petzold, *Staatsmacht und Demokratie in der Syrischen Arabischen Republik* (Berlin: Staatsverlag der DDR, 1975); Picard, "La Syrie", pp 165ff.

8. Cf. particularly: Jean Hannoyer/Michel Seurat, *État et secteur public industriel en Syrie* (Beirut: CERMOC, 1979); Elizabeth Picard, "Clans militaires et pouvoir ba'thiste en Syrie", *Orient*, Vol 20 (1979), pp 49–62; Michel Seurat, "Les populations, l'état et la société", in Raymond, *La Syrie*; Françoise Metral, "Le monde rural syrien à l'ère des réformes", ibid.; Elisabeth Longuenesse, "L'industrialisation et sa signification sociale", ibid.

9. Cf. Michel Seurat, "Vague d'agitation confessionelle en Syrie", and "La société syrienne contre son État", in idem: *L'État de barbarie*, (Paris: Éditions du Seuil, 1989 [originally published 1979, 1980]); Alasdair Drysdale, "The Asad Regime and its Troubles", *MERIP-Reports*, Vol 12 (November–December 1982), No. 110, pp 3–11; Hanna Batatu, "Syria's Muslim Brethren", ibid., pp 12–20; Fred H. Lawson, "Social Bases for the Hamah Revolt", ibid., pp 24–28; Thomas Mayer, "The Islamic Opposition in Syria, 1961–1982", *Orient*, Vol 24 (1983), pp 589–609; Habib Janhani, "al-Sahwa al-islamiyya fi bilad al-sham: mithal Suriya" [The Islamic Awakening in the Bilad al-Sham: The Example of Syria], in *al-Harakat al-islamiyya al-mu'asira fi al-watan al-'arabi* [Contemporary Islamic Movements in the Arab Homeland] (Beirut: Center for Arab Unity Studies, 2nd ed., 1989 [1987]); Raymond A. Hinnebusch, "Syria", in Shireen Hunter (ed), *The Politics of Islamic Revivalism* (Bloomington: Indiana Univ. Press, 1988); Hans Günter Lobmeyer, *Islamismus und sozialer Konflikt in Syrien* (Ethnizität und Gesellschaft, Occasional Papers No. 26) (Berlin: Das Arabische Buch, 1990); idem, "Islamic Ideology and Secular Discourse. The Islamists of Syria", *Orient*, Vol 32 (1991), pp 395–418.

10. Seurat, "L'État de barbarie. Syrie 1979–1982", in idem, *L'État de barbarie* [1983].

11. Cf. Raymond A. Hinnebusch, "State Formation in a Fragmented Society", *Arab Studies Quarterly*, Vol 4 (1982), pp 177–197; idem, *Peasant and Bureaucracy in Ba'thist Syria. The Political Development of Rural Development* (Boulder: Westview, 1989); idem: *Authoritarian Power*; Perthes, *Staat und Gesellschaft*; Eberhard Kienle; "Entre jama'a et classe. Le pouvoir politique en Syrie contemporaine", *Revue du Monde Musulman et de la Méditerannée*, Vol 59–60 (1991), No. 1–2, pp 211–239.

12. Cf. Alasdair Drysdale, "The Succession Question in Syria", *Middle East Journal*, Vol 39 (1985), pp 246–257.

13. Cf. Seale, *Asad of Syria*.

14. Cf. Elizabeth Picard, "Could Salvation Come from Syria", in Nadim Shehadi/Bridget Harney (eds), *Politics and the Economy in Lebanon* (Oxford/London: Centre for Lebanese Studies/SOAS, 1989).

15. Cf. Volker Perthes, "Syrien", in Veronika Büttner/Joachim Krause (eds), *Die Rüstung der Dritten Welt nach dem Ende des Ost–West–Konflikts* (Baden-

Baden: Nomos, 1994).

16. Cf. most outspokenly Daniel Pipes, *Greater Syria. The History of an Ambition* (New York/Oxford: Oxford University Press, 1990); idem, *Damascus Courts the West: Syrian Politics 1989–1991* (Washington D.C.: The Washington Institute for Near East Policy, 1991).

17. Cf. in particular Alasdair Drysdale/Raymond A. Hinnebusch, *Syria and the Middle East Peace Process* (New York: Council on Foreign Relations Press, 1991); cf. further Moshe Ma'oz, "Syrian–Israeli Relations and the Middle East Peace Process", *The Jerusalem Journal of International Relations*, Vol 14 (September 1992), pp 1–21; Muhammad Muslih, "The Golan: Israel, Syria, and Strategic Calculations", *Middle East Journal*, Vol 47 (1993), pp 611–632; Asad Abu Khalil, "Syria and the Arab–Israeli conflict", *Current History*, Vol 93 (1994), pp 83–86.

18. Cf. Eliayhu Kanovsky, "What's behind Syria's Current Economic Problems?", in *Middle East Contemporary Survey 1983–1984*, Vol 8 (1986), pp 280–345; Patrick Clawson; *Unaffordable Ambitions: Syria's Military Build-Up and Economic Crisis* (Washington D.C.: The Washington Institute for Near East Policy, 1989); Volker Perthes; "The Syrian Economy in the 1980s", *Middle East Journal*, Vol 46 (1992), pp 37–58.

19. Cf. 'Arif Dalila, "Tajribat suriya ma' al-qita'ayn al-'amm wa-l-khass wa-mustaqbal al-tajriba" [Syria's Experiment with the Public and the Private Sectors and the Future of this Experiment], in *al-Qita' al-'amm wa-l-qita' al-khass fi al-watan al-'arabi* [The Public and the Private Sector in the Arab Homeland] [Beirut: Center for Arab Unity Studies, 1990; Fred Lawson, "Libéralisation économique en Syrie et en Irak", *Maghreb-Mashrek*, No. 128 (April–June 1990), pp 27–52; idem, "External versus Internal Pressures for Liberalization in Syria and Iraq", *Journal of Arab Affairs*, Vol 11 (1992), No. 1, pp 1–33; Volker Perthes, "The Syrian Private Industrial and Commercial Sectors and the State", *International Journal of Middle East Studies*, Vol 24 (1992), pp 207–230.

20. Cf. Steven Heydemann, "The Political Logic of Economic Rationality: Selective Stabilization in Syria", in Henri J. Barkey (ed), *The Politics of Economic Reform in the Middle East* (New York: St. Martin's Press, 1992); Raymond A. Hinnebusch, "State and Civil Society in Syria", *Middle East Journal*, Vol 47 (1993), pp 243–257; Volker Perthes, "The Private Sector, Economic Liberalization and the Prospects of Democratization: The Case of Syria and Some Other Arab Countries", in: Ghassan Salamé (ed) *Democracy without Democrats* (London: I.B.Tauris, 1994); idem: "Stages of Economic and Political Liberalization in Syria", in Eberhard Kienle (ed), *Contemporary Syria: Economic Liberalization between Cold War and Cold Peace* (London: British Academic Press, 1994); Eberhard Kienle, "The Return of Politics", ibid.

21. Cf. Yahya M. Sadowski, *Political Vegetables? Businessman and Bureaucrat in the Development of Egyptian Agriculture* (Washington D.C.: Brookings, 1991), pp 12, 50; Timothy J. Piro, "Privatization in Jordan: The Political Economy of Public Sector Reform", Paper submitted to the 26th Annual Middle East

Studies Association Conference of North America, Portland, 28–31 October 1992.

22. Cf. e.g. Françoise Chipaux, "Attendant des progrès dans les négociations avec Israël: La Syrie a amorcé une timide libéralisation", *Le Monde*, 3 March 1993; William E. Schmidt, "In a Region Full of War, Syrians Think of Peace", *International Herald Tribune*, 28 June 1993.

23. Cf. Lawson, "External versus Internal", p 31.

24. Cf. in particular Ali E. Hillal Dessouki, "Policy Making in Egypt: A Case Study of the Open Door Economic Policy", *Social Problems*, Vol 28 (April 1981), pp 410–416; Robert Springborg, *Mubarak's Egypt. Fragmentation of the Political Order* (Boulder: Westview, 1989); Sadowski, *Political Vegetables*.

25. Cf. e.g. Perthes, "Private Sector, Economic Liberalization".

26. Cf. Renate Mayntz, "Problemverarbeitung durch das politisch-administrative System: Zum Stand der Forschung", in Joachim-Jens Hesse (ed), *Politikwissenschaft als Verwaltungswissenschaft* (*Politische Vierteljahresschrift*, special issue, No. 13) (Opladen: Westdeutscher Verlag, 1982), p 75.

27. Cf. e.g. R.D. McLaurin/Don Peretz/Lewis W. Snider, *Middle East Foreign Policy. Issues and Processes* (New York: Praeger, 1982); Sa'd al-Din Ibrahim et al., *Kaifa yusna' al-qarar fi al-watan al-'arabi* [How are Decisions Produced in the Arab Homeland?] (Beirut: Center for Arab Unity Studies, 1985); Muhammad Sa'd Abu 'Amud, "Sana' al-qarar al-siyasi fi al-huqba al-sadatiyya" [Political Decision Making in the Sadat Era], in *al-Mustaqbal al-'arabi*, Vol 11, No. 112 (June 1988), pp 112–128; Sa'd Abu Diah, *'Amaliyyat ittikhadh al-qarar fi siyasat al-urdunn al-kharijiyya* [The Decision-Making Process in Jordanian Foreign Policy] (Beirut: Center for Arab Unity Studies, 1990).

28. Cf. the illustrative study on economic policy-making in Egypt by Amani Qandil, *Sina'at al-siyasa al-iqtisadiyya fi misr, 1974–1981* [The Making of Economic Policy in Egypt, 1974–1981] (Cairo: Mu'assasat al-Ahram, 1979), further Denis Sullivan, "The Political Economy of Reform in Egypt", *International Journal of Middle East Studies*, Vol 22 (1990), pp 317–334; Springborg, *Mubarak's Egypt*, Sadowski, *Political Vegetables*. For a study on Syria's agricultural policy-making, cf. Hinnebusch, *Peasant*.

29. Cf. the state-of-the-art review (also containing a critique of more traditional, orientalist approaches to the sociology of the Arab world) by Samih K. Farsoun/Lisa Hajjar, "The Contemporary Sociology of the Middle East: An Assessment", in Hisham Sharabi (ed), *Theory, Politics and the Arab World. Critical Responses* (New York/London: Routledge, 1990).

30. Cf. Mahmud 'Abd al-Fadil, *al-Tashkilat al-ijtima'iyya wa-l-takwinat al-tabaqiyya fi al-watan al-'arabi. Dirasa tahliliyya li-ahamm al-tatawwurat wa-l-ittijahat khilal al-fatra 1945–1985* [Social Formations and Class Structures in the Arab Homeland. An Analysis of the Most Important Developments and Tendencies 1945–1986] (Beirut: Center for Arab Unity Studies, 1988), pp 21ff.

31. Ibid. pp 45f.

32. Ibid., p 192. Concepts derived from the study of European history may

indeed imply particular expectations as to the future development of the social formations in question. Terms such as "kulak" or "rural bourgeoisie" for peasants with medium-sized land property would at least need further specification. And referring, without further explanations, to the Syrian working class as "proletariat" would be problematic since the concept in its common European understanding implies that members of this class do not own any (landed) property.

33. Cf. Hanna Batatu, *The Old Social Classes and the Revolutionary Movements of Iraq. A Study of Iraq's Old Landed and Commercial Classes and of its Communists, Ba'thists, and Free Officers* (Princeton: Princeton University Press, 1978), pp 5ff; 'Abd al-Fadil, *al-Tashkilat*, pp 198ff; Halim Barakat, *The Arab World. Society, Culture, and State* (Berkeley: University of California Press, 1993), pp 81–87.

34. *Wasta*, in Syria as in other Arab states, is an almost all-encompassing concept for the distribution of resources and access through patronage and mediation. Cf. Annika Rabo, *Change on the Euphrates. Villagers, Townsmen and Employees in Northeast Syria* (Stockholm: University of Stockholm, 1986); Frank Czichowski, "'Ich und meine Vettern gegen die Welt...'. Migration, Wastah', Verteilungskoalitionen und gesellschaftliche Stabilität in Jordanien", *Orient*, Vol 29 (1988), pp 561–578.

35. Cf. 'Abd al-Fadil, *al-Tashkilat*, p. 107; Khudr Zakariyya, "al-Mu'ashshirat al-iqtisadiyya al-ijtima'iyya fi al-watan al-'arabi wa-madlulatuha al-mustaqbaliyya li-'amaliyyat al-tanmiya" [The Socio-Economic Indicators in the Arab Homeland and their Future Relevance for the Development Process], *Dirasat 'arabiyya*, Vol 19 (April 1983), No. 6, pp 69–91 (72).

36. Cf. primarily Manfred Halpern, *The Politics of Social Change in the Middle East and North Africa* (Princeton: Princeton University Press, 1963), pp 51–78. For the Syrian case, and from a Syrian perspective, cf. Bu 'Ali Yasin, *al-Sulta al-'ummaliyya 'ala wasa'il al-intaj fi al-tatbiq al-suri wa-l-nazariyya al-ishtirakiyya* [Worker Power over the Means of Production in the Syrian Practice and in Socialist Theory] (Beirut: Dar al-Haqa'iq, 1979).

37. Cf. John Waterbury, "Twilight of the State Bourgeoisie?", *International Journal of Middle East Studies*, Vol 23 (1991), pp 1–17.

38. Raymond A. Hinnebusch, though differentiating and avoiding idealizing the Syrian ruling stratum, comes closest to viewing their activities as driven by reason of state rather than their particular social interest. Cf., in particular, his *Authoritarian Power*, p 324 and passim. Marxist analyses of the development of state capitalism come closest to regarding the state bourgeoisie as an instrument of not yet fully developed capitalist class forces. Cf. Syrian Communist Party (SCP), *Hawl ba'd al-tatawwurat wa-l-tadabir al-iqtisadiyya fi suriya* [Regarding Some Economic Developments and Measures in Syria] (Damascus: SCP, December 1988), pp 5–10; 'Isam Khafaji, *al-Dawla wa-l-tatawwur al-ra'asmali fi al-'iraq 1968–1978* [The State and Capitalist Development in Iraq, 1968–1978] (Cairo: Dar al-Mustaqbal al-'arabi, 1983), pp 38ff.

39. Cf. Hartmut Elsenhans, *Abhängiger Kapitalismus oder bürokratische Entwicklungsgesellschaft: Versuch über den Staat in der Dritten Welt* (Frankfurt a. M./New York: Campus, 2nd ed., 1984); idem, "Dependencia, Unterentwicklung und Staat in der Dritten Welt", *Politische Vierteljahresschrift*, Vol 27 (1986), pp 133–158; Joel Migdal, *Strong Societies and Weak States. State-Society Relations and State Capabilities in the Third World* (Princeton: Princeton University Press, 1988).

40. Cf. 'Abd al-Fadil, *al-Tashkilat*, p 201.

41. Quite characteristic of more recent scholarly works on Syria that overstress the minority question are Mahmud A. Faksh, "The Military and Politics in Syria: The Search for Stability," *Journal of South Asian and Middle Eastern Studies*, Vol 8 (1985), pp 3–21; Martha Neff Kessler, *Syria: Fragile Mosaic of Power* (Washington, D.C.: National Defense University Press, 1987); Pipes, *Greater Syria*; idem, "Syrie: L'après-Assad", *Politique internationale*, No. 59 (Spring 1993), pp 97–110. For a critique of such overstressing of the minority problem cf. in more detail Volker Perthes, "Einige kritische Bemerkungen zum Minderheitenparadigma in der Syrienforschung", *Orient*, Vol 31 (1990), pp 571–582; Elizabeth Picard, "Critique de l'usage du concept d'ethnicité dans l'analyse des processus politiques dans le monde arabe", *Études politiques du monde arabe. Dossiers du CEDEJ* (Cairo: CEDEJ, 1991), pp 71–84.

42. Cf. Picard, "Critique".

43. Cf. Theodor Hanf, *Koexistenz im Krieg: Staatszerfall und Entstehen einer Nation im Libanon* (Baden-Baden: Nomos, 1990), pp 32ff.

44. Cf. Thomas Scheffler, *Ethnisch-religiöse Konflikte und gesellschaftliche Integration im Vorderen und Mittleren Orient* (Berlin: Das Arabische Buch, 1985).

45. Cf. Seale, *Asad of Syria*; Moshe Ma'oz, *Asad. The Sphinx of Damascus: A Political Biography* (New York: Weidenfeld & Nicolson, 1988); Daniel Le Gac, *La Syrie du général Assad* (Bruxelles: Editions Complexe, 1991); Lucien Bitterlin, *Hafez el-Asad. Le Parcours d'un Combattant* (Paris, Éditions du Jaguar, 1986).

46. Cf. Kanovsky, "What's behind", pp 280f; Clawson, *Unaffordable Ambitions*, pp 50ff; Dalila, "Tajribat suriya", pp 393f.

47. In the population censuses, for instance, the active populace is categorized in terms of their status of employment (unemployed, wage-earner, employed without wage, self-employed, employer) and their occupation. On this basis, both the owner of a boutique and a lottery-ticket seller fall under the same category, namely, independent salespersons.

48. Cf. Perthes, "The Syrian Private Industrial and Commercial Sectors", note 21.

49. According to the census of 1970, for instance, there were 748,000 persons employed in agriculture. According to the labour-force sample of 1975, 894,000 persons were employed in agriculture. In 1976, according to the sample of that year, their number had sunk to 678,000; in 1981, according to the census, it was down to 498,000. According to the 1984 labour-force sample,

the number of persons employed in agriculture amounted to 571,000, and in 1991, according to that year's sample, it had risen to an unprecedented 917,000. The differences are almost entirely the result of an inconsistent categorization of female rural labour. The labour-force sample of 1975 counted 262,000 unpaid female workers employed with their family; the 1976 sample counted only 47,000 women in this category. The censuses counted 63,000 (1970) and 39,000 (1981) respectively. The 1984 sample counted a total of 142,000 women working in agriculture, the 1991 sample more than doubled this number to 292,000.

For a critique of the methods used to produce the samples, cf. Amal Husseini, *Profile of Women in Agriculture and Rural Development in the Syrian Arab Republic* (Damascus: unpublished, 1979), pp 52ff. Elisabeth Longuenesse holds that the samples are simply unusable ("Reflexions de methode pour l'étude de la classe ouvrière dans le pays arabe", Paper presented to the symposium on "Les origines et la formation de la classe ouvrière dans le pays arabe", Algiers, December 1978, p 9). I would argue that the census data are doubtless of greater value. The samples have, however, improved and become more realistic since the last census was undertaken in 1981.

50. This is the case regarding the complete absence of military, security or police personnel in all statistics on employment. Also lacking, since 1980, are data on the proportional distribution of national income in terms of income from wages and salaries on the one hand and from property and self-employed activities on the other.

CHAPTER TWO

The Emergence and Transformation
of a Statist Economy

The socio-economic face of Syria has changed tremendously over the 25–30 years that the Ba'th party and Hafiz al-Asad have been in power. In 1963, Syria's population amounted to less than 5 million, in 1970 to 6.3 million. By 1990, the latter figure had almost doubled; by 1993, the Syrian population was estimated at over 14 million, almost half of them under the age of 15. In 1970, more than 57 per cent of the population lived in the countryside; more than half of the population and almost three quarters of its female part were illiterate.[1] By the early 1990s, the proportion of those dwelling in urban areas can be estimated to have reached some 65 to 70 per cent.[2] Illiteracy had dropped to an average 25 per cent, and to less than 40 per cent for the female population.[3]

On the whole, change and development look impressive, if today's Syria is compared with the country at the beginning of the 1970s. The Syria of the 1990s produces fertilizers, iron bars, cables, tyres, electrical engines and a choice of medical drugs and consumer articles. None of these were part of the country's productive spectrum in 1970. The area of irrigated land has increased by some 80 per cent, the total cultivated land under crops by about 40 per cent, and the average yield of Syria's main crops – wheat and cotton – has almost doubled. Per capita GDP increased by three quarters.[4] The picture looks less bright if, rather than the developments of the last two-and-a-half decades, those of the 1980s and early 1990s are scrutinized. Syria experienced a deep economic crisis throughout most of the 1980s, similar in many respects to the crises suffered by a number of comparable Arab and third-world countries which had pursued ambitious state-led import-substituting industrialization programmes during the 1970s.[5] Responding to these problems, Syria pursued a cautious, home-made programme of structural adjustment by which it was able to improve its overall economic performance. The 1980s, nonetheless, remained a lost decade for the country's social and economic development. Per capita income fell, the larger part of the population had to bear substantial losses of income, and the government's room for manoeuvre in development policies and public investments narrowed.

This chapter attempts to analyse the interrelation between economic variables and economic policies in Syria, sketching the basic features of the Syrian economy and the shifting patterns of the regime's development and general economic policies. The analysis centres on the adjustment or transformation process of the 1980s and early 1990s and, because of its significance for this transformation, the changing relationship between the public and the private sector.

1. Macro-Economic Variables and Imbalances

Syria is not a poor country. In World Bank categories, based on per capita GNP, it is regarded a lower-middle-income economy, with, at the beginning of the 1990s, a per capita income of $1,000 to 1,200.[6] The purchasing power of the Syrian average income, if spent on the local market, is larger than this figure suggests: roughly, slightly below that of Turkey, Jordan, or Tunisia.[7]

The country is endowed with fertile soils; however, some 65 per cent of the area is considered arid or semi-arid. About half of the land is steppe and only exploitable as pasture; only a third is regarded as cultivable. Agriculture in the cultivated zones is highly dependent on starkly varying rainfall. Land reclamation and irrigation have therefore constantly been a high-ranking policy goal.[8]

Syria's main mineral resources are oil, natural gas, and phosphates. Phosphate production began in 1971; natural gas has increasingly been used as industrial fuel since the mid-1980s. Mineral oil has been produced on a small scale since 1958 and in commercial quantities since 1968. On an international scale, Syria is still a minor oil producer; oil nonetheless plays a major role in the country's economy. Over the past two decades, Syria has almost quintupled its oil production. In the early 1970s output was less than 120,000 b/d and in 1986 had still not reached 200,000 b/d. By 1993, however, with new oil fields in the Dayr al-Zur area coming on stream from the late 1980s, production stood at some 580,000 b/d.[9] From the early to the mid-1980s, rising local demand for oil products led to more oil imports than exports.[10] Since 1986 the country has again become a net oil exporter, and oil revenues form the largest part of its foreign exchange earnings.

After considerable growth over the 1960s and 1970s, in the 1980s the rate of growth slowed down and fell behind demographic growth.[11] Real per capita GDP, as shown in Table II.1, almost doubled between 1970 and 1980. It began to decrease in 1982, declining by almost 20 per cent between 1981 and 1989. From 1990 onwards, a recovery of the economy could be felt; per capita GDP in that year, however, was still some 10 per cent below its 1980 level. Investment figures reflect the shifting trends of the Syrian economy even more clearly. At constant prices, annual investment increased modestly between 1963 and 1970,[12] then jumped more than fourfold over the 1970s, continued

Table II.1   GDP Development and Indices of Commodity Production

	1970	1980	1985	1990	1992
Real GDP at market prices 1985 constant LS millions	27,965	72,078	83,225	89,485	109,510
Real GDP p/c, LS	4,469	8,281	8,106	7,386	8,451
Index of manufacturing industries output	29	61	100	100	107
Index of oil production and mining	26	99	100	267	334
Index of agricultural production	39	96	100	115	139
Index of gross investments (in constant 1985 prices)	19	85	100	58	77

Source: Statistical Abstracts 1975–1993. 1992 figures are provisional.

Table II.2   GDP Structure and Sectoral Distribution of Employment (%)

	GDP structure					Sectoral distribution of employment		
	1970	1980	1985	1990	1992	1970	1981	1991
Agriculture	20	20	21	28	30	51.0	26.0	28.2
Mining and manufacturing	22	16	15	20	16	13.5	17.7	14.3
Building and construction	3	7	7	4	4	7.3	17.5	10.4
Transport and communication	11	12	10	9	9	4.2	6.8	5.1
Trade	20	25	22	23	24	9.5	9.5	11.6
Finance, insurance, real estate	11	6	5	4	3	0.6	0.9	0.7
Services	13	19	20	12	14	13.8	21.4	29.2
Employed (mill.)						1.46	1.88	3.25

Note: All figures on employment, particularly those for 1991, understate the urban informal sector and omit the military. 1981 figures additionally understate female agricultural labour.

Source: *Statistical Abstracts 1992, 1993; Population Census 1970, 1981.*

to grow, if at reduced speed, till the mid-1980s, and fell to about half their 1985 level by the end of the decade.[13]

Although the Syrian economy has become more diversified, a brief look at the country's macro-economic indicators shows that a structural transformation from an agrarian to an industrial economy has not taken place. Agriculture, as shown in Table II.2, has remained the single most important economic sector, contributing some 25 to 30 per cent of GDP, at the beginning of the 1990s, depending on rainfall. In the 1960s agriculture's share in the GDP fell in the same range. During the 1970s, when largely urban-centred development efforts speeded up and urbanization increased, agricultural GDP decreased in proportion to non-agrarian sectors. Its renewed increase from the late 1980s mirrors both the effects of a gradual, but substantial rise of agricultural procurement prices introduced by the government at that time, and the relative decline of those non-agrarian sectors most heavily affected by recession in the 1980s.

The labour force in agriculture decreased during the 1970s, both proportionately and in absolute numbers. Although agricultural mechanization played a part in producing this, it primarily reflected the abandonment of agriculture by a large number of small peasants for jobs in the cities created by huge development spending – both on industry and infrastructure, as well as public administration and services. In the 1980s, the capacity of the formal urban sectors to absorb high numbers of rural migrants declined. Agriculture continues to employ almost 30 per cent of the labour force.

From the early 1970s, construction boomed; both its share in GDP and in the labour force more than doubled over the decade. The transport sector also grew disproportionately, indicating growing mobility and a substantial expansion of Syria's communications network. The increase of the industrial labour force was more limited, and the growth of industrial GDP remained below the overall growth rate. In the 1980s, all of these sectors receded, proportionately at least. The sharp decline of employment and income generated in construction clearly reflects the acute recession that struck in those years. Industrial GDP still increased; this increase, however, as production indices show,[14] resulted almost exclusively from the growth of Syria's oil sector which employed less than 4 per cent of the industrial work force. While oil production almost tripled in the second half of the 1980s, production in the manufacturing industries remained stagnant. Over the whole period under consideration, the growth of industrial GDP and employment – including the oil sector – more or less corresponded to overall economic and demographic growth. However, industrialization efforts did not result in notable changes to the macroeconomic structure, that is, the sectoral distribution of employment and the origins of value added: both in 1970 and at the beginning of the 1990s, industry employed some 14 per cent of the labour force and generated about one fifth of GDP.

The one sector that, in terms of employment, grew disproportionately over the entire period was the services sector, the major part of which represents public administration and other government services. Comparison of employment and GDP data shows clearly that the expansion of this sector was not accompanied by a commensurate increase in its share of the pie. At the beginning of the 1970s the average income in the service sector ranged around the general average; in the 1990s it had fallen to less than half of it.

The largest share of the non-agricultural GDP, both in the boom years and in the years of recession, was held by the trade sector. Aside from the small and highly profitable real estate and financial business, trade also remained the one sector in which the highest average income was generated. Trade and trade-related services employed only about 12 per cent of the workforce, accounting, however, for some 27 per cent of value added. Little wonder, therefore, that commercial activities attracted an increasing proportion of the economically active population, especially at a time when substantial income losses had to be suffered in other sectors.

Wages and Cost of Living

In the 1970s, most wage earners were able to improve their income substantially.[15] Immediately after taking power in 1970, Asad raised the wages of most wage-earners by granting a family bonus to all permanently employed males; in 1973 and 1974, pay rises of some 15 per cent each were decreed for all public sector employees. With inflation speeding up after the October war, wages remained behind the development of consumer prices. By 1979, wage-earners had to bear real income losses, despite further pay rises in 1975 and in 1978. This contributed to the general popular disenchantment with the regime and the socio-political unrest of 1979 and 1980. A 65 per cent pay rise in 1980 has to be seen in the light of that year's crisis of the regime. Until 1985 then, no further general pay rise was decreed; wages increased only slowly by means of routine promotions and a new system of performance-oriented allowances that was gradually introduced as of 1979. Pay increases in 1985 and 1987 did little to bridge the widening gap between wage and consumer price developments. By 1987, the purchasing power of the average public-sector wage had fallen below that of 1970. Over the 1980s, as Table II.3 shows, retail prices increased about sevenfold, wages not more than twofold. In the late 1980s, a public-sector wage was hardly sufficient to cover food expenses for an average family of six; the entire minimum household expenses of such a family – including rent, clothes, schooling, electricity, heating, and transport – would hover around twice the average income of a public-sector employee, or four to five

Table II.3 Wages and Prices (1970 = 100)

	Wage index	Price index
1970	100	100
1980	450	285
1985	712	525
1990	1,592	2,039
1992	2,079	2,404

Source: *Statistical Abstracts*, various years.

times the minimum wage.[16] More than that, wages were not allowed to deteriorate. Even though wage increases in 1989 and 1991 were accompanied by substantial cuts in consumer price subsidies,[17] the average wage–price ratio improved slightly as of the early 1990s. At the same time, certain groups, particularly university professors, obtained extra allowances, just about doubling their salaries. Still, many public-sector employees were unable to sustain their family from their salary.

Balance Deficits and Resource Gap

Syria's economic development was built on a combination of imbalances quite typical for countries that followed state-led import-substituting industrialization strategies. Traditionally, Syria's trade balance has been in deficit. Since 1970, despite the agrarian character of its economy, Syria has also been a net importer of foodstuffs. From 1973 to the mid-1980s, as Table II.4 shows, the country's balance-of-trade gap increasingly widened, both absolutely and proportionately. In 1986, only slightly more than 40 per cent of Syria's imports were covered by exports. The deficit increase was due primarily to ambitious industrialization efforts, but also to growing imports of consumer goods. Industrial investments needed large quantities of imported capital goods; new industries consumed imported material and spare parts without contributing much to the export side. As the inflow of worker remittances and official aid – which had peaked in 1979 and 1981 respectively – declined in the mid-1980s,[18] Syria's current account also became increasingly negative. By 1986, the country found

Table II.4   Foreign Trade and Oil Exports ($ million)

	1970	1980	1985	1990	1992
Exports	203	2,108	1,637	4,221	3,100
of which: oil and oil products	34	1,662	1,212	1,907	2,151
Imports	350	4,118	3,967	2,062	3,498

Note: 1992 figures are provisional.

Source: World Bank, IMF; *Statistical Abstract 1993*.

itself on the brink of a foreign-exchange bankruptcy. As a result, imports declined sharply and continued to decline till the end of the decade causing severe shortages but easing the balance deficit. From the other side, increasing petroleum and, to a lesser extent, private-sector commodity exports, helped narrow the gap. In 1989, Syria achieved its first positive trade balance for decades. Since then, as yet, the balance has remained more or less even.

By 1992 the situation had improved. This was despite the fact that (1) unaccounted-for smuggling and overbilled exports certainly made the real balance less positive than the official one;[19] (2) debt-servicing commodity exports to the former Soviet Union neither actually produced foreign exchange nor provided a guaranteed outlet for Syrian products;[20] and (3) high invisibles payments, mainly for the product share and service costs of foreign oil companies, turned the current account negative again.[21] The improvement resulted mainly from the steep increase in petroleum production and exports – both crude and refined. From the mid-1970s to the mid-1980s, and again from 1992, oil exports made up some 70 per cent or more of Syria's total export value, which rendered the country heavily dependent on world-market oil prices. The oil-price slump of 1986 cut Syria's petroleum earnings by half and accounted for much of the sudden deterioration that year in the foreign-exchange situation.

Export earnings could not cover imports most of the time; nor could Syria's own industrial resources cover infrastructural investments. The public sector helped to satisfy growing consumption needs, but did not in itself become an instrument for capital accumulation.

Syria's resource gap – the difference between investments and domestic savings – averaged less than 5 per cent of GDP during the 1970s; it increased towards the end of the decade and averaged around 12 per cent over the 1980s[22] – a rather high figure if compared to most other Arab and non-Arab lower-middle-income countries.[23] Domestic savings in Syria rarely accounted for more than 50 per cent of gross investments. Since the public sector, throughout the 1970s and up till 1988, came up with the majority of all investments[24] the resource gap was clearly reflected in government budgets. Foreign grants were of particular importance, however not sufficient to cover the differential between revenues and government expenditures. Even with grants included, Syria ran budget deficits that, according to published data, hovered around 15 per cent of the budget in the early 1970s, and around 20 per cent from the late 1970s to 1986. Due to severe real budget cuts, the deficit then diminished considerably. In some pre-1991 years, budget figures even sported a surplus. Only since 1992 have deficits increased again.[25] As a percentage of GDP, budget deficits ranged around 5 per cent in the first half of the 1970s, between 5 and 10 per cent from 1976 to 1986, and between zero and 2.5 per cent in the 1986 to 1991 period with its relative decrease in public investments and other expenditures. Since then, there has been a renewed upward tendency. These figures also represent a relatively high deficit in comparison with other Arab and non-Arab lower-middle-income countries.[26] The deficits had to be covered by internal borrowing that spurred inflation, and by loans from abroad. It can be estimated that, throughout the 1970s at least, some 65 per cent of all investments, and some 80 per cent of all public investments were actually financed from external resources.[27] Inflation peaked between an annual 35 and more than 60 per cent in the years 1986–88, while otherwise hovering between 10 and 20 per cent.[28]

The Military Factor

Military expenditure as reported in government budgets ranged around 35 per cent of the total from the early 1970s until 1978, increased to peaks of around 40 per cent in the years until 1987, and have since dropped again to some 30 per cent, except for Gulf War year 1991, when over 35 per cent of the budget was spent on the military.[29] As a rule, budgeted military expenditure does not include arms purchases. Arms imports were estimated to average – with stark annual variations – some $570 million per year between 1970 and 1978. They increased sharply from $900 million in 1978 to $2 billion in 1979 – the year of the Egyptian–Israeli peace treaty which virtually removed Egypt from the Arab–Israeli strategic equation, left Syria as the only credible frontline state, and allowed Israel to concentrate its forces on its northern and eastern fronts. In the first half of the 1980s arms imports remained extremely high, averaging more than $2.8 billion annually. In the second half of the decade they decreased, averaging only half that amount.[30] Recent reports about arms shipments to Syria suggest that the early 1990s saw a new increase, if less than that of the early 1980s.[31] As a percentage of GDP, Syria's defence budgets ranged around 10 per cent until the late 1970s, increased in the wake of the Egyptian–Israeli peace treaty of 1979 and further after Israel's 1982 Lebanon war, reaching a peak of more than 16 per cent in 1984. Since 1986, the defence/GDP proportion has again dropped, ranging around 12 per cent.[32]

Though these proportions are high by world standards – not so, as a matter of fact, in regional comparison[33] – it would be misleading to assume that Syria's high defence expenditures were made at the expense of social and economic development, let alone to claim that Syria's maintenance of a large army has translated into economic crises. Military expenditures no doubt represent a waste of resources. In the Syrian case, however, military strength has been employed quite successfully to generate financial resources from abroad, not only for wasteful military consumption, but for civilian use as well.

The major part of Syria's arms imports have been paid for by its Arab allies – mainly the GCC countries and Libya – or financed by the main supplier, the Soviet Union, on a concessionary-loan basis. In general, therefore, these imports did not burden Syria's foreign-exchange balance or budgets.[34] Special Arab aid also covered a substantial part – sufficient data to support any more precise statement do not exist – of the financial costs that Syria's military involvement in Lebanon entailed.[35]

With arms deliveries and Syria's Lebanon engagement largely paid for or financed from abroad, the official military budget can be taken to represent Syria's domestic military expenses.[36] By and large, Syria's budgeted military expenditures have developed in a pro-cyclical manner, i.e. they declined, in real terms, along with the total budget during the years of recesssion. In this respect, it is the economic constraints that have led to cuts in military spending rather than military expenditures being responsible for financial problems.[37] Certainly, these expenditures are high and are covered from domestic sources. In a sense, however, Syria's build-up of military strength and credibility has been a necessary investment to make maximum use of the country's location and its political-strategic position in the Arab–Israeli conflict and become, after Camp David, the most important confrontation state with Israel. The GCC countries in particular have not only paid for Syria's arms imports, they have also provided substantial financial aid for the country's civilian, development-oriented expenditures. Arab funding for Syria has been considerably larger than for comparable countries of lesser strategic importance.[38] Indeed, a large part of Arab financial support for Syria's civilian, economic and development projects would not have been paid, had Syria not represented a credible enemy to Israel. A zero-sum relation between military and civilian aid or between military build-up and civilian development investments did therefore not exist in the Syrian case.[39]

External Resources and Debts

Since 1973, and compared to the 1960s and the early 1970s, Syria has received an enormous inflow of civilian economic assistance. Most of this has come from Arab sources and, during the Iraq–Iran war, Iran. Western countries, international organizations, and the former Soviet Union played a lesser role. Available data on civilian grants and concessional loans are not necessarily accurate, and this is even more true of data on military assistance and private transfers which also increased from around 1973.

Workers' remittances have been largely under-reported since, for the most part, they have not been transferred through official bank channels. The inflow of remittances peaked in the oil-boom years of 1978–81, ranging around an estimated $600–900 million per year. In the years to follow, the amounts Syrians brought home from the Gulf decreased; still, however, a constant inflow of at least $350–400 million can be assumed for most of the 1980s and the early 1990s.[40]

In the 1970s, assistance from the West and from international organizations increased from less than $10 million to some $100 million annually, remaining around that level with variations, before taking an upward tendency from the beginning of the 1990s. Civilian aid from the former Soviet Union and other Eastern European countries was estimated at $50 million annually for the 1970s.[41] We can assume that this level has been maintained to the mid-1980s, then diminishing to all but zero. In sum, Western, international, and Eastern European civilian aid to Syria hardly exceeded some 10–15 per cent of all official assistance.

Most financial assistance accrued to Syria from Arab, particularly Gulf Arab, sources. Considerable Arab aid began to pour into Syria with the October war of 1973. Between 1973 and 1978, official Arab aid averaged close to $600 million per year. Additional unreported grants of some $250 million in cash or kind were extended to Syria in the immediate wake of the war.[42] The Baghdad Arab Summit of 1978, which was called upon to confront the Egyptian–Israeli Camp David accord, pledged to Syria a $1.8 billion annual grant for a ten-year period. A substantial part of this promise materialized, at least in the first years after the summit at least. Net Arab assistance jumped to an annual average of almost $1.6 billion in the 1979–81 period, declining thereafter to an average of $670 million in the years till 1987 and to around zero in 1988 and 1989.[43] The decrease after 1981 was primarily due to political factors, namely Syria's support for Iran during the Iraq–Iran war. Diminishing flows from Arab sources were to a large extent replaced by Iranian grants in the form of free and concessional oil deliveries to the value of up to $1 billion for some years.[44] A more conservative estimate, based on Syrian budget data, would put the figure at between $300–$800 million annually in the 1982–86 period. Thereafter, as the Syrian side lost its interest in concessionally-priced oil and the Iranians tired of granting free oil to a partner loath to pay its liabilities, Iranian assistance decreased, reaching a low of less than $50 million in 1990, then terminated.[45]

Thus, aid flows from practically all sources diminished towards the end of the 1980s. To make matters worse, substantial repayments on loans, both from the West and international organizations, and from Arab agencies, became due. In 1989, Syria's debt service actually exceeded incoming payments. Only with the Gulf crisis and war of 1990/91 did aid flows to Syria increase again. Gulf Arab aid alone was estimated at $1.5 billion for the 1991–92 period; net total civilian assistance in the early 1990s can be assumed to range around an annual $600–700 million or more.[46]

Compared to the high political rent realized by Syria in the wake of Camp David, when total aid flows reached more than $1.7 billion a year, and even $600 million or so in the mid-1970s, an aid flow of around $700 million does not seem too impressive. We have to

consider, however, that international and, particularly, Arab funds have
shrunk enormously since the oil price decrease of the early 1980s.[47] In
the first half of the 1990s, Syria may actually have taken some 20–25
per cent of total Arab financial assistance. Even in relation to Syrian
variables, aid inflows remain substantial. Equalling approximately 4–5
per cent of GNP, foreign assistance is of considerably less importance
than it was at the end of the 1970s and beginning of the 1980s when
it ranged around 10 per cent; however it is still high in comparison to
other middle-income countries of the region.[48] Moreover, aid has
remained the main source from which public investments are financed.
As financial assistance amounts to more than half of Syria's projected
development or investment budgets, it can still be assumed that the
foreign exchange part of public investment is all but completely
covered from external resources accruing to the state. The decrease in
aid flows in the second half of the 1980s did not cause the country's
economic crisis, rather it revealed an unhealthy situation, namely that
the externally-financed investments of the 1970s did not bear the
expected fruits and reduce the dependence on imports.[49]

Since most of the external resources to finance Syrian development
programmes came in the form of grants and concessional loans with
relatively favourable conditions,[50] Syria has unlike many other Arab
or middle-income countries, avoided enormously high civilian external
debts. These debts can be estimated at some $5–6 billion for the early
1990s. Syria's total foreign debt of 1991, however, including its military debt to the former Soviet Union, was put at $16.8 billion, which
about equalled the country's annual GNP.[51] Until 1992, Syria serviced
its debts to the former Soviet Union by subtracting the value of most
of its merchandise exports to that country from its debt account.[52]
Then, in a conflict over further payments, this debt barter was dis-
continued. In particular, Damascus did not acknowledge Moscow's
demand that it repay to Russia its military debt to the Soviet Union.
Soviet arms shipments, the Syrian side argued, had been political
rather than commercial ventures, and, moreover, linked to Soviet
security guarantees laid down in the 1980 Soviet–Syrian friendship
treaty, which post-Soviet Russia could not fulfil. Whether Syria,
therefore, would have a serious debt problem for the rest of the 1990s
and probably beyond, was largely a political question depending on
whether and to what extent Russia would eventually waive its demands
or – what seems more likely to date – write most of them off. *De
facto*, Syria would hardly be able to repay Russia for what its policy-

makers, and most probably Soviet policy-makers too, had always regarded as politically motivated military aid. With debt service consuming some 20–25 per cent of the country's total export earnings, which means one third or more of the export earnings of the public sector, Syria's civilian debts alone represent a considerable, if still manageable, burden.

2. Development Approaches and Public-Sector Economy

Given that external financing played a large role, and given also that seeking for political rents certainly has been a motive in Syria's regional policies, it is notable that Syria has seen little if any direct interference of external actors in its economic and development policy-making.[53] Government development strategies – not necessarily their outcome – followed what the regime considered appropriate at any given period. Under the Ba'th, the political and, to an extent, social interests of the regime elite and its allies have for the most part ruled economic policies. Only in the 1966–70 period did ideological considerations gain considerable influence. The pragmatism in matters of economic policy-making, so characteristic of Asad's rule, can itself be regarded as the expression of an approach that has considered the economy a handmaiden of politics. Insofar as the economy had to work reasonable well to allow the pursuit of political goals, particularly the maintenance of national security and regime stability, economic needs were taken into account and economic crises could so bring about policy changes. This has evidently been the case for the ongoing economic adjustment process of the 1980s and early 1990s.

Background: The Ba'thist Takeover
and its Socio-Economic Content

It has been argued that the coup of 8 March 1963 which brought the Ba'th party to power in Syria was basically a military putsch, like others before and after, rather than a revolution, as official rhetoric would have it.[54] Though the putschist character of the Ba'th and its path to power cannot be denied, the tremendous changes which Syria went through after 1963 must not be overlooked. Not only was the political elite which, with short interruptions, had determined Syria's course since independence, replaced by a new younger elite which

did not share its predecessors' class backgrounds; but also the economic system was substantially remodelled. The socio-political and
economic results of the coup may therefore well qualify as
revolutionary.

Syria's new ruling elite was composed mainly of military officers
from rural backgrounds, and the small-town intelligentsia. Damascene
intellectuals such as party founders 'Aflaq and Bitar held leadership
positions in the first years, but lost out in 1966. Practically all the
military officers playing a role in the regime originated from the
middle class peasantry, that is from families whose income allowed
them to send some of their sons to high school, but not to university.
At that time a high-school degree entitled its bearer to join the
military academy. The background of Hafiz al-Asad – the son of a
petty notable from Qardaha, who knew from his own experience the
backwardness of the countryside and freed himself from its constraints
by going to high school in Latakia and then on to a military career –
is quite characteristic for this group.[55] Like Asad, many Ba'thist officers belonged to religious minorities, primarily the Alawites and the
Druze, which at that time still formed largely compact minorities
inhabiting rather poor and peripheral rural areas. Similarly, most
Sunni officers with Ba'thist leanings came from the country's
periphery, mainly the Hauran, the Dayr al-Zur area, and the north.
Aside from the army officers, there were in the leadership and ranks
of the Ba'th a large number of provincial town school teachers (the
teachers' training colleges, like the military academy, were free of
charge), medical doctors, and lawyers. Since these professionals mainly
stemmed from the provincial middle classes, their social experience
and background was not too different from that of the officers from
peasant families.[56]

The new powerholders did not at the beginning have a clear socio-
economic policy. The *Theoretical Principles*, a document largely written by Syrian Marxist philosopher Yasin Hafiz, which the Ba'th Party's
Sixth National, i.e. Pan-Arab, conference of 1963 narrowly adopted,
called for the socialist transformation of Syria and the other Arab
countries. This would, among other things, involve the nationalization of "all important productive sectors, finance, infrastructure, transport, large real estate, foreign trade and the most important sectors of
internal trade".[57] The apparent radical turn which the Ba'th party
took with its conference decisions raised the fears of the Syrian bourgeoisie and its opposition to the regime; but it did not reflect the

opinions of those Ba'thist politicians and officers who were then at the helm. Indeed, Yasin Hafiz and his ideological followers were driven out of the party a year later.[58] Until 1966, when a more radical and ideologically determined group of Ba'thists took over, the regime's economic policies were the handmaiden of its political goals – on the one hand, the preparation of unity schemes with Egypt and, on the other, regime stabilization and the removal of domestic opposition.

Emulating Egyptian legislation, banks which had been nationalized under the UAR, then reprivatized after Syria's secession from the union in 1961, were renationalized shortly after the 1963 takeover.[59] In the summer of 1963, a revised land-reform law – the first one had been issued under the union and then amended after secession – was promulgated, setting new upper limits for landed property.[60] In the light of such measures and the party's programmatic decisions, attempts by the government to reassure entrepreneurs that "national capital" would not be harmed by their form of Arab socialism remained largely unsuccessful. The local bourgeoisie did not immediately after the coup, as Ba'thists have sometimes argued, go on an investment strike, but they clearly did so from 1964.[61] Already in 1963 and 1964, however, a number of joint-stock and limited companies were dissolved or transformed into less conspicuous and smaller personal establishments as entrepreneurs started to fear growing socialist tendencies and the calls for nationalization from within the Ba'th. Such fears on the part of the urban bourgeoisie were mixed with their contempt for the new men in power who, aside from their provincial middle class origin, often belonged to religious minorities and had laicist tendencies. This and the general notion that the Ba'th was anti-religious helped to strengthen existing ties between the religious establishment, the bourgeoisie, the conservative urban petit bourgeoisie and a large part of the latter's employees. In the suqs and the mosques, the mood became increasingly unfriendly to the regime. In the spring of 1964, in January 1965, and in May 1967, violent anti-Ba'thist protests erupted in more than one city. These protests were led for the most part by the conservative Muslim Brotherhood. In Hama, the protests of 1964 developed into an outright insurgence which the regime was only able to put down with the help of the army.[62]

Responding to the 1964 clashes, the government nationalized eight larger commercial and industrial companies. In January 1965, a complete or partial nationalization of another 120 industrial establishments followed. In the next months more commercial establishments, all cotton ginning factories and the last private power plants were transferred into public ownership. At the same time, a state-sector monopoly of the importation and exportation of certain basic commodities such as cotton, cereals, iron, and drugs was introduced.[63]

The 1964/65 nationalizations were political measures rather than the expression of an economic or development programme. In 1964, evidently, nationalizations came as a reaction to anti-regime disturbances, representing a "means of punishment for bad citizens".[64] At the same time these nationalizations represented a warning that the old elite, already deprived of its political power, might also lose its economic power base if it proved unwilling to cooperate with the new regime. The bourgeoisie understood and prepared itself, mainly by capital flight,[65] for the second round which came in 1965.

Besides being directed against the old elite, the nationalizations were part of the new regime's alliance policies. To stay in power the Ba'th needed to broaden its social base. In the countryside, this was partly achieved by means of the land reform which particularly strengthened those rural strata from which many of the new leadership stemmed, namely medium-sized and small landowners. In the cities, the regime wanted to win over the industrial working class, particularly its unionized part whose mobilization could be essential to gain the upper hand in future confrontations with the old elite and its middle class and proletarian basis in the *suqs*. The unions, however, were extremely radicalized. Union leaders, who refused to accept that there was anything like a national bourgeoise, demanded the bourgeoisie's total liquidation and the establishment of workers' control.[66] It was not the Ba'th party that dominated organized labour, but the communists, and the Ba'th's main rivals in these years, the Nasirites. Nationalizations, the report to the Ba'th Party's 1964 National Conference stated, were a "political necessity" if workers were to shift their loyalty from 'Abd al-Nasir to the Ba'th.[67] The Ba'thist leadership who, in the spring of 1964, had expelled several prominent representatives of the Marxist left, in addition found nationalizations a political necessity in order to stabilize their hold over the party. The loyalty of some party ranks to the deposed leftist leaders, according to the organizational report to the 1965 regional, i.e. Syrian, party conference, "could only be transferred into party loyalty by means of the last nationalization laws".[68]

From a purely economic or development perspective, the nationalizations made little sense and had obviously been decreed in the heat of the day. In contrast to Syria's largest company, the *Khumasiyye*, which was already nationalized when the Ba'th came to power, and the banks which were nationalized in 1963, most of the establishments transferred to public ownership in 1965 were rather small and capital-poor[69] as well as often highly indebted to the country's already nationalized banks.[70] Many owners of the nationalized firms were in fact the technical directors of their establishments which, in some cases, were mere workshops and were returned to their owners after a couple of months.

The nationalization campaign considerably enlarged the public sector. By 1965, the public industrial sector employed about one quarter of the total industrial workforce while public-sector trade establishments controlled some 40 per cent of foreign trade.[71] For the most part, however, the performance of nationalized establishments decreased as skilled staff left with the owners and the government did not, or was unable to, replace them with qualified personnel.[72]

Until 1965, then, the public sector had mainly been expanded by the tranformation of private into state property. Only after the coup of February 1966 which brought the ideologically determined, leftist group of military and civilian Ba'thists around Salah Jadid to power, did the government embark on an ambitious development programme. Economic policy had as its goal a socialist type of import-substituting industrialization *cum* socio-economic development of the country's rural areas and agriculture.[73] Seventy per cent of all and 95 per cent of industrial investments were to be made by the state. The major single investment project was to become the Tabqa Dam on the Euphrates. The project was designed to double Syria's irrigated agricultural land area by the end of the century; the hydroelectric power station at the dam would also help industrialization efforts. Major sums were earmarked for the development of the country's railway system and the oil sector. By 1968, Syria began to export limited quantities of oil. The industrial projects planned included the Hama rolling mill, the nitrogen-fertilizer plant at Homs, the tractor factory at Aleppo, a factory for the production of electrical engines at Latakia, as well as a number of establishments in the textiles and food industries. The main foreign partners in the establishment of these projects were the Soviet Union and the other socialist countries. Some of the smaller industrial units were finished and in operation by 1970, the larger projects completed only thereafter. Already by 1970, however, the public industrial sector employed some 57,000 persons,[74] about one third of the entire industrial labour force. A planning apparatus and a public-sector bureaucracy had been created. With budgeted government expenditures equalling almost 41 per cent of GDP – as compared to some 23 per cent in 1963[75] – the state had become the leading agent in the economy.

The Public Economy under Asad

Defining Development

Hafiz al-Asad's takeover represented a turning point not only in Syria's political history but also for the country's economic and development policies. Though a leading member of the regime he eventually toppled, Asad had been known to favour abandoning that regime's strategy of socialist transformation, reducing Syria's reliance on the socialist bloc and opening up to the West, the conservative Arab states and, internally, to the private sector. Asad's influence in the regime had been growing since the spring of 1969 when he had staged a first, partial coup that enabled him to put some of his loyalists into important government positions, not only in the security, but also in the economic policy field. Some cautious economic policy moves, containing elements of liberalization, were therefore undertaken in 1969 and 1970. A substantial departure towards a new development strategy, however, did not take place before Asad's complete takeover in November 1970.

Under Asad, Syria embarked on a still state-led – albeit state-capitalist rather than socialist – course of import substituting industrialization. Occasional rhetorical reference to socialism notwithstanding, economic policies became more pragmatic or non-ideological in the sense of no longer being geared towards the achievement of a particularly egalitarian, anti-capitalist model of society. Socialism was in fact redefined: in the regime's understanding it stood for increasing industrial employment, an expansion of the role of the public sector, and, at the same time, an activation of the private sector and "productive, non-exploitative" private investments.[76] Development was now basically conceived of as a factor of national strength, development efforts as complementary to other factors that would enhance the country's position in the regional power equation and, though not explicitly mentioned, boost the strength of the regime. Defence of the homeland, steadfastness, and victory, Asad time and again told his compatriots, were impossible without development.[77]

Development itself was understood to mean fast growth and modernization. Syria, in Asad's words, had to "catch up with the caravan" of technological progress.[78] Practically, Syria should cease to be an agricultural economy and become a mainly industrial one instead.[79] Lack of indigenous technical capabilities was to be compensated for by importing complete, turn-key projects;[80] financing was to be secured by increasing as much as possible the exports of oil and other raw materials, by means of foreign borrowing, and Arab aid.[81] Development efforts should rely on all available resources and energies; ideological or social conflicts "aside from the main battle" – i.e. for construction and liberation – had to be avoided.[82] Other than under Asad's predecessors, therefore, good relations with the conservative Arab states and the West were to be established and maintained, the private sector was to be encouraged to play its role, and even foreign capital, where needed to spur technical progress, could be invited. Western companies were not particularly interested in direct investment in Syria, except for the oil sector. This, however, was a highly controversial issue. In 1964, Ba'thist Syria had been among the first countries in the Third World to decide that foreign capital should not be allowed to exploit the country's mineral resources; if necessary, the participation of foreign companies was to be limited to servicing contracts.[83] Government plans to extend drilling concessions on a product-sharing basis to foreign oil companies therefore raised the opposition of the Ba'thist left and the Syrian Communist Party, which was tolerated as a junior partner in the Ba'th party-led National Progressive Front. While the Ba'th party's 1975 congress officially sanctioned the course of the government,[84] the communists' critique remained annoying enough for the regime to practically freeze the work of the National Front.[85] From the time of Asad's takeover generally and after 1973 in particular, Syria's economic policies moved towards what has commonly become known in the Arab context as *infitah* – economic opening, that is, to international markets, to the conservative Arab states and, as will be shown in more detail below, to the domestic private sector.

Build-up and Crisis

This opening remained state-led. Also from 1973 on, as outlined above, Syria attracted substantial Arab aid that enabled the regime to pursue a large-scale investment programme. Industrial development was given absolute priority. In the three five-year plans covering the 1971–85 period, between 29 and 36 per cent of all projected investments were earmarked for industry, including mining and energy production. The real share of industrial as a percentage of total investments was even higher, amounting to 47, 52, and 40 per cent respectively in the three plan periods.[86] The industrial build-up was no doubt impressive, exceeding by far whatever Syria had seen in an equal time period before. In contrast to the previous heavy reliance on Eastern European countries, new contracts were now for the most part won by Western companies. Among the list of projects the government ordered in the wake of the October war were a paper mill, two fertilizer plants, a second oil refinery, a major power plant, two cement factories, four sugar refineries, eight cereal mills, factories for the production of aluminum parts, cables, synthetics, tyres, building materials, china, glass, ceramics, bulbs, drugs, batteries, and a dozen or so plants each in the textile and food industries. In addition, the railway and road networks and Syria's commercial air fleet were expanded.[87] Apart from industry, energy, and communications, dam building and land reclamation were regarded as development priorities. In practice, however, investments for agricultural development purposes remained below expectations and plan goals, amounting to less than 10 per cent of total realized investment in the 1970s, and only slightly above 10 per cent in the 1980–85 period.[88]

The investment and general development pattern of the 1970s has since been much criticized, not only for its relative neglect of agriculture. Project costs were only halfheartedly monitored and exploded practically everywhere. Financial bottlenecks, lack of means of transport, building materials and skilled labour contributed to delaying the completion and bringing into service of all but a few of the projects. While investment in imported technology was heavy, local research and development was practically non-existent; no local machinery-building industries emerged and hardly any estabishments capable of producing spare parts for imported machines emerged. Most of the new industries were capital- rather than labour-intensive, but the labour they needed had to be skilled. With the reliance on turn-key projects, the chance was missed to enable local cadres to appropriate the new technologies while the projects were being built, and a number of the plants remained dependent on foreign specialists. Moreover, many of the new industries were mere finishing industries fitting together imported intermediary products, and the major part of the new industrial base remained reliant on foreign raw material and spares.[89] Industrial plants had, more often than not, been purchased with little attention to sectoral links, quite a number were oversized, and some certainly located in the wrong place.[90] Today, two decades after the take-off of Syria's gigantic industrialization programme of the 1970s, even government ministers may concede that many of these projects were launched without sufficient economic and technical feasibility studies.[91] This, however, is only part of the story. The State Planning Authority had in fact voiced objections against a couple of projects or their details, but these objections had been disregarded.[92] Obviously, the personal interests of members of the regime elite, and kickbacks, accounted for many of the more problematic investment decisions.

Unsound allocations and investment decisions notwithstanding, Syria's public economic sector grew to an impressive scale. By 1985, when eventually all but a few of the industrial development projects launched in the mid-1970s were operating, the public industrial sector employed some 140,000 persons, almost 40 per cent of the country's entire industrial workforce. Public-sector construction companies employed almost the same number. The product range of public-sector industries had become more diversified, including most basic consumer goods and a number of important inputs for agriculture, as well as both public and private manufacturing and construction.

The performance of the public industrial sector, however, remained below expectation. Basically, Syria's public economy faced the almost classical set of problems of such sectors in statist and authoritarian-led economies: it lacked incentives for rational economic behaviour and was burdened with social policy objectives which it could only fulfil at the expense of its productivity and profitability. Products had to be marketed at government-set low prices and public-sector companies had to employ thousands of persons they did not need, thus covering up high unemployment levels. Accordingly, wages and the motivation of the employed remained low, the turnover of workers high. More qualified cadres left for better-paid jobs in the private sector, others remained only to keep the social benefits of a public-sector job. Financial and spare-part bottlenecks, lack of domestic raw materials, and technical problems caused a constant under-utilization of capacity. Political and clientelistic appointments, too many cases of politically loyal but otherwise incompetent managers, a bureaucratic structure that punished initiative and accepted losses as normal, as well as corruption and theft, all aggravated the situation.[93] Evaluating the state of Syria's public-sector industries, the planning authority concluded that, except for the oil sector, "large and increasing losses were a common characteristic."[94]

As mentioned, the import dependence of Syria's industries – both public and private – contributed to a steadily growing deficit in the balance of trade. Furthermore, agricultural development and land reclamation had remained below expectation. From 1970 to 1987, only some 18 per cent of the land was actually brought under the plough in the area that, according to plans, should have been reclaimed in Syria's largest agricultural development project, the Euphrates basin.[95] There was no substantial expansion of irrigated lands until the beginning of the 1990s. Even so, agricultural production increased considerably throughout the 1970s, both as a result of technical modernization and intensification, and an expansion of land under crop. Then, however, until the end of the 1980s, due partly to low agricultural procurement prices and the abandonment of agriculture by peasants, agricultural production became all but stagnant, unable to satisfy the needs of a growing population, and burdening Syria with a mounting bill for imported food supplies.[96]

Even though critical signs, namely foreign-exchange bottlenecks, recurred time and again from the late 1970s,[97] the abundant inflow of external resources generally allowed Syria to live with the structural imbalances of the economy. When the flow of Arab aid and other foreign resources began to decrease in the mid-1980s, however, a serious foreign-exchange and fiscal crisis erupted, translating into unplanned import reductions of consumer goods as well as industrial and agricultural inputs. Shortages of material and spare parts, in their turn, led to production losses and often long stoppages in most branches of the industrial sector.[98] Syria, as is clearly revealed by the economic indicators presented above, found itself in a severe economic recession. Few Syrians could be convinced by their President's insistence that there were only "difficulties", no crisis.[99]

Austerity and Export-Orientation

The problematic aspects of the ambitious, industry-centred growth of the 1970s were not lost on those in charge of economic development and planning in Syria. If Syrian development plans have virtually little value as guidelines for actual economic-policy and investment decisions, at least they reflect the debate in the administration. Notably, the 1981–85 Five Year Plan gave special importance to agricultural development and emphasized the need to establish labour-intensive projects, to integrate new projects with existing economic structures, to concentrate on industries using local rather than imported raw material and, generally, to base investment decisions on feasibility studies.[100] In practice, no major new industrial projects were launched during the 1980s. With few exceptions, industrial investments remained limited to the completion of unfinished projects and to the replacement, repair, and improvement of facilities and equipment. Also, some larger infrastructural projects – such as dam projects, power stations, and the renewal of the sewerage sytem in Damascus and other cities – were postponed for lack of finance.

On the part of the country's political leadership, the basic notion of development as a factor of national strength – of growth and economic progress being needed to achieve strategic parity, or, for that matter, peace – had not changed.[101] However, the economic problems which had to be faced from the beginning of the 1980s enforced substantial alterations to the approach of the 1970s with its reliance on state-led, aid- and deficit-financed import substitution.

From 1981 on, the government embarked on a policy of economic austerity – not necessarily so-called. More often, more encouraging terms were used such as *iktifa' al-dhati* (autarky), *i'timad 'ala dhat* (self-reliance) or *tarshid al-istihlak* (guidance or rationalization of consumption). As the first two terms, for all practical purposes, represented highly unrealistic concepts for an economy so reliant on external economic relations, the last-mentioned was closest to the new economic policies. As the president told his people, since Syrians had been consuming more than they had been producing,[102] state and people now had to tighten their belts. This was not a departure from import substitution towards a new development strategy. As a matter of fact, it is doubtful whether the Syrian leadership in the period under examination ever had a clear economic-policy strategy; rather, it relied on ad-hoc decisions taken in response to needs and opportunities.[103] While the private sector was actually encouraged to expand the production of import substitutes, the state made it clear that it could no longer sustain the costly path of development the Syrians had become used to in the preceding decade, that is: the constant expansion of public services, of employment in the state, and of the range of price-controlled industrial products. Projects that had been envisaged in the 1981–85 plan were never launched, development spending being concentrated rather on the leftovers from previous plans. The 1986–90 plan was rewritten several times during that period, thus following developments rather than guiding them, and was never published. Budget increases remained below the annual rate of inflation, allocations thereby being shifted from development or investment expenditures to the current expenditure budget.[104] Public-sector wage rises remained behind inflation, and employment in the public economic sector and administration was capped. In 1985, a freeze was decreed on employment with the state. Only education and higher education and the graduates of Syria's engineering and nursing colleges to whom the state had promised jobs were generally exempt from the freeze. In other cases, every single appointment needed the personal approval of the prime minister. As a result, employment in the administration and the public industrial sector remained at around its 1985 level until 1990, increasing only slowly thereafter, while public-sector construction companies actually laid off tens of thousands of workers.[105] From 1988, the government began cautiously but – in the light of decreasing real wages – perceptibly to cut consumer subsidies as well as subsidies on agricultural and industrial inputs.

Austerity measures could only relieve the treasury of some burdens; they could not help the economy back onto its feet. On the contrary, reduced public spending contributed to the general slump inasmuch as productive units were allowed to stand idle for lack of inputs and spares, and a substantial part of the population, particularly those living on public-sector salaries, fell below the poverty line. Thus, in response to otherwise unsolvable economic pressures, the government began gradually to adjust its economic policies. As outlined below, policies turned cautiously towards economic liberalization or a second *infitah* after 1983, and more visibly so from 1985. In addition, from about 1986, a new approach regarding the public sector and its economic function emerged. The main task now, in the government's view, was to overcome the foreign-exchange crisis paralysing the whole economy. The public sector, along with the rest of the economy, was therefore to be reoriented towards exportation. Practically, the idea that had ruled the build-up of Syria's public sector since the 1960s, namely that this sector should supply the country and especially its popular classes with all the goods required by a modernizing, indus-trializing society, i.e. import substitution, was thereby set aside, for the time being at least.

First, absolute priority was given to the oil sector and its expansion. Production and exports were rapidly increased. Exports of other raw products, mainly cotton and phosphates, were to be increased where possible.[106] Further, from 1987, the government began to force the state-owned industry to seek foreign-exchange outlets for its produce and to tie imports to exports. As a rule, no foreign exchange was to be allocated for the imports of public-sector units beyond what a particular unit earned from its own exportation. Exports at dumping prices were encouraged; the treasury would cover losses in local currency. Public-sector establishments with no chance of selling their products abroad were to earn foreign exchange by "exporting to the local market", that is, by offering their goods locally for hard currency. In general, exports were to have priority over local supply: while previously the rule had been that the public sector produce for local consumers and try to export what surplus remained, it should now export whatever could be marketed abroad and leave the rest for local consumption. Additional shortages of consumer goods, inflation, and an increase of import smuggling were to be accepted, a foreign-exchange bankruptcy being considered the greater threat.[107] By 1989, this turn from import substitution to export orientation had become a publicly defended economic-policy tenet: "Just as investive spending has been the basic and appropriate feature of the 1970s," ran an official paper from the Ministry of Economy, "today, exports and the concentration on exports are the central element of work and the appropriate feature of the 1980s."[108]

As the renewed growth of the early 1990s pushed back the recession and foreign aid flows increased again, there was a re-emergence of some patterns reminiscent of the growth and investment policies of the 1970s. Many infrastructural investments, postponed under the financial constraints of the 1980s and now put into commission, were obviously needed. This includes the construction of new sewer systems for Syria's four biggest cities and the expansion of the country's power-generating capacities. A couple of mainly industrial investment decisions, however, appeared to have been taken without much regard for economic rationality. In the wake of the Gulf War, much as after the 1973 October War, Syrian officials seemed to have problems coming up with project proposals for all the cash offered for development purposes from Gulf Arab and other sources. The rationale of some projects now planned – such as an iron-and-steel plant and two more large cotton mills – is questionable, particularly in view of existing plants working below capacity.[109] There has been a general, unhealthy tendency among Syrian decision-makers to favour new investments over the renewal and maintenance of existing facilities.[110] In times of relatively easy access to external resources this tendency can be expected to meet little resistance. Yet, foreign aid, oil revenues, and other rents are unlikely to support the Syrian economy to the same extent that they did in the 1970s, when the economy was half today's size and surplus capital from the Gulf was abundant. Some gigantomanic, poorly planned, and occasionally corrupt development spending may therefore recur, but it can only do so on a smaller scale. Moreover, future developments are likely to differ from those of the 1970s, because the relationship between the state and the private sector is different today – the first half of the 1990s – from those two decades ago.

3. State and Private Economy: Patterns and Phases of Liberalization

In his declaration of 16 November 1970, the day he accomplished his coup, Asad in very general terms promised a new relationship between the regime and its citizens, namely the preservation of the citizens' freedom and dignity. Asad's declaration contained no reference to economic liberalization, pointing instead to the deepening and development of socialist transformation.[111] However, Syria's bourgeoisie and the upper middle class were among those who met his takeover with open sympathy, knowing that he was favourable in principle to business interests and to a realignment with Syria's conservative fellow Arab states.

Those who expected an economic opening were not disappointed. As mentioned above, some initial measures towards liberalization had been introduced even before Asad's complete assumption of power. They showed little effect, however, since they seemed not to express the regime's general policy direction. The first decisive moves towards what in hindsight can be understood as Syria's first *infitah* began in 1971. *Infitah* measures were deepened in 1974/75 and began to peter out by 1977. During the 1980s, a second *infitah* followed which brought about a more radical change in economic policies and in relations between state and private business. The term *infitah* was widely used in 1974/75.[112] Later it became somewhat discredited in the official discourse – not so that of businessmen – since it was connected with the specific course of events in Sadat's Egypt.[113]

The First *infitah*: Liberalization in the Shadow
of State-Led Growth

The series of initial measures taken even before Asad's assumption of power was directed mainly towards non-Syrian Arabs and Syrian expatriates, allowing them to open foreign currency bank accounts in Syrian banks, to acquire real estate, giving certain guarantees for their investments in Syria – should there be any – and allowing, under certain conditions, the repatriation of capital invested and profits originating from such investments.[114] In 1971, the government underlined these rather theoretical commitments by joining the Arab Investment Insurance Organization and ratifying an Arab agreement on the facilitation and protection of inter-Arab capital investments. These measures were primarily declarations of principle and good intention, aimed more at a realignment with conservative Arab states and probably at attracting some public sector investments from wealthier Arab countries, than at encouraging private Arab investors to freely test their entrepreneurial skills in Syria. A list of conditions to be met by potential investors made sure that such investments would only be undertaken if the Syrian government were interested in the particular project.

The new regime, after Asad's takeover, initiated a series of measures aimed at gaining the trust and support of the private sector. Immediately after the coup, import restrictions on certain goods were lifted and, early in 1971, registered importers became entitled by means of the so-called quota or Exceptional Imports System to import certain quantities of goods banned in principle from importation.[115] As of 1972, imports without foreign exchange transfers were allowed in order to enable merchants and other persons who had wealth abroad to repatriate some of it to Syria. As early as January 1971, Asad had issued an amnesty on capital flight and other offences against economic laws committed prior to his coup. In the same year, a new authority for Syria's existing two free and future zones was created, aimed at offering entrepreneurs an opportunity to make use of Syria's comparative advantages – essentially cheap labour and the country's geographical location – without being subject to its trade and currency regimes. By thus showing goodwill towards private business without abandoning any element of state control over private-sector activities, the government tried to reassure the private sector in general and to encourage in particular entrepreneurs who had left Syria after the nationalizations of 1964/65 to return and start some new business. In this sense, Syria's 1973 constitution explicitly guaranteed private property, preventing expropriations other than for public use and, where these did happen, with equitable compensation.[116] All these attempts met with some success. A considerable number of new, though generally small, private manufacturing and service establishments were set up, even though this initially triggered a surge of imports, particularly of consumer goods.

The scope of *infitah* was substantially widened after the 1973 October War. Syria's financial capabilities, as shown above, improved considerably through rising oil revenues and increased capital inflows from external sources that helped to finance the government's gigantic investment programme. Development, as noted, was to be led by the state which would, however, assign a role to the private sector. As a rule, private business was to concentrate on less capital-intensive ventures that would secure comparatively quick returns,[117] such as trade and services, light manufacturing industries, and construction, particularly of dwellings and private-sector industrial buildings. Banking and insurance, mining and oil, manufacturing industries defined as strategic, as well as others in which existing public-sector establishments were supposed to cover local demand, remained out of bounds to private capital; in other industrial fields private-sector establishments were to be permitted alongside the public sector.

The private sector was encouraged to take its share from public spending – mainly by importing on behalf of public-sector agencies and by playing an intermediary role between the state and foreign companies – and to expand its activities in manufacturing, construction, services and internal trade. Foreign-exchange controls were virtually abandoned; local businessmen were allowed to operate openly as middlemen trying by various means to have government contracts assigned to foreign companies; and new credit facilities for the private sector were introduced. Even though government policies were more favourable to private trade than they were to manufacturing, the entire private sector grew considerably throughout the 1970s. Private investments increased even faster than those of the public sector, and private industrial and commercial establishments almost doubled.[118]

In 1977, the last substantial measure of Syria's first *infitah* was launched by entrusting private entrepreneurs with a number of important projects for the development of Syria's tourism industry. The principle of assigning to private business economic activities that promised quick returns was thereby fully taken into account. A so-called "mixed" (private-state) sector, consisting essentially of two large shareholding companies was established. These companies were private in all but name. The state held a minority share but did not interfere with the conduct of business. Each of these companies, however, was established by law and thus legally protected against competition. Not surprisingly, they could acquire quasi-monopolistic positions in certain sectors of the tourism industry.[119] Even though their establishment therefore can hardly be referred to as a matter of liberalization, it represented an element of *infitah*, insofar as this means the opening of the regime towards the private sector and includes the possibility of selectively farming out privileges to certain individuals closely connected to the regime.

As of 1977 the government had to reconsider its liberal import policies; this was because of economic constraints, particularly a deterioration in the balance of payments. Gradually, Syria's first *infitah* drew to a close. The private sector was reassured that there would be no return to socialism and expropriations, but import restrictions were imposed, first in 1977 and on a wider scale in 1981 when, after some relief due to rising oil prices, symptoms of economic crisis became increasingly apparent. In the first place, these restrictions applied to more or less luxury consumer items. Instead of importing, the private sector was encouraged to produce them locally, which entailed the importation of machinery and intermediate goods. Furthermore, imports without foreign exchange transfers – a system which had increasingly encouraged illegal currency exports – were banned; importers had again to obtain a letter of credit from the Commercial Bank. Apart from these purely economic measures, the Economic Penalties Law – essentially an anti-corruption law – was updated in 1977,[120] and special economic security courts were established to deal with smuggling, particularly illegal foreign-exchange trade, corruption – particularly bribery and fraud connected to contracts with the state – and other economic offences.

Such laws would not necessarily end the corruption which had spread conspiciously. The regime made it clear, however, that the earlier *infitah* policies were not intended to give the private sector the freedom to determine the course of economic policies. On the contrary, the regime would still be able to define the limits for private business, and individual businessmen remained subject to the good will of the regime. Concessions made to the private sector were revocable, and they could be granted, upheld, or withdrawn selectively – import restrictions being lifted or imposed for certain goods and not for others, investments allowed in a particular sector of a particular industry, and soon. This became particularly clear in 1980. Since 1979, an increasingly violent, Islamist-led anti-regime opposition had once again emerged. Hoping to rally the support of, among others, the leaders of the Damascus business community, the regime lifted a series of import restrictions.[121] This and other measures – particularly a 65 per cent wage increase to maintain the allegiance of those employed in the public sector – were taken, out of purely political as opposed to economic considerations. A year later, in view of a deteriorating foreign-exchange situation, the government imposed new limits on the freedom of importation, circumscribed free-zone activities, and, as noted, began to adopt an austere budget policy. These measures made it clear that the period of state-led growth on which the *infitah* of the 1970s had been founded, had come to an end.

The Second *infitah*: Cutting Back the State

From 1983, initial measures towards a new economic opening were introduced, and by 1986/87, representatives of Syria's commercial class had begun to speak of a new *infitah*. This second *infitah* was qualitatively different from that of the 1970s. Then, public resources had seemed almost unlimited, and the state, leading economic development, opened or expanded existing fields of private-sector activities according to its own socio-political and economic priorities. Throughout most of the 1980s, however, as outlined above, Syria faced severe economic problems – basically a foreign exchange crisis which developed into a general slump. Diminishing public resources and austerity budgets now forced the government into gradually opening up to the private sector, abandoning some of its instruments of control, and surrendering some economic levers to the private sector.

As in the 1970s, this new *infitah* was a phased, gradualist undertaking. Policies were largely home-made, that is, not forced upon Syria from abroad. Obviously, they did not follow a pre-fabricated plan or schedule, even though, eventually, the reforms and changes entailed in the process turned out to be very much in line with structural adjustment programmes (SAPs) that other countries adopted under the tutelage of the International Monetary Fund (IMF) or the World Bank.

The *intifah* was still continuing in 1994. So far, three overlapping stages or bundles of measures can be distinguished; a fourth one is in the making. An initial stage lasted until around 1987/88. Paralleled by the government's austerity attempts, it was characterized by still cautious moves to somewhat relax foreign-exchange regimes and thereby rid the state of a responsibility which it could no longer sufficiently fulfil. Since 1982, it had become increasingly difficult for Syria's state-owned Commercial Bank to provide the private sector with foreign exchange for imports, and by 1984 the Bank virtually declined to open any further letters of credit for private importers. Against this background, the government took a series of measures aimed at enabling the private sector to provide its own foreign exchange and, at the same time, increasing the state's foreign exchange reserves. The most important step in this context was, in 1983, to allow private manufacturers to keep 50 per cent of their hard currency export earnings for their own imports; the remaining half was to be sold to the Commercial Bank at the official or, depending on the class of goods, a more favourable parallel rate. In 1987, this measure was extended to include all private exporters – not only manufacturers, while the percentage of export earnings that could be kept was raised to 75 per cent for a list of export goods compiled and constantly supplemented by the Ministry of Economy and Foreign Trade.[122] Syrians and non-Syrians alike were encouraged to open foreign currency accounts at the Commercial Bank to finance their imports. The foreign exchange deposited was supposed to have originated from property or economic activities abroad, but it was also announced that no questions would be asked about its source. At the same time, the Ministry of Economy and Foreign Trade began once more to gradually open up the field for private importation, lifting, on the whole, more import restrictions than it imposed. In 1985 imports without currency transfers were permitted again. To an extent, the liberalization of foreign trade regimes only sanctioned the *de facto* abolition of effective state control over foreign trade through increased smuggling. Shortages of consumer goods as well as industrial or agricultural supplies resulting from the state's difficult foreign-exchange situation created opportunities for a range of private traders – illegally but effectively – to privatize parts of the public-sector foreign-trade monopolies.[123]

Through all these measures, however piecemeal their introduction, the state's legal monopoly on the disposal of foreign exchange was loosened, and the currency black market boomed. A new law against currency smuggling was promulgated – legislative Decree 24 of 1986. This threatened with severe penalties those who dealt illegally in Syrian currency or foreign exchange. However, since there was a demand for foreign exchange which the official sector could not satisfy, this measure did not put an end to currency black-marketeering; it only served to a concentration of the business.

Apart from foreign-trade and currency regulations, this initial phase of the second *infitah* involved a substantial liberalization of Syria's agricultural economy. In 1986, following the earlier model of mixed tourism and transport companies, the establishment of mixed agricultural joint-stock companies was permitted.[124] Although the more far-reaching demands of Syrian businessmen, such as scrapping the 1958 law on agricultural relations, were not met, the new regulation represented a fundamental departure from the land reform and agricultural policies of the 1960s, which had officially been maintained to that date. Instead of limiting private property in agricultural land, the concentration of vast landed holdings in a few hands was again permitted and even encouraged in order to mobilize private capital – both Syrian and Arab – for productive investments, particularly into export-oriented or otherwise foreign-exchange-earning ventures. With the same purpose, new investments in the tourism industry were encouraged with the offer of tax holidays and exemptions from customs duties, and the restrictions on free-zone investments imposed in 1981 were once more lifted.[125]

The emergence of the mixed agricultural sector marked the transition to a more far-reaching stage of economic liberalization, the main element of which was a phased devaluation of the Syrian currency and a considerable liberalization of trade regimes. In 1986, a new "encouragement" rate for the Syrian pound was introduced, originally for non-commercial transactions. Initially this rate was close to the black- or free-market rate. With the further deterioration of the Syrian currency's value, however, it soon became just another, if more favourable, artificial exchange rate. At the end of 1987, the pound was officially devalued from 3.95 to 11.2 LS/$. In 1989, the Ministry of Supply announced that it would revalue imported consumer goods distributed through its outlets at a pound-rate of 40 LS/$ – a rate close to the then free-market rate. In the same year, the Ministry of Economy and Foreign Trade for the first time officially acknowledged, if still on a limited scale, the validity of the free-market rate as an indicator of the value of the Syrian currency. Exporters of certain agricultural products were granted the "neighbouring countries' rate" – essentially the free or black market rate minus some 10 per cent – for that part of their export earnings which they had to sell to the Commercial Bank.[126] Step by step, the free-market rate was accepted. In 1990, the state offered to buy private export earnings – if exporters did not want to use them for importation – at the neighbouring countries' rate; alternatively owners of foreign exchange could assign it to needy importers through the Commercial Bank.[127] The latter measure represented a qualitative step insofar as it allowed for a limited degree of private foreign-exchange dealings, thus stripping the state of a legal monopoly and an instrument of control. In 1991, the neighbouring countries' rate was officially applied for basically all personal and private-sector transactions, including that part of foreign exchange earnings which exporters still had to surrender to the bank.[128] Certain exports, particularly those of fruits and vegetables, had been fully exempted from the regulation obliging exporters to sell a fraction of their foreign-exchange earnings to the bank. There remained limits on the sale of foreign exchange by the bank, dictated by the scarcity of hard currency, and the official rate was maintained. By applying the neighbouring countries' rate to more and more types of transactions, however, – from 1991, the government also began to calculate certain budgetary items and public-sector imports and exports on the basis of the neigbouring countries' rate – an effective, gradual currency devaluation took place.[129]

This was accompanied by a deregulation of foreign trade. The private sector was allowed to import raw materials for public-sector companies unable to earn their own foreign exchange – such as the Hama iron-and-steel mill and the Dayr al-Zur paper factory – and let these establishments work for their account against a certain percentage of the material or hard-currency payment.[130] In 1990, expatriates were granted special, though still limited, rights to import goods generally banned from importation. Private traders were permitted to import on behalf of public-sector foreign-trade agencies, and the monopoly of public-sector agencies to import and distribute to retailers such basic consumer goods as rice, sugar, tea, coffee and cooking fat, was abandoned. Similarly, public-sector monopolies to purchase certain fruits and vegetables from farmers were gradually relinquished. The state maintained a monopoly over the trade in agricultural products regarded as strategic, such as cotton, wheat, and sugar-beet.

At the end of this phase, the government had largely surrendered its control over foreign exchange to the market; the state-owned banks, instead of being instruments of control over private exports and imports, were gradually reduced to the role of intermediary. While control instruments over foreign trade were maintained, their use was limited, giving way, here too, to market forces; the idea that the state could, by means of its foreign-trade policies, effectively steer the development of production and consumption was abandoned.

The third stage of Syria's second *infitah* comprises a bundle of measures intended to liberalize investment policies and generally encourage private production and investment, particularly in industry. In agriculture, the basic turn to encouraging large capital investments had already been made with the 1986 law on mixed agricompanies. Two years later, the government began to increase considerably agricultural procurement prices for crops which were still to be marketed solely through state agencies; it also began to allow farmers to import agricultural machinery. Both measures had visible effects on agricultural production and supply. Many peasants, who in previous years had left some of their fields uncropped or had tried to smuggle some of their products out of the country, regained their interest in producing the strategic crops which the state monopolized, and in investing in their farms. The increase of procurement prices did not as such represent a liberalization measure; but it did mean the government's implicit acceptance of market principles.

As regards industry, the main thrust towards a liberalization of investment did not appear before 1991. Already in 1986, however, the government had considerably extended the list of industries open to private activities, a measure taken on other occasions, such as in 1981, when private businessmen had been encouraged to produce locally goods banned from importation. By opening new spaces for private activities promising good returns, these measures had positive effects. They did not, however, represent any substantial change in industrial policy: by means of a constantly changeable list of "industries regarded as falling within the activities of the private sector permitted to be licensed in the Syrian Arab Region" the government still widened or narrowed the scope for private industrial activities at will or, in friendlier terms, according to the country's development needs as defined in the five-year plans. Potential investors could never be sure that the establishment of an industrial firm to produce, for example, chewing-gum or herbicides – both added to the list in 1981 – would still be permitted in the following year when the government might have decided that enough producers of this particular item were at work in the country. A change to this approach first became apparent in 1988, when, instead of the list of licensed industrial activities being updated, a negative list was produced which defined those industries to be reserved solely for the public sector, or for either the public or mixed sector. By implication, all other industries lay open to private business. The majority of industries still reserved for the public sector were regarded as strategic, in a few other cases the maintenance of public-sector monopolies was obviously intended to protect existing public-sector establishments against competition.[131]

A qualitative change was brought about after another three years with the promulgation of an investment law, generally referred to as Law No. 10 of 1991. This law has greatly widened the scope for private investment, allowing Syrian, Arab, and foreign investors to launch private or "mixed" investments in basically any field of the Syrian economy. Capital investments must not be below 10 million LS ($240,000), and all projects are subject to authorization from a new Higher Council for Investments, headed by the Prime Minister. Applications from potential investors have to be decided upon within no more than 60 days; decisions should take into account such factors as the project's expected contribution to the national income and to exports, its effects on the labour market, and its modernization effects. An Investment Office was established to consult with investors and to prepare decisions for the council. Approved projects are granted up to seven years' tax holiday, are guaranteed the right to repatriate capital invested and profits, and are widely exempt from import restrictions and customs duties. Parallel to the investment law, a new tax law was enacted which substantially reduced business taxes.[132] Before that, taxes on profits had, theoretically at least, reached 90 per cent or more; private-sector representatives, particularly industrialists, had therefore long demanded that tax laws be reformed. Both the investment law and the tax law granted special incentives – particularly longer tax holidays, easier access to foreign exchange, and lower tax rates – to export-oriented establishments.

After the implementation of the investment and tax laws, *infitah* policies slowed down. Overall economic indicators, particularly Syria's foreign exchange situation, had improved, thus making the need for further reform less visible and pressing. Private sector demands had been satisfied to a large extent. And, as major high-policy decisions had to be prepared in the context of the Middle East peace process, economic reform was not the most urgent issue on the leadership's agenda. Nor was a quick pursuit of further reform steps necessarily expedient, given that many in the military, the party, and the bureaucracy found both the peace negotiations and economic reform hard to digest. But the reform process was not terminated. By 1994, when work on this study was finished, the process of liberalizing import regimes was continuing, preparations to establish a stock exchange were underway, and discussions were taking place about the reform of Syria's banking sector.[133] It was not out of the question that the Syrian currency would move towards convertibility, and that Decree No. 24, which criminalized everyone outside the public-sector banking system who dealt in foreign exchange, would eventually be shelved.

The Structural Results of *infitah*

The most notable result of Syria's second *infitah* was a remarkable growth of the private sector. In 1990, for the first time since 1963, private-sector capital investments had exceeded those of the public sector. The private share of imports had increased from some 25 per cent at the beginning of the 1980s to about 50 per cent in the early 1990s.[134] According to the Damascus Chamber of Commerce, the private sector now contributed some 55 per cent of Syria's gross domestic product, covering 98.6 per cent of agriculture, 72 per cent of transport, 62 per cent of trade, 59 per cent of finance and rents, 50 per cent of building and construction, 37 per cent of converting industries, and 13 per cent of services.[135] By the mid-1980s, as noted, some 40 per cent of the labour force in industry and construction had been employed by the state. In the following years, the employment share of the private sector increased substantially. By 1991, the state employed no more than 30 per cent of the workforce in industry and construction.[136]

The private sector's improved position in the national economy, as reflected in all available statistics, was in the first place the result of the public sector's deteriorating performance.[137] Nevertheless, there was overall real growth in the private sector, accompanied by a partial restructuring within the private economy. Branches that expanded exceptionally were those that had always been regarded as the most profitable and were now, as was the case during the first *infitah*, the prime beneficiaries of the reform package: import-export trade and commissioneering, real estate, internal trade with imported or locally manufactured consumer goods for mainly upper and upper-middle-class use and other services. Industry was, and still is, regarded as the more difficult way to profit, and big business, in Syrian terms, was limited to commercial enterprise. It is notable that the main emphasis of *infitah* policies – as it was in the 1970s – was on freedom for private trade and a gradual deregulation of the foreign-exchange market. Agricultural liberalization centred upon measures to encourage large-scale investments, while the freedom of land reform peasants to make decisions about production and marketing according to their own preferences remained limited. Moreover measures to encourage effectively domestic industrial activities came late. Only since 1985, therefore, has a considerable number of larger industrial establishments, employing a workforce of 50, 100, or even more, begun to emerge. In 1992, average registered employment in the private manufacturing sector was still below three persons per establishment.[138]

This is not to say that private manufacturing did not benefit from the *infitah* of the 1970s and 1980s. Specific opportunities lay in producing for a widening domestic market for light industrial consumer goods, and in exports to the socialist countries, particularly to the Soviet Union. Syria's debt-for-goods swaps with the USSR served practically as a large support programme for private-sector industry.[139] The crisis of the 1980s, however, hit private manufacturing hard while the commercial sector, on the whole, did not lose. Production in the private industrial sector, as in the public sector, suffered palpable cutbacks over much of the 1980s. Gains and losses were unevenly distributed as a number of establishments remained highly profitable. These were, in the main, comparatively large establishments that managed to benefit from protective bans on imported consumer goods and were able to export part of their produce and thus secure their own foreign exchange.[140]

The 1991 investment law represented a qualitative departure, triggering, for the first time, a wave of new, bigger investments. Less than two years after the enactment of the law, more than 700 investment projects had been licensed, some 300 of them in industry, the rest mainly in the services sector.[141] In 1993, plans were underway for private and mixed-sector companies to re-enter or enter such strategic industries as electricity production, notably an industry from which the private sector had been excluded 30 years earlier, and car assembly.[142]

On the whole, we can estimate the number of private, non-agricultural establishments in Syria to have grown to some 400–450,000 by the early 1990s, up to twice the 1981 figure. Some 60 per cent belonged to the trade sector, up to one quarter to industry, the rest was made up by construction, transport and other services. More than half of these establishments were family shops and workshops that did not employ wage labour on a regular basis. Less than an estimated three or four per cent of the private industrial establishments – and a similar proportion can be assumed to apply in the other sectors – were more than petty ventures employing a registered workforce of less than ten persons.[143] Within that fraction, a remarkable group of bigger private establishments has emerged. As the gap between this upper stratum and the vast petty-bourgeois majority of Syria's private sector widens,[144] a limited, yet visible trend towards concentration has become apparent. This trend is supported by the new division between the export-oriented establishments, which practically came to monopolize the foreign exchange legally available for private imports, and others that were producing for the domestic market and finding enormous difficulties in covering the foreign-exchange needs of their production.

The growth of the private sector was accompanied by a substantial reduction in the role of the state. While government budgets had equalled more than 40 per cent of GDP in 1970, and more than 50 per cent from the mid-1970s to 1985, this ratio had decreased to some 25 per cent by the early 1990s.[145] Similarly, as noted, the public sector's share of investments, production, and employment had all become smaller. The capacity of the state to lead the economy and to determine the course of socio-economic development had diminished; this was due both to the quantitative reduction of state economic activity and to the functional cutback of government interference in the economy and, accordingly, to the expansion of private-sector autonomy. One can no longer speak in practical terms of a planned economy in Syria. The 1986–90 Five Year Plan, as noted, was never published; sectoral committees then worked on drafts for a 1991–95 plan, which, however, was never given a comprehensive form. And while the state still sets the frame for economic policy, the abandonment of public-sector trade and production monopolies, the deregulation of trade and currency regimes, and the encouragement of comparatively large private investments have all limited its ability to determine what – and under what conditions – is to be produced, sold, and consumed in the country.

4. Conclusion: Prospects and Limits of Economic Change

The two moves towards *infitah* that the Syrian economy underwent in the 1970s and 1980s were brought about against distinctively different economic backgrounds. In the first case, abundance provided the motive for economic opening; in the second case it was scarcity of resources and the threat of state bankruptcy. In the 1970s *infitah* policies served as a means of distributing Syria's increased political and oil rents; in the 1980s, the objective was to mobilize domestic private resources to compensate for the state's inability not only to maintain state-led growth strategies but also to secure the supply of imported consumer goods and production inputs – both for the private and for the public sector. On the whole, Syria's *infitah* of the 1980s served its purposes, even though the remarkable improvement of Syria's overall economic situation has, to a large part, been due to increased oil exports and Arab aid.

Economic Prospects

Crude oil and oil products are likely to remain Syria's main exportable commodity. It seems reasonable to suppose that oil will continue to make up no less than 60 per cent of the country's export earnings in the foreseeable future. The surge of private-sector manufactured exports in the second half of the 1980s and the extraordinary contribution of these to the balance surplus of the 1989–91 period were mainly a matter of Syria's debt barter with the former USSR, which is unlikely to be resumed on its former scale. Private industries are certainly up for further growth and will try to at least cover their import needs by exportation. Textiles and food production, Syria's traditional industries with their relative labour-intensiveness and high reliance on domestic raw products, offer the greatest comparative advantages and opportunities. However, hard currency markets for Syria's manufactured goods exports are still not easy to find, and an expansion of Syria's industrial exports will therefore most probably be limited. There is a market for Syrian agricultural products, particularly in the Gulf countries, but there are limits to the expansion of these exports, since other and new regional suppliers, including Israel, will try to gain or expand their share of that market. Exportwise, therefore, Syria will most probably remain highly dependent on petroleum and the uncertainties of the world oil market.

Assuming that oil exports will remain around their 1992/93 level – growing local demand is likely to consume further production increases – , that agricultural and industrial exports as well as tourism receipts experience visible but limited, and – as far as weather-dependent agriculture is concerned – unstable growth, and that both capital- and consumer-goods imports will increase under the impact of growing consumer demand, liberalized foreign-trade regimes, and an active encouragement of private investments, we may conclude that Syria's future trade-and-services balance will hover between more or less even and slightly negative. Such a situation would be substantially better than that of the 1980s. It would secure at a reasonable level the inflow of most of the imports needed for consumption and the employment of existing productive capacities. It would not, however, by itself secure the means for big investment-based leaps forward.

Responding to the crisis of the 1980s with a combination of austerity and liberalization, the Syrian government has to some extent managed to streamline public expenditure and to reduce foreign trade imbalances. The big challenge for the period to come will be finding employment for a growing and, in the Syrian case, extremely young population – a task often neglected by the stabilization and adjustment programmes in many Third World countries. Estimates of the number of jobs that have to be created in the near future alone in order to absorb jobseekers range between an official 200,000 and a somewhat exaggerated 500,000 a year.[146] Even if a conservatively estimated annual average of 200,000 to 220,000 new jobseekers is assumed for the rest of the 1990s, and an average of 250,000 to 300,000 in the first decade of the next century, it is hard to see how enough jobs can be found.[147] The public sector may, at best, increase its civilian staff by some 50–60,000 a year; half that figure, however, seems more realistic.[148] An expansion of the military is not to be expected if the peace process continues. In the private industrial and services sector, some 80–100,000 jobs a year may be created under favourable conditions.[149]

Agriculture is not likely to absorb any significant numbers of new jobseekers. Land reclamation and irrigation projects have begun to make visible progress since the beginning of the 1990s and a further expansion of Syria's cultivated area and agricultural production can be expected in the decade to come. As of 1994, new dam-building projects were planned on the Khabur and Orontes rivers,[150] and these with the Euphrates basin project (still to be completed) are most probably the last large-scale irrigation schemes Syria is likely to undertake. Any expansion of agriculture is liable to be accompanied by further mechanization and rationalization. Agricultural employment, therefore, is bound to decrease rather than increase.

Thus, even under favourable conditions (removal of bottlenecks – particularly electricity shortages – that impede full use of industrial capacity, stabilization of oil prices and real growth rates that exceed the demographic increase), unemployment, or rather, marginal underemployment will increase.[151] Furthermore, given that government budgets will remain under strain and heavily burdened with unavoidable expenses for the maintenance of basic services – particularly public health, education, and energy production which suffered during the years of austerity – it is unlikely that public-sector wages will increase enough to make up for the losses of the 1980s. Moderate real growth can reasonably be expected for Syria's forseeable future. However, the limited ability of the state and the private sector to absorb those entering the job market, the lack of a meaningful public social security system, the losses of real income on the part of the majority of those employed by the state, and the growing divide between a small upper stratum and a vast petty-bourgeois basis in the private sector, are all likely to ensure that such growth will most probably accentuate rather than redeem the inegalitarian effects of Syria's *infitah*.

Syria, as outlined, has long relied on external resources for much of its development and security expenditure. In the 1970s, high inflows of external resources and the income from its own oil exports gave Syria all the characteristic features of a rentier economy.[152] Rents accruing to and distributed by the state became the main source of growth; apart from financing the build-up of the public sector and administration, the state, to all intents and purposes, subsidized imports, private trade and, to a lesser extent, import-substituting goods production. It did so by means of overvalued exchange rates, and farming out privileges and monopolies to well-connected entrepreneurs. In the 1980s, as shown, the relative importance of external rents – both as a portion of GNP and of government budgets – decreased.[153] Still, by the early 1990s, oil income represented the main source of foreign exchange and the largest single source of government revenue.[154] As noted, however, the entire government revenue was sufficient only to maintain existing structures and services. Any additional major investments and other public expenditures aimed at precipitating growth, extending public services and employment, and improving the income of state employees or living standards in general, will most probably remain dependent on the state's ability to generate political rents from its regional environment. Playing with the political conditions of the region, as Hannoyer and Seurat noted in their analysis of Syria's political economy of the 1970s, had become as important for the regime as the improvement of the country's economic performance.[155] During the 1980s, the government learnt that such an improvement of the productive base was essential for maintaining the basic functions of the state. Political rents were nonetheless to be sought, mainly to order the economy and to support the regime's room for manoeuvre.

By 1994, given that more than a stabilization of oil prices was unlikely, and that Syria already received up to 25 per cent of all Arab aid, Damascus could not expect any considerable increase in its oil revenue or of Arab financial support. Western financial aid could be set to increase, but not to an extent that would make up for the stagnation – albeit at a comparatively high level – of Arab aid.[156] Also, it was far from clear to the Syrian government whether the ongoing Middle East peace process would evenutally bring a dividend – in terms of both direct financial support accruing to the state and expatriate or foreign investments – equal to the Arab support which it received as political rent for its front-line position in the Arab–Israeli conflict.[157] Whatever the outcome of the peace process, it seems reasonable to suppose that Syria will continue to draw on a relatively decreasing, yet substantial political rent from, in particular, the Arab oil monarchies. Both the loose alignment of Syria and Egypt with the states of the Gulf Cooperation Council under the 1991 Damascus Declaration, and Syria's ability to obstruct unpalatable regional arrangements may help in this respect. Given the limits of the prospective rent income which the Syrian regime can thus be expected to control, its continuous inflow does not invalidate the need for a mobilization of private resources and, generally, an improvement in economic performance. At the same time, the mere existence of this still substantial rent will, among other factors, help preserve the remarkable restraint of the private sector – which itself can expect to benefit directly and indirectly from state-controlled rent inflows[158] – with regard to far-reaching demands concerning the progress of economic reform.

Limits and Rationale of Liberalization

Both the limited *infitah* of abundance Syria pursued in the 1970s and the deepergoing *infitah* of public poverty in the 1980s fall short of the structural adjustment favoured by orthodox economists. No large-scale privatizations have taken place, or are to be expected. There has been, as noted, some quasi-privatization of state land through the establishment of the agricultural mixed sector, and several dozen outlets of Syria's public-sector retail organizations have been closed and sold off to private merchants.[159] More privatizations of this kind may well happen, and some public-sector companies, especially in the services sector, may be transformed into "mixed" companies by injection of private capital. There could also be more privatization by liberalization, whereby private entrepreneurs are allowed to offer goods or services hitherto monopolized by the public sector. A case in point is the public transport system of several Syrian cities. In 1993, private entrepreneurs, after being allowed to import micro-buses, started to set up effective public transport networks and managed to marginalize public-sector bus transport. Public-sector establishments will probably gain more flexibility through some measure of administrative decentralization, but the public sector as such, particularly the industrial sector, seems to be there to stay. Notably, there are no private-sector demands for any large-scale privatization, let alone private-sector interest and ability to take over the larger public-sector companies and invest the capital needed to bring them to a healthy state. There is some economic and a lot of political rationality in maintaining the public sector as a producer of basic commoditites and an employer of a relatively decreasing but substantial part of the labour force. The public sector is certainly not the most cost-effective producer. But its industries have been developing linkage effects on other sectors of the domestic economy; public-sector establishments have been located and offer some employment in the more distant rural areas shunned by private investors; and public-sector production serves to feed and clothe those who cannot afford the higher-quality products of private industry. Whatever its flaws, the public sector still serves as a means of patronage and control, and of rudimentary social security.

Not only has Syria's *infitah* stopped short of any large-scale privatization. Trade, foreign-exchange and investment regimes have been liberalized, but not completely. There is still no discussion about abandoning import-licensing as such, and it would be a mistake to assume that Syria's business community is in favour of such a total liberalization of foreign trade. For the near future, at least, one should not expect investment licensing to be abolished or exchanged for a surveillance system based merely on technical or ecological standards. Even though in practice the government will not stand in the way of reasonable private investment projects, the present licensing system remains an instrument of political control which the regime is unlikely to give away easily.

The changes to the economic structure which Syria's second *infitah* has engendered are nevertheless more than just superficial. The state has definitely given up some levers of the economy, market principles have come to play a larger role, and private sector interests have gained a stronger position than was the case in the 1970s. We can assume that this at least partial deregulation of the economy will not be revoked. Notably, the reform process which began in a moment of deep economic crisis has not been abandoned but deepened since Syria's general economic situation began to improve again from the end of the 1980s. It should be realized, however, that while the state has lost some control over the economy, certainly over production and foreign trade, the regime has not lost control over the reform process as such. The scope and schedule of the reform have been defined by the regime; and the transformation of Syria's heavily statist economy of the 1970s and early 1980s into a more flexible, more market-oriented, and more privately managed development capitalism has neither abolished nor seriously circumscribed the political decision-making power of the regime.

Political as well as purely economic cost-benefit considerations have obviously been taken into account during the entire reform process making the Syrian *infitah* a highly selective affair.[160] The rationale of economic reform was not simply to stabilize the economy but, as noted before, to stabilize the regime. By abandoning some economic functions of the state and increasing the economic autonomy of private business, the regime was able to rid itself of financial burdens and mobilize private resources which otherwise would not have been employed, at least not in Syria. Indemnification from economic failures by making the private sector responsible for a larger part of the economy may also have been a reform incentive.[161] At the same time, *infitah* policies have brought about and furthered what can be understood as a social alliance between the regime elite and parts of the bourgeoisie.

Since there is no clear economic and development strategy on the part of the regime, it is hardly possible to talk of a regime-inspired social project. However, while economic needs have certainly made reform necessary (as emphasized above), the social interests of those in power – and of those without power – must be taken into account as factors influencing the direction of economic change and its social implications. Economic reform is not a socially neutral process. Both the build-up and the ongoing transformation of Syria's statist economy have, as the following chapter will show, produced winners and losers and entailed significant changes generally to the country's social structure.

Notes

1. Cf. Syrian Arab Republic (SAR), Central Bureau of Statistics (CBS), *Population Census in the Syrian Arab Republic 1970*, 2 vols., n.d. (1976). Illiteracy figures relate to persons over ten years of age.

2. According to official statistics, only 50.4 per cent of the population lived in urban areas in 1991. Cf. Syrian Arab Republic, Central Bureau of Statistics (CBS), *Statistical Abstract (Stat. Abs.) 1992* (Damascus, n.d.), p 73. Urbanization, however, is largely understated in official statistics.

3. *Stat. Abs. 1992*, p 75.

4. For figures, see Table II.1. In general, it has to be stressed that Syrian statistics express tendencies rather than giving exact figures. See the introductory chapter above.

5. For a general picture of the problems Arab countries encountered as a result of their import-substituting industrialization policies cf. Alan Richards/ John Waterbury, *A Political Economy of the Middle East*, pp 219ff.

6. Cf. The World Bank, *World Development Report 1992* and *1993*, Table 1.

7. Calculations based on the free market exchange rate of the Syrian Pound (LS) (45–50 LS/$ in the early 1990s) as well the World Bank's computation of GNP p/c (which is based on Syrian statistics, although the official exchange rate of 11,05 LS/$ is adjusted according to the World Bank's own methods) certainly understate the purchasing power of the Syrian currency. The purchasing power estimates of the UN International Comparison Programme (ICP), on the other hand, which classify Syria below Jordan but above Turkey and Tunisia, might overstate the Syrian currency's value since figures for Syria, in contrast to other countries, have been extrapolated from 1975 data. For the ICP figures cf. *World Development Report 1993*, Table 30.

8. Cf. in detail: Wirth, *Syrien*, pp 99ff; Hamash, *Tatawwur al-iqtisad*, pp 28f.

9. Source: The Economist Intelligence Unit (EIU), *Country Report Syria*

(London: The Economic Intelligence Unit, various issues).

10. Until the oil wells in the Dayr al-Zur area went on stream, Syria produced only heavy high-sulphur crude from its northern oilfields. This heavy crude had to be blended with imported light crude.

11. According to World Bank data, annual GDP growth averaged 9.9 per cent in the 1970s and 2.6 per cent in the 1980s. Cf. *World Development Report 1993*, Table 2.

12. According to the *Statistical Abstracts (Stat. Abs.) 1971*, p. 494 (Syrian Arab Republic (SAR), Central Bureau of Statistics (CBS), *Statistical Abstracts* (Damascus, annually), the increase was actually by 50 per cent (in 1963 prices); according to later calculations with changed base years, it amounted to only some 20 per cent. Cf. *Stat. Abs. 1992*, p 502.

13. Ibid.

14. Syrian statistics do not break up GDP into "mining" and "manufacturing." Production indices, though measuring output instead of value added, reveal clearly enough the differential between the growth of oil production and manufacturing industries. See Table II.1.

15. There is no official wage index in Syria. We can, however, assume the average wage index for the industrial public sector – which can be calculated from published data – to be representative of the overall development of wages and salaries.

16. Cf. more detailed: Perthes, *Staat und Gesellschaft*, pp 169f; and Syrian cost-of-living calculations as contained in: General Federation of Trade Unions in the Syrian Arab Republic (GFTU), *Mu'tamar al-ibda' al-watani wa-l-'itimad 'ala al-dhat*, pp 190f; Syrian Communist Party, *Hawl ba'd al-tatawwarat*, p 41.

17. The 25 per cent pay rise of 1 June 1989, e.g., was accompanied by a gradual reduction of subsidies on bread, vegetable oil, petrol, and butane gas. The salary of a public-sector employee of the lowest wage group was raised by 270 LS/month with the pay rise. For a lower-class family of six, the increase in the price of bread alone caused monthly additional expenses of some 180 LS.

18. See below.

19. Cf. David Butter, "Syria's Under the Counter Economy", in *MEED*, 23 February 1990; Perthes, *Staat und Gesellschaft*, p 109; 'Arif Dalila, "al-Qita' al-'amm fi suriya. al-Waqi' wa-l-afaq", in Economic Sciences Association, *Seventh Economic Tuesday Symposium, Issues of the Syrian Economy, Damascus, 28 April 1992 – 27 April 1993* (Damascus, n.d. [1993]), pp 22f.

20. Cf. Perthes, "The Syrian Private Industrial and Commercial Sectors and the State", pp 219f.

21. EIU, *Country Report Syria*, 1/1993, pp 6f.

22. Source: SAR, *Stat. Abs.*, various issues.

23. Cf. *World Development Report 1993*, Table 9; Richards/Waterbury, *Political Economy*, pp 220f.

24. Public sector investments accounted for 60.2 per cent of total gross investments reported for that period. Only in 1989 and 1990 did the public-

sector share fall below 50 per cent. Source: *Stat. Abs.*, various issues.

25. The deficit in the 1992 budget has been calculated at 21, that in the 1993 budget at 35 per cent; cf. *MEED*, 30 July 1993. Had foreign loans been calculated at the free-market rate of the Syrian pound, not – as was done until 1992 – at the official rate, previous budget deficits would have turned out even larger, and surpluses turned into deficits.

26. Source: International Monetary Fund (IMF), *Government Finance Statistics Yearbook* (Washington, D.C.: The Fund, various issues).

27. Cf. Hamash, *al-Iqtisad al-suri*, p. 79. More exact figures are not available because of the under-reporting of grants, the confusion produced by the application of different exchange rates, and the lack of a break-down of data on gross investments into their domestic and foreign-exchange elements.

28. The index of retail prices published in the annual *Statistical Abstracts* which is largely based on official prices is likely to understate real inflation figures. For different estimates on inflation, cf. Munir al-Hamash, *al-Tanmiya al-sina'iyya fi suriya wa-afaq tajdidiha*, p 90.

29. International Monetary Fund (IMF), *Government Finance Statistics* (Washington, D.C., various issues); 1991 preliminary figures are based on Law No. 7, 17 May 1992 (General Budget of 1992). In the budget projects, promulgated by law and summarily published in the annual *Stat. Abs.*, the proportionate share of the Ministry of Defence tends to be lower than its share of actual expenditures. This is mainly so since actual revenues and, accordingly, the expenditures of civilian ministries, often remain below the forecasts – particularly investment expenditures where projects and projected payments are delayed. The Ministry of Defence, in contrast, tends to spend at least the amount to which the annual budgets entitle it.

30. Cf. U.S. Arms Control and Disarmament Agency (ACDA), *World Military Expenditures and Arms Transfers* (Washington, D.C., various issues).

31. Cf. *al-Hayat*, 12 January 1992.

32. Cf. Stockholm International Peace Research Institute (SIPRI), *SIPRI Yearbook. World Armanents and Disarmament* (various issues); ACDA, *World Military Expenditures*. ACDA estimates tend to be slightly higher.

33. Cf. ibid. Syria's defence expenditures as a percentage of GDP range far below those of Iraq and more or less, with considerable annual variations, on the same level with Israel and Jordan.

34. Cf. in more detail: Clawson, *Unaffordable Ambitions*, pp 30ff, 50ff; Perthes, "Syrien". As a matter of fact, neither arms shipments to Syria nor payments on arms are reported in Syria's foreign-trade and balance-of-payment statistics. According to Clawson, military aid to Syria amounted to some $22 billion for the 1977–88 period – enough to cover basically all arms imports.

35. Notably, Syrian budget figures do not show any significant rise in military expenditures directly corresponding to the deployment of troops in Lebanon. Opinions on this issue, however, differ considerably between authors concerned with things Syrian. Eliahu Kanovsky, among others, considers Syria's involvement in Lebanon and other effects of the Lebanese war a burden

on the Syrian economy. Cf. his "What's behind", p 283. Fawaz Traboulsi, in contrast, contends that Syria has been "gaining economically rather than losing" from its military presence in Lebanon. Cf. his "Confessional Lines", *Middle East Report*, Vol 20 (Jan./Feb. 1990), No. 162, pp 9–10. I have pointed out elsewhere that the Lebanese war had quite positive effects, sectorally at least, on the Syrian economy. Cf. my "The Syrian Economy in the 1980s", *Middle East Journal*, Vol 46 (1992), 1, pp 37–58 (56f).

36. Cf. Kanovsky, "What's behind", p 296.

37. The political costs of Syria's high militarization will be discussed below. Cf. chapter IV.

38. From 1973 till the end of the 1980s, Syria received more than 25 per cent of the total concessional assistance Arab countries and funds extended to other Arab countries. Between 1979 and 1987, Syria even obtained an average 30.7 per cent of all Arab concessional aid. Source: Pierre van den Boogaerde, *Financial Assistance from Arab Countries and Arab Regional Institutions* (Washington, D.C.: IMF, 1991), p 67.

39. Cf. Clawson, *Unaffordable Ambitions*, pp 31f; Perthes, "Syrien"; Rizkallah Hilan, "The Effects on Economic Development in Syria", pp 61, 64.

40. Figures represent official estimates which tend rather to be too low than too high. For the 1970s, therefore, these estimates have been upwardly corrected in recent Syrian and IMF statistics. Cf. IMF, *Balance of Payment Statistics* (Washington, D.C.: The Fund, various years).

41. Clawson, *Unaffordable Ambitions*, p 54.

42. On the basis of data published in a Ba'th party conference report, the total civilian aid that Syria received from other Arab countries between the October war and the end of 1974 can be estimated at $1,200 million. Cf. Arab Socialist Ba'th Party (ASBP), *Reports and Decisions of the Sixth Regional Conference convened in Damascus, 5–15 April 1975, Economic Report* (Damascus, 1976), pp 155, 162. Officially reported Arab assistance to Syria amounted to only $945 million for 1973 and 1974; cf. Boogaerde, *Financial Assistance*, p 76.

43. Sources: OECD Development Assistance Committee, *Development Co-operation* (Paris: OECD, various issues); Boogaerde, *Financial Assistance*.

44. Cf. Economist Intelligence Unit (EIU), *Syria: Country Profile 1993/94*, p 53.

45. On the oil deliveries to 1987 cf. Clawson, *Unaffordable Ambitions*, p 55. Syria's 1990 budget was the last one projecting an entry under the title of "Grants and Assistances" which used to stand for the Iranian oil gift.

46. Cf. *World Development Report*; OECD, *Development Co-operation*; *Le Monde*, 5 January 1993; *al-Hayat*, 13 October 1993.

47. Official aid flows from Arab OPEC states decreased from more than $9.5 bn in 1980 to a low of less than $1.5 bn in 1989. In the Gulf crisis year of 1990, the Gulf states increased their payments to over $6 bn; in 1991, however, they were back to $2.7 bn. Cf. *World Development Report 1993*, Table 19.

48. A notable exception is Jordan which traditionally has been highly

dependent on foreign aid flows. Cf. *World Development Report*, various issues; Boogaerde, *Financial Assistance*, p. 81.

49. Cf. Perthes, "The Syrian Economy".

50. In 1991, 78.5 per cent of all Syria's external debts resulted from concessional, i.e. non-commercial, loans; this is the highest ratio of concessional in relation to total debts among all middle-income countries. Cf. *World Development Report 1993*, Table 24.

51. Ibid., Tables 21, 24.

52. Cf. A. Skripkin, "The CIS-Syria: Direct Links Between Enterprises Needed", *Asia and Africa Today* (1992), No. 3, pp 45–46. Exact figures are not available since it is not clear how much of Syria's exports to the former Soviet Union is regarded as credit repayment.

53. See Chapter V below.

54. Cf. Petran, *Syria*, p 167.

55. Cf. the sympathetic biography by Seale, *Asad*.

56. Cf. Batatu, "Some Observations"; Drysdale; "Syrian Political Elite"; Hinnebusch, *Authoritarian Power*, pp 81–119.

57. ASBP, National Command, *Ba'd al-muntaliqat al-nazariyya allati aqarraha al-mu'tamar al-qawmi al-sadis fi tishrin al-awwal 1963*, pp 73f.

58. On the power struggles in party and state, cf. Horst Mahr, *Die Baath-Partei*; Rabinovich, *Syria under the Ba'th*; Van Dam, *Struggle for Power*; on the ideological dimension: Kamal Abu Jaber, *The Arab Ba'th Socialist Party*.

59. Legislative (Leg.) Decree 37/2 May 1963.

60. Leg. Decree 88/23 June 1963.

61. This is evident from Syrian statistics. In 1963 and 1964, private capital investments more or less remained at their 1962 level which indicates that the bourgeoisie initially was not totally inimical towards the new regime. Cf. *Stat. Abs. 1963*, p 396, and *1969/70*, p 496.

62. Cf. Rabinovich, *Syria*, pp 109ff; Batatu, "Syria's Muslim Brethren"; Mayer, "Islamic Opposition".

63. Cf. Syrian Arab Republic (SAR), Ministry of Information, *al-Qarrarat al-ishtirakiyya fi suriya*.

64. Hans Henle, *Der neue Nahe Osten*, p 327.

65. Members of Syria's old bourgeoisie, interviewed 25 years later, confirmed that after the nationalizations of 1964 they expected more measures of that kind and made their preparations. Reliable figures on capital flight are not available.

66. Cf. e.g. Khalid al-Jundi, "al-Raja'iyya awwalan" [The Reaction First], in *al-Ishtiraki*, 6 September 1965.

67. Cf. Hannoyer/Seurat, *État et secteur public*, p 15.

68. Quoted from: Bu 'Ali Yasin, *al-Sulta al-'ummaliyya*, pp 44f.

69. The total capital of those 108 industrial establishments that were nationalized in 1965 and remained with the state amounted to some LS 230 million (LS 1 equalling $0.26 in 1965). The total number of persons employed in the establishments nationalized in 1965 amounted to some 20,000. Cf.

Hamash, *al-Iqtisad al-suri*, p 209; Mohammed Adnan Schahbandar, *Probleme der Entwicklung*, p 38.

70. Cf. Yasin, *al-Sulta al-'ummaliyya*, pp 46f; Syrian Communist Party (SCP), *Documents of the Third Conference of the SCP* (n.p., n.d.), p 135.

71. Cf. 'Isa Darwish, *al-Sina'a wa-l-taqa fi al-jumhuriyya al-'arabiyya al-suriyya*, p 40; Hamash, *al-Iqtisad al-suri*, p 410.

72. Cf. SAR, Ministry of Information, *Suriya al-thawra fi 'amiha al-sadis* [Revolutionary Syria in its Sixth Year] (Damascus, 1969), p 78. The appointment of persons who were unfit to do the job was not only a matter of favouritism by means of which many military officers were promoted to directors' positions in the public sector. In 1965, according to the 1969/70 *Stat. Abs.*, there were no more than 804 civil engineers, 150 electrical engineers, and 111 mechanical engineers in Syria. This lack of technical cadres created objective difficulties in filling technical leadership positions in more than 100 industrial establishments – and thus gave a further incentive to distribute such positions to loyal officers.

73. Cf. SAR, Ministry of Planning, *al-Ittijahat al-asasiyya fi al-khitta al-khamsiyya al-thaniya li-l-tanmiya al-iqtisadiyya wa-l-ijtima'iyya 1966–70* [The Basic Tendencies of the Second Five Year Plan for Social and Economic Development 1966–70] (Damascus, 1966).

74. Cf. *Stat. Abs. 1975*, p 295.

75. Cf. *Stat. Abs.*, various issues.

76. Cf. SAR, State Planning Authority, *Fifth Five Year Plan for Economic and Social Development, 1981–85* (Damascus, 1981), p 3.

77. Cf. e.g. Asad's speech to parliament, 8 March 1978, *al-Ba'th*, 9 March 1978, or his speech of 8 March 1986, *al-Ba'th*, 9 March 1986.

78. Speech to trade unionists, quoted in: General Federation of Trade Unions in the Syrian Arab Republic (GFTU), *Proceedings and Decisions of the 17th Conference of the GFTU in the Syrian Arab Region, Damascus, 20–23 September 1972* (Damascus, n.d.), p 30.

79. Cf. 'Abd al-Muhaimin al-Khattib, *al-Sina'a wa-tatawwuruha fi suriya* [Industry and its Development in Syria] (Damascus: author's edition, 1979), p 51. Khattib was then director of planning in the Ministry of Industry.

80. Cf. Asad's speech at the 1978 trade union congress where he reprimanded trade unionists for having voiced criticism against the increasing pattern of buying turn-key projects from foreign companies: GFTU, *Proceedings and Decisions of the 19th Conference of the GFTU in the Syrian Arab Region, Damascus 15–19 November 1978* (Damascus, n.d.), p 44.

81. Khattib, *al-Sina'a*, p 51; ASBP, *Sixth Regional Conference. Economic Report*, pp 42, 101.

82. Cf. the Political Decisions of the Sixth Regional Conference (1975) of the Ba'th Party, quoted in: ASBP, National Command, *Nidal hizb al-ba'th al-'arabi al-ishtiraki* [The Struggle of the Arab Ba'th Socialist Party] (Damascus, 1978), p 160.

83. Cf. Hisham Mitwalli, *Abhath fi al-iqtisad al-suri wa-l-'arabi* [Studies

on the Syrian and the Arab Economy] (Damascus: Ministry of Culture, 1974), pp 75ff.

84. Cf. ASBP, *Sixth Regional Conference. Economic Report*, p 42.

85. Cf. SCP, *The Fifth Conference of the SCP, May 1980. Documents and Decisions*, (Damascus, n.d.), p 20.

86. Source: SAR, State Planning Authority, *Mudhakkira hawl: al-takhtit li-l-tanmiya al-iqtisadiyya wa-l-ijtima'iyya fi al-jumhuriyya al-'arabiyya al-suriyya* [Memorandum: Planning for Social and Economic Development in the SAR] (unpublished mimeograph, 1987), p 23. Cf. also, if without figures: Hamash, *al-Tanmiya al-sina'iyya*, p 81. For a statistical profile of the sectoral distribution of investments according to Syria's five-year plans, cf. Perthes, *Staat und Gesellschaft*, pp 69, 89.

87. For a detailed overview of the industrial and communication projects launched after 1973 cf. SAR, CBS, *Dirasa 'amma 'an qita' al-sina'a wa-l-mu'ashshirat al-ra'isiyya, 1971–75* [General Study on the Industrial Sector and the Main Indicators 1971–75] (mimeograph, October 1977); ASBP, *Reports and Decisions of the Fifth Extraordinary Regional Conference convened in Damascus, 30 May – 13 June 1974* (Damascus, 1974), pp 99–107; idem, *Sixth Regional Conference 1975. Economic Report*, pp 19f, 57, 65.

88. Cf. SAR, State Planning Authority, *Mudhakkira hawl: al-takhtit*.

89. Cf. in general: Khattib, *al-Sina'a*, pp 102f; Chatelus, "Croissance économique"; Hilan, *al-Thaqafa*; 'Isam Khuri, "Rabt al-tijara al-kharijiyya"; Hamash, *al-Tanmiya al-sina'iyya*.

90. Cf. in more detail: Perthes, *Staat und Gesellschaft*, pp 105f.

91. Cf. Ahmad Nizam al-Din, "Waqi' al-sina'at al-suriyya wa-afaq tatawwuriha". For earlier critiques along this line cf. GFTU, *Proceedings, Decisions and Recommendations of the 18th Conference of the GFTU in the Syrian-Arab Region, Damascus, 21–24 September 1974* (Damascus, n.d.) pp 174f; ASBP, *Reports and Decisions of the Seventh Regional Conference convened in Damascus, 22 December 1979 – 6 January 1980. Economic Report* (Damascus, 1980), pp 8f.

92. Cf. SAR, State Planning Authority, *Taqrir taqwim al-khitta al-khamsiyya al-khamisa 1981–85, qita' al-sina'at al-tahwiliyya*, p 10.

93. The most thorough insider critique of the performance and management of the public sector has been brought forward by the trade unions. Cf. in particular: GFTU, *Mu'tamar al-ibda'*.

94. SAR, State Planning Authority, *Taqrir taqwim al-khitta al-khamsiyya*, p 80f.

95. Cf. GFTU, *Mu'tamar al-ibda'*, p 336.

96. Cf. *Stat. Abs.*, various issues; Khuri, "Rabt al-tijara al-kharijiyya", p 308.

97. Cf. Kanovsky, "What's behind", pp 302ff.

98. Cf. Perthes, "The Syrian Economy", pp 40f.

99. Cf. Hafiz al-Asad's speech at the 1986 trade union conference, 16 November 1986, *al-Ba'th*, 17 November 1986.

100. Cf. SAR, State Planning Authority, *Fifth Five Year Plan*, pp "d", "h", 9.

101. Cf. Hafiz al-Asad's speech of 8 March 1986, *al-Ba'th*, 9 March 1986.

102. Cf. Hafiz al-Asad's speech of 16 November 1986.

103. Cf. below, Chapter V.

104. Development expenditures as a percentage of the total budget had shrunk from 50 per cent in 1980 – and around 60 per cent in the second half of the 1970s – to less than 40 per cent by the end of the 1980s. Cf. *Stat. Abs. 1992*, p 426.

105. Cf. *Stat. Abs.*, various issues.

106. Cf. *al-Thawra*, 27 March 1987.

107. Author's interviews, Ministry of Economy and Foreign Trade, Damascus, 1988.

108. Quoted from Amal al-Humsi, "Adwa' 'ala nadwat tanmiya al-sadirat al-suriyya al-mun'aqida fi dimashq" [Spotlights on the Symposium on the Development of Syrian Exports convened in Damascus], *al-Iqtisad*, No. 308, June 1989, pp 3–8 (5).

109. Author's interviews, Damascus, 1992. Cf. also Hamash, *al-Tanmiya al-sina'iyya*, p 178.

110. Cf. Dalila, "Tajribat", p 409.

111. The declaration of Asad's "Correctionist Movement" of 16 November 1970 is documented in: ASBP, National Command, *Nidal hizb al-ba'th*, pp 115–121.

112. Cf. e.g. Hafiz al-Asad's speech of 8 March 1974, *al-Ishtiraki*, 11 March 1974; ASBP, *Sixth Regional Conference. Economic Report*, p 84.

113. This section draws largely on my article "Stages of Economic and Political Liberalization".

114. Cf. Minister for Economy and Foreign Trade (MEFT), Decree 779/1970; Leg. Decree 183/1969; Leg. Decree 265/1969.

115. Cf. MEFT Decree 267/1971.

116. Cf. Article 14 of Syria's "Permanent Constitution" of 13 March 1973.

117. Cf. ASBP, *Sixth Regional Conference. Economic Report*, p 122.

118. The number of private establishments increased from some 130,000 in 1970 to about 220,000 in 1981. Cf. in detail: Perthes, "Syrian Private Industrial and Commercial Sectors", pp 211f.

119. Cf. ibid., p 215.

120. Leg. Decree 40/1977.

121. According to Seale, *Asad*, p 326, Asad's successful attempt to win over the Damascus Chamber of Commerce actually turned the tide in favour of the regime.

122. Cf. Prime Minister (PM) Decrees 1791/1983; 375/1987; 595/1987; MEFT Decree 279/1987.

123. Quite naturally, there are no official data on smuggling. The main goods that were illegally imported throughout the 1980s were cigarettes, iron, wood, drugs, tyres, salt, and electronics. Illegal cigarette imports – cigarettes had been banned from importation in 1981 – were estimated at some 660 million packs a year by the Syrian authorities before the import of cigarettes through

a public-sector trade organization was again legalized in 1992 (cf. *al-Nahar*, 1 June 1992). According to conservative estimates, illegal imports made up some 25 per cent at least of Syria's total in the second half of the 1980s; with the gradual liberalization of foreign-trade regimes, the illegal import sector is likely to have decreased substantially. Cf. Perthes, *Staat und Gesellschaft*, p 111.

124. Legislative Decree 10/1986.

125. Cf. PM Decrees 186/1985 and 1817/1987.

126. Cf. MEFT Decree 1048, 1593/1989.

127. Cf. MEFT Decree 2184/1990.

128. Cf. MEFT Decree 70/1991.

129. The application of different exchange rates to different operations of the same actor thoroughly confused Syrian trade and payment statistics. In 1992, for instance, grants accruing to the budget were calculated at the neighbouring countries' rate of 43 LS/$, while foreign loans were still calculated at the official rate of 11.2 LS/$, i.e. at about one quarter of what their real burden amounted to. Only from 1993 were loans also calculated at the more realistic neighbouring countries' rate. Also in 1993, however, the returns from oil exports and some exports of public-sector agricultural products, as well as some public-sector imports, were still computed at the official rates while some other public-sector exports were calculated at the neighbouring countries' rate. So were all private-sector exports and imports.

130. Cf. MEFT, Decrees 158, 160/1989; Perthes, "Syrian Private Industrial and Commercial Sectors", p 222.

131. Still reserved for the public sector were, among other things, the production of sugar, iron and steel, cables, matches, cotton yarn, beer, and tomato pulp. Cf. Ministry of Industry, Decree 4342/1988.

132. Law 20/1991.

133. See below, Chapter V.

134. Cf. *Stat. Abs.*, various issues. The percentage of private-sector transactions in foreign trade as a whole was subject to stark annual variations, mainly depending on the amount and value of oil exports as Syria's, and the public sector's, main export commodity.

135. Cf. Damascus Chamber of Commerce, *al-Taqrir al-sanawi 1990*.

136. There is of course a large informal sector whose data are collected neither by the Central Bureau of Statistics nor any other data-collecting institution such as the Ministry of Finance. Even the formal private sector is often underestimated, since entrepreneurs, fearing taxation and other cuts from their profits, tend to hide parts of their activities.

137. Gross fixed capital formation (investments) may serve as an example: private-sector investments, in constant prices of 1985, dropped from 6.7 billion LS (35 per cent of all investments) in 1983 to 4.7 billion (52 per cent of the total) in 1990; in current prices private investments increased from 5.9 billion to 21.3 billion LS. Public sector investments dropped from 12.2 billion LS to 4.3 billion respectively, still increasing in current prices from 11.6 to 19.5 billion LS. Cf. *Stat. Abs. 1991*, pp 502f.

138. Source: Ministry of Industry, Directorate for Private Industry and Industrial Artisanery, Registration and Statistics Division. Even if we assume that the workforce in private establishments is 50 per cent under-reported, average employment does not exceed five persons per establishment.

139. In 1989, exports to the USSR jumped from an annual average of $200–300 million to about $1 billion. At least 20–30 per cent of these exports were made by the private sector. Cf. Perthes, "Syrian Private Industrial and Commercial Sectors", pp 219f.

140. Cf. in detail: Perthes, "Syrian Private Industrial and Commercial Sectors".

141. Source: Prime Minister, Investment Office.

142. Cf. *al-Hayat*, 30 September 1993, 19 October 1993; *MEED*, 3 December 1993.

143. Employment figures are not as telling for commercial and service establishments as they are for industry. The figures and estimates here provided are based on my "Syrian Private Industrial and Commercial Sectors"; more recent data from the Ministry of Industry, Directorate for Private Industry and Industrial Artisanery; and SAR, CBS, *Nata'ij bahtay al-istiqsa' al-sina'i li-l-qita' al-khass li-'amay 1989–90* [Results of the Studies of the Investigation of the Private-Sector Industry Survey for Years 1989 and 1990] (unpublished mimeograph, June 1992).

144. This is illustrated, among other things, by the growing differentials in the invested capital of industrial ventures. The average capital of private industrial projects not falling under the special provisions of investment law No. 10 of 1991 that were established between 1991 and June 30, 1992 amounted to less than $25,000. The average capital invested in new industrial and service companies established under the investment law up to the end of 1992 exceeded $2.5 million. Source: Ministry of Industry; Prime Minister, Investment Office.

145. Cf. *Stat. Abs.*, various issues. Since actual government expenditures tend to remain below budget figures, actual government finance as a percentage of GDP also tends to be somewhat lower than the figures here presented.

146. The former number was given by Syria's Minister of State for Planning Affairs in a statement to parliament, the latter number, which actually represents the annual population increase in the early 1990s, not the number of persons entering the job market, has been traded by parliamentarians. Cf. *al-Hayat*, 24 June 1993; Muhammad Ihsan Sanqar, "Mudakhala hawl taqrir mashru' al-muwazana al-'amma" [Intervention on the Draft Budget] (mimeographed, 3 May 1993).

147. Our figures are based on the assumption that the annual net increase of the labour force equals about 60 per cent of the increase of the number of persons over 15. The estimate is conservative, since for the decade to come it does not assume any significant increase of female participation in the labour force.

148. In 1992, according to the Minister for Planning Affairs, 67,000 persons

were newly employed in the public sector and administration (*al-Hayat*, 24 June 1993). In the whole period between 1988 and the end of 1992, however, only some 120,000 jobs, i.e. an average of less than 25,000 a year, were created in the state sector. Exact figures are not available as not all groups of government employees (presidential staff, security, employees of the public-sector construction companies) are always listed in the *Stat. Abs*.

149.   This would represent an annual increase of about 5 per cent. The estimate assumes that an annual 20,000 or so jobs could be created by large investors making use of investment law No. 10 while twice that number could be indirectly initiated by these investments. Another 20,000 or so could be initiated in the small-industries and trade sector and the informal sector.

150.   In 1993, the total irrigated area was officially estimated at more than 1.1 million hectares which represents a more than 50 per cent increase over the 1991 figures given in the *Stat. Abs. 1992*. Cf. *The Middle East*, December 1993, pp 32ff.; *al-Hayat*, 13 December 1993.

151.   Official unemployment figures and estimates – some 6.8 per cent in 1991 according to *Stat. Abs. 1993*, p 72 – do not tell us much since persons without formal employment rarely register as unemployed. A more common, but difficult-to-measure feature is constant underemployment of day labourers waiting for the occasional job, and a far-from-gainful self-employment at the margins of the informal sector.

152.   For a general characterization of the rentier state phenomenon in the Middle East, cf. Hazem Beblawi, "The Rentier State in the Arab World", in: Giacomo Luciani (ed), *The Arab State* (London: Routledge, 1990).

153.   Once more, the existence of different exchange rates and under-reporting make it impossible to give exact data. Roughly, net oil income and aid can be estimated to make up some 10 to 15 per cent of GNP.

154.   The oil revenue is not identified on the revenue side of the budget. The entry in line 8207 "Different Revenues", however, approximates the oil export earnings if calculated on the basis of the official exchange rate.

155.   Cf. Hannoyer/Seurat, *État et secteur public*, p 133.

156.   Commercial loans could probably be obtained on a larger scale. In view of its existing debt load, however, the unresolved problem with its Russian debt, and its strong sense for maintaining Syria's sovereignty against any possible interference of foreign actors in its policy–making, the government had good reasons to be wary of contracting further debts.

157.   In a post-war Middle Eastern economy, large foreign capital investments will flow to Israel, Palestine, and probably Jordan rather than Syria. Syrian expatriates are likely to increase their investments in Syria, if so on a limited scale. Syrian expatriate capital has been estimated at some $50–75 billion (cf. *Financial Times*, 5 November 1992, *al-Hayat*, 21 January 1994). Capital transferred from abroad under the provisions of the 1991 investment law were planned to amount to $1.5 billion for the projects licensed in 1991–92. Probably, 30–50 per cent of this amount will be realized.

158.   For instance, the private sector benefits from a credit scheme financed

by the Kuwaiti Fund for Arab Economic Development and channelled through the public-sector Industrial Bank, and it has for a long time been able to benefit from interest rates on bank credits below inflation.

159. Cf. GFTU, *The 22nd Conference of the General Federation of Trade Unions in the Syrian Arab Republic, Damascus, 7–11 December 1992. General Report*, Vol. II, p 327.

160. Cf. Heydemann, "Political Logic".

161. Cf. Jean Leca, "Social Structure and Political Stability: Comparative Evidence from the Algerian, Syrian and Iraqi Cases".

CHAPTER THREE

Social Structure and
Class Relations

Since Asad took power more than two decades ago, Syrian society has experienced a rapid process of change. Among the most visible has been the numerical and relative decrease of the agricultural workforce. In 1970, the main occupation of about half of the economically active population was in agriculture; in the first half of the 1990s this is true of less than 30 per cent. Despite a higher birth rate in the countryside, there has been a continuous decline in the proportion of the rural population, with the shift of the generally most active elements to the cities and other economic sectors. Among the most conspicuous changes in the cities is the growth of both the wage-earning middle classes and the marginalized strata – the former primarily being a feature of the 1970s, the latter of the 1980s. The growth of the working class, particularly of workers in modern industries, has remained relatively limited. The proportion of the traditional middle classes – independent craftsmen, retailers, and other small entrepreneurs – has been increasing slightly, in contrast to what might have been expected, namely a decline of small goods production in the course of a modernizing development.

1. Rural Relations

Land Reform

The most decisive event for the development of the social structure of the Syrian countryside was the implementation of the land reform law – originally issued in 1958 and amended several times – and the law on agrarian relations.[1] When the Ba'th assumed power in 1963, the implementation of the reform laws began in earnest. By 1969, some 4,500 landowners whose individual property, including that of their wives and children, exceeded 120 hectares of irrigated or 460 hectares of rainfed land,[2] had been stripped of some 1.5 million hectares. This amounted to about half of their property – except for those parts of their land that had been sold or distributed before the implementation of the law – and to some 17 per cent of Syria's total cultivable land at that time. Expropriated land was to be distributed within the villages such that the property of beneficiaries would not exceed 8 hectares of irrigated or 45 hectares of rainfed land. Since the law did not prescribe any lower limit for the allocation of expropriated land, some peasants received extremely small parcels of land which were hardly sufficient for subsistence. On the other hand, land was not only distributed to small or landless peasants, but also to peasants with medium-size property. More often than not, it was allocated to people not legally entitled to benefit from the reform, such as the sons of big landowners, state employees and other persons not working in agriculture.[3] Land reform land was heritable, but it could not be sold or rented, nor fragmented by inheritance. Beneficiaries were obliged to work their land themselves, to become members of a cooperative, and to pay to the cooperative a transfer fee for the land in 20 annual instalments.

In fact, only some 446,000 of the 1.5 million hectares of expropriated land and some further 432,000 hectares of state land and recently reclaimed marshland in the Ghab area were distributed to around 100,000 families. What was not distributed became state land, or was sold as building land or allotted to cooperatives, state farms and other public-sector establishments. Some 180,000 families employed in agriculture remained landless.[4]

In 1980, a new law further reduced the upper limit for land property to a maximum of 200 hectares.[5] In pursuit of the law, another 42,700 hectares were expropriated. Distribution of the land was initially planned, but was not implemented. Most of the land was rented.[6]

As a result of the reform, the area of land in the possession of smallholders and holders of medium-sized plots increased, the distribution of holdings thereby approximately equalling the distribution of legal property.[7] According to different estimates, prior to the land reform some 13 to 17.5 per cent of all private land had been smallholdings of less than 10 hectares, some 38 to 45 per cent had been

Table III.1 Holders of Private Agricultural Land by Size of Holdings, 1970 and 1981

Size of holding	1970				1981			
	no.	%	area	%	no.	%	area	%
Smallest holdings less than 1 ha	75,500	16.1	36,700	0.8	76,200	17.0	35,900	0.9
Small holdings 1–6 ha	215,400	46.0	596,400	12.7	216,900	48.6	585,400	14.3
Medium-sized holdings 6–50 ha	165,300	35.3	2,563,900	54.8	143,600	32.2	2,118,200	52.0
Large holdings 50 ha and over of which:	12,500	2.6	1,477,500	31.6	9,400	2.1	1,331,900	32.7
100 ha and over	4,300	0.9	957,100	20.5	3,100	0.7	816,800	20.1
300 ha and over	900	0.2	448,300	9.5	700	0.16	476,700	11.7
Total	468,000		4,674,600		446,200		4,071,400	
Agricultural holders mainly occupied in agriculture	438,500	93.6			290,100	65.0		

Note: Figures rounded.

Source: Agricultural Censuses 1970 and 1980.

holdings between 10 and 100 hectares, and the rest had been large holdings of 100 hectares or more. In 1970, some 75 per cent of all landholders were in the possession of holdings of less than 10 hectares size and held somewhat less than a quarter of all private land. A quarter of all landholders were in the possession of medium-sized holdings between 10 and 100 hectares, and less than one per cent were big landowners, still holding some 20 per cent of all land. On the average, realities of Syrian agriculture are better reflected if the dividing line between small and medium-sized holdings is drawn at the 6-hectare mark and that between medium-sized and large holdings at the 50-hectare mark. If we apply these categories, some 62 per cent of all holders of agricultural land are seen to have been smallholders, having less than 14 per cent of all private land at their disposal; some 35 per cent were holders of medium-sized property, possessing around 55 per cent of the land, and almost 3 per cent were big landowners with more than 31 per cent at their disposal.

According to the census, there were few changes to the picture over the next decade. By 1981, the number of smallest smallholders – those with less than one hectare each – had increased slightly, as had the proportion of smallholders to the total number of holders, whilst medium-sized holdings and their proportion to the total had somewhat decreased. Within the group of big landowners, a slight tendency towards concentration can be seen, particularly as far as landowners holding 300 hectares and more are concerned. This is the only group which, despite the decrease in the total area of agricultural land, had more land at its disposal in 1981 than in 1970. We might consider most of the smallest holders – those with less than one hectare – as being mainly occupied outside agriculture and therefore exclude them from our calculation. Nevertheless, we find that the 700 wealthiest landowners were in possession of more land than the poorer half of all holders. Also, a substantial number of landowners had obviously been able to accumulate or maintain landed property far exceeding the upper limits defined by law.[8] The tendencies displayed through the data available for the 1970–81 period are likely to have developed further in the following decade.

Small Peasants

In fact, rural property and production relations have undergone changes larger than those indicated by official statistics. Agricultural

censuses and samples do not convey an exact picture of these changes,
partly because, according to the law they should not happen, partly
because they have not been studied. These changes have been due
mainly to the difficulties of small peasants, particularly those who
possessed only the piece of land they had obtained through the land
reform. In many cases, the holdings of these peasants were simply
too small to secure the subsistence of a family. Just a few hectares of
rainfed land planted with fruit trees, or one hectare of horticultural
land or greenhouses can support a family. Most smallholders, however, were too poor to make optimal use of their land, which generally was not of the best quality. The land reform had provided them
with land but not with machinery. Access to water, too, was a problem many smallholders were left to solve by themselves.[9] Frequently,
peasants became indebted for seeds and fertilizers, and they were
certainly not able to invest in irrigation devices or long-term projects
such as fruit tree plantations that would have made their plots profitable. Loans from the Agricultural Cooperative Bank were difficult to
obtain for smallholders who could not provide sufficient security.
Generally, smallholders were forced to plant crops subject to governmental central production plans,[10] that is, crops which had to be sold
to the state at fixed procurement prices.[11] With holdings being small
and possibilities to improve one's land limited, government procurement prices became the central problem for smallholders. Between
1973 and 1977, and once again from the early 1980s to 1988, the
development of agricultural procurement prices stayed far behind the
rapid increase in consumer prices. In the late 1970s, the development
of agricultural procurement prices held pace with the general consumer price index, and, as of 1988/89, the government once again
tried to make up for losses in terms of purchasing power that peasants
had had to cope with in the years before by substantially raising
procurement prices for strategic crops. In the meantime, however,
peasants who had to plant centrally marketed crops faced severe
difficulties. "The pricing policy", the Peasant Union mildly put it,
"has not given [peasants] any encouragement to actually increase the
production of crops, such as cotton, the production of which was
planned to be increased."[12]

Even the official statistics of the Ministry of Agriculture revealed
that for several years in the mid-1980s, procurement prices for wheat,
barley, chick-peas, sugar-beet and other crops ranged below production
costs.[13] The surplus that could be gained from planting wheat or

cotton was generally too low to support a smallholder family. Several studies have shown that villages mainly planting centrally marketed cash crops could not sustain themselves from their produce.[14] Holders of medium-sized and large estates could live with the system of governmental price regulations; their income was higher in absolute terms, and agriculture of some scale reduced costs considerably.[15]

Facing these difficulties, many small beneficiaries of the land reform were unable to remain independent peasants. Many became indebted to merchants or usurers, or to the previous owners of their land. Some entered into what was legally a partnership relation (*musharaka*) with a financier or investor providing credit, machinery, or water and thereby becoming entitled to a share in the harvest. Others sold their land or part of it – illegally if they had obtained it through the land reform – remaining as sharecroppers or paid labourers or leaving the countryside. Still others rented their property, permanently or for a couple of years during which they would render their military service or seek employment abroad to big landowners or to other peasants, thereby themselves becoming mini rent-capitalists.[16] Some beneficiaries of the land reform also lost their holdings because it was returned to its previous owners.[17]

As mentioned above, such changes to the structure of Syria's rural society are not evident from official data. The agricultural censuses do not provide any information on, for example, how much of the land held by smallholders has changed from one holder to another between 1970 and 1981. It is notable, however, that the number of holders who state that their main occupation is outside agriculture has increased dramatically, with the number of full-time peasants decreasing from 440,000 in 1970 to 290,000 in 1981. These data show that a substantial number of smallholders have given up their agricultural work, sometimes leaving it to their wives and children. Where smallholdings cannot support a family, these plots are increasingly worked by females.[18] This phenomenon does not improve conditions for agricultural development: though women may work the land, they do not gain control over it; important decisions are still taken by men, although they may be absent as producers.[19] Agricultural production becomes a mere source of additional income, allowing those members of the smallholder's family who work as wage-labourers to offer their labour more cheaply than landless peasants and urban labourers.

Agricultural Workers

Since small landed property was no guarantee against impoverishment and even smallholders were frequently forced to work outside their plot in order to maintain their property, dividing lines between self-employed smallholders and agricultural labourers or landless peasants are anything but clearcut. Some of the smallholders had been landless before the land reform. And where a family plot was too small to support more than one heir and his family, the brothers of that heir who could not find non-agricultural work or who remained in the countryside inevitably became agricultural wage labourers, seasonally at least. The proportion of self-employed peasants to paid agricultural labourers has decreased from approximately 3:1 in 1970 to approximately 2:1 in the early 1990s. This reflects both the impoverishment of agricultural smallholders and the increased use of wage labour in modern capitalist agriprojects established by wealthier landowners and investors. In this respect, demands to facilitate the cancellation of share-cropping contracts or to scrap altogether the 1958 law on agricultural relations altogether have been brought forward by potential agricultural investors[20] – still cautiously, since such demands could stir up the Peasant Union and their realization would go against the historical social contract between the Ba'th and the peasantry.

Agricultural labourers are among the poorest classes of Syrian society and the socially least protected stratum. Agricultural workers are not included under the stipulations of the Syrian labour code, but they do appear under the law on agricultural relations. While this law improved the situation of sharecroppers, it did not better the conditions of wage-labourers.[21]

Middle Peasants

The beneficiaries of small land reform also experience difficulties because the cooperatives which they have to join do not in fact reflect their interests. In 1974, the land reform cooperatives were integrated into the Peasant Union, a regime-sponsored popular or mass organization founded in 1964. Not only land reform beneficiaries but almost everyone employed in agriculture was entitled to join: agricultural labourers, sharecroppers, peasants and farmers whose legal property did not exceed 16 hectares of irrigated or 90 hectares of rainfed land,

and agricultural engineers. The rural poor – namely landless peasants and smallholders – were thereby deprived of an organization serving their own interests. Neither the Peasant Union nor the cooperatives represent the interests of all members equally. Rather, they have become organizations serving the interests of their wealthier members, i.e. peasants with medium-size holdings. Most leadership cadres of the cooperatives and the Union are middle class peasants who more often than not manage to exploit their position for the negotiation and distribution in their own interest of credit, machinery, seeds etc.[22]

Many middle class peasants, in fact, have more interests in common with landlords whose property exceeds the limits of those peasants entitled to join a cooperative than with smallholders and agricultural labourers. Middle class peasants may themselves be employers or petty landlords renting some part of their land to a sharecropper. As noted, holders of medium-sized and bigger estates could cope with the government's agricultural procurement prices. They would get credit more easily, they could often afford to buy their own machinery, they were preferentially served by machine contractors. Such advantages made it possible to collect the harvest in time and cash bonus payments for early delivery. Many owners of medium-sized holdings were able to plant fruit trees on parts of their land – naturally a long-term investment, since these trees would not bear for years – or invest in irrigation devices, or erect some greenhouses, thereby considerably increasing the returns from their land. The government has successfully been encouraging and supporting such improvements.[23] Throughout the 1980s in particular, large areas of farmland were converted into fruit tree plantations.[24] Also, owners of medium-sized holdings, particularly in the eastern regions of the country, could often extend their holdings by renting state land, in much the same way as the big landowners and agricultural entrepreneurs.

On the whole, medium-sized landholders were the real winners – economically, socially and politically – of the land reform and post-reform agricultural policies. The distance between this agricultural middle class and big landowners has narrowed. While the latter frequently were cut to size by the land reform, the economic situation of the peasant middle class has improved. Thanks to their position in the cooperatives, the Peasant Union and the party, they have become politically the leading class in the countryside without, however, at the same time becoming its wealthiest stratum.

Big Farmers, Landlords and Agricultural Entrepreneurs

Following the implementation of the land reform considerably large landed properties were still in evidence, both in the hands of urban absentee landlords and of local sheikhs and aghas (local chiefs) whose ancestors had been registered as the owners of the villages they represented at the beginning of the century. Many urban landlords still have their estates cultivated by sharecroppers; and local landlords often farm part of their land themselves, leasing the rest to share-croppers; the land reform and the law on agricultural relations did not abolish share-cropping. Rent income, however, was reduced, encouraging landlords to manage their estates as a single unit and to introduce modern and more capital-intensive methods.

As early as in the 1940s, a new group of landowners – not more than several hundred – had been emerging. They rented or bought vast areas of land in what was to become Syria's corn-belt, i.e., the country's north-eastern province, the Jazira. These entrepreneurs imported machinery and set up modern agricultural establishments relying on professional management and a limited number of wage-labourers. Few of these entrepreneurs stemmed from the old land-owning classes; most of them were urban merchants with little or no landed property.[25] In the 1970s and 1980s, a new generation of entrepreneurs began to follow this pattern. Since they rented state land instead of acquiring legal property their estates did not fall under the terms of the agricultural reform laws. According to a Soviet scholar, the major part of the state land in Syria's north-east had been privatized by the mid-1970s, agricultural entrepreneurs either renting it or simply "laying their hands on it" (wada' al-yad) – to use the Syrian legal term. Generally, the authorities welcomed such private initiative, expecting modernization effects and increased production.[26]

Where agriculture trespasses the frontiers of cultivable land and encroaches on the steppe without actually introducing irrigation and drainage systems, desertification can ensue.[27] Ploughing the steppe has therefore been forbidden, apart from in areas close to settlements. Despite official governmental concern, however, ploughing is frequently tolerated and occasionally permitted in recognition of old tribal property rights. This obviously contradictory behaviour of the authorities can only partly be explained by short-sighted economic considerations. Of greater importance, it seems, is the fact that many of those who illegally or semi-legally lay their hands on the steppe occupy positions of influence, either "traditional" or "modern". They may be tribal chiefs, officials of the Peasant Union or the party, or simply well connected to high-ranking state, party or military officials. A rare and open critique of the phenomenon could be read in a newspaper interview with the head of the Ba'th party's peasant committee in the province of Dayr al-Zur in 1988. Ploughing the steppe, he said, whether with or without permission, not only created ecological damage; it also enabled "a small group to acquire enormous wealth at the expense of the peasant class, and it creates a new class of feudalists (*iqta'iyyun*) – including everything this word and the term 'class' involves."[28]

Apart from agricultural entrepreneurs with relative large holdings, there is an increasing number of contractors – some 500 to 700 in 1970 and some 2000 by 1981[29] – not holding any land but owning agricultural machines and employing a number of wage-labourers to work the machines on other people's estates. Like the merchant-entrepreneurs who, in the 1940s and later, began to establish large estates in the Jazira, these contractors have been pioneering the implementation of agricapitalist relations in the Syrian countryside. In contrast to the former, their background is rather middle class. Many have been migrant workers in the Gulf states to gain the capital they need to set up their establishments. To some extent, these entrepreneurs are reproducing and completing on a modernized, capitalist basis, traditional relations between the urban middle class and the countryside. Such relations – including the financing by urban merchants of seeds or other inputs, their ownership of irrigation devices used by agricultural smallholders or their ownership of some sheep in the herds of sheep-breeding beduin[30] – have never been severed. Rather, such relations have coexisted alongside state–countryside relations built up by the Ba'thist regime.

There are two other notable tendencies which have influenced the evolution of the socio-economic structure of the Syrian countryside, namely the increase of medium-sized landed estates owned by military officers, and the establishment as of 1986 of agricultural joint-stock companies. Since the mid-1970s, officers and a limited number of other civil servants who had been able to gather some wealth began to purchase small or medium-sized rural plots, later building there good-sized houses, setting up fruit tree plantations, poultry farms or greenhouses, more often than not using military manpower. Plantations and farms were subsequently to be worked by hired labour.

While it is difficult to estimate their number, these estates, which are generally known as *mazari' al-dubat* (officer farms), have increased to at least several thousand. Even though such estates are producing for the market and are employing wage-labour, we can hardly, or only with reservation, call their owners agricultural entrepreneurs. The objective of these enterprises, for the founding generation at least, is rarely entrepreneurial activity and capital accumulation, but rather representation and rent-seeking. In a sense, these officers, who for the most part are the sons of Syria's middle class peasantry, are returning to the countryside usually as petty absentee landlords of sorts.

The establishment of mixed-sector agricultural joint-stock companies was permitted in 1986, following a pattern which in Syria had first been introduced for the tourism industry. These companies are managed as private enterprises even though the state owns a certain proportion, usually 25 per cent, of the stock. Mixed companies have been granted far-reaching privileges, and they have mainly been established by representatives of a new class of businessmen whose ascent was connected to the expansion of the state sector in the 1970s. The positive effects of these companies on the Syrian economy in general and on rural development in particular have yet to be proven. By early 1994, less than a handful had actually gone into production; and early positive balances and their claimed contribution to the reduction of the country's balance-of-trade deficit were somewhat dubious.[31] Greater employment opportunities in the countryside had not been created, and profits were flowing into the cities instead of helping to improve rural infrastructure and living conditions.

The Land Reform as an Instrument of Change

Whether the land reform and the Ba'th's agricultural policies in general have been successful in terms of the social, economic and political goals of their proponents is questionable.[32] For the purposes of our analysis in this book, greater importance lies in the fact that the land reform has initiated a far-reaching process of socio-economic change in the Syrian countryside. New rural structures which had been evolving largely as a result of Ba'thist agricultural policies have to be taken into account as a variable of the transformation policies implemented since the mid-1980s.

The land reform was the regime's main instrument for breaking the absolute power over the countryside of Syria's absentee or local landlords. These remained as fairly big landowners, but their economic and social power was circumscribed and their political power broken, although the latter was due more to the fall of the Ancien Régime in 1963 than the land reform as such. By the early 1990s, local big landowners living on their estates and cultivating at least parts of it came to form the upper strata of a broad agrarian middle class which comprises some 15 to 17 per cent of those whose main occupation is in agriculture. This agrarian middle class as a whole can be regarded as the leading class in the countryside. Its interests are generally vested in preserving social conditions as they are, and they constitute a strong power base of the regime.

The main line of social conflict, therefore, is no longer the dividing line between peasants on one hand and landlords, agrarian entrepreneurs and the state on the other, but rather that between the generally well-off middle class and the rural lower classes consisting of smallholders and landless peasants. The rural middle class – farmers with medium-sized and bigger holdings – have been able to find a mutually satisfying arrangement both with that part of the urban bourgeoisie who, either as merchants or by means of investments and contractor services, participate in the division of agricultural income, and with the state. The state not only skims off parts of the agricultural surplus, it also offers services in return – credit, subsidized inputs, infrastructural investments and land. This division of labour has generally been advantageous to the rural middle class, less so to the lower classes. Many of the latter certainly acquired land through the land reform; but this did not necessarily secure their existence as independent peasants. Most smallholders, though landed proprietors, had to seek additional or alternative sources of income in order not to fall back into traditional social and economic dependencies.

Capitalist modes of production have expanded at the expense of traditional rural modes of production, i.e., production is increasingly designed for local and international markets, production decisions are subjected to market principles, wage-labour has been increasing, and agricultural entrepreneurs are gradually taking the place of landlords. Yet, we have to assume that a certain traditional or "pre-capitalist" element, including some agricultural subsistence production[33] and a considerable number of particular share-cropping relations, will persist for some time. Share-cropping contracts, according to which land is let for a certain part of the harvest, are likely to decrease gradually as large-scale agricultural production involving contractors and wage-labourers increases. Partnerships between urban rentiers and peasants, however, whereby the former holds a share in the latter's land or finances his machinery, are still seen as a proper form of investment and financing. Such partnerships are traditional as far as their legal form is concerned. They are not necessarily anti-modern, however, since they can contribute to the modernization of agricultural production.[34] For the rentier, such partnerships represent a form of investment which involves little effort; for the peasant they are a means to secure agricultural credit more easily than through the banks and more cheaply than through a usurer. The peasant will have to pay a comparatively high rent to his financier, but he remains without debt even in the case of bad harvests. Both partners may regard it as advantageous that their contract does not involve the state. As far as the investor is concerned, this is one of various ways of concealing wealth. Peasants who have observed how public services are more likely to benefit wealthier peasants than themselves, how most inter-actions with the bureaucracy need *wasta* (mediation) and who distrust state agencies, may in consequence favour such traditional forms of finance over a loan from the agricultural bank. Share-cropping con-tracts cannot, of course, protect smallholders from eventually being pushed aside by bigger, capitalist enterprises that can produce more cheaply for the same markets.

The "capitalization" of an economy and the disappearance of pre-capitalist forms of production is neither positive nor negative in itself. From a normative perspective, the important question – as far as agriculture is concerned – is whether the dominant mode of production contributes to satisfying increasing demand for food and to improving the living conditions of both the rural and the urban population, or whether it contributes to the impoverishment of parts of the peasantry and thereby to an unorganized rural–urban migration which only increases urban poverty. From this viewpoint, the land reform and agrarian policies, particularly those of the 1970s and early 1980s, can-not be regarded as too successful. The stagnation of agriculture, and of cereal production in particular, has to be seen partly as the result of an agricultural policy which created a large number of proprietors without at the same time creating the conditions for them to produce, and produce increasingly, for the market. Even though the agrarian middle class has been strengthened considerably and is performing well, their increased output could not compensate totally for the losses resulting from the impoverishment, proletarianization, and migration of a substantial part of the small peasantry. Agriculture has, by means of indirect taxation, been one of the important sources of finance for the state budget and public investment in other fields of the national economy.[35] Although the state has invested in rural infrastructure and subsidized agricultural inputs, it has, for a long time, not done enough to prevent this source from drying up. New agricultural policies as introduced since the mid-1980s, particularly the raising of procurement prices and, to a lesser extent, the encouragement of agricultural joint-stock companies may contribute to an increase in the flow of this source of domestic accumulation once again.

Syrian planners and administrators have frequently stressed, and rightly so, that rural living conditions have improved remarkably under the Ba'th, particularly as regards transport and communication, electrification, and the expansion of the educational system.[36] The social and material infrastructure of the Syrian countryside has no doubt improved, and rural living standards have risen. Compared to the cities, however, services in the Syrian countryside, particularly its more distant regions in the east, north and south of the country, remain poor. The gap between countryside and cities, as any examination of housing conditions, health services, or education shows, has remained wide.[37] Syrian newspapers frequently report the lack of drinking water and drugs in rural regions, or the lack of teachers and physicians. First and foremost, however, the Syrian countryside lacks opportunities for gainful employment.

Migration

Migration from the countryside to the cities has therefore remained a problem. Syrian statistics reveal little either about internal migration or labour emigration. We can assume, for instance, that a majority of the inhabitants of Greater Damascus are still registered in their villages or towns of origin where they may have some land or a family house – the discrepancy between official and semi-official data is striking.[38] Official data on the proportion of rural to urban inhabitants – according to which the urban population increased from 43 per cent of the total in 1970 to 47 per cent in 1981 and 50.4 per cent in 1991 – are therefore indicative of the direction of internal migration but not necessarily of its extent. Damascus is without doubt the country's largest centre of migration. Additionally, there is constant migration from within the rural provinces toward the provincial capitals. In the late 1960s and early 1970s the province and town of Raqqa, where the Euphrates Dam was constructed, attracted many migrants. So, for a while, did Banias and Tartus whose ports were expanded in the early 1970s.[39] Syrian studies often stress that rural–urban migration decreased throughout the 1970s as a result of a policy of rural growth.[40] In fact, the main factor behind this trend was temporary emigration to the Arab OPEC-states.[41] When job opportunities in the Gulf became scarce and Syria's agricultural economy began to run into crisis in the early 1980s, rural–urban migration most probably increased again.

Realistically, we have to assume an annual flow of some 50,000 to 100,000 migrants to Damascus. There are four main channels of migration to the capital and to other cities: the search for employment, military service, higher education, and family members joining their breadwinners. Smallholders or their sons who move to the cities to seek employment are not necessarily migrating completely, let alone immediately intending to do so. Many of them remain peasant–workers, become worker–peasants, or continue to work in agriculture seasonally. Also, the majority of the 30,000 or so young men annually drafted from the countryside to complete their two-and-a-half-year military service, and who are for the most part sent to one of the larger cities, do not necessarily plan to leave their villages for good. The same is true of some 15,000 students of rural origin who annually join Syria's universities and colleges; although a substantial number do tend to remain in the cities. Easy access to college education represents a real improvement in the life-chances of young people from the lower rural classes and for as long as the economic and infrastructural gap between countryside and city remains or even increases, only a few of those who move to the city to study will afterwards feel inclined to return to the countryside. Graduates of teachers' colleges and medical schools are obliged to do three years' rural service after graduation; but the need to enforce this rule shows how much employment in the countryside is still regarded as a period of probation or as a punishment. This, in its turn, does not help to improve the situation in Syria's rural regions.

2. Urban Society

Syria's cities, or, more precisely, Syria's non-rural society shows even greater and more evident signs of social change than does her rural society. Rural and urban change are, of course, interrelated. In the same way that agrarian reform and agrarian policies have been major determinants of societal developments in the countryside, the development of Syria's urban society has largely been determined by political decisions and actions, particularly by the expansion of the state apparatus and its regulative functions, and by both *infitah* and austerity policies. By the early 1990s, almost one-third of the workforce, including military and security, was employed by the state, and the majority of the urban population, particularly the salaried middle classes and the working class, was directly dependent on the government and its wage and employment policies.

The Urban Working Class

In comparison with other social strata, the growth of Syria's urban working class has remained relatively limited – regardless of how broad or narrow a concept of working class is applied. Since it is important to take into account both status and living conditions, the term working class is operationalized here to include not only workers in production but also transport workers, guards, and servants. If the lower ranks of the security forces – military, police, and security services – are included, in 1970 the working class in the broadest sense consisted of some 24 per cent of the economically active population. By 1980 its proportion had increased to around 35 per cent. Over the 1980s, the growth of the working class no longer exceeded that of the total labour force; its proportion to the whole remained more or less static.[42]

The Syrian working class is in no way uniform. Only a small part of it has, in Marxist terms, become a class "for itself"; the majority have no such experience or tradition and have not developed a working-class consciousness.[43] The first group mainly consists of those working in Syria's traditional industries, particularly the textile factories of Aleppo and Damascus, some of which were established under the French mandate.[44] These large establishments, which nowadays belong to the public sector, have been fertile ground for a working-class movement of mainly urban origin which from the 1930s fought for the social and material interests of its members and participated in the political struggles of the mandate and independence period.[45]

Most workers who became employed in the 1970s and 1980s were of rural origin. Many continued to work part-time in agriculture, either on their own plots or seasonally on others' and must be seen as worker–peasants or peasant–workers, still very much connected to rural society through family ties or through their own work patterns. For many of this group, industrial work and the urban, industrial environment remain of secondary importance so far as their family income, life style, and social values are concerned. But even those who have given up agricultural work completely have developed little proletarian consciousness, preferring to regard their wage-labour in industry, construction, or services as transitory. Most migrants from the countryside seek some sort of independent activity rather than wage-labour. Many try to become self-employed after some years of wage-labour or seek some independent or quasi-independent employment in addition to their main job.[46]

This is partly due to the high social prestige any independent activity – in contrast to wage-labour – enjoys in most Arab societies. At least as important, however, is the fact that the material situation of the Syrian working class has neither enabled migrants to sever their ties to agriculture, nor bound them to industry. Nevertheless, wage-labour increased the income of migrants, particularly if they continued to cultivate their own piece of land or had it cultivated by their family. Furthermore, working-class living standards were generally on the increase until the mid-1970s. By the late 1970s, however, the situation had worsened. As mentioned above, wages remained far behind prices throughout the 1980s. At the beginning of the 1990s, the average wage of a public-sector worker covered about one third of the necessary expenses of a family of six.

Conditions for private-sector workers differ from those of their public-sector colleagues in more than one aspect. The private sector employed some 80 per cent of the working class in 1970, slightly less than 60 per cent in 1981, and rather more than 60 per cent in 1991.[47] As noted, most of those employed in the private sector work in small establishments, or very small establishments with no more than 12 employees. Before the enactment of the 1991 investment law, only an estimated 2,000 or so private industrial establishments employed ten persons a shift, or more, regularly.[48] The low average of workers per establishment is due, on the one hand, to increased use of machinery and, on the other, to the tendency of skilled workers to set up their own establishment after some years. Moreover, private textile manufacturers in particular tend to use female home-based workers for some of their work. Small manufacturers and traditional, patriarchal artisan-type establishments generally prevail. Half of all workers employed in the private sector work in family establishments where the employer adds the labour of one or more paid hands to his own and that of his family; an estimated 85 per cent work in establishments which employ less than ten persons. In both cases, employers and employees work closely together, and there is no great difference between the living standards of qualified workers in such establishments and those of their employers.

As a rule, Elisabeth Longuenesse's remark that private-sector workers are better paid but more exploited than workers in the public sector still holds true.[49] Syria's trade unions complain continously that the majority of those employed by the private sector are not covered by social security, that ten-year-olds are working like grown-ups, and that other stipulations of the labour code – on holidays, sick-leave, or protection against wrongful dismissal – are simply ignored. Private-sector wages are generally higher than those in the public sector; but wage differences in the private sector are large: unskilled labourers are rarely paid more than the minimum wage; many small workshops rely on unpaid family labour or minimally paid apprentices; yet skilled workers, particularly in modern establishments, can easily earn 60 per cent more in the private sector than they would in the public sector, and highly qualified workers are paid twice or three times and in some cases five or eight times the wage they would receive in the public sector.[50] Such earnings can enable a worker to set up his own establishment after some years, or to become a partner in a workshop, a taxi, or a commercial venture.

Thus, public-sector wages are anything but attractive if compared to those of the private sector. Public employment, however, has several advantages: almost total protection against dismissal; old-age pensions; free medical care and continued, though somewhat reduced, wage payment during sick-leave. Many public-sector establishments have kindergartens and consumer cooperatives, and free transport is often available to and from the under-serviced suburbs where most of the working class live. In the private sector only large, modern establishments offer similar benefits and services; a couple of these outdo those of the public sector.

A considerable proportion of public-sector workers, however, are deprived of what are generally seen as the advantages of a public-sector job. Public-sector construction companies which employ almost half of all workers in the public sector rely almost entirely on seasonal labourers, who are not covered by pension schemes, nor entitled to the other benefits enjoyed by their colleagues. Even in other parts of the public sector, there are constant complaints about benefits not being paid, services not being rendered, health and safety regulations being ignored, and working conditions generally remaining below legal requirements. The oil, foodstuffs and chemical industries all have particularly poor records in this regard.[51]

Qualified workers, therefore, find little to recommend public- over private-sector employment. Public-sector directors frequently complain that workers view their employment in the public sector merely as an opportunity to take advantage of its social benefits while spending their energies elsewhere, or to gain professional experience for later private-sector employment. Eventually the public sector has to employ those with little or no industrial experience and minimal education, and keep those whose qualifications are insufficient for employment in the private sector.[52]

The Syrian working class is a young working class insofar as most of its members have not been born into it. Its level of education and training is generally low. Despite reasonable progress with literacy and schooling campaigns, some 60 to 65 per cent of production and service workers had no school certificate in 1981.[53] Working-class living standards did not improve in the 1980s, mainly due to both continued migration from the countryside – which put pressure on the cities and created a reservoir of cheap labour – and to the economic crisis of the 1980s. The main part of the working class has settled down in rapidly growing suburbs, particularly around Damascus. Since these settlements have been neither planned nor licensed, they are often lacking most basic infrastructural services. Social security is insufficient.[54] Most importantly, public-sector workers and a substantial part of those working in the private sector earn wages below the subsistence level. In most working-class families mothers are not gainfully employed, i.e. family income depends on the work of the father as the main breadwinner and, probably, that of some of the children.[55] Public-sector workers, construction workers regardless of their employer, and even some industrial and service workers employed in the private sector are forced to seek additional income; qualified and active workers seek to give up wage-labour for some independent – and mostly unproductive – activity. A large part of the working class, as noted, regards wage-labour and their working-class existence as temporary. This attitude, insufficient income, the extreme fragmentation of a working class, the major part of which is employed in small family enterprises, and, additionally, the state of Syria's trade unions[56] render working-class interests comparatively weak and less well defended than the social and economic interests of other strata – particularly if one considers the numerical strength of this class.

The Semi-Proletariat

While the growth of the urban proletariat has been limited, partly as a result of the limited capacity of urban and rural industries to absorb an increasing number of job seekers, the mainly urban semi-proletariat has been growing rapidly. Any of the terms used to name this stratum – sub-proletariat, lumpen-proletariat, the marginalized – are to some extent misleading. Those belonging to this stratum are not generally distinguishable from the proletariat or working class by features that might be implied by prefixes such as "sub" or "lumpen". Neither is their social status necessarily below that of wage-labourers, nor are rags and shabby clothes restricted to this stratum. To speak of marginalization for a group which may consist of up to one quarter of the urban population is also unsatisfactory. Here, therefore, the term semi-proletariat is used, taking into account the similarity of the living conditions of this stratum and the working class, although a substantial part of this semi-proletariat would probably see themselves as members of the petty bourgeoisie. Research has to acknowledge, at times, that social realities are not easily contained within, and social developments do not follow, sociological definitions.

This semi-proletarian stratum consists of those economically active members of the population and their families who are neither employed, at least not permanently, nor employ others, nor live off some rent income, nor own any means of production or parts of it except when it has little or no value. The semi-proletariat thus comprises the two large groups of casual workers, i.e. those whose permanent unemployment can often be interrupted by temporary engagements, and, secondly, self-employed sales- and servicemen offering their largely marginal products and services not in a permanent shop or shack but rather, as the Arabic expression goes, *bi-l-rasif*, on the pavement: these include vendors of small items, cigarettes, smuggled goods and other things in short supply, as well as lottery-ticket sellers, shoeblacks, beggars and others. Part of this stratum are also petty criminals or members of the entourage of local strongmen who are not formally employed by the state or the military, as the retinue of political or military bosses usually are. Members of this stratum frequently change from one gainful activity to another, many of them work seasonally in agriculture. Many a street-vendor or day-labourer may work informally for one of the security services. Pointing to this feature and exaggerating somewhat, an opposition publication sarcastically stated that the prevalent pattern of rural–urban migration in Syria was not taking rural youth from agriculture to industry but rather from "agriculture to the security services".[57]

The numerical strength of the semi-proletariat is even more difficult to assess than that of other social strata; being underestimated and hardly identifiable in official statistics is itself a feature of social marginality. Very roughly estimated, their number doubled between 1970 and 1980, and increased another 150 per cent or more over the 1980s. At the outset of the 1990s, the semi-proletariat can be estimated at around 15 per cent of the total population.[58]

The main source of the semi-proletariat is recent migration from the countryside. Its growth accelerated with the economic crisis of the 1980s which substantially reduced the capacities of both the private and the public industrial and construction sectors to absorb rural migrants, demobilized conscripts, and the children of the urban working class as well as of the middle classes.

The unemployed casual workers who can be found at particular spots in all Syrian cities waiting to be offered a job for the day, mainly in construction, constitute the poorest layer of urban society.[59] On the whole, however, the living conditions of the semi-proletariat are not necessarily worse than those of the working class or the lower stratum of the wage-earning middle classes. The working class and the semi-proletariat share their village origin and dwell, for the most part, in the same poor quarters and suburbs. The living conditions and income of someone selling cigarettes on the streets all day may be little different from that of a skilled or semi-skilled worker who has to find some casual moonlighting work. The income of parts of the semi-proletariat, particularly those casual black-marketeers, smugglers, and well-organized street-vendors who, responding to shortages and demand, deal in American cigarettes, Lebanese jeans or Hungarian drugs, is certainly better than that of factory workers, and their social prestige is higher too. The same may be true of a driver who casually runs a taxi for some 30 per cent of the fare, legally being a self-employed partner of the taxi owner and thus lacking any job security and any social protection in case of sickness, accident, or old age. Not all members of the semi-proletariat are therefore part of the urban poor. On the whole, however, the spread of marginal activities is indicative of economic developments unfavourable to the poorer strata of society.

Given that the major part of the semi-proletariat stems from the rural proletariat, that it can no longer be counted within this group, but has not yet become part of the working class or the petty bourgeoisie, dividing lines between these strata are blurred and fluid. The social and material conditions of the semi-proletariat are as varied and unstable as their activities and employments. Politically, this stratum can be assumed to be extremely unhomogeneous and unsettled. One cannot exclude that, under certain conditions, it may be mobilized for anti-regime movements; such mobilization would be more probable if it were supported by traditional ties and if stress were laid on traditional values, both of which offer the illusion of stability and security lacking in the majority of this stratum.

The Self-Employed Middle Classes

The academic and political discussion about the character and basis of the Syrian Ba'thist regime and similar regimes in the Middle East has often focussed, during the 1970s in particular, on the middle classes or petty bourgeoisie, frequently hiding behind the breadth of the concept. Regarding the importance which in Arab – and other – societies is given to the independence of occupational position as a criterion of social stratification,[60] it is necessary to draw a clear analytical line between the wage-earning or salaried and the self-employed or independent middle classes. This latter stratum, the essential small or petty bourgeoisie, consists of self-employed craftsmen and industrialists, small merchants with their own shops, and other small entrepreneurs in similar conditions – with or without paid employees – as well as self-employed professionals.

Between 1970 and 1991, this stratum has grown from some 140,000 to around 410,000 economically active persons and their families,[61] the growth-rate of the 1980s thereby exceeding that of the 1970s. Its proportion to the entire population has increased slightly from around 9 to some 11 per cent. Around one quarter of this group are active in manufacturing, some 70 per cent in trade, transport, construction, and other services; the rest are self-employed professionals. Some two-fifths of this petty bourgeoisie employ paid labour, some three-fifths do not. Thus, despite the modernizing and industrializing efforts of the state, Syria's independent middle classes have been able to maintain their societal position. This is particularly so as regards social ranking and the prestige of self-employed, independent activity, and is also true of their numerical strength. Temporary effects of the 1980s crisis notwithstanding, the material conditions of craftsmen, small manufacturers and industrialists have remained comparatively good, both where they have to compete with modern public-sector industries and, even more so, where a certain division of labour has been established between public- and private-sector industries. In these cases, the public sector is mainly producing intermediate products and lower-quality consumer goods, while the private sector is concentrating on finished and higher-quality products.[62]

It is striking that Syria's private manufacturing sector remained rather small-scale throughout the 1970s and 1980s while the absolute number of private establishments increased continuously. Middle-class entrepreneurs in Syria tend to refrain from enlarging their establishments above a certain size. This may be out of fear that any expansion would cause increased difficulties with the bureacracy or arouse the envy of those in power; or it could be from simple consideration of the labour and social security regulations that apply to bigger establishments. The numerical increase of smaller establishments, and thus, of the number of middle-class industrialists, is therefore partly a mushrooming process in the course of which members of one family set up several small establishments in the same industry rather than one large factory. Apart from that, this middle class recruits most of its new members from its own employees. Many of those who work in these small establishments will try to set up their own workshop after some years of training and, more often than not, with a loan or the financial participation of their former employers. Tendencies to concentration within the private industrial sector which became evident during the 1980s and increased as a result of new investment regulations introduced between 1988 and 1991, have therefore nevertheless remained limited.[63]

Doubtless, entrepreneurial activity in commerce, transport, and construction has been more profitable than in industry. Different from the prevailing pattern in manufacturing, the recruitment into a partially new commercial petty bourgeoisie has not always been exclusively from its own environment. The social background of Syria's petty traders and small entrepreneurs in construction and services is rather varied. Apart from members of the traditional strata of petty merchants and entrepreneurs, there are climbers from the semi-proletariat, returning labour-migrants who buy, or participate in, a taxi or a truck, open a shop or engage in real-estate speculation, and there are the sons of civil servants and military officers preferring an entrepreneurial career facilitated by their fathers' connections to an employment with the state.

Longuenesse assumed at the end of the 1970s that the Syrian petty bourgeoisie was an ascending class, rather than a class bound to lose importance, which contrasts with the picture given by Western capitalist modes of development. Longuenesse concluded that the growth of this class had transformed it from an enemy into a base of support to the regime.[64] Her introductory assumption holds true, even in the early 1990s; her conclusion, however, has to be qualified.

The Syrian bourgeoisie, particularly its traditional urban nucleus, is for the most part staunchly conservative. Hanna Batatu has correctly called it "the most religiously oriented class in Syria".[65] It has strong ties with the religious establishment; frequently still, craftsmen or merchants in older parts of the cities exercise some subordinate function in their neighbourhood mosques, and many of these small entrepreneurs contribute to funds covering the costs of mosques and religious institutions. Ties between the traditional bourgeoisie of Syria's cities and smaller merchants and manufacturers have been maintained to a considerable extent all through the revolutionary and state-socialist phases of Nasserism and Ba'thism. In general, these small entrepreneurs share the social conservatism of that bourgeoisie as well as – despite partly diverging economic interests – their conviction that state interference in the economy should be limited. Since the mid-1960s, when the Ba'thist regime nationalized a large number of private establishments and the influence of Alawi officers in the political leadership began to increase, members of this petty bourgeoisie have therefore been among the staunchest opponents of the regime and formed the nucleus of the Islamic opposition. Parts of the petty bourgeoise remained wary of the regime even after Asad's takeover and the beginning of his *infitah* policies. In the eyes of many of its members, Asad, despite his attempts to present himself as a pious and orthodox Muslim, remained the boss of an Alawi regime that suppressed the Sunni majority and allied itself with the enemies of Sunni Islam: with Lebanon's Maronites in 1976, and with Iran during the Iraq–Iran war. As a rule, this conservative petty bourgeoisie did not contribute the militants who repeatedly clashed with the regime even before the uprising of 1982. Parallel to the worst clashes, however, many petty merchants and craftsmen went on strike, and in general they are supposed to have lent their financial support to the opposition.[66]

All this did not prevent a substantial part of the petty bourgeoise from coming to terms or even making their peace with the regime. This was particularly so for the petty bourgeoisie and the bourgeoisie of Damascus whom Asad had tried to accommodate since his takeover in 1970. As a result, the merchants and manufacturers of Damascus did not lend open support to the opposition during the conflicts of 1979 to 1982. After the defeat of the Hama uprising of 1982, the petty bourgeoisie of Hama, Homs, and Aleppo had also, *nolens volens*, to come to terms with the regime.

Asad has certainly been able to win support among the newer segments of this petty bourgeoisie, particularly merchants and manufacturers who owed their existence to *infitah* policies or to valuable connections with leading civil servants and officers. On the whole, the petty bourgeoisie of the 1980s and early 1990s has not yet developed into a stable basis of the regime. They would not, that is, try to defend it if it was about to fall. Inasmuch, however, as its members are doing well economically, as there does not seem to be any alternative to the regime in power, and as this regime secures political stability, this class no longer poses a threat to Asad and his leadership.

The situation is somewhat different for the small, yet growing number of Syria's self-employed professionals. This stratum of mainly doctors, lawyers, and some members of technical professions, differs in more than one respect from the rest of the self-employed middle classes. Their educational level is generally higher, and only rarely do they stem from the craftsmen–merchant petty bourgeoisie. Since Syria's educational system has been opened up and widely expanded under the Ba'th, today's generation of professionals consists of children of all classes and regions. Being self-employed, these professionals are generally better off economically than the majority of the Syrian intelligentsia employed by the state, but less well off than merchants and manufacturers. Only the medical professions – physicians, dentists, pharmacists – earn an almost guaranteed high income. These are the professions young Syrians dream of; and access to the three faculties which train them is limited to students with excellent grades or connections. It is striking that there is almost no high official who does not have at least one son or daughter studying or practising pharmacy, medicine, or dentistry.

Despite the difference between their living conditions, many members of both parts of the intelligentsia – those employed by the state and those working independently – share an unsatisfied wish for greater political and intellectual openness and freedom, and they often share a more or less critical stance towards the regime and its policies. They have, on occasion, tried to challenge the regime on civil liberties and human rights issues. In 1980, without joining the violent uprising of the Islamists, whose ideology and goals were not in fact theirs, lawyers and other professionals tried through their unions to pressure the regime into introducing a minimum degree of rule-of-law. The respective union executives were dissolved, their members imprisoned. Similarly, in 1991, a group of lawyers and other members of the intelligentsia made an equally unsuccessful attempt to establish a human-rights committee and to question the 99.9 per cent result of the referendum on Asad's re-election.[67] Syria's intelligentsia represents an oppositional potential, but not one that the regime would seriously have to fear.

The Wage-Earning Middle Classes

The wage-earning or salaried middle classes comprise all those employed in the private or public sector who, according to First World categories, are regarded as white-collar employees. This includes employees in academic professions, teachers of all categories, leading or subordinate employees with administrative, office, financial, or accountant functions, technicians and nurses, officers and non-commissioned officers in the armed forces, sales personnel as far as they are wage-earners, and other employees rendering various personal services. The category thus includes office boys as well as directors of government agencies. Not included is the political and military leadership. Some 70 per cent of the salaried middle classes are regarded as *muwazzafin*, civil servants and senior staff, including both secretaries and clerks as well as public- and private-sector managers and executives. The other 30 per cent are regarded as *mustakhdamin*, petty officials and employees. They usually hold a primary or, at best, a secondary school certificate, and render subordinate services. In 1970, around half of the wage-earning middle classes were employed with the state, twenty years later this proportion has risen to approximately two-thirds.[68]

Throughout the 1970s, the wage-earning middle classes grew faster than any other stratum of Syrian society. In the 1980s, however, their growth lagged behind that of the semi-proletariat. From 1970 to 1980, the wage-earning middle classes more than doubled in number, increasing from some 160,000 to around 370,000 economically active persons. Within the state-sector their number almost tripled from 85,000 to 255,000. During the 1980s, this stratum grew further, although at reduced speed. In 1991, the salaried middle classes could be estimated at some 640,000 persons employed plus their families, representing more than 17 per cent of the whole population.

The wage-earning middle classes were the stratum which most intensively determined the Syrian scene throughout the 1970s. In a sense, their numerical growth indicated the particular direction and the extent of social change taking place at that time. The majority of those joining and enhancing this stratum during the late 1960s and 1970s were of rural origin. This was to some extent the result of increasing opportunities for the children of peasant families to obtain higher education; but it was also, particularly as far as the public sector and public administration were concerned, a matter of politics. With state functions increasing, there were plenty of vacancies which could be filled with those loyal to the new people in power. Given that the Ba'th party's main sources of support lay in the countryside, not in the larger cities, the employment of educated young rural migrants became a means of strengthening the Ba'thists' hold over the state apparatus and weakening bureaucratic resistance to their rule.

This new echelon of socially mobile state employees, clearly embodied all the dominant perceptions of development and modernization the regime was pursuing. Most had obtained a high level of education and an increasing number had studied abroad. For the most part, they left their rural traditons behind, adopting "western" modes of dwelling, consumption and social behaviour,[69] thereby developing demands for consumer goods local industries could not easily satisfy. The needs and demands of the wage-earning middle classes found their expression in the first *infitah* which encouraged both the import of modern consumer goods and import substitution, i.e. their local production.

Differences between petty officials, on the one hand, and high-ranking public- or private-sector employees remained large. On the whole, however, the salaried middle classes were a privileged group. In the 1970s, the income of a civil servant, even a petty official, would not only support him and his family but also allow for the purchase of some goods and services that previously would have been viewed as part of a "bourgeois" lifestyle.[70] The living standards of the salaried middle classes were further increased in comparison to, for instance, skilled workers, since they had on average fewer children and a comparatively higher percentage of women in gainful employment.

Since the early 1980s, as public-sector wages ceased to keep pace with inflation, differences within the wage-earning middle classes have become sharper. Younger members of this stratum, who started their career after the beginning of the austerity policies of the 1980s, have not been able to share the benefits of those who joined the bureaucracy ten or 15 years earlier. Their salaries would hardly cover the daily needs of their families, let alone the acquisition of an apartment or furniture.[71]

As a result, the wage-earning middle classes have become increasingly differentiated. At the top, there is a small layer of private-sector managerial staff and of high-ranking civil servants just below the political and administrative leadership. This bureaucratic top group earns salaries which, like the salaries of the rest of public-sector employees, have lost their value. Their income, however, is not dependent on their salaries alone; to a large extent it depends – illegal gains excluded – on privileges connected with their functions. Such privileges include cars, travel abroad and travel allowances, privileged access to goods and services in short supply, scholarships and grants for their children, extra pay, and expenses and allowances for participation in government committees and for functions in the party or in mass organizations. In contrast, the intermediate layer within the wage-earning middle classes, had to learn, during the 1980s, to cope with decreasing real incomes and to change some of the consumer habits it had acquired in the decade before. Many of its members felt forced to look for a source of additional income to maintain some of the standards they had become used to. Still, a majority had in the past acquired certain securities, particularly real estate, and so the group has been protected against outright impoverishment.

This has not been the case for the generation of public-sector employees first employed during the 1980s, and for lower-level officials. Even though a young teacher would still earn some 35 per cent more than an office boy, their living conditions would become increasingly similar given that neither of them could support a family on their income. By the early 1990s, that sector of middle-class state employees whose wage was below subsistence level had grown to an estimated 40 per cent. As a rule, members of this layer were either living with their parents or other relatives, unable to afford their own housing, or living in the crowded neighbourhoods of the urban poor. If they had to support a family their employment with the state became simply the source of a secondary income – illegal gains once again excluded – moonlighting becoming the main source. Those who were unable to find a second job could not even be sure of being able to secure their families' basic needs. They constitute what Waterbury calls a "lumpen-salariat"[72] dependent on the support of others, on casual jobs, petty trade, or even their children's labour.

Thus, between the late 1960s and the end of the 1970s, the wage-earning middle classes formed the largest group on the winners' side of a rapid process of social change. Despite considerable differences of status and income within this stratum they could almost entirely be regarded as the largest urban source of support to the regime. Many state employeees are still, in the early 1990s, committed to the political goals of the Ba'th party – that is, to Arab unity and some sort of socialism. However, the wage-earning middle classes no longer form a social stratum largely united by common interests in and common benefits from the course of political and economic development. The upper layer of this stratum, politically influential and more or less unaffected by the economic crisis of the 1980s, has generally remained close to the regime and is interested in defending its own and the regime's position. The middle layer, except for its younger generation, has been losing economically without becoming impoverished. Its members are able to rationalize at least parts of these losses; they are prepared, to some extent, to understand the need for austerity and to swallow the fact that Syria has for some time been living beyond its means. In this group, loyalty to the regime, a strong interest in maintaining stability and securing and defending their own position as well as a certain preparedness to share in the country's economic burden, are mixed with complaints about objectively reduced levels of consumption and unease over political conditions in general. There is particular concern about the lack of participation and political freedom as well as about the regime's renunciation, in all but rhetoric, of the Ba'th party's and the state's lofty national and social goals. Apparently such unease on the part of state employees has been increasing the more economic advantages connected to their position have shrunk. As long as living standards rose, political conditions were not viewed too critically. The regime most likely took into account this relationship between the middle classes' economic situation and their tendency to political quietism when, in 1990, singling out university professors – many of whom had become quite outspoken in their criticism of the regime – for special pay rises. However, this intermediate layer of the salaried middle classes, particularly that part employed by the state, has become a less reliable basis for the regime than it was in the 1970s.

It seems that the regime has lost much of its legitimacy and credibility for similar reasons within the lowest layer of the wage-earning middle classes. Officials whose basic needs are no longer provided for by the state can hardly be relied upon as potential defenders of the regime in power. Over the 1980s, parts of the bureaucracy have thus turned into a potential threat to the regime. A freeze on recruitment decreed in 1985 for most of the public sector and administration – and only gradually lifted with economic conditions improving as of the late 1980s – has therefore had its political as well as its economic rationale. At least it prevented a segment of dubious loyalty within the bureaucracy from growing during the worst years of economic crisis.

The Bourgeoisie

Thirty years after the Ba'thist "revolution" of 1963, and despite the nationalizations of the 1960s, an upper class has emerged both greater in number and wealthier than the bourgeoisie of the pre-Ba'thist era. Lack of appropriate data makes it difficult to estimate their number accurately. At the outset of the 1990s, we might estimate the upper class, or bourgeoisie, including agricultural entrepreneurs and big landowners, at around one per cent of the population. The most illustrious group within this stratum is doubtless the one frequently referred to in Syria as the new class (*al-tabaqa al-jadida*), the top layer of Syria's new commercial bourgeoisie.[73] There are also the remnants of Syria's pre-1963 bourgeoisie, and a new industrial bourgeoisie as well as the so-called state-bourgeoisie.[74]

What today is considered the old bourgeoisie is that stratum of business people that consists of the survivors and offspring of Syria's pre-1963 entrepreneurial class. Most of them stem from the less prominent and less wealthy part of the pre-Ba'thi bourgeoisie. This class was the leading class, both economically and politically, since independence. It received its first blow with the land reform of 1958, was pushed out of government by the Ba'thists in 1963, and received its most serious economic blow with the nationalizations of 1963, 1964 and 1965.

As a rule, merchants were less affected than industrialists by the nationalizations. Their businesses survived, although they reduced operations for some time. After Asad's assumption of power, their role was largely restored. Even though they had to abandon some of their activities to the state – particularly banking, wholesale trade in cotton and other main agricultural goods, and the importing of particular goods now traded by specialized public-sector agencies such as the General Organization for Fodder or the General Organization for the Trade of Pharmaceuticals – Asad's *infitah* policies, the huge development programmes of the 1970s and the growth of the salaried middle classes with their new consumer habits opened up large and profitable opportunities for their businesses.

Since most private industrial establishments of any scale had been nationalized in the 1960s, only a very small number of Syria's old industrial bourgeoisie were able to maintain their businesses. Many left the country right away or left industry, shifting to trade, brokerage or other activities. A limited number of industrialists set up new, smaller establishments immediately after the nationalizations, and some returned to the country, or to industry, after 1970. Individual descendants of those who left the country in the 1960s started to invest some money in Syria from the late 1980s, particularly from 1991 under the provisions of the new investment law.

As the state pursued its *infitah* policies, and public and private spending rose during the 1970s, new groups caught up with and surpassed the old bourgeoisie in wealth and influence. Belonging to one of the old notable families ceased to be the main guarantee of bourgeois class status. Although some members of these new groups began their climb earlier, it is only since 1970 that they have been able to secure social positions into which they have not been born. Most new industrialists stem from the petty craftsmen or merchant bourgeoisie, some from the wage-earning middle classes. Quite similar to the old bourgeoisie when it emerged during the mandate period and after independence, these young industrialists, in the 1970s and 1980s, benefited from new technologies, a growing population, changing consumer habits and, during the 1970s, increasing mass purchasing power. In contrast to Syria's industrial bourgeoisie of the independence period which, among other things, had established some basic industries such as electricity and water plants, cement factories, sugar refining, cotton ginning, and textile weaving plants, the new industrialists were almost entirely restricted to light finishing industries producing consumer goods for upper and middle class use. This was due mainly to the regime's industrialization policies which, as noted, defined a particular division of labour between the private and the public sector until the early 1990s. Entrepreneurs, however, would rarely complain, since business opportunities offered within the space delimited for private industrial activities were generally regarded as good.

That sector of the bourgeoisie, however, which benefited most from the economic policies pursued under Asad's regime, was Syria's new commercial bourgeoisie and particularly its top layer, the so-called new class. The social background of the new commercial bourgeoisie and this new class is varied. With their new wealth and a certain social respectability, members of this new class often try to upgrade their family history somewhat. But in fact very few derive from the old commercial class, a larger part descends from the petty bourgeoisie, others from the wage-earning middle classes, and some even from the military or from the semi-proletariat. The rise of this new class has been closely related to two factors, namely to their personal relations with people in power and to soaring public expenditure – the latter factor being advantageous to the commercial class as a whole. Almost everything ordered and purchased by the state and public sector – whether consumer goods for distribution through the public-sector retail network, cars, machinery and raw material for public-sector industries or entire turn-key factories – entailed opportunities for merchants, middlemen and commission seekers.

This is not to imply that all deals concluded with Syria's authorities or the public sector involved corrupt practices. Thousands of members of Syria's commercial class were able to benefit from contracts with the state, even without greater manipulations. What can truly be called the new class consists of no more than several hundred persons. They have been making, and make, most of their big deals by virtue of their connections, frequently entering into silent partnerships with influential bureaucratic, military or political figures. Some of their activities – such as smuggling and contraband trade – are illegal or semi-legal;

illegal or manipulative methods may of course be used in the running
of what are otherwise entirely legal businesses, such as the representation of foreign companies, which in itself is entirely legal. In addition
to representation and middlemanship, new class members are also
traders and contractors, and they may under certain conditions invest
their money in agricultural, industrial or service projects.

Members of the new class, however, are not simply bigger and less
scrupulous than the rest of the commmercial bourgeoisie. Their main
characteristic is their dependency on a state which controls large parts
of the national economy without being able to forgo certain services
by private businessmen, and whose bureaucracy is not subject to
democratic control. All principal activities of the new class have in
some way or other been related to the state, utilizing its authoritarian
nature. What has constituted the source of complaints of other entrepreneurs – namely government control over foreign exchange, imports, exports, and prices; state tutelage over the economy in general;
the anarchy of import regulations – has allowed new class businessmen to make profits that could hardly be made in free-market systems.
By virtue of their connections and influence, they have been able to
secure for themselves special exemptions, monopolies and quasi-
monopolies.

This symbiotic relationship between the new class and the state
has found its clearest legal expression in the mixed sector, that is,
those privately managed joint-stock companies in which the government or the public sector hold a minority share. With a range of
privileges, such as exemption from foreign-exchange and import regulations, success is almost guaranteed for any company established
under the conditions of an at least partly state-controlled economy.
Since their establishment involves public money, mixed-sector companies can only be founded by law or, according to the law on the
agricultural mixed sector and to Investment Law No. 10, by a decree
of the Prime Minister. Competition is thus largely reduced. Notably,
the first two mixed-sector companies set up, the Syrian Arab Company for Touristic Establishments and Transtour, became quasi-
monopolistic corporations for a certain sector of the tourism industry,
with their respective founders and managers, 'Uthman al-'A'idi and
Sa'ib Nahhas, emerging as the two most prominent and influential
new class businessmen in Syria in the 1970s and 1980s. The privileges connected with the mixed sector made it an ideal instrument for
the new class to pursue and cover a broad spectrum of deals which

were not necessarily legal or part of the functions originally assigned to the company in question. Besides that, the mixed sector strengthened the ties between the new class and the bureaucracy, hence constituting a particularly attractive instrument for all parts of the Syrian bourgeoisie that were interested in close cooperation with the state.

Syria's bourgeoisie is uniform neither in its appearance nor in its attitude toward the regime. Generally speaking, the old bourgeoisie, including its younger generation, can be said to be socially and politically conservative, often harbouring reservations about the regime elite and its social and confessional background. Syria's old bourgeoisie, industrialists in particular, and members of the new industrial bourgeoisie tend to be more opposed to the regime and less eager to cooperate with it than the commercial class. Many of them privately complain about the burdens of dictatorship and bureaucracy, and criticize what they regard as the government's bias in favour of commercial activities; they also object to the anarchy of frequently changing and sometimes contradictory regulations on trade, production, and prices which all make investment decisions difficult. Syria's commercial bourgeoisie, in contrast, was relatively quick to give up the disdain many of its members initially felt toward the Ba'thists, and to disguise it behind economic interests, responding positively to the demonstrative friendliness the Asad regime displayed towards the merchants, particularly those of the Damascus Chamber of Commerce.

The new commercial bourgeoisie in general, and the new class in particular, have been among the main beneficiaries of the political and economic developments to take place in Syria since the early 1970s. They managed to benefit both from the boom of the 1970s and, to some extent, from the crisis of the 1980s. On one hand, this crisis allowed many of them to engage in crisis-related ventures such as contraband trade, on the other it helped to remove political obstacles to a gradual economic liberalization. The members of this new commercial bourgeoisie do not share the reservations harboured by parts of the old bourgeoisie towards the regime elite. They have, instead, become one of the regime's main partners.

The State Bourgeoisie

The growth of both private commerce and private industry has been, as mentioned above, directly connected to the expansion of state functions and state employment, particularly to the growth of the wage-earning middle classes and their demand for consumer goods. At the top of the state apparatus, there emerged an upper stratum which soon distanced itself in terms of economic and social status from those who formed the main body of that apparatus. This top group consists of the highest echelons of government and party, that is, the Ba'th party's Regional Command, provincial governors (*muhafizun*), government ministers and deputy ministers, the secretaries of the provincial party organizations, the heads of the mass organizations, the highest ranks of the military, the police and the secret services (*mukhabarat*), and the top managers of the public sector. Membership of this group usually requires some direct connection to the President. A large number of its members have gained powerful political positions, and many have been able to acquire – by legally, illegally or semi-legally exploiting their positions and privileges – personal wealth which often far surpasses that of Syria's old bourgeoisie. Many of them, with some notable exceptions, hold a university degree or have passed through the military academy. Most stem from the rural and small-town middle classes, some from the small peasantry. Asad has recruited some members of the urban bourgeoisie also into this group.

Although the concept is controversial, the group is referred to here as the state bourgeoisie. State bourgeoisies, as John Waterbury has pointed out, are functional strata,[75] rather than classes which would necessarily try to reproduce themselves and the mode of production to which they owe their existence. The Syrian state bourgeoisie, like its equivalent in other countries of similar development experience, does not derive its position from the formal ownership of means of production; it was not "born from the market but has ripened and grown in offices and barracks".[76] It monopolizes, however, the control over the public economic sector and hence, irrespective of legal ownership, has become the effective proprietor of the country's main means of production, deciding over the distribution of the surplus generated and controlling a significant part of the labour market. Since it is located at the top of the political power structure, controlling the media, the public administration, and the security organizations, it is able to deeply influence social developments according to its own interests.

There is some probability that this state bourgeoisie, or parts of it, will gradually become transformed into an authentic bourgeoisie which, in addition to or in lieu of its control over the public sector, acquires legal ownership rights to means of production by investing inside its own country, rather than simply spending, some of the wealth it has accumulated. This does not imply any planned, let alone collective self-transformation; the state bourgeoisie has, if at all, developed a limited consciousness of its common social interest.[77] Any change that does take place is likely to be because individual members of this stratum do not find a better alternative for securing their own current social position in a future where the public sector may have lost much of its importance, and the regime may have become a feature of the past. Continued austerity policies that would further reduce the opportunities for private accumulation of public resources and for providing lucrative jobs for offspring are likely to fuel such a process. Various relationships that have been established between the state bourgeoisie and the private bourgeoisie would ease their partial and gradual amalgamation. Such a process would neither be historically unique – consider the descent of much of Syria's old bourgeoisie from an Ottoman bureaucracy which transformed its control over state land into private property rights – nor exceptional in comparison with other states of the region, Egypt for instance.[78] First signs indicating the possibility of such a development are clearly visible. Few of the sons and daughters of high Syrian officials would start or contemplate starting a career similar to that of their fathers, that is, in the public sector, the administration or the military. Like military officers, many high state officials have acquired land, and established agricultural projects of some scale.[79] Representatives of the state bourgeoisie whose children or close relatives are openly investing in local – or in Lebanese – industrial, commercial or service ventures are still mainly to be found among those occupying the highest political positions, and among military officers. Most probably, members of this group have little fear that someone might dare to inquire into the source of their capital. We may assume that a considerable part of the state bourgeoisie has covertly invested parts of its wealth in private-sector ventures. However, the number of those who transfer their wealth to foreign countries both to provide for a refuge outside, should that become necessary, and for a rentier existence can hardly be underestimated.

3. Conclusion: Social Structures and Political Alliances

Income and Employment

Since 1970, Syria's urban society or, more precicely, that part of society which is not mainly employed in agriculture, has become more polarized. Both the proportion of the urban upper and upper middle classes – that is, Syria's urban bourgeoisie, middle class entrepreneurs and the upper stratum of the salaried middle classes – and of the lower classes have increased slightly at the expense of the middle and lower middle classes. More important, however, than this stratification by status (according to which a school teacher, for instance, would be regarded part of the middle classses) are real differences of living conditions.

Poverty and wealth are relative categories. We regard as relatively poor those who cannot cover the basic needs of their family – food, clothing, habitation, and a minimum of expenses for education and health – from the main income of the main breadwinner. There may be additional income from moonlighting, the labour of other family members, support from the extended family or from a family plot in the countryside. Living below the poverty line, in this sense, does not therefore necessarily mean being unable to secure the family's subsistence. It means, however, being unable to support it from the main breadwinner's regular work. Those falling under this category are referred to in Syria as persons with limited income (*mahdudin al-dakhl*). As a rule, such limited income entails physical and psychological strain, and more often than not poor nourishment. In many cases it also entails children being taken from school after the sixth grade, or even before, to contribute to the family income.[80] Given that the public system of social security does not even come up with what is stipulated by law, an increase in absolute poverty, involving malnutrition and homelessness on a large scale, is only prevented because traditional social relations are still strong – making it possible to rely on the support of one's extended family in case of sickness and unemployment. Traditional family relations and the dependencies that go with them declined somewhat with the enormous social changes of the 1960s and 1970s, but they have, as a matter of fact, been strengthened again with the economic crisis of the 1980s.

In the early 1970s, the line of relative poverty ran approximately between the urban lower and middle classes, with petty employees still living above this line. In the early 1980s, it came to separate the lower and intermediate strata of the middle classes, while at the beginning of the 1990s, with parts of the civil service becoming a lumpensalariat, it ran right through the medium strata of the middle classes. The proportion of those with limited income can be estimated to have risen from less than 60 per cent of the urban population in

1970 to some 70 per cent in the early 1990s. Some 7 per cent of the urban population may be regarded as wealthy or well off, less than a quarter as belonging to the medium-income strata. The distance between the upper and the middle classes has increased considerably.[81]

On the whole, in both its urban and rural sectors, Syrian society has seen a considerable growth of its upper and upper middle classes over the two decades between 1970 and the early 1990s. The proportion of the middle classes has increased slightly, that of the lower classes has decreased as a result of the upward mobility and migration of a substantial number of young people from small peasant backgrounds, particularly during the 1970s. The small peasantry has decreased by absolute number and in proportion to the entire population as many peasants abandoned agriculture as their main occupation. The proportion of those living on a limited income, or below the line of relative poverty, decreased over the 1970s – primarily as a result of the expansion of the public sector – and increased again over the 1980s. At the outset of the 1990s, these relatively poor constituted some 70 per cent of the population.[82] The gap between the prosperous and the poor has become larger since wages, salaries and agricultural procurement prices have lagged far behind the overall rate of inflation during the 1980s. Although precise data are not available, there is no doubt that a considerable redistribution of wealth took place from wage- and salary-earners to property-owners.[83]

During the 1970s, perpetuating a development of the 1960s, the proportion of wage-labour to the entire work-force rose considerably from some 42 per cent in 1970 to more than 55 per cent in 1981. In the following decade, this proportion remained almost stagnant, ranging around 56 per cent. This stagnation is mainly due to the partial freeze on state-sector recruitment after 1985. The increase of wage-labour reflects that capitalist relations of production have generally been growing at the expense of pre-capitalist ones.

Although one of the main social goals of the Ba'th party had been to create, by means of the land reform, a large number of cooperatively organized family farms, which were supposed to then form the basis of a non-capitalist agricultural development, actual agricultural policies did not provide the frame for a successful performance of the co-operatives and for a secure existence of small peasant holdings. Many of the small peasants gave up their independence, left agriculture, or turned their plot into a source of secondary income. The picture in Syrian agriculture has become increasingly determined by medium-

Table III.2 The Social Structure of Syria

	1970		1981		1991	
	1,000s	%	1,000s	%	1,000s	%
Upper Class						
Big landowners and agricultural entrepreneurs; industrial bourgeoisie; commercial bourgeoisie and new class; state bourgeoisie	10	0.6	20	0.9	40	1.1
Middle Classes						
Middle class entrepreneurs (employing wage-labour)	40	2.4	80	3.4	160	4.3
Middle class peasantry	170	10.0	140	6.0	130	3.5
Petty bourgeoisie (self-employed, not employing wage-labour)	100	5.9	140	6.0	250	6.7
Upper and middle stratum of wage-earning middle classes	110	6.5	280	11.9	480	12.9
Lower stratum of wage-earning middle classes	50	2.9	90	3.8	160	4.3
Lower Classes						
Working class	410	24.1	830	35.3	1,300	34.9
Semi-proletariat (rural and urban)	100	5.9	220	9.4	550	14.8
Small peasants	270	15.9	150	6.4	140	3.8
Unpaid agricultural labourers	300	17.6	300	12.8	360	9.7
Paid agricultural labourers	140	8.2	100	4.3	150	4.0
Total	1,700		2,350		3,720	

Note: All data and estimates refer to economically active persons, including military personnel.[84]

Sources: Population Censuses of 1970 and 1981; Agricultural Censuses of 1970 and 1981; Statistical Abstracts 1970–1992; Industry Survey for 1970; Private-Sector Industry Surveys for 1982, 1983, 1984, 1989/90; Survey of Economic Establishments for 1981 (all published by: SAR, CBS); SCP, Documents of the 6th Conference; General Federation of Trade Unions; Higher Council of Public-Sector Construction Companies; Ministry of Industry; The International Institute for Strategic Studies, The Military Balance, various years.

sized and larger farms that employ more capital and less labour than before, by agricultural contracting firms of various sizes that rent their machinery and workers to the peasants, by large agricultural investors, and, since the late 1980s, by a number of joint-stock agri-companies. A substantial part of the rural population has become proletarianized, the productivity of agricultural labour has increased, and employment opportunities in agriculture have became scarce.

In contrast, and during the 1970s in particular, employment opportunities increased in the service sectors, mainly with the state, and in the modern public industrial sector. Only from the mid-1980s has the private industrial sector been growing faster than the public-sector industries. In 1970 the public sector employed some 40 per cent, in 1981 around 50 per cent, but in 1991 an estimated 45 per cent or so of all wage-earners in manufacturing industries.

Within the private sector, as noted, larger establishments have been increasing in proportion to the rest. However, the private sector is mainly determined by small establishments with the owner present on the shop floor. Some of these small establishments have become virtu-ally dependent on wholesalers who are legally or illegally importing raw materials and are marketing the products of these smaller firms. This has particularly been so since, in the early 1980s, the state began to refrain from providing foreign exchange for imports to private manufacturers and to reduce its own imports of raw material for distribution to the private sector.

On the whole, the proportion of those who own the means of production has shrunk considerably. Except for marginal means of production such as a shoeblack's box, the proportion of those who own the means of production ranges around 19 per cent at the begin-ning of the 1990s, whereas it lay over 37 per cent twenty years earlier.

After an egalitarian push in the 1960s, differences of class became more pronounced throughout the 1970s and 1980s. The gradual loss of importance of traditional relations of production has contributed to this development. Nonetheless, little class consciousness has emerged within the working class, the semi-proletariat, or the small peasantry. This is due partly to the fragmentation of each of these strata and partly to the fact that – as a result of rapid social change – class lines are cutting straight through families. The dominant socio-economic position of the state adds further to the lack of class consciousness and class-conscious behaviour on the part of workers and peasants. The state is by far the largest employer and, as a purchaser of much of the agricultural product, part of the agricultural relations of production. The social and economic interests of wage-earners and peasants have to be voiced and defended vis-à-vis the state rather than vis-à-vis a private entrepreneurial class. Trade unions and the Peasant Union, however, are committed to state and regime interests at least as much as they are to the interests of their membership. Since fragmentation and individualization is also a feature of Syria's still large self-employed middle classes, policy-makers do not have to fear any collective action of scale on the part of either of these groups.

Class Structures and the Social Basis of the Regime

Since the Ba'th assumed power in 1963, the social basis of Syria's political leadership and the stance of various social groups toward the regime have undergone changes. The revolutionary Ba'th of the 1960s found the largest part of its basis in the countryside. Most of the officers leading the party's course were sons of the middle rather than the small peasantry. The party, however, had a considerable source of support within the small and landless peasantry, and it had a narrow but active basis in the urban intelligentsia.[85]

Thirty years after the Ba'th party's assumption of power, the middle peasantry was still a stable source of support to the regime. These peasants have become relatively well off; they have gained secure social and material positions; they are largely integrated into regime structures; and they still form an important basis for the reproduction of the regime – not only through the army, but to a large extent through the Peasant Union and the party apparatus. The small peasantry, in contrast, has lost weight; many of them having abandoned agriculture at least as their main occupation. Those who still make their living from the land they originally possessed or have acquired through the land reform are certainly not in opposition to the regime. Their support, however, is rather lacklustre, mixed with a strong element of mistrust towards the state, the party, and towards the Peasant Union which presents itself to this group as an instrument for implementing regime policies rather than an interest organization.[86]

The rural proletariat and the urban semi-proletariat, on the whole, are lacking any political direction. Parts of these strata are linked to the regime or – mainly through traditional tribal or sectarian ties – to some of its outstanding figures. The emergence of local movements of landless peasants, squatting or trying to squat the land of old or new landlords, cannot totally be excluded.[87] By incorporating the landless peasants into the Peasant Union, however, the regime has provided against the emergence of any syndicalist rural protest movement.

Members of the urban semi-proletariat will most probably seek individual, as opposed to collective, solutions and gains. The emergence of an organized movement aimed at improving the conditions of this stratum is unlikely. Only if the economic situation should deteriorate such as to endanger the supply of basic food items to popular quarters, could spontaneous "bread riots" be imagined. The regime has clearly realized that austerity policies must not go that far, and it has as yet always managed to avoid a complete breakdown of basic supplies. Only in the spring of 1988, during the worst phases of the economic crisis, did bread shortages on some days seem to lead the country to the brink of uncontrollable public unrest.[88] Under certain conditions, the semi-proletariat may be mobilized against the regime, particularly, as was the case during the 1978–82 period, by religio-political movements.

In the working class, in the wage-earning middle classes, and particularly in the intelligentsia, the regime lost popularity and support over the 1980s. These groups benefited from the expansion of the state and the public sector in the 1960s and 1970s, experiencing personal social and economic advancement. This was the case even for industrial workers who could not sustain their families from their industrial work alone, since many of them relied on some additional income from agriculture. Until the mid-1970s, both groups formed a strong basis of support to the regime, the wage-earning middle classes even more so than the working class. The latter were partly fragmented over a multitude of private family workshops where they to some extent shared the conservative attitudes of their employers, while Communists and Nasirists found a strong base among those who worked in the modern industrial sector. As both groups suffered real income losses during the 1980s, and discontent with regime policies grew, the regime had to realize that it could no longer totally rely on these strata. From this perspective, the regime's own interest to further enlarge the public sector and, even more so, the public administration, declined.

In contrast, Syria's political leadership has been able to improve its standing within both the petty and the grand bourgeoisie, particularly within its commercial segments. But Syria's bourgeoisie cannot be regarded as a firm, and certainly not as a reliable basis of support to the regime. However, it can be assumed that this class's interest in the maintenance of stability and in the preservation of current socio-economic relations has increasingly come to predominate over the desire for political change harboured by some. Even conservative, Islamic opposition forces would be unable to count on the unqualified support of the bourgeoisie. Indeed, if oppositional groups appeared to have only a limited chance of toppling the regime, the bourgeoisie would most probably favour the dominant order. This was clear during the 1979–82 unrest when the *suq* of Damascus no longer joined ranks with the Islamist-led opposition. There is large sympathy for Islamist causes as a true expression of social conservatism within Syria's bour-geoisie and petty bourgeoisie. But there is an even greater interest in maintaining and improving commercial and political relations with the West, which has become wary of Islamist movements; and the bourgeoisie is not likely to support any movement that could throw the country into political chaos. In its majority, therefore, the bour-geoisie will favour a re-Islamization from above – even at the hands of an Alawi if need be – and a general reorientation towards conservative values and habits, to any seemingly revolutionary push towards Islam.

Regarding class structures, the social base of the regime became narrower during the 1980s. We have to take into consideration, how-ever, that the social base of the regime – or, for that matter, of an opposition – is not determined by class structures alone; nor do regime policies necessarily reflect the structure of its social base. Traditional social relations still play a considerable role, determining loyalty struc-tures and, to an extent, politics. And being the most important agent of social change itself, the state enjoys considerable autonomy from its social base. Changing class structures do nonetheless influence the ability of different social groups to pursue their particular interests and are thus important variables in the power equation underlying political decisions.

Notes

1. The Syrian law on agrarian relations (Law 134/4 May 1958), defining different forms of production and share-cropping, is largely based on tradi-tional rural relations of production. "Partners" contribute labour, land, or finance (including machinery or pumps), or any combination of these factors. Each partner is entitled to a certain share of the harvest in exchange for the

factors he contributes, and this in varying percentages according to local customs, natural conditions, and the particular crop planted. Apart from share-cropping contracts regulated by Law 134, land can be rented on a monetary basis. Such rent contracts are subject to the civil code. Law 134 on agrarian relations considerably improved the position of peasant sharecroppers. Still, a peasant contributing only his labour had to leave the largest part of the harvest to the landowner. The law made it more difficult, however, for landowners to get rid of peasant sharecroppers; unilateral decisions on the part of the land-owners were made illegal. At least, landowners had to pay compensations if they terminated share-cropping contracts, and compensations were fixed by arbitration committees generally favourably inclined towards the peasants.

2. Or any combination thereof. Cf. more detailed: Mohamed Hosry, *Sozialökonomische Auswirkungen der Agrarreform in Syrien*, Table 10.

3. Author's interviews at the Ministry of Labour and Social Affairs, Damascus. On the implementation of the land reform cf., e.g.: Metral, "Le monde rural", pp 298 ff; Bu 'Ali Yasin, "'Alaqat al-intaj fi al-rif al-suri ba'd tanfidh al-islah al-zira'i", pp 374f; A. Filonik, *Su'ubat al-zira'a al-suriyya al-haditha*, p 40.

4. Cf. Filonik, *Su'ubat*, 1987, p. 43; Hinnebusch, *Peasant*, p 98. A Syrian author gives a higher figure of 250,000 agriculturally employed families remaining without land property: Khudr Zakariyya, *al-Tarkib al-ijtima'i li-l-buldan al-namiya*, p 310.

5. Legislative Decreee 31/14 May 1980. Limits on property were staggered according to soil quality, rainfall and mode of irrigation. The maximum of 200 hectares applied only to rainfed land in the eastern provinces. The upper limit for rainfed land in areas with more than 500 mm annual rainfall, for example, was set at 55 hectares, the limit for land in the eastern provinces irrigated by wells at 45 hectares, etc.

6. This according to the Minister of Agriculture answering a parliamentary interpellation. Cf. *al-Ba'th*, 19 May 1987. The law was not enforced strictly, a considerable number of proprietors could evade its implementation.

7. Syrian agricultural censuses do not give an exact picture of land distribution in terms of legal property rights. The most one can learn from the censuses is how holdings are distributed that are entirely, or more than 50%, or less than 50% owned by their holders. These data convey only approximate information on the distribution of legal property. In fact, in Syria as in other Arab states, holding rights, i.e. the power of disposal (*hiyaza*), are more important for the determination of rural relations of production and power than legal property rights (*mulk*). Through history, land has frequently been the legal property of the Sultan or has been common property, while the important question was who would have the right of disposal over it. The land reform law defined upper limits for legal properties, not for holdings. Big holdings, exceeding 300 hectares, could therefore exist legally even after the implementation of the land reform. All data on land distribution are computed on the basis of SAR, CBS, *1970–1971 Agricultural Census Data. First Stage –*

Basic Data in Syrian Arab Republic (Damascus: CBS, 1972), and SAR, CBS, *1981 Agricultural Census Data* (Damascus: CBS, 1986), 14 vols.

8. Among the 700 wealthiest landowners there were 400 persons with full legal property rights over their land. The holdings of this group averaged 625 hectares per owner. Taking into consideration that the maximum of 200 hectares can legally be owned only if the land in question is rainfed and situated in Syria's eastern provinces, whereas in all other cases ceilings imposed on land property are lower, we have to assume that far more than these 400 persons maintained landed properties exceeding the legal limits. This assumption is supported by civil servants who had been occupied with land expropriation and distribution. Source: *Agricultural Census 1981*, Tables 26 of Vols 1–14.

9. A notable exception was the Ghab project west of Hama. In this previously marshy reclamation zone, irrigation was organized by a public agency set up to administer the project. In addition to that, some peasants benefited from irrigation projects on the Euphrates and other places during the 1970s and 1980s. Cf. Günter Meyer, *Ländliche Lebens- und Wirtschaftsformen Syriens im Wandel*, pp 161ff; Françoise Metral, "State and Peasants in Syria: a Local View of a Government Irrigation Project".

10. Agricultural plans are worked out annually in a top-down process reaching from the Higher Council of Agriculture to the local authorities and co-operatives. The plans define how much of which crop is to be planted in each specific planning entity. Loans from the Agricultural Cooperative Bank are made subject to the implementation of agricultural production plans. Most producers try to evade these plans at least partly; cooperatives and smallholders, however, can least afford to do so. On the system of central agricultural production planning, see Hans Hopfinger, *Öffentliche und private Landwirtschaft in Syrien*, pp 40ff; Hinnebusch, *Peasant*, pp 51f.

11. These crops included grains, lentils, chick-peas, tobacco, sugar-beet, peanuts, cotton, silk, maize, i.e. the most important cash crops and, at the same time, those local crops needed for the basic diet of the poor: bread (grains) and sweet tea (sugar). In the case of both products, any government would have an interest in keeping procurement prices low.

12. General Federation of Peasants (Peasant Union), *The Sixth Conference of the Peasants, Damascus, 8 March 1986* (Damascus, 1986), pp 68f.

13. SAR, Ministry of Agriculture and Agrarian Reform, *The Annual Statistical Abstract 1985* (Damascus, n.d. [1987]), Tables 111ff; idem, *The Annual Statistical Abstract 1988* (Damascus, n.d. [1990]), Tables 126, 128.

14. Cf. Rabo, *Change on the Euphrates*, pp 50f; Metral, "State and Peasants", p 348, Meyer, *Ländliche Lebens- und Wirtschaftsformen*, pp 76ff; Hopfinger, *Öffentliche und private Landwirtschaft*, p 80.

15. Hinnebusch, *Peasant*, pp 153ff, stresses that, on average, i.e. regardless of the different conditions of rich and poor peasants, procurement prices did leave a margin for profits, at least throughout the 1970s. Smaller peasants, however, were likely to get comparatively lower returns than bigger producers.

A more detailed picture, in this respect, is drawn by Hopfinger, *Öffentliche und private Landwirtschaft*, pp 102ff, 204ff. Hopfinger gives several examples of peasant and farm households from one area cultivating holdings of different sizes. Providing concrete cost/income calculations, he proves that smallholders subject to central agricultural planning can hardly sustain their living from their agriculture.

16. Cf. Yasin, "'Alaqat al-intaj", pp 371ff; Meyer, *Ländliche Lebens- und Wirtschaftsformen*, pp 194ff; Filonik, *Su'ubat*, pp 49ff; Hinnebusch, *Peasant*, p 95; and occasional reports in the Syrian press, e.g., Bashshar al-Hajali, "Ma hikayat al-ard wa-l-fallah fi 'Ain al-'Arab" [What's the story of peasant and land in 'Ain al-'Arab], *al-Thawra*, 23 May 1988.

17. After Asad's takeover, the government revised some cases of landowners who claimed that they had been expropriated excessively. Since the Syrian countryside had not been completely surveyed until recently and data on property frequently relied on estimates, there were plenty of causes for such complaints. Corruption may sometimes have played a role too. Some 100,000 of initially 1.514 million hectares expropriated were returned to their previous owners. Additionally, in the mid-1980s, the authorities returned the lands of some 350 former landlords that had been sequestered in 1966 as a measure of punishment against persons refusing to cooperate with the land reform authorities (Author's interviews, Damascus).

An internal statistics of the Authority for State Land and Land Reform (*Sijjil harakat aradi al-istila'* [Register of expropriated lands]) of 1987 lists a total of 1.265 million hectares of expropriated lands. This contrasts with the official data on expropriations carried out according to land reform laws 161/1958 (1.401 million hectares after the revisions of 1971–5) and 31/1980 (42,700 hectares) which add up to 1.444 million hectares.

18. Cf. Rabo, *Change on the Euphrates*, pp 52ff; Metral, "Le monde rural", p. 320; Khalid 'Alush, "Dawr al-mar'a fi al-nishat al-iqtisadi: waqi'uhu wa tatawwuratuhu", pp 29ff.

19. Rabo, *Change on the Euphrates*, p 57.

20. Author's interviews, Damascus 1989, 1992.

21. Agricultural labourers are not protected against dismissal, they do not have to be covered by social security, and only labourers working on machines have, legally, to be insured against industrial accidents. Children below the age of 12 – the minimum working age according to the labour code – may legally be employed as agricultural workers. Most of the protective regulations provided for women by the labour code do not apply to female agricultural labourers.

22. Cf. Filonik, *Su'ubat*, p 104; Hinnebusch, *Peasant*, p 184, and idem, *Authoritarian Power*, p 214; and frequently articles in the Syrian press, e.g.: Ziad Malud, "al-Jama'iyya al-fallahiyya li-tarbiat al-asmak fi Riqqa" [The Fishery Cooperative in Raqqa], *Tishrin*, 11 April 1988; Fahd Diab,"Mukhassasat 5000 ghanam - ila ayn tadhhab" [Where does the Allocation of 5000 Sheep go to?], *al-Thawra*, 28 January 1989; Haitham Yahya Muhammad, "Mukhalafat

wa-akhta' fi jama'iyyat Shubat al-fallahiyya bi-Tartus" [Violations and Mistakes in the Shubat Cooperative of Tartus], *al-Thawra*, 4 July 1992.

23. For instance, Law 31/1980, setting new limits on landed property, ruled that land recently irrigated or planted with fruit trees be considered as normal rainfed farmland, thus allowing landowners to own larger areas than originally permitted in the case of irrigated or tree-planted land. The rationale was that farmers improving their property should not be punished.

24. The total area planted with fruit trees increased from 497,000 in 1981 to 774,000 in 1991 (*Stat. Abs.* 1986, p 156, 1992, p 118). Cf. with a regional study of this phenomenon: Anton Escher, *Sozialgeographische Aspekte raumprägender Entwicklungsprozesse*, pp 218ff.

25. Cf. with some interesting details of how, in the 1940s, Damascene businessmen began their run on agricultural lands in the Jazira, the memoirs of Badr al-Din Shallah, *al-Tarikh wa-l-dhikra, qissat jahd wa-'umr.*

26. Cf. Filonik, *Su'ubat*, pp 67ff. In the 1980s, the authorities were even prepared to recognize what legally remained an occupation of lands by entrepreneurs as an established right of sorts.

27. Cf. e.g. "Dirasa hawl al-tasahhur fi suriya" [A Study on Desertification in Syria], *al-Ba'th*, 22 December 1991.

28. *al-Ba'th*, 12 December 1988.

29. Estimates on the basis of the agricultural censuses of 1970 and 1981.

30. Cf. Meyer, *Ländliche Lebens- und Wirtschaftsformen*, pp 270ff; Rabo, *Change on the Euphrates*, pp 60f.

31. Cf. Hans Hopfinger, "Kapitalistisches Agro-Business in einem sozialistischen Land", pp 157–176; idem, "Problems of Privatization in Syria's Agricultural Sector".

32. The question is not to be answered here. For critical assessments of the land reform from a perspective generally defending the initial socialist or, at least, egalitarian goals of the reform, cf. Bu 'Ali Yasin, *Hikayat al-ard wa-l-fallah al-suri* [The Story of the Syrian Land and Peasant], (Beirut: Dar al-Haqa'iq, 1979); Filonik, *Su'ubat*. More apologetic is Muhammad Kaffa, *Tahawwulat al-iqtisad al-zira'i fi suriya.*

33. No data or detailed studies on the importance of pure agricultural subsistence production in Syria are available. Yasin ("'Alaqat al-intaj", p 384) assumes that 40% of all smallholders (with less than 10 ha) are producing for subsistence only, i.e. not for the market. This estimate is most probably too high, since land-reform smallholders are subject to agricultural plans and – for that reason at least – are producing for the market.

34. Cf. Metral, "State and Peasants", pp 346ff.

35. Cf. Dalila, "Tajribat".

36. Cf. e.g. Qasim Miqdad, "Tatawwur al-qita' al-khidmi fi al-iqtisad al-suri".

37. In 1981, for instance, 94% of all registered, occupied dwellings in the town of Damascus were connected to the public fresh-water net, 97% were connected to the sewage system, and some 90% were equipped with a flush

toilet. In the rural areas of Damascus province, 69% were connected to the fresh-water net, 55% to the sewerage system, and 48% had a flush toilet. In the rural parts of Dayr al-Zur province, 2,034 out of 39,000 dwellings, i.e. 5.2%, were connected to the public fresh-water net, and 633, i.e. 0.8%, to a sewerage system. Out of 205 mother-and-child health centres distributed over Syria's 14 provinces, a total of 12 were to be found in the three eastern provinces of Hassake, Raqqa, and Dayr al-Zur, with two out of these 12 in the countryside. And whereas, on the national average, only 1.5% of all girls were not enrolled in primary schools, this proportion rose to 3.2% in the province of Hassake, to 10.7% in Raqqa, and to 12.8% in Dayr al-Zur province. Cf. SAR, CBS, *Nata'ij al-ta'adad al-'amm li-l-masakin 1981*, 14 vols. (Damscus, 1986); Laila Abu Sha'ar, "al-Mar'a wa-l-tanmiya fi 'aqd al-mar'a al-dawli", in: General Union of Women, *al-Mar'a al-'arabiyya al-suriyya fi 'aqd al-mar'a al-dawli 1975–1985*, p 122.

38. According to the *Statistical Abstracts 1993*, the total population of Damascus and the Damascus countryside province did not exceed 2.9 million in that year. In 1992, Syrian media had noted that some 4.5 million persons were actually living in Greater Damascus (Cf. *Tishrin*, 19 December 1992). Official data had been questioned before too; cf. e.g. Ahmad Shukri, "al-'Ilam wa-l-wad' al-sukkani" [Information and the Demographic Situation], *al-Ba'th*, 18 August 1991.

39. Cf. Taufiq al-Jarjur, *al-Hijra min al-rif ila al-mudun fi al-qutr al-'arabi al-suri*, pp 83f; Sufuh Khayr, *Suriya. Dirasa fi al-bina' al-hadari wa-l-kiyan al-iqtisadi*, pp 112ff.

40. Cf. ibid.; Ibrahim 'Ali, "al-'Alaqa al-mutabadila bayn tauzi' al-sukkan wa-l-tanmiya fi al-qutr al-'arabi al-suri", in SAR, CBS and United Nations Fund for Population Activities, *al-Nadwa al-dawliyya hawl al-sukkan wa-l-tanmiya wa-ahammiyat al-raqm al-ihsa'i, Homs, 25–27 October 1983*, p 128.

41. Cf. Khudr Zakariyya, *al-Hijra al-dakhiliyya fi Suriya – Nushu'uha wa-tatawwuruha*), p 57.

42. All data on the numerical strength of different social strata are compiled from the sources mentioned in Table III.2.

43. Cf. the work of Elisabeth Longuenesse, particularly "The Syrian Working Class Today", *MERIP Reports*, Vol. 15 (July-August 1985), No. 134, pp 17–24, "État et syndicalisme en Syrie. Discours et pratiques", *Sou'al*, No. 8, Feb. 1988, pp 97–130; further Hannoyer/Seurat, *État et secteur public*, pp 93f; Bu 'Ali Yasin, "Mauqi' al-tabaqa al-'amila fi al-mujtama' al-suri", *Dirasat 'arabiyya*, Vol 7 (Oct. 1971), No. 12, pp 7–29.

44. Cf. Longuenesse, "L'industrialisation", p. 355.

45. Cf. 'Abdallah Hanna, *al-Haraka al-'ummaliyya fi suriya wa-lubnan 1900–1945*.

46. Cf. Elisabeth Longuenesse, "Structure de la main d'œuvre industrielle et rapports de production en Syrie", p 16; Hisham Bashir, "Hawl izdiwajiyyat wila' al-yad al-'amila bayn al-qita'ayn al-sina'i wa-l-zira'i" [On the Ambivalent Loyalty of the Workers between Industry and Agriculture], *Tishrin*, 8

May 1989.

47. Military persons excluded.

48. CBS estimates hovered around less than half that number. Cf. SAR, CBS, *Nata'ij bahtay*. For a short critique of the CBS's industrial data cf. Perthes, "The Syrian Private Industrial and Commercial Sectors", p 228, n 21.

49. Cf. Longuenesse, "L'industrialisation", p 350.

50. In 1993, the average monthly income in the public sector was estimated at about 3,000 LS, that in the private sector at about 5,000 LS. Some workers in the private sector would earn up to 15,000 LS a month. Cf. *al-Hayat*, 30 November 1993.

51. Cf. e.g. Wasif Mihna, "al-'Ummal fi huqul Rumaylan" [Workers in the Rumaylan Oil-Fields], *al-Ishtiraki*, 10 and 24 September 1973; GFTU, *21st Conference 1986. General Report*, p 140; 'Amil [Worker], "Lana al-kalima" [Give Us the Word!], *al-Ishtiraki*, 12 September 1988.

52. Cf. e.g. Amin Habash, "al-Waqi' al-'ummali wa-l-iqtisadi wa-l-intaj fi qita' al-sina'at al-ghadha'iyya" [The Situation of the Workers, the Economic Situation and the Situation of Production in the Foodstuff Industries], *al-Ishtiraki*, 5 September 1988; Jihad al-Ahmar, "Azmat al-naql al-dakhili fi tariqiha ila al-hall" [The Local Transport Crisis on the Path of Being Solved], *al-Ba'th*, 29 December 1991; Tamir Habil; "Qita' al-ghazal wa-l-nasij fi suriya – Nash'atuh, tatwwuruh, waqi'uh" [The Textiles Sector in Syria – Its Emergence, Development and Current Situation], *al-Ishtiraki*, 13 August 1992.

53. Compared to 70–80% in 1970. Cf. *Population Censuses*, 1970 and 1981.

54. It is notable that Syria's public system of social security is still based on the Social Security Law and the Labour Code promulgated in the UAR-period. The system covers only parts of the population – esssentially all registered wage-earners outside agriculture. Persons employed with small firms as well as seasonal workers – the latter category includes the entire private and public construction sector – have only to be insured against industrial accidents and occupational diseases. Establishments with more than five employees are obliged to register their staff for the old-age pension scheme of the official Syrian Insurance Company. According to the labour code, permanent employees in the public sector and in private establishments of over 50 employees are entitled to free medical care. In addition, medical treatment in public health centres is generally free; drugs are, however, frequently to be purchased and paid for by the patient. Public health institutions being understaffed and poorly equipped, patients are frequently sent to private doctors, laboratories, and clinics. There is no general health insurance and no unemployment insurance scheme. Cf. GFTU, *Marahil sarayan ahkam qanun al-ta'minat al-ijtima'iyya wa-ta'dilatih*; Aziz Saqr, *Dirasat ishtirakiyya fi al-dimanat al-ijtima'iyya wa-l-tijariyya*, pp 181ff.

55. A 1984 study by the Syrian CBS showed that only 7.7% of urban females of working age were economically active. Almost three-quarters of these women were teachers, employed in the health service, or clerks; less than 40% of the employed women were married. This suggests that working-

class women, with few exceptions, are not gainfully employed except before marriage. Cf. 'Alush, "Dawr al-mar'a".

56. See below, Chapter IV.

57. Mahmud Sadiq, *Hiwar hawl suriya*, p 103.

58. My estimates are based on population census data of 1970 and 1981, the results of the employment surveys of 1984 and 1991 as published in *Statistical Abstracts 1989* and *1992*, taking into account given data on unemployed, own-account production, service, and sales workers, and on data from the 1981 survey of economic establishments: SAR, CBS, *Nata'ij hasr al-munsha'at al-iqtisadiyya fi al-qutr al-'arabi al-suri li-'am 1981*.

59. In the early 1990s, about half of these casual workers and other low-income people were estimated to earn a daily income of no more than 40 LS (*al-Ba'th*, 10 April 1991). This was less than $1 at the free market rate of the Syrian pound and represented the price of two kg of beans or tomatoes, or 200 g of red meat.

60. Cf. Barakat, *The Arab World*, pp 86f.

61. Analyses based on the census data for 1970 and 1981 are likely to overestimate the numerical strength of the petty bourgeoisie. Many of those who according to the census are self-employed craftsmen or merchants should rather be reckoned within the semi-proletariat, since they do not possess a shop or workshop. Census and employment data have therefore to be crosschecked with the censuses of economic establishments and private-sector industry surveys.

62. Private producers of clothes, for instance, purchase most of their locally produced intermediate products (fibres, cotton-yarn, certain fabrics) from public-sector firms.

63. Cf. above, Chapter II.

64. Cf. Longuenesse, "The Class Nature of the State in Syria. Contribution to an Analysis", *MERIP Reports*, Vol 4 (May 1979), No. 77, pp 3–11 (pp 5, 11).

65. Batatu, "Syria's Muslim Brethren", p15.

66. Cf. ibid., p 15f. I do not agree, however, with Fred Lawson's suggestion that the petty bourgeoisie of, particularly, Homs, Hama, and Aleppo were hurt by the state's industrialization policy and therefore driven into the oppositional camp. Cf. his "Social Basis for the Hamah Revolt" and "Comment le régime du président el-Assad s'emploie à remodeler l'économie syrienne", *Le Monde Diplomatique*, January 1984. Lawson seems to underestimate the fact that Syria's public-sector industries have rarely been competing with private manufacturers, that, wherever there was an element of such competition, the private sector has been doing well, and that the number of private industrial and commercial establishments has been growing considerably throughout the 1970s and 1980s, not only in Damascus but in Aleppo, Homs, and Hama as well.

67. In March 1992, the founders of this Committee for the Defence of Democratic Freedoms and Human Rights in Syria, an Alawite lawyer from Latakia and other intellectuals, were sentenced to long prison terms.

68. For 1970, we regard as belonging to the wage-earning middle classes employed by the state all those who, according to official statistics, are regarded as civil servants and state *mustakhdamin*, plus roughly 10% of those employed in the public economic sector. Since the 1980s, Syrian statistics have no longer distinguished between *muwazzafin* and *mustakhdamin* nor between employees in the public administration and employees in the public economic sector. Instead, persons employed by the state are roughly classified by type of work. All those who are classified as administrators and clerks, legislators and specialists can be regarded as part of the salaried middle classes. In this study, different from the approach chosen by Longuenesse ("The Class Nature"), transport-workers, cleaning personnel and guards are not counted among the wage-earning middle classes but rather, in view of their social status and conditions, among the working class.

69. Some of these changes become evident in the study of Muhammad Sufuh al-Akhras, *Tarkib al-'a'ila al-'arabiyya wa-waza'ifuha. Dirasa maydaniyya li-waqi' al-'a'ila fi suriya*. Being extremely apologetic about social developments in Syria, the author tries to prove the modernity of Syrian society and of Islamic societies in general without paying too much attention to methodological accuracy.

70. This included things such as refrigerators and for the most part some other electrical household appliances, some industrially manufactured furniture, and the consumption of imported foodstuffs. *Muwazzafin* would usually participate in a housing cooperative so as to own an apartment after a couple of years. A private car was not part of what civil servants could afford, except for some senior officials and persons earning a second income besides their salary. A television set would be regarded as normal for almost any urban household. Cf. Bu 'Ali Yasin, "Adwa' 'ala al-hayat al-thaqafiyya li-tabaqa al-'amila al-suriyya", pp 115–128.

71. In the early 1990s, a locally produced refrigerator cost around four times a teacher's monthly pay, and the monthly subscription to a housing cooperative would just equal his or her salary.

72. John Waterbury, *The Egypt of Nasser and Sadat*, p 250.

73. Generally, in political science, "new class" does not refer to the commercial bourgeoisie or parts of it but, in the sense of Milovan Djilas and others, to the layer of intellectuals dominating socialist systems. In the same sense, the concept has been applied to Syria by Ibrahim Hasan, "La Syrie de la guerre civile", *Peuples méditerranéens*, Vol 12 (July–September 1980), pp 91–107. In this study, we follow the more popular use of the term in Syria, where "new class" refers to what, in the Egyptian case, Springborg and Sadowski call "parasitic bourgeoisie" and "crony capitalists" respectively. Cf. Springborg, *Mubaraks's Egypt*; Sadowski, *Political Vegetables?* In Syria, at times, the more pejorative term "parasitic bourgeoisie" (*burjwaziyya tufailiyya*) has also been used.

74. This section draws largely on my "A Look at Syria's Upper Class: The Bourgeoisie and the Ba'th". Information was mainly gained from interviews

with Syrian businessmen, conducted from 1988 to 1993. See also the detailed study of Joseph Bahout, *Les Entrepreneurs Syriens. Economie, affaires et politique* (Les Cahiers du CERMOC No 7, 1994).

75. Waterbury, "Twilight".

76. 'Abd al-Fadil, *al-Tashkilat*, p 122.

77. Cf. Waterbury, "Twilight", p 14.

78. On the transformation of parts of Egypt's state bourgeoisie into private-sector managers and entrepreneurs, cf. e.g. Amani 'Abd al-Rahman Salih, "Usul al-nukhba al-siyasiyya al-misriyya fi al-saba'inat: al-Nash'a wa-l-tatawwur", *al-Fikr al-istratiji al-'arabi*, Vol 26 (October 1988), pp 9–50; Springborg, *Mubarak's Egypt*, pp 70f.

79. Cf. Hinnebusch, *Peasant*, pp 33f.

80. Primary-school attendance has been made obligatory and the employment of children of primary-school age has been forbidden under Law No. 35/1981. Nonetheless, truancy is a problem in Syria. Reasons for dropping out of school are both "cultural", i.e. parents taking girls from school after grade four or five, and economic. Cf. Ma'mun Duwaihi, "Mushkilat al-tasarrub fi al-marhala al-ibtida'iyya" [The Problem of Truancy in the Elementary Stage], *al-Thawra*, 1 August 1992.

81. Poverty and wealth are reflected, among other things, through housing conditions. The housing census of 1981 gives a picture of the urban social structure resembling the one drawn above. Consider the data for Aleppo which seem to be more representative for the urban structure in general than, e.g. those for Damascus, since administrative Aleppo contains almost the whole of the urban area of Aleppo, whereas parts of Greater Damascus are part of the Damascus Countryside province. According to the Aleppo census, 1.3% of the population were living in dwellings with two rooms (except bathrooms and kitchens) or more per person, 8% in dwellings with between one or two rooms per person, 28.7% in dwellings with more than one, but not more than two persons per room. The living conditions of these almost 40% may be considered as comparatively tolerable. 62.1% were living with more than two persons per room, mainly in two-room flats inhabited by seven, eight, or more persons, or in three-room flats with between seven and ten inhabitants. 30% of this group, i.e. some 20% of the population, were living in dwellings with more than four persons per room. Ten years later these conditions had worsened rather than improved.

82. It is assumed here that besides the urban strata living on a limited income, paid and unpaid agricultural workers and about half of the small peasantry fall into this category.

83. In the mid-1980s, according to a conservative estimate of the Syrian Communist Party (SCP), less than 30% of the national income accrued to some 65% of the population, that is, to what roughly represents Syria's lower classes, while more than 42% accrued to the next 30% of the population and more than 28% to an upper class of less than 5% of the entire social pyramid. Cf. SCP, *Conference Documents from the Sixth Conference of the SCP, mid-July*

1986. Economic Report (Damascus, n.d.), p 14. Cf. also Iliyas Najmah, "al-Mas'ala al-iqtisadiyya fi al-qutr al-'arabi al-suri", in *Economic Sciences Association, Fifth Economic Tuesday Symposium on Economic Development in the Syrian Arab Region, Damascus, 14 January – 29 April 1986*, p 167.

84. In comparison to an earlier version of this compilation, published in my *Staat und Gesellschaft*, p 217, totals regarding the number of unpaid agricultural workers have been changed for 1970 and 1981, this time relying on the labour-force samples rather than the population censuses to set off the latter's considerable underestimation of female agricultural labour.

85. Cf. among others: Batatu, "Some observations"; Hinnebusch, *Authoritarian Power*, pp 81–105.

86. Cf. Hinnebusch, *Peasant*, pp 160f; Filonik, *Su'ubat*, pp 121, 126.

87. During the 1970s in particular, there were some incidents in which landless or expelled peasants tried to squat on the land of big landowners or got into violent conflicts with landlords recovering land that had been distributed with the land reform. Cf. Hinnebusch, *Peasant*, p 40; Yasin, *Hikayat al-ard*, pp 106f.

88. Even the official papers reported that the situation outside the bakeries and public-sector bread stalls "sometimes necessitated the intervention of police patrols". Cf. *al-Ba'th*, 24 May 1988.

CHAPTER FOUR

The Structure of Authoritarianism

Under the rule of Hafiz al-Asad, Syria has developed into a strong national-security state; that is, its *raison d'être* – in the design of those who control it – has been primarily to serve both national and regime security.[1] The political system that was built after Asad's takeover differed both from the unstable and putsch-ridden liberal system established in the post-independence period and from the fragile military-party regime with its trial-and-error system of government that characterized the initial phase of Ba'thist rule from 1963 to 1970.[2] Asad's regime may best be characterized as an authoritarian presidential system with distinct neo-patrimonial traits. The system is authoritarian in the sense that political power is highly centralized, with the military and bureaucracy playing a dominant role, while the space for pluralistic competition and civil society is narrowly circumscribed, and political participation, at best, selectively granted. The personalistic rule of the President, the extensive use for political as well as social and economic interests of clientelistic networks, and, thus, the high importance of personal, often traditional or primordial loyalties and ties, all give the regime its patrimonial face.

A main feature of this political system is the high measure of control which the state exercises over society, both by authoritarian and patrimonial means. This control has certainly provided for the extraordinary stability and longevity of the regime so frequently stressed by observers. It has also, however, created an atmosphere of lethargy and stagnation not uncharacteristic of authoritarian regimes.

The institutional foundations of the system were laid in the first years of Asad's rule. The system has not remained entirely unchanged since, but has gradually been developed. To the extent that the participation of societal interests was considered necessary, developments followed a model of authoritarian-corporatist group representation. It has been pointed out that while the concept of corporatism has not, or has only recently, entered the Arab political discourse, the logic of corporatism with its rejection of both class struggle and liberal pluralism is certainly not alien to Middle Eastern regimes.[3] Authoritarian corporatism conceives of society as an organic body whose different functional groups fulfil specific tasks under the leadership of the government. According to the model, the functional groups into which society divides – agricultural producers, workers, merchants, the military and so on – should be organized in compulsory, noncompetitive, functionally differentiated, hierarchic associations exclusively representing the members of that functional group and their legitimate interests vis-à-vis the state. The state may entrust these associations with certain quasi-governmental functions in regard to their membership and functional sphere, and selectively coopt their leadership into the formal institutions of government. As a rule, bargaining for the allocation of resources is not to take place between these different groups, but between each group and the government as the "brain" of the body politic and final arbiter between competing interests. Ideally, competition cannot develop into antagonistic conflict, since any healthy body cannot be in conflict with itself and any of its parts can only move in coordination with all others; coordination, of course, being the business of the government.[4] There is, accordingly, in corporatist systems a strong tendency to seek consensual solutions that include every group which, for its part, accepts the higher interest of the whole and the right of the leadership to define this higher interest. As it tends to organize society in functional groups that cut across class lines, and to prevent a liberal, pluralistic competition of voluntarily organized interests, ideas, and demands, corporatism can serve as a means of control and containment of those societal groups and strata that do not receive their fair share of the pie.[5] And to the extent that the increasing complexity of socio-economic structures demands a refinement of political institutions, corporatist mechanisms allow a selective involvement of key groups into decision-making processes without actually democratizing the system.

Asad and his lieutenants have not at any stage referred to corporatism or made corporatist examples a model for the Syrian regime.

Asad has, however, occasionally expressed corporatist notions. Thus, in a discussion about the future of the Ba'th party and the state which he reportedly initiated before his eventual takeover in 1970, Asad proposed that the party be organized sectorally, along professional groupings, rather than geographically.[6] More than once has he implied that the popular organizations in Syria actually were or should be in charge of matters related to the work of the group they represent, and that popular participation take place through these organizations. Explicitly, in a speech in 1980, he stated that whatever concerned agriculture and whatever concerned labour and industry were to be decided by the Peasant Union and the trade unions respectively.[7] The popular organizations were not given legislative powers, of course, but trade unions and the Peasant Union were in the same year incorporated into the Progressive National Front which formally features as a political steering body. According to the official reading, the establishment of the Front itself was to serve the goal of furthering the unity and cohesion of the people,[8] a notion very much in line with the corporatist vision of the state as a body with no internal divisions.

1. Institution-Building and Political Development: An Overview

Insofar as Asad's assumption of power marked the beginning of a far-reaching restructuring of the political system, it represents more than simply the capture of the state by another *jama'a*, clique or gang, as the neo-patrimonial approach would suggest. Instead, the scope of the state and its hold over society were expanded, new institutions were built, and existing ones transformed so as to fit the emerging hierarchical and authoritarian structure.

There was no resistance to Asad's takeover. He could rely on the army which he had successfully purged of supporters of his rival Ba'thists during his time as Minister of Defence. Parts of the party, of the unions, and of those younger intellectuals who had supported the radical regime now overthrown had to be reckoned with as potential opponents. They were not in a position, however, to resist the coup. Asad, after all, was in firm control of the means of coercion. The upper stratum of society, as mentioned, welcomed his takeover, and there was some popular support too. Weary of the radical leftist course which the toppled regime had been following, many Syrians wanted a change, and Asad was promising a new departure.

Among the most important elements of this restructuring were the installation, in 1971, of a parliament, the establishment, in 1972, of the Progressive National Front (al-Jabha al-wataniyya al-taqaddumiyya) (PNF), and the promulgation, in 1973, of a new constitution. These measures had been promised by Asad in his declaration of 16 November 1970, the day on which he undertook what later came to be called his Correctionist Movement.[9]

Asad himself was first appointed Prime Minister by the new provisional Regional Command of the Ba'th Party which he formed with his coup. Then, in March 1971, he was elected President in an uncontested referendum. At the same time, the provisional constitution of 1969 which had vested legislative powers in the cabinet was changed so as to make the system a presidential one.

By establishing a parliament and the PNF, and having a new constitution passed, Asad tried both to broaden his basis of support and to legitimize his regime by institutionalizing it. Equally important for the stabilization of his regime, as will be outlined, were a restructuring and transformation of popular organizations such as the trade unions, and of the party. Parallel to the remaking of the political-institutional frame, and particularly from 1973, when Arab aid and Syria's own oil revenues vastly increased the state's financial capabilities, the public administration, the military, and the internal security apparatus were expanded on a hitherto unprecedented scale.

The combination of economic liberalization and growth which the country experienced in the first half of the 1970s, and the political victory of the 1973 October War, gained considerable popularity for the regime. There was political opposition, though, both from the left and from conservative, Islamist tendencies. Occasional violent protests took place, particularly in the traditionally conservative city of Hama, a town whose notables had been hard hit by the land reform. In 1973, Islamist groups, suspicious of the laicist tendencies of the regime, called for strikes and demonstrations against the allegedly un-Islamic character of the draft constitution. After a series of clashes, the regime bowed partly and modified the draft so as to stipulate that the religion of the president is Islam.

Only from 1976, however, did serious and country-wide tensions become tangible on a large scale. The income of the largest part of the population, as mentioned, was affected by inflation; the corruption, nepotism and illegal enrichment of the regime elite became conspicuous; Syria's intervention in Lebanon was highly unpopular; and complaints over the virtually unlimited power of the security services increased.

Oppositional forces were not able to organize politically and were thus driven to violence. In the years 1979–82, Syria experienced a situation close to civil war. The anti-regime opposition was led by, though not solely composed of, Islamist forces, particularly the Syrian branch of the Muslim Brotherhood, who tried and partly succeeded in giving the conflict a sectarian or confessionalist (Sunni-majority against Alawi-minority) character. Among other things, hard-core members of the opposition deliberately murdered Alawi intellectuals, regardless of whether or not they were close to the regime. Unlike previous phases of heightened tension and open conflict between the Ba'thist regime and Islamist groups, the regime was now unable to gain the upper hand quickly. Instead, it found itself threatened not only by recurring clashes with and violent uprisings of Islamist elements but, moreover, by a loss of allegiance among large parts of society that previously had been counted among the wider regime base: public-sector workers, members of the liberal professions and parts of the salaried urban middle class.[10] The regime reacted with increased repression. The bureaucracy was purged of persons deemed disloyal, and arbitrary encroachments of the security services on the life, freedom and other property of citizens reached an unprecedented level.[11] The final showdown, and a lasting defeat for Syria's militant Islamist opposition, came in the spring of 1982 when the regime brutally ended a three-week uprising in the city of Hama – destroying some 30 per cent of the town and leaving probably more than 10,000 inhabitants dead.[12]

Already two years earlier the government had crushed the most important elements of the liberal opposition. In April 1980, the executive committees of the lawyers', the engineers' and the physicians' unions were dissolved, their members arrested, and new executive committees formed from regime loyalists.[13] The three associations had failed to declare their support for the regime in the ongoing conflict with the Islamist opposition, and the lawyers' union, long critical of the regime's handling of human rights, had even called for a one-day strike in demand for an end to the state of emergency.[14]

During the same period, while it clamped down on those parts of civil society that had still maintained their independence from the state, the regime strengthened its corporatist structures. Most importantly, a Committee for the Guidance of Imports, Exports and Consumption was set up to discuss and pre-decide important economic policy matters. Essentially a government committee headed by the Prime Minister, it incorporated representatives of the party, the trade unions, and, for the first time, the Chambers of Commerce and Chambers of Industry. At the same time, as mentioned, trade unions and the Peasant Union were incorporated into the PNF.

From the defeat of the Hama insurrection in 1982 till the late 1980s, Syria's internal political scene remained almost stagnant. Indifference and cynicism were probably the most salient features of popular attitudes towards politics and the regime. Then, however, the Syrian regime could not but in some way respond to the sweeping changes in Eastern Europe which the Syrian public watched attentively. After the fall of Ceaucescu's regime in the last days of 1989, graffitti appeared in Damascus referring to the Syrian president as *Sham*-cescu.[15] Asad's response was a three-pronged attempt: first, to bring home to his people that Syria could not be compared to the socialist, or former socialist, countries of Europe; second, to allow for a token relaxation of political control; and third, to introduce a limited re-balancing within the political institutional framework. Instead of "popular democracy", a term borrowed from the socialist countries of Europe and long used to denote the character of the political system, Syria's official rhetoric now changed to speaking of "pluralism" (*ta'addudiyya*). With the Correctionist Movement of 1970, so the argument went, and the establishment of the PNF, Syria had long ago implemented a "pluralistic" multi-party system. Syria's economy, with its public, private, and mixed sectors, was equally pluralistic. There was no way, therefore, of putting Syria in one category with the socialist countries, and no need for fundamental changes.[16] Adjustments might neverthelesss be necessary. In particular, the scope of emergency laws should be limited to matters of state security.[17]

In fact, most "economic crimes", such as offences against price regulations, were transferred from special security courts to the civil jurisdiction,[18] a measure which actually represented an element of economic rather than political liberalization. In 1991 and 1992, thousands of political prisoners whom the regime deemed to be of little danger were set free. Although these amnesties did not mark an end to political imprisonment – in fact, thousands of political prisoners remained in jail, and new ones entered – they represented more than a pure propaganda move vis-à-vis the domestic and foreign public. Mainly they expressed a certain relaxation of domestic political strain. There were no oppositional forces around that, in all seriousness, could have challenged the regime, and the overall improvement of the economic situation translated into a somewhat more positive public mood than that of the 1980s.

So far as the political institutional frame is concerned, the most important development was a significant upgrading of the parliament from the legislative elections of 1990. Parliament was given a more visible role in policy-making, and it was expanded so as to include a substantial number of independent deputies from outside the PNF. Many of these independent parliamentarians represented Syria's business community, whose increasing economic relevance thus found political-institutional expression.

2. The Institutional Framework

Observers have tried to catch the special character of Syria's authoritarian presidential system established since Asad's takeover by referring to it, among other things, as a presidential monarchy,[19] or an absolute presidency. Both constitutionally and practically, there is no doubt that the President is at the helm, and that all strings of power end in his hands.

Constitutionally, the President is at the same time the supreme commander of the armed forces, he is head of the executive and, in consultation with the Council of Ministers, defines general government policies.[20] He appoints his deputies, the Prime Minister (President of the Council of Ministers), the government ministers and their deputies, officers of the armed forces, high civil servants, and judges. The government is answerable to the President. The President submits bills to parliament (*majlis al-sha'ab*), he promulgates laws that the parliament has passed, but he has the right to veto these laws. Parliament can, theoretically, overrule his veto by a two-thirds majority. The President, however, may then, or on any other occasion, dissolve the assembly. When parliament is not in session, as well as in cases of extreme need or when national interest so demands, the president can exercise legislative powers himself. He may submit important matters to popular referendum. Constitutional amendments need a three-quarters majority in parliament *and* the approval of the President.

The President is elected by popular referendum; the only candidate for the position is to be nominated by parliament on the proposal of the Regional Command of the Ba'th Party. Asad has been the secretary general of the Syrian Regional Command and of the Pan-Arab National Command of the party since 1970 and 1971 respectively. While the constitution does not explicitly demand a personal union of secretary general of the Ba'th party and president of the republic, the charter of the PNF practically does so. It rules that the "president of the republic, secretary general of the Arab Socialist Ba'th Party" is also the president of the front.[21]

Thus, Asad ultimately commands and controls in person the three apparatuses or centres of power of state and regime, namely the bureaucracy, the military and security or intelligence services (*mukhabarat*), and the party. These apparatuses are all centralized hierarchical structures which, to varying degrees and partly parallel to each other, reach from the regime leadership down to the village or neighbourhood. Thus, at provincial level, the President is represented by the governor (muhafiz). Directly responding to the President, Syria's 14 provincial governors are superior to, and control the work of, the provincial and local departments of the central government ministries and public-sector units. The governor is chief executive of the local administration and *ex officio* president of the provincial council. In emergency situations, he is also in command of the police and the military forces stationed in his province.[22] Parallel to the governor, the secretary of the provincial branch of the Ba'th party also represents central power. Provincial party secretaries are hand picked by, and report directly to, the president in his function as secretary general. The party branches monitor the work of the provincial bureaucracy and public sector; the party secretary may act for the governor in the latter's absence. The activities of party and administration, on all administrative levels, are additionally monitored by the three or four most important security services.

The structure allows for a high measure of state and regime control over the whole country. The organizations of civil society – that social space, whose individual and institutional actors are not directly part of the political system – have almost totally been penetrated by the state, transformed into quasi-corporatist institutions or, at least, brought into line. The trade unions will serve as a particularly illustrative case in point. Participatory elements have been introduced only according to the perceived needs of the political leadership; they have not been meant to be or to become a means of societal control over state and regime.

The Bureaucracy

Since 1963, and since 1970 in particular, all spheres of societal life have seen increasing state interference and, partly at least, regulation. This growth of the state included, as outlined, the build-up of the public economic sector, the expansion of public education and public health, of water and electricity networks, and the establishment of a still inadequate social security system. Also, a planning apparatus and a comprehensive public administration reaching from ministerial down to village level came into being, and the agencies of security and control were expanded.

By the early 1990s, almost 700,000 civilians were employed by the state, more than five times as many as in 1970. More than 420,000 of these can be referred to as the bureaucracy, that is, those working in the public services sector and public administration. The number of the bureaucracy had thus increased more than twice as much since 1970 as had the total workforce or the population.

Obviously, the objective increase of state functions can only partly account for the growth of the bureaucracy. Till the mid-1980s, the

Table IV.1   Persons Employed in Public Administration and in the Public Economic Sector

	1965	1970	1980	1991
Civilian employees[c] of which:	70,000	136,000	457,000	685,000
Public industrial sector	28,000	57,000	110,000	145,000
Public construction cos	[a]	[b]	120,000[c]	120,000
Military[d] and security [c]	65,000	100,000	300,000	530,000
Total	135,000	236,000	757,000	1.215,000
Total workforce (millions)	1.1	1.7	2.3	3.7

[a] none   [b] figure unknown or insignificant   [c] approximate figure
[d] includes conscripts

Sources: see Table III.2.

public payroll was one of the most important instruments for members of the regime elite to extend favours and make or placate clients. Moreover, public employment has been a means of political as well as social control. After each of the coups of 1963, 1966 and 1970, the respective new power-holders flooded the bureaucracy with new recruits, partly at least to create friendly majorities in its central branches. Conversely, in the latter part of the 1980s, as noted, it was expedient to reduce new recruitment and thereby keep the number of severely underpaid and perhaps unreliable young civil servants under control. By expanding the bureaucracy and public services, state and regime have made their presence felt even in the remotest village. The growth of the bureaucracy has facilitated access to the state, particularly for the rural population, although at the same time people also need more of this access. Today, it is advisable for citizens all over the country to accommodate themselves with the state, to build connections with authorities and civil servants. Such connections can even be essential to achieve one's legal entitlements – whether to secure acceptable care in a government hospital or the full amount of the subsidized rationed foodstuffs every family is entitled to. Since most extended families in Syria have at least one of their members permanently employed by the state, the growth of the bureaucracy and the public sector has also served as a factor of national integration.

To the extent that Syria's bureaucracy, including that of the public sector, has grown, it has also acquired a poor record. Even high-echelon bureaucrats admit, privately at least, that the overall performance and efficiency of the public administration are dismal. For one thing, public sector and public administration are overloaded with superfluous employees, particularly in administrative positions. According to trade-union data, only some 70,000 out of a total of 140,000 persons employed in the public industrial sector in 1987 were workers,[23] the rest were administrative and service personnel in the widest sense.[24] More importantly, a considerable number of unqualified persons have been brought into leading positions, clientelism and corruption are widespread, a multitude of agencies exercise tutelage over lower-level administrative and economic units, and the decision-making structure is extremely centralized.

Few directors of public-sector establishments have been trained in business and management.[25] Party or military status, or personal relationships with members of the regime elite were often qualification enough. The appointment of military officers to public-sector leadership positions was mainly a feature of the 1960s and 1970s. However, even in 1992, a report of the Ministry of Economy was demanding that new administrative cadres be properly qualified and that "personal considerations and ties" no longer play a role in the appointment of public-sector officials.[26] Regarding tutelage from above, the work of administrative units and public-sector establishments, according to the summary description of a trade-union report, is not only subject to the control of the Central Audit Office and the respective ministerial department, but also to that of the General Organization – the highest subministerial level in the public-sector hierarchy —, the individual minister, the party and trade unions as agencies of "popular control", the security services, and others.[27] Reportedly, the more political of these agencies, i.e. the unions, party, and security services, and the minister or even the prime minister, interfere frequently in the affairs of individual units or establishments. Often, such interference takes place through personal networks rather than the official channels of command, and low-level officials may feel, or actually are, forced to secure the interests of some high-echelon patrons rather than those of their company or authority.[28]

Legally, public-sector units and companies enjoy a limited degree of entrepreneurial freedom;[29] in practice, even this limited sphere is rarely taken advantage of. On the one hand, provisions defining the competences of each administrative level have often been overruled by administrative decree from the ministry in charge or the Prime Minister,[30] on the other, lower-level officials have simply shirked responsibility. Overcentralization and attempts to escape and disclaim responsibilty are in fact complementary. "Stark centralization", ran a report of the Planning Authority, "has created a sort of dependence in lower administrations and led them to relinquish some of their competences."[31] Many government ministers insist on personally looking into any decision taken by their ministry. Directors of ministerial departments are often stripped of virtually all competence, and some ministers do not allow even their deputies to take routine decisions. The Minister of Industry, to give but one example, regularly presides over many of the annual board meetings of the 90 or so companies under the ministry's supervision. Even the detailed problems of public-sector firms are frequently discussed and decided upon at very high level – such as the Prime Minister's office or a government committee. By chairing personally almost all permanent government committees, the Prime Minister is directly involved, among other things, in the distribution of high-school graduates among the country's universities or the licensing of private investment projects.[32] Public-sector projects are decided upon at highest government level, legally in the Planning Council, and sometimes above that – by the President or by persons in his entourage outside the formal administrative structure. In some cases, special government committees deal with or supervise particular projects. When, for instance, work began in 1991 on the overhaul and expansion of the sewerage systems of Syria's four biggest cities, a supervisory committee was formed for each project, and each commitee was chaired by either the Deputy Prime Minister for Economic Affairs or the Deputy Prime Minister for Services.

Regarding administrative performance and efficiency, this over-centralization is highly counterproductive. In her insightful study on the authority managing Syria's largest development scheme, the Euphrates basin project, Annika Rabo has shown how far this once enthusiastic agency has been transformed by centralized and authoritarian structures into a conservative institution; it has no say concerning the plans it has to execute and, in turn, expects the local population to accept these plans without debate. "Taking an initiative," she writes, "has become almost dangerous for many employees, and many have become accustomed to doing as little as possible ..., thereby not threatening any superior nor the status quo." Observers are left with the impression of total incompetence.[33] The trade unions themselves, as the main representative of bureaucracy and public-sector interests, have repeatedly criticized anarchy, indifference, escapism, irregularities, and corruption in the public administration and emphasized that all these phenomena have caused a general loss of confidence in the bureaucracy.[34]

All this does not deny that technocratic-rational orientations exist within the Syrian bureaucracy and public sector.[35] There are no doubt differences between particular ministries and agencies in the degree of bureaucratization, centralized decision-making and authoritarianism. To a great extent, and largely because of the authoritarian nature of the system in which the respective boss of an institution very much determines its character, these differences depend on the personality of the minister in charge. And there are also differences in the degree to which particular authorities and public-sector companies are allowed to develop a certain independence from bureaucratic tutelage. It is evident that the Syrian Petroleum Company and some other foreign-exchange-generating public-sector establishments are run much more efficiently than, for instance, Syria's General Company for Retail Trade, which is notorious for its poor service and high level of corruption. Obviously, in the first case, the economic costs of allowing clientelism, corruption, overemployment, and mismanagement to take their toll would far outweigh their political benefits while, in the second case, these costs are considered tolerable.

Generally, as much as there is a political rationality in maintaining an overstaffed bureaucracy, there is also a political rationality in its overcentralized decision-making structure. From a regime perspective, efficiency is not the only criterion by which the performance and value of the bureaucracy is to be judged. It is just as important that the bureaucracy, in exercising its various functions of service, management, resource extraction, and control, itself remain under control and not develop independent centres of power, particularly given that, as a whole, it is not a reliable support base for the regime. Little ideological cement is left since government policies have come increasingly into conflict with the ideological tenets of the Ba'th party; the party itself, as will be shown, has been de-ideologized; and loyalty to the regime has become a matter of material interest rather than ideology. There is no doubt that the deterioration of the living conditions of the younger and lower strata of state-employees has caused increasing indifference towards the regime, if not silent opposition, from within the ranks of the bureaucracy. Many of these younger and lower strata in particular still connect their interest to the state and the public sector – most of them hardly have a personal private-sector alternative —, but not necessarily to the regime. In contrast to many high-echelon civil servants, they would, on the whole, not lose if the regime was to change.

The perceived need for control over the bureaucracy is therefore one of the factors that has so far precluded, and is likely to further preclude, any more than cosmetic structural reform of the public administration and public sector. In addition, any substantial attempt to raise the efficiency and quality of bureaucratic performance would involve the regime elite or state bourgeoisie – those, that is, who would have to initiate the process – themselves losing patronage, decision-making power and other material and non-material privileges. The deficiencies of the bureaucracy are thus largely systemic. They are not, as various reports and reform proposals from within the apparatus might suggest, curable diseases, but partly functional, intrinsic elements of Syria's authoritarian regime structure.

The Security Apparatus

Syria's military forces, security or intelligence services (*mukhabarat*), and police, are certainly the central and, on the whole, most reliable instrument of power the regime has at its disposal, and the strongest institutional actor on the scene. Even before the Ba'thist coup of 1963, Syria's military and security services had a long record of interference in politics. Syria, from its full independence in 1946 until 1970, was notorious for being the most putsch-ridden Arab state. Even when the armed forces were not themselves at the helm, the state was not really in control of its military.[36] During the first seven years of Ba'thist rule, all important changes of regime and policy were brought about by military pressure or coup. The Ba'th itself had come to power through military force; it had extended ideological legitimacy to the military's meddling in politics by speaking of an "ideological army" as an avant-garde force and "school of socialist revolution",[37] and it had to rely on the military and the intelligence services that were beginning to proliferate under its rule in order to stay in power. This military–party alliance, or rather duality of power between the civilian and the military party organizations, as has been described by both insiders and outsiders, was highly conflictual.[38] Only Asad's takeover ended this duality of power, bringing the party apparatus and the state under the control of the military leadership.

Under Asad's rule, Syria's armed forces have been expanded and strengthened such as to become, for the first time, a credible threat to and, to an extent, a deterrent against Israel, and to allow Syria a limited regional power projection. Since 1976, the Syrian army has been on its mission in Lebanon, and in the 1990/91 Gulf Crisis and War, Syrian army units were deployed in Saudi Arabia. At the same time, Syria's entire security apparatus – military, mukhabarat, and police – has become an important agency of socialization and social control, an economic power in its own right, and an instrument of political control with its own corporate interests.

Until the mid-1980s, the security apparatus grew at about the same speed as did state employment as a whole, or even somewhat more rapidly. The regular armed forces increased from some 80,000 in 1970 to over 400,000 by 1985. After that, the number of active troops remained steady. By the early 1990s, Syria's armed forces, including the Syrian contingent of the Palestine Liberation Army and the gendarmerie, numbered some 430,000 troops.[39] Police and mukhabarat, for which no data are available, may employ another 100,000 or so.[40]

Over and above that, some 60,000 civilians are employed in three large companies belonging to the Ministry of Defence. This military economic sector consists of a couple of industrial establishments, belonging to the Organization of Military Factories, that assemble arms and produce uniforms and spare parts both for military equipment and for civilian industries, and of two large construction companies. One of the latter, the Establishment for the Execution of Military Construction, Muta', was founded in 1972 to undertake engineering and construction works for the army, and the other, the Military Housing Establishment, Milihouse, was founded in 1975 to provide housing for members of the security apparatus. Both companies have undertaken far more than they were originally designed for. Among other things, they have built streets, bridges, and irrigation schemes, schools, hospitals, sport stadiums and representative buildings such as the Asad Library in Damascus, and they work as subcontractors for foreign companies. Milihouse also produces industrial equipment, furniture, and some agricultural produce. The military companies have been given wide entrepreneurial freedoms. In particular, they are free to hire and fire, they have been practically exempt from foreign-trade and currency regimes, or have simply ignored them by virtue of their military status; moreover they offer attractive pay. Milihouse has become the country's largest company by far; in good times, it employed up to 70,000 persons. In the early 1990s, it still had 46,000 on its payroll, more than one third of all persons working with the public construction sector. Muta' employs almost another 11,000.[41] Together, the two companies probably consume more than half of all funds the government assigns to Syrian construction companies.

The military also offers attractive opportunities for the best of Syria's science students, namely to be sent abroad for graduate study and then to work in the so-called Centre for Scientific Studies and Research, a largely secretive institution engaged in research for military purposes. Not only do salaries in this institute exceed by far what an ambitious young scientist could earn elsewhere in Syria, it is also the only scientific research institute in the country worth mentioning.

In sum, the security apparatus gives work to almost half of all persons employed by the state, or some 15 per cent of the total workforce. Amongst these, there are 60,000 or so conscripts drafted into the army or police each year for their military service which lasts up to 30 months. For many a young villager, the army represents a chance to leave his rural environment behind, and a career opportunity; many conscripts receive their only professional training during their military service. All of them receive intensive political indoctrination. The military is also in charge of the obligatory military training at high schools and universities,[42] and it organizes and commands volunteer militias attached to the Ba'th party, the Peasant Union, and the trade unions.[43] In addition, it spreads its message through its own media and special radio and television programmes.

While so far the state of war between Israel and Syria, and Israel's occupation of Syrian territory have provided the legitimatory background for a large army and even a strong armed forces presence in public life, it is not lost on the Syrians that a substantial part of the security apparatus has been built to defend the Syrian regime rather than Syria's borders. Naturally this applies to the security services in the first place, but it also applies to most of the special forces and elite units of the army, to the President's 10,000-or-so strong praetorian Republican Guard, and to the militias of the party, workers, and peasants. Given that most agencies and the police are commanded by high-ranking military officers, that much of the mukhabarat structure is part of the military, and that the army and the militias are an important field of recruitment for the security services, dividing lines between military, security services, and police are blurred.

Despite the high degree of militarization and the militaristic socialization which the younger generation has received in Syria's schools and universities, it is to be doubted that the regime and its security apparatus have actually captured the hearts and minds of more than a quarter or so of the population. Even so, the security apparatus has certainly suceeded in conditioning the behaviour of most Syrians. The mukhabarat structure has deeply penetrated society, and dealing with the ubiquitious security services has become part of people's lives and strategies for survival. The four most important services operate a wide net of surveillance in all parts of society, including the bureaucracy, the party, and the army.[44] As the competences of these services overlap, they also check one another. Military Intelligence, for instance, deals with civilians as well as with military persons, and the party's Security Bureau does not restrict its activities to party members. Mukhabarat surveillance is generally a pretty open rather than a secret affair. The objective is, apparently, to maintain an atmosphere of fear and compliance rather than to hide the omnipresence of the services. The mukhabarat keep records of passenger movements on domestic overland taxi and bus routes; they have their own controls at the airports and border posts; they tap phone lines and control international correspondence. University students working for the services openly note political comments their teachers may make; citizens need mukhabarat clearance for, among other things, employment in the bureaucracy, party membership, and a passport. All services have their own prisons, and they question, arrest, and detain people without legal checks. They may hand over people to the judiciary or to the special security courts, but the judiciary cannot interfere with the activities of the mukhabarat. There is no agency to which citizens can complain about arbitrary arrests, torture, the detention or disappearance of relatives, or, even, the murder of detainees. Even though up to 4,000 political prisoners were set free in the early 1990s, the number of persons detained for political reasons was still estimated at several thousand.[45]

The general atmosphere in Syria was more relaxed in the early 1990s than it had been during most of the 1970s and 1980s. Fears of being summoned by the mukhabarat or being arrested for a loose word in a café or other public place, for instance, had evidently receded. But there were still no illusions about the virtually unchecked powers of the security services and the all but total absence of rule-of-law.

People have generally adapted to the ubiquitousness of "security". They take it for granted that even petty mukhabarat officials can and will use their position to enrich themselves and to exercise some power over their environment; but they also make use of the ability of such officials to deliver access to higher echelons in the structure, or to help where mediation with the bureaucracy is needed. It is advantageous to have a military or mukhabarat officer as a relative, a neighbour, a customer, or a colleague, and to preserve good relations with him. It is a myth, though, that anybody who runs a shop or business needs a patron from the mukhabarat or military, a myth much traded by those who seek such patronage in order to secure special gains.

There is no doubt that the security apparatus accounts for much petty and grand corruption and other illegal business in the country. Most of the military and security bosses have become patrons of and partners in private business, or have taken commissions on contracts between the state and international suppliers. Smuggling has, to a large extent, been in the hands of the military, and has been enormously facilitated by the presence of the Syrian army in Lebanon. Syrian officers have extracted protection money and sponsored, as well as participated in, the illegal-drugs business in Lebanon. A majority of the apparatus may be uncorrupted, but corruption and similar business are not restricted to the highest echelons. Many officers have become conspicuously wealthy. Some officers may use the manpower under their command to build a villa, and to run some petty business or, at least, a taxi. Non-commissioned officers and privates may engage in petty smuggling and corruption.[46]

Even without such illicit gains the security apparatus offers considerable privilege to its personnel. Officers and soldiers are provided with subsidized imported goods through the military's own consumer cooperative; officers can acquire cheaply comparatively high-standard family houses in what are called the Asad suburbs, suburban settlements for military personnel. Higher-ranking officers all have their private limousines, and often more than one; lower-ranking and non-commissioned officers frequently use military vehicles for private purposes. Access to a car is a special privilege in a country where the import of automobiles has been severely restricted for more than a decade, and where even higher civil servants can hardly afford a second-hand car. Military and security personnel do not pay income tax; their pay is considerably higher than civil-service salaries and officers may make several times what a civilian state-employee earns.[47]

It seems that it is the privileged position of the security apparatus in the regime and the material privileges extended to its members that in general make it, more than anything else, a reliable arm of the regime. The personal loyalty to the President of officers in leading positions and of much of the rank and file of the Republican Guard and other key units, as well as the balancing of different services, ensure that Asad remains in control of the apparatus. Few coup attempts have been made since Asad's takeover; each was easily discovered and crushed.[48] Asad's praetorian guard – the Defence Brigades commanded by his brother Rif'at until 1984, and the subsequently expanded Republican Guard under Asad's cousin-in-law, 'Adnan Makhluf, and, from the early 1990s until his sudden death in 1994, Asad's son Basil – together with the Special Forces and other particularly loyal elite units have been an effective counterweight to any potential threat from the rest of the armed forces. At the same time, praetorian guard and army elite troops have checked one another, as have the different security services. Asad thus remained the final arbitrator. The events of 1984 – when Special Forces and other army units moved in against Rif'at, who had apparently prepared himself to succeed his brother, should the latter's then critical health have made the succession question acute, or to challenge his brother's position – proved that the system worked, even under the extremely critical conditions of a threat from within.[49]

Ideology, much the same as in the bureaucracy, no longer plays a significant role in the security apparatus.[50] Ideological indoctrination in the army has, at any rate, been reduced to a particularly intensive personality cult around the President. There still is a military left, a couple of high-ranking officers close to the trade unions and with strong anti-imperialist leanings. A much larger group within the military establishment forms part of what has been labelled Syria's military–commercial complex,[51] the alliance of military officers and the new business class. On the whole, other than in the 1950s and 1960s, when a large part of the military was still felt to have a socio-political – nationalistic, anti-feudalistic, and reformist – mission, this is no longer the case today. The security apparatus has so far accepted all the regime's major policy changes, and is likely to continue to do so; this includes accepting peace with Israel, provided that its corporate interests and the well-being of its members are not put at risk.

The numerical strength of the security apparatus and the high grade of militarization notwithstanding, Syria is not a purely military dictatorship; but it is a dictatorship in which the military constitutes the single most powerful and, in sum, least fragmented corporation. Asad is not only formally commander-in-chief, he has also remained Syria's highest military officer. In questions of security and foreign affairs in particular, high officers such as military-intelligence boss 'Ali Duba, chief-of-staff Hikmat al-Shihabi and others are counted among the most important advisors to the President. Those of the President's own family who have been among his closest aides were all military officers – his brother Rif'at until his ouster in 1984, then his son Basil until his death, and 'Adnan Makhluf. Five members of the Ba'th party's Regional Command which Asad hand-picked in 1985 and at least 22 on the party's central committee stem from the security apparatus. The first and third of Asad's, to date, six prime ministers was a general; the Ministry of Defence has been in the hands of Asad's old comrade, General Mustafa Tlas, since 1972; and the ministries of interior, local administration, agriculture, and supply have often been headed by people with military or security backgrounds.

Other high-echelon officers serve as deputy ministers of foreign affairs, interior, and local administration.

The security apparatus therefore does have a strong influence in all matters concerning state and regime security in the widest sense. But it no longer, as will be shown in the following chapter, interferes much in economic policies or other "civilian" policy fields. At the same time, it does not allow the government and bureaucracy to interfere in the affairs of the military or security services. The government has no say over the defence budget, nor has the Ministry of Finance any control over the military debt which is administered by the Defence Ministry alone. Also, the security apparatus and its administrative or financial performance is out of bounds to the government's Central Committee for Inspection and Control and the Central Audit Office. Only the services themselves can check on the security apparatus and its members. The economic establishments of the Ministry of Defence, as noted, are not subject to the rules applied to other public-sector companies, and virtually not controllable by the government.

A conflict that broke out in 1986 between then prime minister 'Abd al-Ra'uf al-Kasm and the military was quite significant for the relation and power equation between the government and the security apparatus. While other questions were at stake too, particularly the corruption and involvement in smuggling of large parts of the security apparatus, the Milihouse company and its free-handed economic dealings centred as the main object of the row. Kasm accused the company of purchasing large sums of foreign exchange from the black market and thus putting additional strain on the Syrian economy. The director-general of Milihouse, Colonel Khalil Bahlul, did not deny the accusation and justified his dealings by the need to complete government projects on time. But he reacted by launching into a limited public a memo implicitly accusing the Prime Minister of favouritism for the benefit of foreign companies that had won some big construction contracts.[52] Bahlul was sacked, and made off to Switzerland, but Kasm himself lost his job a couple of months later. Reportedly, the military bosses urged the President not to reappoint the Prime Minister, or actually vetoed his planned reappointment.

The relationship between the security apparatus and the President is one of mutual dependence. Each individual military leader owes his position to the President and is dependent on his patronage. Who falls from grace, or appears to become disloyal, will also lose office.

There is no doubt that the security services and the military form the strongest centres of power in the country. The Milihouse-Kasm incident showed that the President bowed to the military's collective and strong opposition to a man of his choice. Asad has managed, though, through his balancing of forces and building ties of dependence, to prevent the emergence of *independent* centres of power from within or without the security apparatus – the emergence of someone, so to speak, who could copy Asad's own example of monopolizing military power and then overthrow the regime he is part of.

The President has repeatedly proved that he can strip any military and security strongman of his position. Prominent examples are the commander of the air force and head of the National Security Bureau, Naji Jamil, a close collaborator of Asad from the latter's time as airforce chief, who was removed from his position in 1978, air-force intelligence boss Muhammad al-Khuly, who was temporarily moved to a less prestigious position in 1987, and Ali Haidar, the general commanding the Special Forces, who was sacked in 1994.[53] He has also proved capable of dissolving power centres that tended to become independent. The case of Rif'at who, after the 1984 showdown, was promoted to vice president, stripped of virtually all his power, and exiled, with short interruptions, until 1992, is the most prominent one. Similarly, Jamil, another of the President's brothers, who had tried to build himself an independent political support base in Latakia and in the north-eastern regions of the country, was put in his place.[54] And Asad has shown that he is prepared to set limits to, or even restrict the appropriation of public resources by, the individual members of the security apparatus if expediency so demands. The decision in 1993 to allow the regular importation of foreign-brand cigarettes through a public-sector agency represented a significant move against the vested interests of some high-ranking officers who, since the legal importation of cigarettes had been banned in 1981, had controlled most of their illegal importation. Similarly, some of Syria's highest military and security officers in Lebanon were deprived of much of their income when, in 1992/93, obviously with the encouragement of the Syrian presidency, the Lebanese authorities took action against, and in fact managed to reduce, hashish cultivation in the Syrian-controlled Beqaa valley. And the security apparatus as a whole, as noted, had *nolens volens* to consent to the *de facto* reduction of its budget since the mid-1980s.

At the same time, the President is also dependent on the collective support of the security apparatus. In general, even though he may occasionally have to compromise on detail, he has this support, and he is likely to maintain it as long as he remains in control. The military itself, as a corporation, shares the President's interest in preventing the emergence of independent power centres or any other threat to the power edifice and the stability of the regime. Rif'at's apparent bid for power in 1984 constituted such a threat, and was therefore opposed by practically all other military barons. As long as none of these military leaders under Asad gains clear supremacy over the rest – a situation which is best preserved by maintaining the established balance and Asad's unchallenged position at the top – they may well, when the succession question eventually arises, collectively decide with whom to throw in their lot. With no political mission of their own, they could even let the country's civilian institutions work. In any case, however, they can be expected to reserve for themselves a say in this question.

The Ba'th Party

The same may not apply to the Ba'th party. According to Syria's 1973 constitution, the Ba'th is the leading party in state and society, and it is the party's Regional Command (RC) that proposes to parliament the candidate for the presidency. Since the 1963 takeover, the party has grown impressively. Party membership did not exceed a couple of hundred in 1963, and was estimated at around 8,000 in 1966.[55] In 1971, it already numbered some 65,000 members.[56] Asad, who had been in a minority position in the party leadership that he overthrew in 1970, was wary of the party and its political weight. Reportedly, he had contemplated dissolving it, but this might have been too large an objective and not even advisable if he wanted to build a political substructure for his newly established regime. Instead, the party was transformed: it was further inflated such as to neutralize those who had supported the overthrown leftish leadership, it was de-ideologized; and it was restructured so as to fit into the authoritarian format of Asad's system, lose its avant-garde character and become an instrument for generating mass support and political control. It was also to become the regime's main patronage network. In addition, an institutional frame was built which, if needed, would allow Asad to balance the party against other political forces.

Thus, since 1970, the doors of the party have been opened wide, even admitting ex-Muslim Brethren and rural notables who occasionally managed to take over local party functions besides their traditional village leadership.[57] The civilian membership of the party reached 163,000 in 1974, 373,000 in 1979, and 537,000 in 1984.[58] Some 102,000 of the latter number counted as active or full members, the rest having candidate status. Members usually have to be probationary candidates for several years before – their loyalty proven – they are promoted to full membership. By 1992, party membership was put at around one million, a quarter of them full members.[59] The military still operates an independent Military Committee within the party; military membership can be estimated at around 10 per cent of the total.[60]

In 1984, almost half of the civilian membership were high-school and university students, some 14 per cent each counted as workers and peasants, 9 per cent as employees, 7.5 per cent as teachers.[61] The social structure of the party is not likely to have changed much since. We can estimate roughly that, not counting students, some 16 per cent of the party members belong to the military, some 23 per cent are peasants and farmers, and about 52 per cent work with the public sector and bureaucracy. Only the small remainder is made up by independent professionals, other self-employed outside agriculture, and private-sector employees.

Almost from the moment of Asad's takeover the party was reorganized along quasi-military, hierarchical lines. In 1971, the principle of collective leadership was replaced by that of the individual leader: "The leadership has realized," went a decision of the first party conference after Asad's coup, "that the people ... emphasize the necessity for a leader, rally around the leader, and consider comrade Hafiz al-Asad the leader they seek."[62]

From that time on, the leaderships at subordinate party level were no longer elected from their membership, but appointed by the RC. The party's 1980 Regional Conference recommended that the old pattern, namely the election of the party's subordinate leadership bodies, be reinstated, but with the amendment that the RC propose two or more able candidates for each position. Even this modest proposal, however, was not put into practice, as was critically noted in the organizational report to the 1985 conference.[63] The RC supervises the work of the subordinate party levels. The organizational principle of democratic centralism, which the party considers itself to apply, requires the membership to elect the delegates to the Regional Conference, which then chooses the Regional Command. In practice, the

RC itself exercises substantial influence on the election of conference delegates.[64] Until 1975, the conference elected the RC directly; in 1980, the conference only chose a central committee which then elected the RC from its ranks.[65] In 1985, Asad was empowered by the conference to appoint the central committee himself.[66]

The RC, at least in its own perception, forms the political leadership in Ba'thist Syria. In practice, as far as actual political decision-making goes, it has lost power since Asad has been at the helm, to the benefit of both the president and, as we shall see in the following chapter, the government. Even today, however, the RC includes most of the top members of Syria's political elite, it is regularly informed about government policies and discusses them, sees the President regularly, and has remained the main reservoir for top government posts. The Pan-Arab National Command (NC) of the party, in contrast, though formally superior to the Syrian and all other regional party leaderships, has become a mere honorary board. A seat in the NC is a sinecure, but no longer a powerful position as it had been until 1966. The President, who is also secretary-general of the pan-Arab party organization,[67] has no time for the body, sending his vice-president for party affairs, Zuhayr Mashariqa, and occasionally 'Abd al-Halim Khaddam to keep its members informed.[68]

Parallel to its restructuring, the party has practically become a state institution. Its leading role, as noted, is constitutionally acknowledged. The ideology of the party itself has in this sense been institutionalized: its trilogism "Unity, Liberty, Socialism" forming part of the preamble of the constitution. The party enjoys special legal protection; a law on the "Security of the Arab Socialist Ba'th Party" threatens attempts to steal party documents, to prevent the party from pursuing its tasks, and parallel membership in another party with prison sentences, or with capital punishment if such deeds were instigated from abroad.[69] The party is largely financed from public sources. In 1983, more than 80 per cent of its LS 129 million budget income featured as allowance from the state.[70]

Ironically, with its institutionalization and growth, the party has also lost its ideological and political leadership. It still represents the left wing of the regime; its membership – as its social composition implies – and its leading functionaries have shown a strong public-sector orientation, and their discourse has remained full of Arab-nationalist, anti-imperialist, and socialist sentiment. Reports to party conferences, as well as discussions on these occasions, have been quite critical of socio-political developments.[71] Policy recommendations, however, mostly remained rather vague and have not had a large impact. In 1985, the party's control commission reported that many decisions of the 1980 conference had not been respected, for example: the decision to list all party members whose wealth exceeded certain limits; the decision to examine existing laws as to whether their stipulations contravened the principle of equal rights for men and women; and the decision to hold party conferences bi-annually instead of once every four years.[72] In fact, after the 1980 conference, the rhythm of party conferences was extended to five years. More importantly, from 1985 to date, no conference of the Syrian party organization has been convened at all; the last national pan-Arab conference was held as far back as 1980. RC members, asked why the party had failed to convene a conference after that of 1985, said they themselves did not know or referred to the "general circumstances".[73]

Important policy shifts are obviously not decided upon by the party but commanded and disseminated through the party from the top down, the party with its large membership being an effective channel to transport the message into even remote parts of the country. For instance, within less than a week of the 1989 Arab summit at which Syria had made a major regional-policy turn by supporting Egypt's re-admission to the Arab League, a series of political meetings was announced to bring the new policy directive home to the party and the public. First the RC and then the PNF leadership met with the President. Then, the RC met with the secretaries of the party branches. This was followed by meetings of the branch leaderships with the leadership bodies of the respective sections and subsections. Finally, the subsections met in plenary session to inform "the comrades about the summit decisions ..., whereby Syria's salient role under the leadership of militant comrade Hafiz al-Asad was underlined."[74]

While policy orientations are thus transmitted through the apparatus, and political discussions do still occur within the party, such discussion is not allowed to question the general line as defined by the President.[75] There is a general trend to de-ideologize the party and its discourse, or rather, to reduce party ideology to ever new attempts at popularizing the personality cult around the President that makes Asad the source of and measure of the party's ideological discourse.[76] The President himself has, as long as he has been in office, played around with elements of almost all available ideological tendencies, including conservative Islamist themes. In a speech to religious leaders, for instance, Asad stressed that in Syria's Islamic past, "we do not find anything but weal, pride, glory, justice, and culture. With our Islam ... we were able to bring the world ... the most excellent culture ... When we were victorious in the past, we were far fewer [than today], and we were weaker, but our faith was stronger."[77]

Thus, while the party no longer offers a mobilizing myth or ideological cement that would bind the masses, or strategic societal groups at least, to the regime, its basic function has become to serve both as an instrument of control and a network of patronage. Organized parallel to the administrative structure of the state and the public sector, the different party levels exercise what is referred to as "popular control" over the respective level structure of the bureaucracy. Party cells in public-sector factories, for instance, would regularly report to the economic office of their party branch on performance and productivity, problems and complaints. The provincial economic offices, for their part, give a detailed report every three months to the Economic Office of the RC on the economic situation in their province. The same applies to other administrative entities and party offices.

This procedure allows a controlled measure of critique and informational inputs to move from the regions to the centre, and to sideline bureaucratic channels which are likely to block or filter certain information. Ideally at least, the party command can then approach the government and help to redress defects where it realizes that things are not functioning as planned. Equally important is the fact that this system makes the bureaucratic structure dependent on the political apparatus.

At the same time, the party structure and its system of regular reporting function as a political early warning system of sorts, providing the leadership with a picture of the public mood, and of signs and potentials for opposition and unrest. More than simply reporting on the general feeling in a particular company or agency, party cells actually spy out and report the political orientations of their respective colleagues. Obviously, the objective is eventually to obtain a detailed political mapping of almost Orwellian dimensions of the entire working population. The organizational report to the Ba'th party's 1985 conference gives an impression of how much in this sense political control and surveillance actually occupy the party. In a series of statistics, the political orientations of the membership of different professional groups in the country are listed by number. The reader may learn, for instance, that in 1985, according to the party's assessment, of 2,538 lawyers in the country, 300 were Ba'thists, 99 were with the official Communist party (SCP), 113 with other PNF parties, 12 with an illegal wing of the SCP, 17 with the Muslim Brotherhood, 88 with the Syrian Nationalists, 9 with Kurdish nationalists, and four with a semi-legal Nasirist group. Of the lawyers, 926 were regarded as neutral, 158 as rightists, 66 as reactionaries, four as opportunists.[78] Data of the same kind are listed on engineers and medical doctors, pharmacists, journalists and others, as well as on Syria's workers.[79] The party's own membership is also closely watched. Between 1980 and 1985, according to the same report, more than 130,000 candidates were expelled from the party ranks; only 517 were later readmitted on the basis of party branch recommendations and positive "security evaluations".[80]

Here, obviously, the dividing lines between the party as a political organization and the security apparatus become blurred. There is, however, no clear separation between the functions of both in the first place. Consider that, to give but a few examples, the Indoctrination Office of the RC works as a censorship authority on political litera-ture, that even non-party members have to obtain clearance from their party branch if they want to be employed in certain public-sector positions, and that the Ba'th party's Armed Battalions (*fasa'il al-ba'th al-musallaha*), an army-commanded militia, played an active role in the suppression of Islamist insurgents during the 1979–1982 period.

Apart from but related to its political control function, the party has a function of patronage and, thereby, social control. Whilst, as will be shown in the following chapter with regard to economic policies, any influence over policy matters by individual members of the party leadership, who do not at the same time occupy high gov-ernment office, is limited, RC members have a decisive influence over personnel affairs. Here lies the real importance of the different offices of the RC, each headed by one of the leadership members. The RC member in charge of the Higher Education Office, for instance, vets each academic appointment in Syria's unversities and colleges. The Economic Office, the author was told by one RC member who had once been in charge of it, appointed the general directors of public-sector companies but did not otherwise interfere in the regular work of particular ministries. The first part of this statement has to be qualified insofar as the government formally appoints public-sector directors; general directors of state companies are even appointed by presidential decree. In practice, high-level appointment committees are formed whenever important public-sector positions are to be filled, frequently comprising the respective RC member, the minister in charge, and a member of the trade-union executive.[81] The party, in short, controls personnel more than policies.

Given this function, each member of the party leadership is a powerful patron, and considerable patronage is also vested in lower-level party positions. Even petty party officials can exercise remarkable influence at the local level. They can meddle in the affairs of the local bureaucracy, they are the ones who write reports to the party branch or the leadership in Damascus, and they can, thanks to their function in the political substructure of the regime, mediate access to officials in high government positions. They can and often do use their influence to push forward the interests of their neighbourhood, village, or company as well as their own or their family's interest, or to secure privileges and illicit gains. Corruption of party cadres is an oft lamented problem. Take for instance, the report to the 1985 party conference:

> Opportunists have penetrated the party and formed a dangerous phenomenon. They do not fail to attend meeetings, nor to pay their membership dues; they demonstrate obedience, loyalty, and commitment ... They do not have an opinion on any matter ... What they are concerned with is to arrive at positions of leadership and responsibility to realize material and immaterial gains and to accumulate wealth at the expense of the party's champions and its reputation ... They exploit the opportunities for illicit gains, such as the appropriation of dwellings, valuables, and farms, dealing in real estate, brokerage, smuggling, and the use of equipment belonging to party and state for their personal aims ...[82]

Despite such official lamentation, and despite the constant condemnation of opportunism and corruption, the phenomenon should be considered systemic rather than anomic. The party forms a network of patronage that provides the regime with a mass basis that can be calculated.[83] Obedience and loyalty, as the above quotation implicitly confirms, are traded for goods and services. Corruption is tolerated to bind party members to the regime and also to have them under control. Signs of disloyalty may entail an investigation, whereas the demonstration of loyalty involves material opportunities. Enthusiasm may not go very deep; even party members cannot be forced to believe the slogans they chant – slogans of Asad's eternal leadership, the preparedness for personal sacrifice for the President, etc. Lack of inner conviction is acceptable as long as every single party member and official is prepared to demonstrate publicly his/her commitment to party and President, to repeat and become identified with the slogans that demonstrate this commitment, and have others repeat them in public: at party or trade-union meetings, in the army, or in schools and universities.

The subordination of the party to the President and its unquestioned acceptance of his leadership are not in doubt. At the same time, however, the discourse behind the slogans which, as noted, has remained largely anti-bourgeois, and strongly anti-imperialist and anti-Zionist, has increasingly fallen out of line with actual regime policies. The Ba'th today, with its high percentage of members from the public sector and the bureaucracy, represents to a large extent those societal forces that find themselves at the losing end of the restructuring process. To the extent that the party is still needed as network of patronage and instrument of control – and cannot simply be disposed of – its "pre-modern" radical appearance does not fit with the attempts at encouraging the private sector, opening up to the West, and making peace with Israel. From the early 1990s, therefore, the party has been somewhat demobilized. Posters and banners and other outward signs of the party's presence have been reduced. During the campaign for the referendum on Asad's re-election in 1991 – a large mobilizational carnival – the party was conspicuously absent, whereas great importance was given to demonstrations of loyalty by professional organizations, chambers, and independent, i.e. non-party, personalities. On the day of the referendum, the party was publicly relegated to second place. While the RC and many government ministers waited for the President in a military school-turned-polling-station to cast his vote in their midst, Asad showed up in the bourgeois Malki district of Damascus, close by his office, accompanied not by party or government officials but by Badr al-Din Shallah, the veteran president of the Damascus Chamber of Commerce. The symbolism of the act was not lost on the Syrians.

3. Representation and Control: Front Parties, the Legislative, and Popular Organizations

According to the Syrian regime's own presentation, Syria's popular democracy, democracy, or pluralistic system – terms have changed over the years – manifests itself, and political participation is secured, through the Progressive National Front, the popular or mass organizations (*munazzamat sha'abiyya*), and the parliament.[84] These organizations and institutions structure the space between the government and regime on one hand, and the private and family sphere on the other. This intermediate sphere includes elements that are part of the political system, namely the parliament and the PNF, and others which are normally counted within civil society, such as unions and professional organizations. Since the regime, as will be seen, has largely penetrated these organizations, they have lost much of their "civil", non-state character. However, all these organizations and institutions which the regime euphemistically depicts as participatory have a somewhat ambivalent nature – serving as instruments of social control, and even political repression, as well as, to varying degrees, as channels of interest representation.

The Progressive National Front

The PNF, as noted, was established in 1972. Its charter and by-laws were worked out by a high-level committee which Asad had established a year earlier, comprising the Prime Minister and a couple of other members of the Ba'th party RC, and one representative each of five other parties or party groups officially considered "patriotic" and "progressive". These groups were already represented in the government and the appointed parliament of 1971. Individual representatives of some of them had also been given minor ministerial portfolios in several of the pre-1970 Ba'thist-led governments.

The explicit function of the front was to join these patriotic and progressive forces together to achieve "a greater measure of cohesion and unity" and thereby strengthen the state in its confrontation with the "Zionist occupation".[85] In practice, the installation of the front has primarily served regime-stabilizing functions, namely the neutralization of an oppositional potential, particularly of groups which traditionally have been regarded as competitors of the Ba'th, and the expansion of the President's political support base beyond his own party. It has also allowed the regime, euphemistically though, to depict the political system as pluralist.

The parties that joined the front were the Syrian Communist Party (SCP); the Arab Socialist Union (ASU), a Nasirist group which initially regarded itself as the Syrian branch of Egyptian President 'Abd al-Nasir's own party; the Movement of Socialist Unionists, a breakaway Ba'thist group established after Syria's secession from the UAR in 1961; the Democratic Socialist Unionist Party, a breakaway group from the latter, founded in 1974; and the Arab Socialist Movement, another breakaway Ba'thist party founded in 1964.

Only the Communists, which since a split in 1986 have been represented in the PNF as two separate parties of the same name led by Khalid Bakdash and Yusuf Faisal respectively,[86] can be regarded as a party in their own right – with an independent political and ideological profile and a mass base. Faisal's party may have as many as 10,000 members or more, Bakdash's considerably less.[87] The decision, in 1972, to join the PNF was not too popular among the Communists and led to a first major split in the party.[88] Even as an official ally of the Ba'th party, the SCP has repeatedly fallen out of line with the regime. In 1974, for instance, it voiced strong opposition against the decision to allow foreign oil companies to become active in Syria, and it was also against Syria's Lebanon invasion of 1976. Recurring demands from within the membership to leave the PNF were defeated by the leadership. During the unrest of the late 1970s and early 1980s, the party stood with the regime. However, it considered much of the popular anger against the regime justified, criticized the brutality with which the opposition was put down, and had to concede that many the party counted among its faithful, though not taking sides with the Islamists, took a wait-and-see attitude towards the conflict between the regime and the insurgents.[89] In 1981, the party withdrew its candidates from the PNF list for the parliamentary elections, made them stand as independents, and published its own electoral platform. None of its candidates suceeded; most probably, fraud played a role. In 1986, the party stood on the PNF list again; in 1990 and 1994, both SCPs did so, each being assigned four of the communist contingent of eight deputies. The party has been quite critical of the socio-economic developments and policies of the 1980s.[90] Since its split, the Faisal-wing has acquired a somewhat more modern, the Bakdash-wing a more conservative Stalinist, appearance. While Bakdash's party, for instance, voted against the 1991 investment law in parliament, Faisal's party supported it. At the same time, the latter group is more outspoken in its criticism of human rights abuses, demanding that the constitution be respected, the emergency laws abandoned, and a party law issued.[91]

Apart from the SCP, the ASU, which may still have a couple of thousand members, also had a rather independent profile and, as the Syrian branch of organized Nasirism, a considerable popular base, until 1980. During the 1970s, the ASU's incorporation into the system was based on an uneasy alliance with the Ba'th, and large parts of the party shared much of the criticism which the militant opposition held against the regime. In 1980, a major split occurred, one wing of the party dropping into semi-illegality, the other remaining with the front and associating itself neatly with the regime. The Socialist Unionists may have a few thousand, the Arab Socialist Party probably less than 2,000, the Democratic Socialist Unionists a couple of hundred members. The Arab Socialist Party has tried to maintain a modicum of distinct political profile and may occasionally ask for the "deepening" of democracy and personal freedom in the country or for the abandonment of the emergency laws; however it still yearns for, in the wording of its secretary-general, a reunification with the Ba'th.[92] The other three parties can qualify as Asadist rather than anything else: the Socialist Unionists consider Asad the "symbolic leader"; their "Democratic" offspring bases its ideology on the thought of 'Abd al-Nasir and Asad; the ASU has declared itself a follower of the "theoretical school" of Hafiz al-Asad.[93] ASU boss Safwan Qudsi has even compiled a book on the President's thought.[94]

Little wonder therefore that Syria's front parties, except for the Ba'th party itself and the SCP, are popularly often referred to as *al-ahzab al-shakliyya* – the pro-forma parties. They have not, as noted, all had this character from the beginning, but their incorporation into the PNF has largely neutralized their oppositional potential, even the SCP's. The parties of the front, as spelled out in the PNF charter and by-laws, have accepted that the Ba'th party's programme and its conference decisions are the basic guideline for the front's polices, and that the Ba'th leads the front and has an absolute majority in all its bodies. Consequently, the other parties cannot even force an issue onto the agenda of a PNF meeting. Moreover, the non-Ba'thist parties have agreed to refrain from any political activity in the armed forces. According to the PNF charter, they also committed themselves to stop their activity among students; this commitment, however, has been silently ignored. By forming common election lists, the Ba'th's allies in the front are represented in parliament as well as on provincial and local councils, and each party holds one or two minor ministerial posts. As a rule, the front parties do not have the right to decide who of their members is appointed a cabinet minister; instead they present two or three candidates from their ranks and the President chooses one of them. They have no access to the electronic media and the daily papers, and even the circulation of their own information organs is restricted. Their influence on regime policies is negligible, a fact conceded in private by most of their functionaries.

By tying themselves to the Ba'th, the other PNF parties have lost much of their credibility and popularity. Moreover, in the SCP and the ASU, the question of credibility and to what extent the parties could acquiesce in regime policies even when these contradicted their own ideological essentials has been the main source of internal friction and splits, and thus further weakened them. In the 1950s and 1960s, Communists and Nasirists as well as, for certain periods, the Ba'thist splinters, found their popular base among largely the same societal groups as the Ba'th, particularly among the middle peasantry and land-reform beneficiaries, army officers, and the salaried middle classes in general. In 1970, SCP and ASU may still have had more support in the trade unions and among students than Asad himself. After two decades of work in the front, the Faisal wing of the SCP alone has maintained a limited popular attractiveness and can still recruit the occasional member, even from the younger generation. In the other parties, party functionaries and the party's representatives and deputies in local and provincial councils, PNF leadership bodies, executives of different popular organizations, the parliament, and the cabinet tend to outweigh the rest of the membership. The internal life of these parties has become ossified, their leadership aged.[95] As one party leader put it, his own party would certainly be better off in terms of membership and popularity if it had at some stage left the PNF.[96] Breaking with the front and the regime, however, would entail not only the loss of ministerial positions and other privileges, but also the move into illegality or semi-illegality.

Since the Ba'th's PNF allies all owe their legality and privilege to the President, Asad has not only kept under control potential competitors by integrating them into the front and the government, but also broadened his patronage basis. Asad has occasionally mentioned that additional parties might be allowed into the PNF. One candidate for such an expansion of the front would be the Syrian Social Nationalist Party, a pan-Syrian party which has, under Asad, achieved semi-legal status. In the elections of 1990 and 1994, one of its members was elected to parliament, standing formally as independent. Another possible addition to the PNF could be an Islamic party, formed from those remnants of the Muslim Brotherhood who have made their peace with the regime, and from parts of the religious establishment. Already in 1990, a member, or ex-member, of the Brotherhood, also running as an independent, was elected to parliament; and the regime had tried, but failed, to convince a professor from the Shari'a faculty in the University of Damascus to form an Islamic party loyal to the regime which would be incorporated into the PNF. Any expansion of the front, however, would not by itself change the nature of politics in Syria; such a change could only be brought about by a dissolution of the front or by a party law allowing the establishment and activity of parties outside the front. The front stands for a system that basically denies the existence of conflict,[97] and thereby restricts the chances for their political settlement by competition, that is, open debate, negotiation, and compromise.

Parliament

Syria's parliament or People's Council (majlis al-sha'b), as noted, has been somewhat upgraded since the legislative elections of 1990. Still more a *shura* (consultative) council than a sovereign policy-making body, this upgrading has provided for a widened representation of interests and introduced a new element of political participation by forces outside the regime elite.

Asad first appointed a parliament in February 1971. His pledge, when he assumed power, to install a parliament or, in his words, council of the people, implied a return to a pattern of political representation earlier exercised under the Ba'th rather than to pre-Ba'thist parliamentary-democratic practices. Already in 1965, a corporatist-structured National Council had been appointed comprising the party leadership, representatives from the military, the unions, the Peasant Union, the Women's Union, and professional organizations, as well as "progressive citizens", namely unofficial representatives of the SCP and Ba'thist splinters and some unorganized leftists.[98] This council was dissolved after the coup of 1966. Asad's first parliament resembled that of 1965; however the parties that were to form the PNF were now officially represented, as were representatives of the religious establishment and the chambers.

Parliamentary elections were first held in 1973, then approximately once every four years.[99] In most of these elections, voting was relatively free; only in 1981 were votes reputedly massively rigged. Lesser manipulations most probably happened in other years too. Choice was limited in the first place since candidatures were widely manipulated.

Since the establishment of the PNF, the division of seats between the front parties has been arranged prior to each election. Parties outside the front were not allowed to run. Independent candidates have generally had little chance of being elected if they were not on good terms with the regime or not actually running on the front's list. The notable exception of four oppositional candidates elected to parliament from Aleppo in 1973 only proved the rule; no outright oppositional figure has succeeded since. Independents received around one-third of the seats in 1973, less than a-fifth in 1977, none in 1981 – when SCP candidates ran as independents and the general political climate was particularly strained – and 35 out of 195 in 1986. A scholar closely connected to the regime remarked correctly that these independent deputies could not be considered an independent tendency, but "supporters of the programmes of party and regime".[100] The party itself has held an absolute majority of seats in all parliaments elected to date.

There was more freedom of choice in local and provincial elections. The first elections for provincial councils, in 1972, brought home a defeat for the regime and served as a warning that uncontrolled national elections could become dangerous. Local and provincial councils, however, have completely unpolitical functions. The regime did not, and does not therefore insist on a majority for the parties of the front, and has often left these councils to local notables whose work would in any case be controlled by the provincial governor.

Parliament itself has remained very much on the margins of political life.[101] From the mid-1970s to date, all laws that were passed by parliament have been introduced by the government, and never have government bills been defeated. Not surprisingly, electoral participation in legislative elections remained low, generally well under 20 per cent.[102]

The installation of a parliament, whatever its powers, and the regular holding of legislative and local and provincial elections, as well as of presidential referendums, represented an element of regime legitimation by establishing legal institutions and formalized procedures. The distribution of parliamentary seats was, of course, also a means of patronage. Deputies were supposed to, and usually did, rubberstamp government projects, and not challenge the government on its policies. For the deputies who in their majority represented both the local party structures and the popular organizations – trade unions, Peasant Union, Women's Union and others all having their contingent among the Ba'th party candidates – parliament has been a place to establish and cultivate connections; it supplies *wasta* (mediation) for the deputies' clientele and constituencies and, quite importantly, draws attention to forgotten local problems. The greater part of parliamentary interventions has dealt with issues of distinctly local character such as problems of supply in one province, lack of medical treatment in another, mismanagement in a particular factory, or sluggish progress in a development project. Parliament has thereby been exercising a certain control function, not over policies or politics, but over administrative performance. Regarding the centralized decision-making structure of Syria's bureaucracy, local problems may only be tackled if they are brought to the attention of a government minister or other high regime officals; deputies who do this may in fact be effective representatives of their local constituency, regardless of whether they were elected freely or appointed to their position.

With the legislative elections of 1990, parliament was enlarged from 195 to 250 deputies, and around one-third of the seats were reserved for independent candidates not running on the PNF list. The regime expended considerable effort in encouraging independent candidatures. There was no competition between independents and front-party candidates, and voters still had no choice as far as the PNF list was concerned. It was clear in advance that the PNF would secure seats for all its candidates and maintain about the same number of deputies as it had presented in the outgoing council. But there was considerable competition among non-PNF candidates. Of course, every candidate had to be approved by the authorities. Many candidates had marked views and independent opinions, but none of them represented an anti-regime opposition. Most candidates actually confirmed their allegiance to the President, crediting him as the leader who had put Syria on its "path to democracy".

The 1990 election nonetheless represented not only a numerical, but also a social and functional expansion of parliament. There was still an absolute majority of Ba'thists securing the representation of all those forces that form the traditional support base of the regime: the party itself, Peasant Union and trade union establishment, the bureaucracy and the public sector. Nominally, there were between 82 and 84 independent deputies, which still left the front with a majority of about two-thirds. Certain deputies who are doubtless regime figures, such as the President's brother Jamil, were in some accounts listed as Ba'thists and in others as independents.[103] Except for a couple of such formally independent relatives of high-ranking officials, the independent element represented social forces who hitherto had not been represented or had been under-represented in parliament and other state institutions. Basically, three groups could be distinguished: a score of tribal leaders and landowners, several of whom had already served as independent deputies in previous parliaments; a group of urban professionals and academics, including a couple of men of religion, for the most part from respected city families; and, as the most conspicuous change to the picture, a group of businessmen, especially from the new commercial bourgeoisie. The incorporation of private-sector representatives into parliament was both an expression of the increased economic weight of this group and, concomitantly, the relatively decreasing importance of the public sector, and a sign that the interests of private business were considered legitimate and should have a visible place within the political system.[104] The legislative elections of 1994 accentuated the picture. The numerical destribution of seats between the PNF parties and the independents remained largely the same – in fact, one seat was added to the lot of the PNF to accommodate a new grouping that had split from the Socialist Unionists – and within the group of independents, the business element was strengthened at the expense of some more critical voices from leftish backgrounds.

Parliament has maintained its function of administrative control, its character as a place to mediate between local constituencies and the government, and its patronage function. Significantly, the number of independent deputies has not been increased at the expense of the Ba'th and its front allies, but by expanding the parliament. In addition, the inclusion of the business-class element in particular has given parliament a new, consultative-participatory function. The council has still not developed into a counterweight to the government, and it is not supposed to do so. The concept of a separation of powers fits ill with the regime's corporatist notion of how the state should function. Also, parliament has still no influence on security, foreign affairs or the regime's handling of human rights. Even the budget, which is incomplete in the first place, is not under its control. And there are certain red lines, well known to everyone, which must not be crossed, neither in public nor in parliamentary discussion. Any critique of the President, of the personality cult around him, or of his policy directions is off-limits, as would be a discusssion of the role of the security apparatus, the sectarian composition of its leadership, the spread of corruption among central regime figures, and several foreign and military-policy questions such as, for instance, Syrian policies and behaviour in Lebanon. These questions are, in the first place, not considered to be parliament's business. According to the regime's notion of the matter which to date has not been challenged, parliamentary participation shall chiefly deal with issues that do not feature as high policies, or are even considered non-political, namely, in the wording of Prime Minister Zu'bi, the economy and the daily affairs of the people.[105] The parliament as a whole is supposed to support the supreme authority of the President and his policies, and has duly done so by unanimously nominating him for re-election in 1991. But parliament may discuss, even critically so, economic and social policies and the performance of the government, and may take initiatives in this respect. While, as will be examined in the following chapter, its direct impact on even economic and social policies is limited, it has thus developed into a forum for interest articulation and representation with notable influence on the political discourse.

Popular Organizations

Already in the 1963–70 period, but more consistently thereafter, the regime has endeavoured to organize society along functional lines, i.e. to organize the active and politically important segments of the population into corporatist and regime-dependent, streamlined associations. Partly, new organizations were established for this purpose; partly, existing organizations of civil society were transformed. The aim was to establish a framework of popular or mass organizations which, according to the regime's own reading, would "include all groups of citizens, and work for the interest of these groups in the frame of the higher national interest of the country".[106] More accurately, the function of these organizations is a triple one of representation, mobilization, and control. They shall first ensure that the legitimate interests, especially the particular social and cultural concerns, of society's functional segments are represented in the political system. The political leadership, of course, is to decide what the higher national interest is and which segmental interests are to be considered legitimate. The organizations shall, secondly, mobilize their respective societal segment behind the regime or, as it reads in some of the laws on the establishment of such organizations, "the aims of the revolution", as well as for the development and productive efforts and the general political agenda of the state, and shall also "watch over the fulfilment of the duties" of their respective segment.[107] They are, thirdly, instruments to establish social control over these segments and to contain them politically.

The most important of these organizations are the trade unions and the Peasant Union, the latter established in 1964 with the explicit corporatist notion of associating in one organization almost everyone who was an agricultural producer – agricultural labourers and sharecroppers as well as middle class farmers. There are the Pioneers of the Ba'th, the Revolutionary Youth Organization, and the National Union of Students. Pioneers and youth organization are quasi-compulsory organizations for primary-school students and preparatory and high-school students respectively; the students' union, though not compulsory, features as the organization of all Syria's university students. Further, there are the Women's Union, the Teachers, the Artisans, and the Writers Unions. Also regarded as popular organizations are the various professional organizations – of lawyers, engineers, physicians, journalists, etc. – which for the most part had existed before 1963 and were only gradually brought under Ba'thist tutelage. The chambers of commerce and industry are not normally referred to as popular organizations, and not only because they do not represent any part of the popular classes. While as the more traditional type of corporatist interest organizations they fit into the general framework and are acknowledged as representatives of the private sector, they have maintained a greater measure of organizational independence and are not per se regarded as a mobilizational tool of the regime.

Practically all popular organizations and unions have been developed into hierarchical bodies whose inner structure reflects the authoritarian nature of the political system under which they have been designed or redesigned. Consequently, their leadership is chosen by the regime rather than by their membership. The organizations are non-competitive, i.e. each one is exclusively in charge of a particular societal segment. They all exercise some quasi-governmental functions vis-à-vis their membership, and most of them also offer subsidiary social services to their constituency. They represent their constituency in official committees and bodies, and in parliament; except for the chambers, the heads of all organizations also hold party positions.

While in principle all these organizations have an ambivalent character as both a power instrument of the regime and an interest organization, the degree to which the former or the latter quality materializes, and the measure of autonomy they enjoy, varies from one organization to the other. The Revolutionary Youth Organization (shabibat al-thawra) and the Students Union come closer to being an instrument of repression and control more than anything else. Youth and students' organizations participate in organizing military training in schools and universities, the youth organization also organizes voluntary elite military and intelligence training.[108] Armed members of the youth organization have occasionally been used as police reserves, and the students union has been praised for its help in detecting among the students "forces inimical to the party and the revolution", to "evaluate politically" Syria's students abroad, and to monitor "inimical elements" among them. Any student who wants to register for graduate studies needs political clearance from the organization.[109] Active members of both organizations are entitled to some privileges; most importantly, 25 per cent of all places at universities are reserved for cadres of the youth organization and graduates of their elite training programmes.[110]

The chambers, on the other hand, with a history dating back to before the French mandate period, have largely retained their character as self-ruled corporatist organizations of Syria's traders and industrialists. Ideally representing the common interest of these functional groups, there is no doubt that members of the chamber executives and boards, by virtue of their access to cabinet ministers, their membership on government committees, and their prestige, can and do use their position to further their private interests. Competition for chamber positions is usually fierce. Chamber executives are elected from the entire chamber membership. The regime lets these elections run comparatively free, though candidates considered unacceptable might get a sign to withdraw. The government has the right to appoint a number of members to each chamber executive – six out of eighteen in the case of the Damascus Chamber of Commerce – formally to represent public-sector companies. These are enough votes to guarantee that the boards of the chambers and their presidents, whom the executives elect from within their ranks, are those the government prefers. Where particularly prestigious and influential positions are concerned, the Prime Minister will usually make known whom he favours. Such a position is certainly that of the president of the Damascus Chamber of Commerce, who is also an ex-officio member of the cabinet Committee for the Guidance of Imports, Exports, and

Consumption, an important economic policy-making body. It is unlikely that a chamber executive, in whose interest it is to have good working relations with the government, would fail to follow the Prime Minister's recommendation. The chambers are not supposed to challenge the government on its economic policies or demand substantial policy, let alone political changes; and they have, like others, to prove their loyalty to the President. They are not, however, an agency for regime control over the private sector, but, within the limits of the system, independent actors.

The place of the other popular organizations and unions is somewhere in between. Until 1980, a couple of professional organizations maintained a high degree of autonomy from state and regime, similar to or exceeding that of the chambers. Then, as noted, when the lawyers, engineers, and physicians unions openly opposed the regime, their executives were dissolved by governmental decree, and the associations transformed into docile, corporatist organizations. Like other popular organizations, the lawyers union, for instance, was now legally obliged to follow the political line of the regime.[111] Like others, too, it still has a service character and represents the professional interests of its membership. The following excursus will focus on the trade unions as one of the most important popular organizations, certainly so with regard to the process of economic change and economic policy-making, in order to explain in more detail the role and ambivalent function of these organizations in the political system.

The Trade Union Example

The General Federation of Trade Unions (GFTU, *al-Ittihad al-'amm li-niqabat al-'ummal*) comprises almost all public-sector employees. In the private sector, unionization is officially said to be at about 44 per cent. In practice it is likely to be lower; with a significant degree of unionization only in bigger establishments.[112] Private-sector employees make up less than a quarter of the total trade-union membership of, by 1992, some 540,000.[113]

A Syrian labour movement had already emerged in the 1920s. In the 1940s and 1950s the trade unions became a political force largely dominated by Communists, Ba'thists and neutralists. From the late 1950s, as mentioned, Nasirites became the Ba'th party's main competitors and remained so even after the Ba'thist takeover of March 1963. Compared to the Ba'th which in practice only started to reorganize after its takeover, the trade unions represented a considerable organized social force. Although "no ruling wing of the Ba'th party ever accepted a union leadership leaning towards another wing of the party,"[114] and takeovers within the Ba'th regime were usually accompanied by purges in the trade unions, this force could not be ignored.[115] The union's demand that workers participate in directing public-sector companies, for instance, was taken account of by introducing workers' representation on the boards of these firms; however, a more far-reaching law of 1964, stipulating the "self-administration" of public-sector units, however, was not implemented.[116]

After Asad's coup of 1970, the trade unions were gradually transformed from an organization that prioritized what it regarded as working-class interests, to one which, if necessary, would represent and enforce regime policies in its membership. The 1972 Conference of the GFTU defined the role of the unions in the Ba'thist state as "political" in contrast to what it called "postulative" or "demanding" (*matlabi*) unionism. Practically, and despite its sound, this "political unionism" meant the abandonment of an independent political role for the unions. The organization's new duties were, as declared in a speech of GFTU President Ghazi Nasif, to "deepen the unity of the working class; increase production; protect, support, and develop the public sector" as well as fight red tape, develop the administrative apparatus of the modern state and expand social services for the working class.[117] "Postulative" struggle, such as had been necessary under capitalism, was to be regarded as counterproductive under the now-existing "socialist" system. Even more so, such postulative struggle had to be viewed as "sabotage" of the socialist path.[118] Two years later, Nasif's successor Mahmud Hadid declared that, since the working class had realized the credibility of the leader Asad,

> for us as leaders of the working class the proper climate has come, for the first time, to no longer speak about working-class rights and the struggle for these rights, but about working-class duties and about how we will have to struggle in order to fulfil these duties.[119]

The transformation of the trade unions did not go ahead without opposition. Hadid conceded that it had been difficult to put through the new line, and that there had been resistance from parts of the membership, particularly from the communists.[120] Hadid himself was not entirely prepared to abandon the trade unions' responsibility of publicly pointing to the basic needs of their membership. "Some comrades in power," he complained, thought that political unionism meant the working class had no more demands. Struggling for better living conditions for the workers, however, since ultimately serving the aim of increased production, could not be dismissed as "postulative".[121]

Only in 1977, when Hadid was succeeded by 'Izz al-Din Nasir, was an entirely hand-picked and docile trade-union leadership established.[122] Under Nasir's presidency, the trade unions' apparatus has been widely expanded, and the organization has developed into a corporatist institution. The trade unions have taken on some executive functions, they perform far-reaching functions in the fields of social security and public health, they are represented on all government committees that deal with labour and public-sector affairs, as well as in the leadership of the PNF and, much like a ministry or public agency, they have been included in Syria's five-year development plans. Lines of conflict no longer necessarily run between the trade unions as, theoretically, the collective organization of the working class on the one hand, and public-sector management and private entrepreneurs on the other, but rather cut across the trade-union structure, whose leadership has become part of the regime elite. In order to maintain their control over their membership, elements of internal democracy have been cut down, and the executive has been strengthened vis-à-vis the membership and the subordinate levels.[123] The GFTU leadership and most cadres on the intermediate and partly even on the lower levels of the hierarchy are appointed rather than elected to office.[124] Still, the unions are more than simply a power instrument of the regime. The strengthening of the executive, the incorporation of its leadership into the regime elite as well as the corruption of quite a number of its members can rather be viewed as expressions of the regime's attempt to maintain control over an organization which, due to its numerical strength and its roots in the public sector and in the bureaucracy, contains a critical potential.

The main *political* function of the trade unions has become to mobilize their membership for continuous productive efforts, including unpaid days of voluntary labour, to generate support for regime policies in the working class, and, if necessary, to defend the regime in critical situations. Thus, shortly after Asad's takeover, members of the GFTU executive toured the provincial organizations in order to "explain the communiqué of the Correctionist Movement" and "close the ranks of the labour movement". A similar tour was carried out in 1976, in the wake of Syria's largely unpopular military intervention in

Lebanon, in order to "explain the developments of the current situation".[125] In 1980, when the regime faced its hitherto severest crisis, workers' militias were set up under the control of the party and the military. In 1982, these militias participated in putting down the Hama uprising.[126] An important step to achieving social control over the public-sector work-force – a step which the GFTU hailed as one of the greatest achievements of the working class – was the promulgation in 1985 of a new labour law for all persons employed by the state.[127] With the unification of regulations for the public-sector work-force and those working in the public administration, public-sector workers and employees were turned into quasi-civil servants. Consequently, employment in public sector was defined as a function (*wazifa*). Workers as, in this sense, state-functionaries are obliged to pursue the political aims of the Ba'thist state, "unity, freedom, and socialism"; strikes are explicitly declared illegal.[128] The merger of civil service and public sector has facilitated the unionization of civil servants, thereby strengthening the trade-union apparatus and further bureaucratizing it.

At the same time, the unions fulfil important *social* tasks to the benefit of their membership and other parts of the population. Such services, especially in the field of public health, have become the main incentive for workers and employees to enlist in a union, particularly so in the private sector where unionization is a completely voluntary affair. More than two-thirds of the union membership are also members of union social support funds which pay small sums of money in case of a member's sickness or death, on the occasion of important family events, and to the aged.[129] By 1992, the unions were running three hospitals, some 25 health centres and more than thirty pharmacies, mainly in working-class quarters and in industrial zones. Services provided by these establishments were either free of charge or at least comparatively cheap. Since there exists no general health-insurance system, the fact that these services are open not only to union members but also to their families, gains special importance. Apart from health services, union committees organize kindergartens, and several unions run public restaurants, theatres, and cinemas usually more cheaply and, as regards cultural establishments, better in quality than commercial ones.[130]

On the shop floor, union committees or some of their members are doubtless attempting to serve and defend the interests of their membership. Conflicts between union committees and the directors of public-sector factories are not so rare. These conflicts are generally over the implementation of industrial security regulations and over working conditions in general, and there is regularly some disagreement between union committees and directors over the implementation of the rudimentary form of workers' participation that is demanded by law, namely trade-union representation on the management committee of each public-sector firm, and on the consultative production committees.[131] In firms that belong to the Ministry of Defence not even the establishment of trade-union committees is allowed. All public-sector construction companies, both civilian and those of the military, have repeatedly been subject to harsh criticism from union sources, mainly because of poor working conditions and frequent violations of social-security and labour-code regulations.[132] Notably, the union leadership does not support such criticism, and even dismisses it as communist propaganda.[133]

Generally, the loudest public critique of economic and social policies, and of particular societal developments in Syria is raised from within the trade unions, whereby lower level functionaries tend to be much more outspoken than the national executive. Sober accounts of working-class living conditions and of the situation of public-sector establishments, such as are frequently rendered by union committees, provincial union executives, in conference debates, and in the columns of the unions' weekly *al-Ishtiraki*, often represent strong charges against the official rhetoric of socialist achievements. The unions' paper and their conference reports have frequently analysed economic policy decisions very critically, certainly not overstepping the red lines of tolerated criticism, but touching these lines. A GFTU-organized conference in 1987 on "National Creativity and Self-Reliance" became, albeit against the organizers' plans, a forum for sharp criticism of the regime's economic and social policies. At the union base, also, there doubtless exists a considerable degree of uneasiness with undemocratic structures, red tape, and corruption in their own apparatus. Occasionally, such uneasiness has become evident through union elections on the lowest, sometimes even on the intermediate level, where independent candidates not running on the official list of the Progressive National Front or the Ba'th party happen to be elected. Usually, however, oppositional candidates will be kept away from running for office.[134] At times, criticism from within the unions has been made public. In 1989, for instance, the Printers' Union demanded the introduction, both in their own union and in the national federation, of new methods that would serve as "the basis for a democratic union practice", as well as demanding that the phenomenon of functionaries committed to their own interests rather than to the unions' be fought.[135] Union conferences and publications can thereby serve as a safety valve where steam is let off.

Syria's trade unions thus function as a service more than an interest organization for their membership. They no longer play a direct role as wage-negotiators.[136] Their role-model of a "political" as opposed to a "postulative" union entails as their primary function the support of regime policies, not active measures on behalf of their memberships' demands. Strikes in the public sector are forbidden anyway. The union leadership has in a few cases endorsed token strikes in private establishments to ensure that the owners of these firms raise wages in step with public-sector pay rises.[137] In 1983, in a rare case of far-reaching trade-union protest, the Union of Service and Tourism Workers publicly warned against employment with a hotel company that, as a mixed-sector company, had been exempted from all labour laws.[138] With these exceptions, strikes, boycotts and other active measures are not endorsed by the union leadership. There has, nevertheless, been occasional unorganized workers' action even in public-sector establishments. In all cases that became known, protests were directed against poor working conditions. The trade unions not only refrained from supporting such strikes but cooperated with the security agencies to suppress them.[139]

From the standpoint and in the discourse of the trade unions, workers' action in the public sector would be both unwarranted and unnecessary. The public sector, so they argue, has to be defended against any attempts to dissolve it, privatize parts of it or subject it to private interests – it is not to be fought against. Problems that admittedly occur between the management of public-sector establishments and their workers should and can be solved through the unions' mediation. But there can be no antagonistic conflicts between the workers and the public sector which, by definition, is their own. Has not the President repeatedly said that the workers own the factories, that they are in the position to develop the public sector and its production, and that their unions are practically in charge of labour and public-sector affairs? And is not the trade-union executive represented for that purpose in the PNF leadership and in parliament?[140]

This discourse is more than a euphemistic jingle of words. The trade unions, or more precisely, their leadership, has in fact substantial influence in public-sector matters and is considered to represent public-sector interests – whereby no distinction is made between workers and employees of that sector and its management. Legally, of course, public-sector directors are themselves employees. According to the regime's corporatist logic, management and workers are all nothing but pro-ducers, parts of one single functional segment of the social economy. Notably, there exists no professional organization of public-sector managers. Many of them are union members, or members of the engineers' union. More important, the trade-union leadership has a say in the appointment of public-sector directors. As mentioned, high-level party-union-government committees select candidates for leading public-sector positions. As a rule, such decisions are taken amicably: apart from being professionally qualified, it is sometimes still more important that a candidate should be acceptable to all sides; support for another side's client will be repaid in kind on another occasion. Since their future career could be influenced by the trade-union leader-ship, public-sector directors have, in general, a strong interest of their own in maintaining good relations with the GFTU executive. Occa-sionally, trade-union leaders themselves have been appointed public-sector managers.

Such patronage of the trade-union executive over public-sector managers is not likely to help rationalize communication structures in the public sector or enhance public-sector performance.[141] However, it does ensure that public-sector managers are generally open to trade-union requests and proposals, and that many a problem or conflict actually finds a consensual solution – even if this is often anything but effective.[142]

Moreover, public-sector directors and trade-union leaders share a range of common socio-political interests. Both are interested in achieving an acceptable public-sector performance; in securing and defending the resources of the public sector against the Ministry of Finance, private interests or others; and in maintaining this sector as a source of patronage. Both groups are also, in general, interested in strengthening the authority of state and regime, and in keeping the union base under control: radical opposition that might exploit work-ers' grievances for anti-regime propaganda should be suppressed, while scope for shop-floor union activities is to be upheld so as to maintain the safety-valve and early-warning functions of the organi-zation. "Reasonable" demands from the base may, as outlined, be dealt with through direct contacts between the trade-union executive and the respective public-sector management. As a matter of fact, public-sector directors may themselves use the trade-union track to push their demands. It is the trade unions that have organized workshops and conferences such as the "Self-Reliance" Conference of 1987 dealing with public-sector problems and public-sector development. GFTU-executive members rather than public-sector managers participate in all political discussions on public-sector reform, adjustment, or economic liberalization, sit on the respective committees, and have an apparatus that allows them to prepare their own memoranda and studies.

Apart from their service function for both public- and private-sector workers and employees, the trade unions have thus, in a sense, developed into a "chamber" of the public sector, i.e. a corporatist institution, that is, representing the public sector in the political system, just as the chambers of commerce and industry represent private producers. Both represent legitimate interests which, ideally at least, should not be in conflict with one another. Both have, as such, a place in the political–institutional framework and participate in political decisions that are regarded as their legitimate concern – primarily, of course, social and economic policies. Their participation, as will be seen, remains controlled[143] – and it is granted from above rather than achieved through pressure and negotiation.

4. Conclusion: Patrimonialism, Authoritarian Rule, and the Strong State

Since Asad's assumption of power great efforts have thus been expended to build a structural frame that supports the authoritarian regime through a range of safety devices; such devices prevent parts of the system from revolting against its leadership and, at the same time, legitimize this system through the establishment of legal institutions. Asad's personal rule over the system has, in addition, been secured by the deliberate employment of patrimonial instruments such as, in particular, personal loyalties and patronage. Such elements of patrimonial rule do not conflict with the authoritarian structure of this edifice of power; rather, the prevailing, authoritarian nature of political behaviour in the system gives particular importance to clientelistic networks and all sorts of more or less traditional ties and loyalties. And while the existence and employment of such networks and ties may conflict with economic rationalities, they are not necessarily at odds with the rationality of regime maintenance.

Clientelism, Confessional Ties, and Corruption

As noted variously above, clientelistic or patronage networks pervade the structure of Syria's bureaucracy and public sector, as well as that of the party or popular organizations. Access to resources, be they services, employment, licenses, other material or non-material benefits, or political influence, often needs *wasta* (mediation), and *wasta* is best obtained through vertical patronage networks as well as through less hierarchical family relationships and regional or ethnic ties which, of course, often form the very lines along which patron-client relations are knit. Patronage, as a technique of power, is based on the exchange of resources, or access to them, for loyalty or obedience.[144] Patronage thus establishes a hierarchical relationship by definition. And while the spread of *wasta* may create an egalitarian illusion – namely that everybody can somehow get access to decision-makers and can thereby participate in political processes or even manipulate the state – it is in fact an extremely inegalitarian instrument. *Wasta* is unevenly distributed, creates dependencies, and individualizes political and social action, thus impeding the development of class-based solidarities and, to an extent, obscuring power relations. "Who is the ruler and who is ruled is obvious to all ..., but the line between the two becomes blurred when individuals act vis à vis specific bureaucrats, officials, or party functionaries because of the seeming mutuality in *wasta*."[145]

For the regime, the spread of patronage networks through the institutions of the modern state is not only tolerable. Given the distributional functions of a modern state, and the need for practically all members of society to have access to it, patronage also serves as an extremely useful means of control, and it has been cultivated as such. Patronage binds strategic groups such as the military and parts of the bourgeoisie to the regime; it even helps to create a regime basis in societal groups which otherwise would not be among the regime's supporters; and given its highly selective nature, it also contributes to the fragmentation of these groups.

Often, though not exclusively, patronage relies on and instrumentalizes traditional or primordial ties, particularly regional, tribal, and confessional solidarities.[146] The confessional composition of the regime elite, the strong Alawi bias particularly of the *jama'a*, the group surrounding the President, has often been described.[147] Confession as such, however, is not the criterion for membership in this circle; loyalty to the President is. All strategic positions, particularly those of immediate relevance for regime security, are occupied by persons with strong personal ties to the President. Members of Asad's own family and clan, and from the Alawi sect, can be said to have a comparative advantage in this respect, so to speak. Immediately after Asad's take-over, his brother Rif'at was entrusted with the command of the so-called Defence Brigades (*saraya al-difa'*) which until 1983 were the President's main praetorian guard. After the demise of Rif'at and subsequent dissolution of his Defence Brigades, the second major praetorian guard became the Republican Guard. This was placed under the authority of 'Adnan Makhluf, Asad's cousin-in-law, with Basil, the President's son, becoming second- and, in practice, first-in-command in the years before his death in 1994. Other relatives of the President hold further central security positions; all military units as well as most security services that might be in a position to stage a coup are under the command of Alawi loyalists from the President's own tribal and regional background. Not all important positions are in the hands of Alawis. Notably, Chief-of-Staff Hikmat al-Shihabi, Minister of Defence Mustafa Tlas, Vice-President 'Abd al-Halim Khaddam, and, as yet, all prime ministers who served under Asad, have been Sunnis.[148] These and other Sunni members of the President's inner circle, such as, for instance, party vice-secretaries 'Abdullah Ahmar and Sulayman Qaddah, have not – as is occasionally suggested[149] – obtained their positions as alibi-Sunnis or in order to please the Sunni majority. Nor do Asad's Alawi strongmen hold their positions because they are Alawis. They are all there because they have been Asad's friends, comrades, and loyal followers for a long time. Tlas was a comrade of Asad in the military academy; Khaddam and 'Abd al-Ra'uf al-Kasm, who was Prime Minister from 1980 to 1987 and then became head of the party's National Security Bureau, have known Asad and been among his comrades since his activist days in Syria's students union.

The group around the President represents the top of a pyramid of patronage networks that reach through all levels of society. Anyone in the President's inner circle owes his position to Asad. By being the President's men, however, the members of this group have become powerful secondary patrons who all have their networks of clients and followers in the army, the party, or the bureaucracy. Members of the party RC outside the immediate core group, cabinet ministers in charge of important ministries, or the heads of popular organizations are in a similar way, if on a lesser scale, entitled to patronship.

It is not at all unusual to find public-sector directors or high administrative officials being tied and loyal to a high-ranking patron from their own sect rather than their formal superior; and to find such officials giving family, confessional, or regional ties preference over qualification in their employment practices. Alawis, largely under-represented in government service before the Ba'thist takeover, have certainly profited over-proportionally from the fact that key positions in the regime have been occupied by Alawi officers since 1966. Similar advances were made by members of other predominantly rural societal groups among which the Ba'th had a strong foothold – especially Sunnis from the Hauran, from the rural regions of Aleppo, and from the Dayr al-Zur area. Still, therefore, while Alawis are no doubt over-represented in the officer corps,[150] the same does not apply, at least not significantly so, to civilian government service. Rather, the visible advancement of Alawis and other previously underprivileged groups through the ranks of bureaucracy and public sector has helped to achieve a roughly proportionate representation of regions and sects.[151]

The conspicuous high positioning of numerous Alawis in the regime structure has made many observers depict the Syrian regime as an Alawi minority dictatorship, or view the Alawis as the new "ruling elite of Damascus".[152] There is no doubt that the moderniza-tion of Syria's socio-economic structure has not invalidated confes-sional and regional affiliations as one important category of identity among others; nor is there any doubt that such affiliations have been an important element of intra-elite conflicts in Ba'thist Syria, and that they still play a role in determining the composition of patronage networks. Distinctions have to be made, however, between politics and policy contents, in order not to fall into the trap of overstating the obvious – namely the high concentration of Alawis in regime positions, particularly in the security field. The Alawi community, or, for that matter, any other, is by no means a homogeneous bloc. Since the 1960s particularly, the Alawi community has undergone a rapid process of social diversification, especially through education, migra-tion, and the emergence of an urban Alawi middle class; and it is not, and has never been, politically uniform. A group of Alawis is in power, not the Alawis. There is in fact a substantial measure of anti-regime opposition among the Alawi community, and all major political conflicts, within the regime elite and even between the regime and the opposition, have so far transcended ethnic lines.[153]

The exploitation and manipulation of confessional bonds has remained part of the political game in Syria, for the regime and individuals in the regime elite, as much as for some opposition groups. The absence of an open political space that would allow political organization and competition along ideological lines makes the utilization of ethnic ties an expedient strategy for the individual or collective pursuit and the settlement of interests and conflicts.[154] Given the employment of confessional ties is likely to foster confessional tensions and provide the ground for confessionalist agitation, it is a dangerous means of politics. Confessionalism remains a means, however, not a political end.[155]

Most importantly, the regime has not pursued social or economic development policies that would have specially advanced or favoured the Alawis or the coastal region from which the majority of Syria's Alawi community originates.[156] Intensive, if only partly successful, efforts were spent, particularly through the 1960s and 1970s, to bridge the urban–rural gap, namely to bring electricity, schooling, and health services to the countryside. The coastal region and its rural parts have benefited from these measures, as have other underprivileged areas. However, living conditions in some Alawi mountain villages are still extremely poor.[157] The region that has profited most from the government's investment and development policies has been Damascus and its surroundings, not the coastal area.[158] Some particularly large investments in the provinces of Latakia and Tartus, namely the expansion of both cities' ports and of the oil terminal in Banias, have certainly been in the interest of the Syrian national economy as a whole. The main growth axis in the country still extends along the Damascus–Homs–Hama–Aleppo road, with only secondary axes having emerged between Latakia and Aleppo, and from Aleppo over Raqqa to Dayr al-Zur. Private sector investments, too, have been largely concentrated in Damascus and Aleppo. Had the coastal regions been privileged in terms of public infrastructural investments, or had their population become particularly wealthy, one should assume that they would also have attracted larger portions of private capital investments. Latakia, the main Alawi province, where approximately 6 per cent of Syria's total population live, has attracted less than 3 per cent of all private and only 4.2 per cent of all public-sector industrial investments. The province contains 6.5 per cent of all primary schools,

5 per cent of all hospitals, and 4 per cent of all physicians in the country.[159] It has occasionally been suggested that Syria's Alawi community and the regime might seek to prepare the establishment of an Alawi mini-state in Syria's coastal provinces for the time after Asad.[160] Given that economic policies have not been confessionally or regionally biased, and that Syria's Sunni urban bourgeoisie has fared considerably well under Asad's rule, there is little empirical substance to such claims in the first place. Any such attempt would also clearly contradict Asad's persistent endeavour to build a strong Syrian state and further the country's national integration. While the political exploitation of confessional bonds for the stabilization of his own, personal rule, has been counterproductive in this latter respect, Asad's attempt, at the ideological front, to cultivate good relations with the Sunni religious establishment and present himself as a pious Muslim cannot be overlooked. There have also been, and particularly from the mid-1980s, significant moves from within the Alawi community to remove confessio-psychological barriers between their sect and ortho-dox Islam. Consider, for instance, the building of mosques in Alawi villages, or the publication of a series of books, by Alawis or others, that seek to lift some of the secrecy around the Alawi faith and to prove that the Alawis are part of the Shia, not a heterodox sect.[161] In a sense, this attempt at an ideological integration only expresses the fact that the Alawis have definitely lost their status and character as a mainly rural, largely underprivileged, and geographically concentrated or "compact" minority. Those Alawis who have migrated to Damascus and other cities, and even more so their progeny, have become as Damascene as other migrants to the capital. It is here, in a social environment which has little in common with their or their parents' village of origin, that they make their living and seek to survive, no matter to what extent they may thereby rely on regional ties and confession-based networks of patronage.

While confessional, regional or other bonds that can serve to establish a group identity are employable to form networks and patronage relations, they do not, in the long run, suffice to maintain loyalties. Patronage necessarily involves a selective distribution of privileges. Borders between patronage and corruption are therefore extremely fluid. Opportunities for corruption are widespread, and they are graded. Wherever a deal is struck with the state, where licences are needed, or where jobs can be provided, illicit gains can be made. Where high-ranking military or civilian officials make sure that a public-sector contract is won by a particular foreign company, kick-backs of millions of dollars may be in play; where a custom official closes his eyes to some illicit private import, he might be rewarded with a *baqshish* of no more than a dollar's equivalent. Bribery is ubiquitous. Given the general feeling that both the regime elite and the business community are thoroughly corrupt and that petty state employees do not earn what they need for their living, Syria's general public does not regard petty corruption as particularly wrongful.[162]

It has been noted that Syria's political elite has indeed developed a strong tendency to "treat the state as their private property".[163] Persons in the immediate vicinity of the President, namely members of his family, his vice-presidents, party vice-secretary-general Ahmar, and other members of the party RC seem to have a fairly unlimited licence for corruption. Even larger scandals have not cost members of this group their positions, and they can, for their part, allow a measure of grand corruption to their own clientele.[164] Notably, Rif'at al-Asad did not lose his power in 1984 because of his notorious involvement in corruption and smuggling, and his patronage over some of the most dubious elements of Syria's business community, but because of his attempt to form an independent centre of power and challenge the President's authority.

Recurrent, sometimes almost permanent, anti-corruption campaigns which occasionally reach as high as a government minister[165] cannot hide the fact that corruption is tolerated or even planned. A wide net of corruption, as noted, binds those who are involved to the regime, if only by keeping them under threat of investigation, and ensures that lower officials do not try to uncover the illicit practices of their superiors. Anti-corruption campaigns are necessary, both to make the threat of prosecution credible and thus maintain the instrumental character of planned corruption, and to avoid this instrument getting out of hand – in other words, to prevent ecoomic damage exceeding political benefit.

The regime has, by and large, managed to check the greatest sys-temic danger which planned patronage and corruption involve, namely the self-consumption of the system through the greed of its main beneficiaries.[166] More than once, for instance, especially in 1984 and 1992/93, the regime has set limits to militarily patronized contraband trade. In the latter period too, as noted, effective measures were per-mitted against the hashish and opium cultivation in Lebanon's Biqaa valley, a business in which the Syrian army was heavily involved.

Increased international criticism of Syria's sponsorship of and participation in the Lebanese drug trade had made this affair a political
liability; its reduction can therefore be understood as an attempt to
ward off Western reproaches rather than one to deprive parts of the
military of their income. It proved, however, that the regime has remained capable of reining in corruption and other excesses, and of
cutting deeply into the privileges of some of its high-echelon patrons
where the interests of self-preservation so demand.

Strong State, Weak Institutions

The regime's ability to rein in the patrons and strongmen it had itself
created, and enforce legality where necessary indicates that a
comparatively strong state has been built. Also, if a strong state is
characterized by its ability to make people comply with its demands,
participate in state-run and state-authorized institutions, and accept
its legitimacy,[167] the Syrian state has to be considered fairly strong.
Already in the first years of Ba'thist rule, after the "revolution" of
1963, the substructures of the Ancient Régime were liquidated. Its
parties were banned, its leading representatives driven out of the
country, its landed and industrial bourgeoisie seriously weakened
through the implementation of land-reform measures and nationalizations, and its bureaucracy was flooded with ambitious and often
politically committed migrants from the countryside. The new regime,
however, was internally fragmented, split between different networks
and groups, and weakened by the struggle for power of various military and party leaders. The regime was not in control of its military,
whose involvement in politics it had itself furthered and legitimized.
It weakened principal allies, such as the trade unions, through recurrent purges of their leadership, and antagonized the entire private
sector, not only the big bourgeoisie. The regime was unable to create
a legitimizing myth or, more importantly, to defend the country when
the battle with the "Zionist enemy" finally occurred – a battle which
the Ba'th's radical nationalists had promised would indeed come and
lead to the liberation of Palestine. Nor was the regime able to establish legal institutions. Attempts that were made in this direction, such
as the promulgation of a provisional constitution and the appointment of a National Council, were sooner or later aborted through the
internal power struggles of the regime elite.[168] The successive Ba'thist
regimes before 1970 were able to prevent a return to power of the

pre-Ba'thist elite and to thwart the bid for power of their Nasirist competitors. Also, despite the political instability of that period, notable developmental achievements were made or set in train. None of these regimes, however, managed to establish more than a feeble measure of political and social control.

Only after Asad's takeover was a new, consistent structure of power and control set up. With the military and the security services as its strongest element, the new regime set out to introduce quasi-military patterns of command into the party in particular, as well as into other organizations and agencies. The expansion of the bureaucracy, the centralization of its decision-making structures and the creation of a system of corporatist popular organizations, all contributed to the establishment of regime control over the largest part of active society; further, they helped to ensure that such local or sectoral strongmen as still existed or were to emerge – old and new village notables, heads of agricultural cooperatives, trade-union leaders, directors of public-sector companies, party-section and party-branch bosses, and others – would only rise through regime-controlled organizations. The regime has gained wide-ranging, if by no means total autonomy from society. Although it has secured a considerable rent income, it is anything but independent from domestic resources, and it cannot survive politically without a social basis of support. It has managed, though, not to make itself dependent on the support of one particular societal stratum alone. Loss of support from the salaried middle classes in particular could be compensated by increasing support from the business community. Most importantly, the regime has kept its own apparatus, the popular organizations it has created, and the forces of civil society under control. Any outright anti-regime opposition, as soon as it tried to organize and to challenge the regime, found itself virtually at war with the state, and was crushed.

Those old and new strongmen, however, who were allowed to gain local and sectoral influence or, moreover, to become national power-brokers and patrons, had to exercise their influence through channels provided or, at least, controlled by the state, and thereby invest their own power resources in the system. A village notable, for instance, who joined the Peasant Union and the party, became head of a cooperative and was thereby able to divert some of its resources for his family's and his personal clientele's well-being, would at the same time strengthen regime control: he would enhance, by means of his local position and standing, the execution of government programmes and production plans in the village, would mobilize his clientele for elections and use these and other occasions to prove his and his clientele's support for party and President. He would, in other words, comply with and make his environment comply with the demands of government and regime, and participate in the organizational structure that state and regime provide. Similarly, a businessman who ran and suceeded as an independent candidate for parliament would certainly increase his personal prestige and influence, would probably become able to mediate access to the government, and to raise issues in parliament that he considered important. At the same time, he would enhance the legitimacy of a parliamentary body whose rights remain closely circumscribed and defined by the executive.

The state does not, despite its deep penetration into society, control, let alone regulate, all spheres of life. The state, under Asad's regime, has become authoritarian, not totalitarian. There is no all-encompassing ideology which state and regime would offer or try to enforce on the population. Ba'thism and Arab nationalism, as noted, have been watered down so as not to stand in the way of the pragmatic realpolitik of the regime. The personality cult around the President, including attempts at fabricating a charisma that extends to his offspring, does not make an ideology. Asadism, so to speak, depoliticizes: it implies that Syria's future is guaranteed as long as Asad is at the helm, and that neither the party, nor government, parliament or civil society should worry about or deal with the country's high policies as long as the leader does so. The regime demands that everyone pay respect to its symbols and refrain from questioning the absolute leadership of the President. Those who speak in a public function should, moreover, make their allegiance to the President known, and preferably do so with proper emphasis. The regime does not, however, prescribe what people should believe, whether they orient themselves to Western modes of living and behaviour, stick to Arabism or some form of *tiers-mondisme*, or – as Syrians have increasingly done, particularly from the mid-1980s – embrace a politically quietistic, but otherwise outspoken form of Islam, including a demonstrative public piety and the strict application of the norms of Islamic morality.

The regime has also never seriously attempted, since Asad's assumption of power, to establish an outright centrally planned economy. Only in agriculture has the government tried to enforce production plans on the private sector; otherwise, state plans were only binding for the public sector – whatever that meant in practice.

The regime aimed at leading the national economy by means of the public sector, maintaining a public-sector monopoly over certain "strategic" fields of the economy, and controlling the allocation of scarce resources, especially foreign exchange. On the whole, it was not too successful in this respect, and economic space has been largely negotiable. In general, as outlined, not economic and development questions but national and regime strength, and the maintenance of control have been the prime concern of the regime.[169] Syria has therefore, as will be shown in the next chapter, successfully sought to prevent any foreign interference in its economic policy-making. However, the regime has not, as a rule, prevented Syria's businessmen from doing business as long as that did not affect, or threaten to affect, its political control. Economic rationalities were, in case of doubt, subjugated to a rationality of control and regime maintenance. The regime would not, for instance, simply to attract more foreign or expatriate investment, cut the powers of its security services, grant independence to the judiciary and establish the rule of law. It would instead, and probably armed with better knowledge, seek to claim that the regime's stability and longevity were essential elements of a proper investment climate.[170] Similarly, as outlined, the regime has tolerated, if not actually fostered, the spread of corruption and clientelism and thus allowed serious misallocations of resources. In view of the patronage networks that frequently cut across legal-bureaucratic chains of command, the need for *wasta* to secure access, or the arbitrary exercise of control by the security services, enervated Syrians occasionally claim that there is virtually "no state" in Syria. In fact, what they see and deplore is not the absence of the state but rather the weakness of its institutions – even of those institutions which the regime itself has created as constitutional links between state and society. What the current role of these institutions and of the country's main political actors in a specific field of policy-making is, the following chapter will try to examine.

Notes

1. The one, of course, is closely related to the other: the fear, on the part of those who are at the helm that a breakdown of their control over society might increase external threats is not totally without substance, particularly in a tension-laden environment. Cf. Migdal, *Strong Societies*, p 24.

2. The experimental character of the system during that period may be illustrated by the fact that highest political and legislative authority was consecutively exercised by such different institutions as a mainly military National Council for Revolutionary Command, an appointed legislative council known as the National Council of the Revolution, a Presidential Council elected by this latter Council, the Ba'th party's pan-Arab National Command, its Syrian Regional Command, and the cabinet. Cf. Petran, *Syria*, pp 167ff; Rabinovich, *Syria*, pp 171ff; Amin Isbar, *Tatawwur al-nuzum al-siyasiyya wa-l-dusturiyya fi suriya, 1946–1973.*

3. Cf. Richards/Waterbury, *A Political Economy of the Middle East*, p 337. Cf. also Robert Bianchi, *Unruly Corporatism*; Khaldun Hasan al-Naqib, *al-Dawla al-tasallutiyya fi al-mashriq al-'arabi al-mu'asir*, pp 183ff, 337f.

4. Cf. Ulrich von Alemann/Rolf G. Heinze, "Kooperativer Staat und Korporatismus", in: Ulrich von Alemann (ed), *Neokorporatismus*; Richards/ Waterbury, *Political Economy*, pp 337ff.

5. Richards/Waterbury, *Political Economy*, p 338.

6. Cf. Yusuf Murish, *al-Jabha al-wataniyya al-taqaddumiyya wa-l-ta'addudiyya fi al-qutr al-'arabi al-suri*, p 37.

7. Cf. Asad's speech of 10 March 1980, *al-Ba'th*, 11 March 1980. Cf. also his speech of 14 December 1992, *al-Ba'th*, 15 December 1992.

8. Cf. e.g. the contribution of Syrian vice-president Zuhayr Masharqa in the series "al-Ahzab al-suriyya wa-as'ilat al-marhala" [The Syrian Parties and the Questions of the Present Stage], *al-Hayat*, 3–6 June 1993 (3 June).

9. Documented in ASBP, National Command, *Nidal hizb al-ba'th*, pp 115–121.

10. Cf. Mayer, "Islamic Opposition"; Drysdale, "The Asad Regime"; Seurat, "L'État de barbarie, Syrie 1979–1982", in: idem, *L'État de Barbarie* (Paris: Seuil, 1989); Lobmeyer, "Islamic Ideology".

11. Cf. e.g. Michel Seurat, "Terrorisme d'État, terrorisme contre l'État", in: idem, *L'État de Barbarie*; Middle East Watch Committee (ed), *Syria Unmasked*, pp 8–21.

12. Estimates on the death toll vary considerably. Patrick Seale estimates the number at 5,000 to 10,000. Cf. his *Asad*. Oppositional sources put the number as high as 46,000. Cf. Sadiq, *Hiwar*, p 167.

13. Council of Ministers, Decisions Nos. 1, 2, and 3/1980.

14. Some of the arrested lawyers remained imprisoned till 1989. Cf. Middle East Watch, *Syria Unmasked*, pp 85ff.

15. *Sham*: Arabic for Syria or Damascus.

16. Cf. e.g. Hafiz al-Asad's speech to parliament, 12 March 1992, *al-Ba'th*, 13 March 1992; Prime Minister Zu'abi's policy statement of 18 November 1992, documented in *SWB/ME*, 21 November 1992. The new discourse has also found its expression in political literature; cf. e.g. Murish, *al-Jabha al-wataniyya.*

17. Cf. Asad's speech at the Fifth General Conference of the Revolutionary Youth Organization, 8 March 1990, *Tishrin*, 9 March 1990.

18. Cf. Legislative Decree 2/1990.

19. Hinnebusch, *Authoritarian Power*.

20. Syria's "Permanent Constitution" of 13 March 1973 is documented, in English translation, in the *Middle East Journal*, Vol. 28 (1974), pp 53–66. Articles 83–114 deal with the powers and functions of the president of the republic.

21. Article 9. The introduction of the PNF Charter and its by-laws are documented in Murish, *al-Jabha*, pp 150–158. The complete text was published in *al-Thawra*, 8 March 1972.

22. Cf. Petzold, *Staatsmacht und Demokratie*, pp 108f.

23. GFTU, *Mu'tamar al-ibda'*, p 240.

24. The *Umaya* Co. for Paints in Damascus may serve as a particularly illustrative example. In 1989, some 250 persons were on its payroll, 80 of them working in production, the same number in clerical jobs. There were 26 guards and eight persons running the party cell; the rest were drivers, cleaners, caretakers, doormen, and office boys. For further examples, cf. Hinnebusch, *Peasant*, p 297; Hannoyer/Seurat, *État et secteur public*, p 88.

25. Cf. the statement of former Minister of Industry, Husayn al-Qadi, in: Economic Sciences Association, *Fifth Economic Tuesday Symposium, On Economic Development in the Syrian Arab Region, Damascus, 14 January – 29 April 1986* (Damascus: n.d. [1986]), p 78; GFTU, *Mu'tamar al-ibda'*, p 39f.

26. Cf. MEFT, *Taqrir hawl asalib tatwir al-qita' al-'amm* [Report on the Methods of Developing the Public Sector], unpublished typescript, undated (1992), p 4.

27. Cf. GFTU, *Mu'tamar al-ibda'*, p 41.

28. Cf. ibid., p 254; MEFT, *Taqrir*, pp 2f.

29. The structure of Syria's public sector and the functions of each administrative level have last been defined by Legislative Decree 18/1974 on the organization of the industrial public sector, and Law 1/1976 on the organization of the public construction companies.

30. Cf. MEFT, *Taqrir*, p 2.

31. SAR, State Planning Authority, *Taqrir taqwim al-khitta al-khamsiyya al-khamisa, 1981–1985*, p 186.

32. Among the permanent government committees headed by the Prime Minister, there are the Committee for the Guidance of Imports, Exports, and Consumption,*ᶠ* and the Higher Councils for Planning, for Agriculture, for Companies (in charge of the public-sector construction companies), for Investment (in charge of licensing private investments falling under the 1991 investment law), for Tourism, and for Capacities (istia'b) (in charge of distributing students among the institutions of higher education).

33. Rabo, *Change on the Euphrates*, p 134.

34. Cf. GFTU, *Mu'tamar al-ibda'*, p 37.

35. This has been particularly emphasized by Raymond Hinnebusch. Cf. both his *Peasant* and *Authoritarian Power*.

36. Cf., among others, Fadia Kiwan, *La tradition des coups d'État*.

37. Cf. ASBP, National Command, *Ba'd al-muntaliqat*, pp 6of.

38. Cf. Rabinovich, *Syria*; Sami al-Jundi, *Attahaddi ... wa-attahim*; Munif al-Razzaz, "al-Tajriba al-murra", in: idem, *al-A'mal al-fikriyya wa-l-siyasiyya*.

39. Source: International Institute for Strategic Studies (IISS), *The Military Balance* (London: Brassey's, various years).

40. Some two-thirds of this number may be with the police, the rest with the security services. An additional 30,000 or so mukhabarat full-timers can be estimated to be with the military security services, and thus part of the regular military. This very rough and conservative estimate of not more than some 60,000–70,000 full-time agents of the security services remains much below figures traded by oppositional groups. For an equally conservative estimate, cf. Middle East Watch, *Syria Unmasked*, p 41. Sadiq's, *Hiwar hawl suriya*, a well-informed though not always reliable, and sometimes inconsistent source, speaks of 360,000 full-timers with the security services at one place, and of 250,000–300,000 at another (pp 84, 129). There is no doubt that the total number of those working for the security services in one form or another, including part-timers and occasional collaborators and informers, amounts to several hundred thousand.

41. 1991 figures. Source: GFTU, *22nd Conference*, p 314.

42. Compulsory military education was introduced in 1974. Cf. e.g. Sa'id Matar/Kabri'il al-Shami, "Athbat al-talaba qidratahum 'ala haml al-kitab bi-yad wa-l-silah bi-l-yad al-ukhra" [Students Have Proved Their Ability to Carry the Book in One Hand and the Weapon in the Other], *Tishrin*, 14 August 1989.

43. These militias and the permanent army reserve add up to about the same number as the standing military force.

44. These four services are the General Intelligence (al-Mukhabarat al-'amma) which formally belongs to the Ministry of Interior but practically constitutes an independent state-security authority; Political Security (al-Amn al-siyasi) which is an agency of the Ministry of Interior; Military Intelligence (al-Mukhabarat al-'askariyya); and the National Security Bureau (Maktab al-amn al-qawmi) of the Ba'th party Regional Command. All of these agencies have mainly domestic control functions; all, except for the party's Security Bureau, are headed by military officers. The heads of each service report directly to the President. There are a couple of other and special-purpose services such as the Air Force Intelligence, as well as quasi-independent sub-branches of the General Intelligence and the Military Intelligence. For a directory of Syria's security services, cf. Middle East Watch, *Syria Unmasked*, pp 48–51.

45. Cf. the annual reports of Amnesty International (London); *al-Hayat*, 24 February 1994.

46. Evidence for the spread of corruption and other illicit gains inside or outside the security apparatus is, quite naturally, largely anecdotal. Cf., e.g., Yahya M. Sadowski, "Cadres, Guns, and Money. The Eighth Regional Congress of the Syrian Ba'th", *MERIP Reports*, Vol 15 (July–August 1985), No. 134, pp 3–8; Seale, *Asad*, pp 317ff.

47. Cf. Elizabeth Picard, "Arab Military in Politics: From Revolutionary Plot to Authoritarian Regime", in Luciani (ed), *The Arab State*, p 210. Precise data on military and civilian salaries are not available. On the basis of unpublished data from the Ministry of Finance, we may estimate the 1993 average monthly salary in the military and security – excluding conscripts who only receive a virtual pocket money – to hover around LS 5,000. The average salary in the public administration ranged around LS 3,000–3,500.

48. Cf. Seurat, "Les populations", pp 135f.

49. On the events of early 1984 cf. Drysdale, "The Succession Question"; Seale, *Asad*, pp 419 ff.

50. Cf. Seurat, "Les populations", pp 135f.

51. Cf. Elizabeth Picard, "Clans militaires", p 62.

52. Cf. SAR, Ministry of Defence, Mu'assasat al-iskan al-'askariyya [Milihouse], "Mudhakkira ila al-sayyid ra'is majlis al-wuzara'" [Memo to the Prime Minister] (March 1986, xeroxed typescript).

53. Cf. Seale, *Asad*, pp 323, 482. The replacement of Jamil and Haidar was reportedly due to signs of disloyalty, that of Khuly to the involvement of the airforce intelligence in acts of international terrorism, *Le Monde*, 18 August 1994.

54. Cf. Seale, *Asad*, p 427.

55. Cf. Kamel S. Abu Jaber, *The Arab Ba'th Socialist Party*, p 144.

56. Cf. ASBP, *Reports and Decisions of the Fifth Extra-Ordinary Regional Conference convened in Damascus 30 May – 13 June 1974* (Damascus, 1974), p 33.

57. Cf. Lobmeyer, "Islamic Ideology", p 398; Yahya M. Sadowski, "Ba'thist Ethics and the Spirit of State Capitalism, in Peter J. Chelkowski/Robert J. Pranger (eds), *Ideology and Power in the Middle East. Studies in Honor of George Lenczowski* (Durham/London: Praeger, 1988), p 167.

58. Cf. ASBP, *Fifth Regional Conference*, p 33; idem, *Reports and Decisions of the Eighth Regional Conference convened in Damascus 5 – 20 January 1985. Organizational Report*, pp 47, 57.

59. Author's interview with ASBP RC-member Ahmad Dirgham, 1992.

60. Exact data are not available. The estimate is based on data in ASBP, *Reports and Decisions of the Seventh Regional Conference convened in Damascus 22 December 1979 – 6 January 1980. Organizational Report*, p 28.

61. Cf. ASBP, *Eighth Regional Conference. Organizational Report*, p 47.

62. Quoted from ASBP, National Command, *Nidal*, p 127.

63. Cf. ASBP, *Seventh Regional Conference. Organizational Report*, p 115; *Eighth Regional Conference. Organizational Report*, p 313.

64. Cf. Sadowski, "Cadres, Guns, and Money".

65. Cf. ASBP, *Seventh Regional Conference. Organizational Report*, pp 15ff, 113ff; *Eighth Regional Conference. Organizational Report*, pp 30f.

66. Cf. Seale, *Asad*, p 439. For a general, broader overview of the party structure, cf. Hinnebusch, *Authoritarian Power*, pp 166ff.

67. There is another Ba'th party NC in Baghdad, headed by Saddam Husayn.

68. Author's interviews with members of the National and Regional Command of the party.

69. Law No. 53/1979.

70. Cf. *Eighth Regional Conference. Organizational Report*, pp 303f. Later data are not available. Government budgets do not show this allowance to the party which, in 1983, about equalled the budget of the Ministry of Finance.

71. Cf. Sadowski, "Cadres, Guns, and Money"; and ASBP, *Seventh Regional Conference. Economic Report*; *Eighth Regional Conference. Economic Report*.

72. Cf. *Eighth Regional Conference. Organizational Report*, pp 313f.

73. Author's interviews, 1992.

74. *Tishrin*, 8 June 1989.

75. At the 1979/1980 party conference, the limits of inner-party democracy were frankly defined. There was, it went in the conference report, a misunderstanding of democracy, according to which some comrades had thought they could even criticize the general strategy of the party "offending thereby the spirit of democratic centralism and exceeding the competences of the democratic institutions in the party." Cf. ASBP, *Seventh Regional Conference. Organizational Report*, p 19.

76. Quite expressive for this tendency was a symposium which the Indoctrination Office of the RC organized in 1992 on the "Methodology, Constants, and Visions of President Hafiz al-Asad". Cf. *al-Kifah al-'arabi*, 1 June 1992. Still in 1986–88, an attempt had been made to lead a somewhat more deepgoing ideological discussion in the party and between the party and the public. For this purpose, the same party office organized a series of three symposiums on, respectively, Arab unity, freedom, and socialism. The symposiums were well attended but not really successful from the perspective of the party leadership which had to listen to many critical remarks and could not convincingly prove that its policies had brought Syria or the Arab world closer to either unity, freedom, or socialism. The experiment was not repeated.

77. Cf. *al-Ba'th*, 27 May 1987.

78. Cf. ASBP, *Eighth Regional Conference. Organizational Report*, pp 258f.

79. Ibid., pp 98f. According to the report, there were 579,883 workers in Syria. Among this number, more than 260,000 are listed as being of unknown political leanings. These all either work abroad or are employed by the private sector, particularly in transport and construction (where people work individually, as drivers, or where small family companies with largely seasonal labour prevail). This implies that the party assumes it knows the political orientation of every worker in the public sector and of a large part of those in bigger private-sector entities.

80. Cf. ibid., pp 16, 37.

81. Author's interviews, 1992–93. Cf. also Hamash, *al-Tanmiya*, p 151.

82. ASBP, *Eighth Regional Conference. Organizational Report*, p 313. Cf. also *Seventh Regional Conference. Organizational Report*, p 19.

83. Cf. Sadowski, "Ba'thist Ethics", and section 4 of this chapter.

84. Cf. e.g. Syrian vice-president Zuhayr Masharqa in *al-Hayat*, 3 June 1993.

85. Presidential Decree No. 35/22 May 1971, quoted from Murish, *al-Jabha al-wataniyya*, pp 117f.

86. Faisal's party is also referred to as the United Syrian Communist Party since its inclusion in 1991 of members of a party group under the leadership of Murad Yusuf that had broken away from the mother party in 1974.

87. Estimates on the strength of the parties are based on author's interviews and the assessment of the Ba'th party in ASBP, *Eighth Regional Conference. Organizational Report.*

88. In 1972, Riadh Turk broke away from the official SCP, taking with him, according to SCP (Faisal) politburo member Maurice Salibi, some 5–6,000 of then 12,000 party members. Author's interview, 1990. Turk and other leading members of his group have been imprisoned since 1980 or longer.

89. Cf. SCP, *Fifth Conference*, pp 47f; Khalid Bakdash, *al-Taqrir al-siyasi ila al-mu'tamar al-sadis li-l-hizb al-shuyu'i al-suri awasit tamuz 1986*, p 25.

90. Cf. e.g. SCP (Bakdash), *Hawl ba'd al-tatawwurat wa-l-tadabir al-iqtisadiyya fi suriya.*

91. Cf. e.g. the interview with Khalid Bakdash in *al-Hayat*, 4 April 1993; the contribution of Yusuf Faisal in the *al-Hayat* series on Syrian parties, 4 June 1993; and in the same direction the contributions of Ya'qub Karm in *Tishrin*, 10 March 1992, and Daniel Na'ama in Murish, *al-Jabha al-wataniyya*, p 256.

92. Cf. the contribution of 'Abd al-Ghani Qanut, *al-Hayat*, 6 June 1993.

93. Cf. the contributions of the party leaders in Murish, *al-Jabha al-wataniyya*, pp 233, 241, 245.

94. Safwan Qudsi, *al-Batal wa-l-tarikh.*

95. The youngest party leader, Safwan Qudsi of the ASU, assumed the leadership of his party in 1983. Ahmad al-As'ad has been at the head of the Democratic Socialist Unionists since 1974. 'Abd al-Ghani Qanut has led the Arab Socialists since 1964, Fa'iz Isma'il the Socialist Unionists since 1963. Unbeatable is Khalid Bakdash (born 1912) who has been the secretary-general of the SCP since 1937. His rival Yusuf Faisal, secretary-general of his own wing of the SCP since the party split of 1986, has himself been a member of the SCP central committee since 1954. Cf. in general the somewhat fragmentary biographical notes in Murish, *al-Jabha al-wataniyya*; on Bakdash, also briefly, *al-Hayat*, 4 June 1993.

96. Author's interview, 1992.

97. Socialist Unionist leader Isma'il, for instance, holds that with the establishment of the PNF "the phenomenon of party conflict and negative competition was overcome once and for all." Quoted from Murish, *al-Jabha al-wataniyya*, p 265.

98. Cf. Rabinovich, *Syria*, pp 172ff; Isbar, *Tatawwur*, pp 98ff.

99. 1977, 1981, 1986, 1990, and 1994.

100. Isbar, *Tatawwur*, p 103.

101. Elizabeth Picard, "Syria returns to Democracy".

102. Cf. ibid.; and Picard, "L'emprise du général Assad sur l'État syrien se renforce", *Maghreb-Mashrek*, No. 80, pp 13–14; and "La Syrie de 1946 à 1979"; Seurat, "Les populations". No data were available on electoral participation in the 1980s and 1990s. The fact, however, that all these elections, like previous ones, were held on two consecutive days – which automatically happens if less than 50 per cent of those eligible to vote participate on the official (first) polling day – indicates that participation remained low.

103. Officially, the 1990 legislative comprised 134 Ba'thists, 32 deputies for the rest of the PNF, and 84 independents.

104. Cf. more detailed Volker Perthes, "Syria's Parliamentary Elections. Remodelling Asad's Political Base", *Middle East Report*, Vol 22 (January/ February 1992), No. 174, pp 15–18.

105. Cf. *al-Thawra*, 1 January 1992.

106. Vice-president Zuhayr Masharqa in *al-Hayat*, 3 June 1993.

107. Cf. e.g. Trade Union Law 84/1968 and amendments (Law 29/1986); Law 21/1974 on the Peasant Union; Law 33/1975 on the Women's Union; and SAR, Ministry of Information, *Suriya al-thawra fi 'amiha al-rabi' 'ashar*, pp 242ff.

108. Cf. ASBP, *Eighth Regional Conference. Organizational Report*, p 197.

109. Cf. ibid., pp 218f, 231.

110. Cf. ibid., p 198.

111. Cf. Law 39/1981 on the Lawyers Union.

112. Cf. GFTU, *The 22nd Conference*, p 22; author's interviews.

113. Cf. GFTU, *22nd Conference*, p 23. Public-sector employees are unionized almost automatically, occasionally without even having to apply for membership; cf. Longuenesse, "Syrian Working Class".

114. Ahmad Suwaydan, *Ma'ziq al-'amal al-niqabi fi suriya*, p 106.

115. Cf. Rabinovich, *Syria*, pp 173f.

116. Law 55/16 April 1964.

117. GFTU, *Proceedings and Decisions of the 17th Conference*, pp 16f. These duties of the trade unions as listed in Nasif's speech partly resembled what Trade Union Law 84/26 June 1968 called for. Nasif, however, fell behind that law which also stipulated the unions' obligation to "serve the material interests of the workers" and "defend their rights" (article 17).

118. GFTU, *17th Conference*, p 15.

119. GFTU, *Proceeedings, Decisions and Recommendations of the 18th Conference*, p 34.

120. Ibid., pp 35f.

121. Ibid., pp 36f.

122. 'Izz al-Din Nasir, an Alawi from Banias, is regarded one of Asad's closest civilian followers and a powerful secondary patron himself. He and his closest aides have been at the top of the GFTU for an unprecedented long period. In 1977, Nasir became GFTU president for the first time, in 1992, he was last re-elected for another five years. Of the nine-member executive

committee of the GFTU elected in 1978, eight members were still in office after the 1992 conference, one had died. Nasir became a member of the Regional Command of the Ba'th party in 1980.

123. The lowest organizational level of the trade unions is the shop-floor or local committee. The next organizational level is made up of the provincial unions for each industry. There is a countrywide federation of unions for each industry, and a provincial federation of trade unions bringing together the different industrial unions in a particular province. The central level, superior both to the provincial federations and the industrial federations, is the General Federation of Trade Unions. The centralization, bureaucratization and strengthening of the trade union apparatus becomes evident if one follows successive trade-union laws and their amendments. Thus, for instance, union functionaries became ex-officio members of their respective union conferences through a 1971 amendment of Trade Union Law 84/1968. In 1971 too, public funding of trade unions became regulated by law. Since 1980, public sector firms have been obliged to deduct union membership fees directly from the salaries. In 1982, the share in membership fees accruing to the GFTU executive was raised by law from 15 to 20 per cent at the expense of the subordinate levels. As of 1974, workers' representatives on the boards of public sector establishments had to be appointed by the union leadership instead of – as had been the case before – being elected by the workers. In the same year, the electoral period of the executive committees on all levels was made four instead of two years; in 1980, it was made five years. The central executive closely monitors the activities of the subordinate union structures. The General Report to the 1982 20th Conference, for example, stresses the need for the "highest union authorities ... to compare the minutes of meetings of subordinate sections with (its) own knowledge and to make sure that (the lower levels' work) is in accordance with the general program" (p 120).

124. Author's interviews, and observations at the GFTU's 21st Conference in 1986. Cf. also Longuenesse, "État et syndicalisme", pp 104f.

125. al-Ishtiraki, 26 December, 1970, 14 June 1976, 21 June 1976.

126. Cf. GFTU, *The 21st Conference of the General Federation of Trade Unions in the Syrian Arab Republic. General Report*, pp 123f.

127. Law No. 1/1985: Unified Labour Law for Those Working with the State.

128. Ibid., articles 64, 65.

129. Cf. *22nd Conference 1992*, pp 128ff.

130. Cf. in general: GFTU, *al-Khidmat al-ijtima'iyya al-'umaliyya. Suwwar wa-arqam*; GFTU, *21st Conference 1986*, pp 124ff; *22nd Conference 1992*, pp 99ff.

131. Such committees are to be constituted in each factory or public-sector unit; they are to consist of the directors, the trade union committee, the party committee, and some excellent workers chosen by the director. Despite their merely consultative functions, there are, according to the complaints of unionists, still many directors who prevent their establishment or ignore all their

proposals. Cf. e.g. GFTU, *21st Conference 1986. Economic Report*, pp 85f.; *22nd Conference 1992*, p 376; cf. also with a quite optimistic assessment of the production councils, Hannoyer/Seurat, *État et secteur public*, pp 33ff.

132. Cf. e.g. Tamir Habil, "Ma huwa dawr sharikat al-insha'at al-'amma?" [What's the Role of Public-Sector Construction Companies?], *al-Ishtiraki*, 12 January 1981; Amin Habash, "Jawla midaniyya fi qita' al-bina' bi-Dimashq" [A Tour through the Construction Sector of Damascus], *al-Ishtiraki*, 3 June 1983.

133. Author's interview with GFTU secretary-general 'Auda Qasis, 1988.

134. Cf. Seurat, "Les populations", pp 133f; Longuenesse, "Syrian Working Class", p 24.

135. Isma'il Jaradat, "Niqabat 'ummal al-tiba'a wa-l-thaqafa wa-l-i'lam tada' tasawwuratiha li-tatwir al-mustawa al-tanzimi wa-l-fikri" [The Union of Printers, Cultural Workers and Media Workers lays down its Ideas about Raising the Organizational and Intellectual Level], *al-Thawra*, 9 Feb. 1989. Cf. also Longuenesse, "'État et syndicalisme".

136. Until 1985, the trade unions were occasionally able to negotiate collective labour contracts with the management of public-sector companies. Since the Unified Labour Law (Law 1/1985) has practically turned everyone in the public sector into a civil servant, subject to unified wage categories and tables, there is no longer any space for such negotiations. Still, the trade-union leadership may bargain for wage rises with the government; the decision, however, is in the hands of the government and the President.

137. Author's interviews.

138. Cf. *al-Ishtiraki*, 6 June 1983. To the author's knowledge, this unsuccessful venture has been the only attempt on the part of a union to boycott a private employer.

139. Cf. Hannoyer/Seurat, *État et secteur public*, p 64; Seurat, "La société syrienne", in idem, *L'État de barbarie*, p 77; Longuenesse, "État et syndicalisme", p 108.

140. Author's interviews with GFTU secretary-general Qasis and other trade unionists, 1988–93. For Asad's remarks on workers' participation and their ownership of the public sector see his speeches of 10 March 1980 and 16 November 1986, *al-Ba'th*, 11 March 1980, 17 November 1986.

141. Not surprisingly, therefore, the Ministry of Economy, which itself has little influence over the public sector, has complained that trade-union interference in public-sector affairs exceeds their representation on the company boards. Cf. MEFT, *Taqrir*, pp 9f.

142. The often-heard argument of Syrian trade-union, party, or government functionaries that there are no conflicts or problems between the party, the unions, the government, the public-sector management, and its workforce (in any combination) contains therefore an element of truth, namely the strong interest in finding not necessarily democratic, but consensual, non-conflictual solutions. As a matter of fact, "democratic" in the discourse of Syrian party or government functionaries, often simply means consensual.

143. Cf. below, chapter V.

144. Cf. Sadowski, "Ba'thist Ethics", and idem, "Patronage and the Ba'th: Corruption and Control in Contemporary Syria", *Arab Studies Quarterly*, Vol 9 (1987), pp 442–461.

145. Rabo, *Change on the Euphrates*, p 170.

146. There are cross-sectarian and cross-regional networks too, based on other than primordial ties, namely common education, professional or political background, membership in popular organizations, affiliation to a particular military unit or government authority, or business. Most prominently, Rif'at al-Asad used to patronize a large confessionally mixed business-and-military network. The network of Jamil al-Asad, who figures as the local patron in Latakia, is similarly confessionally diverse. Elizabeth Picard notes that "les associations financières entre militaires et civils ... utilisent de préférence les solidarités ethniques, mais ne connaissent pas de frontière ethnique." Cf. her "Critique de l'usage du concept d'ethnicité dans l'analyse des processus politiques dans le monde arabe", in *Études politiques du monde arabe. Approches globales et approches spécifiques* (Cairo: CEDEJ, 1991), p 80.

147. Among the bulk of more recent articles that deal with Syria's regime elite, only few have analytical depth. Cf. particularly Kienle, "Entre jama'a et classe"; Picard, "Critique".

148. Cf. Kienle, "Entre jama'a et classe"; Seale, *Asad*, pp 427ff.

149. Cf. Pipes, "L'après-Assad", p 103.

150. According to Kienle, "Entre jama'a et classe", p 218, the Alawi proportion among cadets of the military academy in Homs may reach up to 90 per cent.

151. There are no data on the sectarian composition of the staff in government service; evidence stems from author's interviews and observations. As regards party leadership and cabinet positions, van Dam has shown in his study on the 1963–76 period that the proportion of Alawis – who might constitute some 10–15 per cent of the total population – rose enormously after 1963, peaked in the 1966–70 period, and decreased again after Asad's takeover. Only from 1966 to 1970 were Alawis represented proportionately or somewhat over-proportionally in the government; before that they were heavily, after that slightly under-represented. In the RC, they were significantly over-represented from 1966–70, and have been somewhat over-represented since. In the RC constituted at the party's 1985 conference, four out of 21 members, including the President and his brother, were Alawis. Cf. van Dam, "Sectarian and Regional Factionalism"; Drysdale, "Syrian Political Elite"; Elizabeth Picard, "Y a-t-il un problème communautaire en Syrie?", pp 7–21.

152. Daniel Pipes, "The Alawi Capture of Power in Syria", *Middle Eastern Studies*, Vol 25 (1989), pp 429–450. Cf. also Mahmud A. Faksh, "The Alawi Community of Syria: A New Dominant Political Force", *Middle Eastern Studies*, Vol 20 (1984), pp 133–153, and others.

153. Cf. Picard, "Critique", p 77; Drysdale, "Syrian Political Elite", pp 15f.

154. Cf. Picard, "Y a-t-il un problème?", p 18.

155. Cf. Drysdale, "Syrian Political Elite"; Nikolaos Van Dam, "Middle Eastern Political Clichés.

156. Some authors claim the opposite. Cf. Michel Seurat, "Vague d'agitation confessionelle en Syrie", in idem, *L'État de barbarie*, pp 65ff; Kienle, "Entre jama'a et classe", pp 218f. Kienle correctly notes that such a favouring the coastal provinces is difficult to prove on the basis of official statistics, referring this to statistical manipulations, however, rather than to lack of factual evidence.

157. Cf. Kienle, ibid., p 219.

158. Cf. Sufuh Khayr, *Suriya. Dirasa fi al-bina' al-hadari wa-l-kiyan al-iqtisadi*, pp 137, 303ff.

159. Figures are for 1988. Source: Samu'il 'Abud, "ikhtilal tawazzu' al-tanmiya makaniyan wa-dawr al-takhtit al-iqlimi fi i'adat tawazuniha fi al-qutr al-'arabi al-suri" [Regional Imbalances of Development and the Role of Regional Planning for its Rebalancing in the Syrian Arab Region], (mimeographed paper, Training Course for Planning Cadres, 30 November – 12 December 1991, Planning Institute for Social Development, Damascus). More recent figures do not show any different trends. Thus, for instance, only ten of 428 large private investment projects licensed under the provisions of the 1991 investment law till mid-1992 were located in the province of Latakia.

160. Cf. Robert D. Kaplan, "Syria – Identity Crisis", *The Atlantic*, p 27. The existence of a group of Syrian Alawis who under the French Mandate (1920–1943/46) supported the French divide-and-rule policies which included the establishment of an Alawi state (or State of Latakia) on the Syrian coast does, however, not really prove that the Alawis are eternal separatists. Nor does the fact that a (minority) faction among Syria's Druze population at that time attempted to sever the Jabal Druze region from Syria and make it part of (Trans)Jordan speak for such separatist tendencies of Syria's contemporary Druze, as Kaplan suggests. Cf. Birgit Schäbler, "Der 'Drusenaufstand' in Syrien. Zum Verhältnis von Ethnizität und sozialer Bewegung", *Blätter des iz3w*, (February 1994), No. 195, pp 37–41.

161. Cf. Hashim 'Uthman, *al-'Alawiyun bayn al-ustura wa-l-haqiqa* [The Alawis between Myth and Truth] (Beirut: Mu'assasat al-a'la li-l-matbu'at, 2nd ed. 1985); 'Abd al-Rahman Khayyir, *'Aqidatuna wa-waqi'na nahn al-muslimin al-ja'fariyin al-'alawiyin*; idem, N*aqd wa-taqriz kitab tarikh al-'alawiyin;* idem, *risala tabhath fi masa'il muhimma hawl al-madhhab al-ja'fari al-'alawi.*

162. It should be noted that both petty and grand corruption are anything but a Syrian, or a Third-World phenomenon. Even highly industrialized and democratic states such as Germany or Italy have lately been forced to face the problem of excessive civil-service and government corruption. Since public resources in a country like Syria, however, are more limited, corruption drains them more intensely and affects these countries' economies more heavily. Moreover, the lack of publicity, public control, and government accountability, adds to corruption in Syria and comparable countries its particular political dimension.

163. Hinnebusch, "Syria under the Ba'th", p 185.

164. On Rif'at al-Asad and his record of corruption, cf. e.g. Stanley F. Reed, "Dateline Syria: Fin de Régime?", *Foreign Policy* (Summer 1980), No. 39, pp 176–190; Drysdale, "The Succession Question"; on Ahmar: Tammam al-Barazi, "Syrian Corruption", *The New Statesman*, 5 September 1980; Sadiq, *Hiwar hawl suriya*, p 70.

165. In 1987, Industry Minister Nabulsi lost his job, among other things, because of corruption charges.

166. Cf. Sadowski, "Ba'thist Ethics", p 183.

167. Cf. Migdal, *Strong Societies*, pp 32f.

168. The provisional constitution of 1964 was suspended, and the National Council of 1965 was disbanded with the party-and-state coup of February 1966.

169. Cf. above, Chapter II.2.

170. Author's interviews, Damascus. Cf., with the same argument, the interview with Minister of Industry Ahmad Nizam al-Din in *al-Thawra*, 16 April 1994; Munir al-Hamash (ed), *al-Istithmar fi suriya. As'ila wa-ajwiba*, p 34.

CHAPTER FIVE

Economic Policies and Political Decision-Making

Syria's policies of economic transition present a particularly interesting case for the study of economic policy formation and decision-making because they have been largely home-made. In other words, as the reform and adjustment policies pursued by Syria since the mid-1980s have been designed with little if any help or interference from international financial agencies or other external actors, economic policies in Syria can be regarded as primarily a function of local factors. Syria can serve as a laboratory case of sorts, displaying, to a certain degree, the internal dynamics of an adapting authoritarian system whose state-capitalist strategy of development was bound to run into crisis.

1. The Absence of External Interference

In contrast to countries like Egypt, whose development path is seen by many a Syrian observer as the model Syria is following with something like a decade's time lag, and unlike most other adjusting countries in the Arab world, Syria has never, to date, allowed bilateral donors or international financial institutions to interfere in any substantial way with its economic policies, nor negotiated aid for economic reform programmes. Even during the worst years of the crisis of the 1980s, the Syrian government did not ask for IMF standby credits or other IMF facilities that would have involved commitments to a particular reform course, or concluded any agreement on structural adjustment programmes with the World Bank. It seems that the alternative of doing so has never seriously been considered among Syrian policy-makers.[1] The refusal to negotiate their economic policies with international donors or financial institutions may result as much from the Syrian leadership's fear of losing control over domestic affairs as from their fear of jeopardizing what was left of its patriotic or national credentials. Whatever the main reason, where choices had to be made, Syrian policy-makers have certainly placed their ability to make their own decisions regarding the scope and timing of unavoidable reform measures before the short-term relief of liquidity problems that an agreement with the World Bank or the IMF might have brought. They have also foregone the opportunity – which other adjusting Third World regimes have often embraced – to blame the social hardships resulting from economic adjustment on those international institutions. The Syrian regime was prepared to take the blame for adjustment effects itself rather than risk the accusation of tampering with national sovereignty by letting external actors determine its policies.

IMF and World Bank missions were invited and sent to Syria regularly for routine and other consultations, presenting their reports and recommendations to the Syrian government.[2] Discussions took place, including Syria's economic policies, but no negotiations about policy changes. World Bank officials regularly discussed with their Syrian partners their main problem with Damascus, that is, Syria's arrears on World Bank development loans which had been building up since 1986, reaching some $400 million by 1993.[3] In most Arab countries, indebtedness has given international actors a stick with which to push these countries towards policies of economic reform.[4] Syria, however, despite its debt, has quite successfully managed to block this route. Since the Syrian government paid only small installments on its World Bank debts, just enough to avoid being declared insolvent, and otherwise did not seem to be overly concerned about the World Bank's cancelling of all its Syrian programmes, there was little the Bank could do to put pressure on the country. The same applies to other Western donors in their relation with Damascus. Syria has been regarded as an unreliable debtor whose officials would simply refuse to talk to their creditors when the latter tried to negotiate Syria's arrears.[5] As a result, since the mid-1980s many Western banks have avoided extending credit facilities to Syria. Mostly, however, the Syrian government, exploiting its geopolitical position and importance, has been able to find alternative and more lenient donors, namely Arab governments and funds,[6] which would not pressure too hard for re-payments let alone for reforms the Syrians did not want to embark on themselves.[7] Unlike many other Third World countries therefore, Syria was not forced to consider the World Bank or the IMF a last resort.

This is not to say that Syria has not sought the advice of bilateral or multilateral donors, including the World Bank and IMF. Sectoral studies have been made by the World Bank or UN organisations on, among other things, the state of Syria's public-sector industries or its energy sector.[8] A study on development options for Syria's banking sector was undertaken, on behalf of the Syrian government, by *GTZ*, Germany's semi-governmental development agency. Such reports to the Syrian government have to be regarded as inputs into the decision-making process. In some cases their recommendations have been used to support a particular position on issues, and sometimes they have even been put into practice. Syrian leaders also accepted, in the mid-1980s, an offer by Saudi–Lebanese businessman Rafiq al-Hariri, later Lebanese Prime Minister, to finance a comprehensive report on and reform proposals for Syria's crisis-ridden economy; they were thus, albeit indirectly, accepting interference in the Syrian leadership's eco-nomic policy debate. The Syrian authorities, however, have never allowed such external actors to become directly involved in their decision-making and policy formation. In 1992, a West European government offered to place an economic advisor in the Syrian State Planning Authority to assist in the design and implementation of Syria's own economic reform programme. Negotiations about the issue came to nought.

The Soviet Union and Russia as its successor, though Syria's main creditor, were neither in the position nor actually interested to press the Syrians for economic reform. Rather, Moscow's main interest has become making Syria recognize and service its Soviet debts. Further-more, Syria's economic reform process cannot be explained as a reaction to the breakdown of the socialist economies in Eastern Europe. The economic transition of the former socialist-bloc countries has certainly accelerated and made easier economic reform processes in Syria, but it has not initiated them. By 1985, when Gorbachev assumed power in Moscow, Syria's second *infitah* had already begun. And while global and regional developments such as, in the 1980s, the worldwide increase in interest rates, the balance problems of the main Arab oil exporters, and the decrease of worker remittances, have no doubt all been influencing economic-policy decisions in Syria and have somewhat limited the country's options, the actual design of Syria's economic policies has remained in the hands of Syrian decision-makers.

2. The Institutional and Procedural Framework

To examine decision-making processes that concern Syria's economic reform moves of the 1980s, two levels of analysis will be combined. First, we are going to focus, rather narrowly, on the institutional framework and formal government structures to delineate the regular procedure of political decisions on particular reform elements, such as laws or decrees. Since economic reform is an incremental process, boundaries between day-to-day administrative decisions and "reform" cannot always be drawn clearly.[9] Reform[10] may materialize in visible policy shifts – such as the decree allowing the establishment of mixed-sector agricompanies, or Syria's 1991 investment and tax laws – as well as in ministerial decrees which, for instance, lift public-sector monopolies by allowing the private sector to import certain goods. On the second level, the style of policy formation – as far as Syria's economic transition process is concerned – will be focussed upon. We will examine the particular manner in which economic policies are decided upon in Syria, including patterns of consultation, interest articulation, and policy debate. Finally, the inter-relation of economic reform and decision-making structures will be touched on briefly. This means outlining how the role of institutions and interest groups – the focus here will be on organized labour and business – in economic-policy decision-making structures has developed along with the economic adjustment process.

From the late 1980s or so, Syrian officials have been claiming that Syria actually is a state of institutions (*dawlat mu'assasat*). This term, in the way it is used in the Syrian discourse, is both meant to denounce accusations that policy-making in Syria is largely a matter of personal networking and corruption, and to remove the notion that everything in Syrian politics is of the President's own making. Since Asad's takeover in 1970, as outlined, the institutional structure of Syria's political system has in fact developed and become more complex, particularly if compared to the government of Asad's immediate predecessors. This includes the establishment of a parliament, of the PNF and of local administrative bodies, as well as the expansion and diversification of public administration and government. Given the need for *wasta* in the pursuit of even simple and legal bureaucratic matters, the absence of an independent judiciary, the arbitrariness of the security apparatus etc., the term "state of institutions" sounds rather euphemistic, and the role of existing institutions is often more limited than their names might suggest. Their existence itself, however, makes a difference inasmuch as it allows the development of institutional corporate interests, and influences – i.e. delays, accelerates, refines or enriches – decision-making and policy implementation. Some institutions or institutional elements may not, at a given time, play their full role; they may, however, stand by to develop their own life and role more fully under changing political circumstances.

As a rule we can say that economic policy-making, compared to matters of high policy such as security and foreign affairs, is a broader, more complex process that involves a relatively high number and large spectrum of institutional and individual participants. Regarded as mainly low policy, economic policy-making processes tend also to be somewhat more open to academic scrutiny.

The analysis of the formal, structural and procedural aspects of economic-policy decision-making process – as illustrated in Figure 1 – reveals clearly the central role of a centralized bureaucracy, with the Prime Minister and his office as the nodal point. The President, although he only occasionally decides on economic policy elements, hegemonizes the structure and may intervene where things obtain a political – in the meaning of high policies – or conflictual dimension. The functions of the Ba'th party leadership and of parliament are clearly secondary. Private sector and trade unions participate, to varying degrees, in parts of the decisions.

Ministerial and Government Committee Work

The formal way for a particular economic-policy element to be legislated or decreed begins in the *administration*. A draft law or decree, involving minor or major alterations to a given policy, would be drafted – by order of the minister – in the Ministry of Economy and Foreign Trade or another concerned ministry. Government ministers in Syria are regarded as top civil servants, not political figures. If, therefore, such a move were considered to constitute a substantial change in the policies or rules so far applied, a minister generally would not act upon his own initiative but follow a request from the presidency or

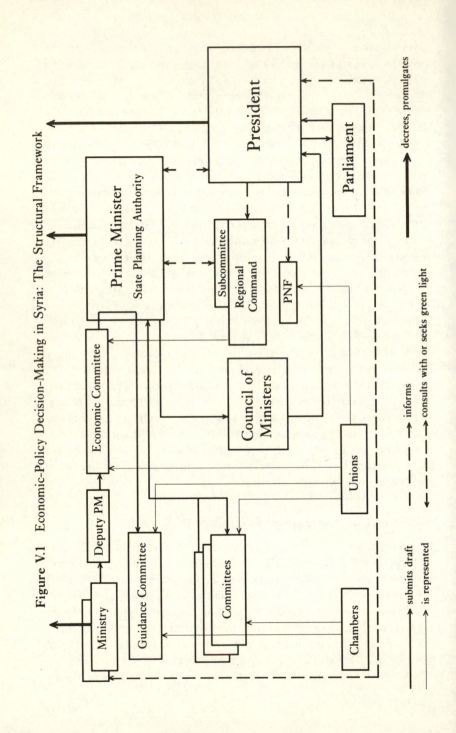

Figure V.1 Economic-Policy Decision-Making in Syria: The Structural Framework

President

Parliament

Prime Minister
State Planning Authority

Subcommittee
Regional Command

PNF

Economic Committee

Council of Ministers

Deputy PM

Unions

Ministry

Guidance Committee

Committees

Chambers

→ decrees, promulgates

– – → informs

◀– –▶ consults with or seeks green light

→ submits draft

→ is represented

the Prime Minister. Only some more active or ambitious ministers would try to push things forward themselves and for that purpose then seek a green light from the President. Thus, to give but one example, Minister of Economy Muhammad al-'Imadi, before initiating the drafting of the legal framework for a reform of Syria's banking system that would allow the establishment of mixed-sector – and probably, at a later stage, private – banks, sent a memorandum to the President explaining the background and reasons for such a move and waited for the latter's go-ahead. This was done even though 'Imadi and others had been discussing the issue in public for several years.[11] The President's consent alone, however, would guarantee that a legislative initiative in this respect would not be blocked prematurely by its opponents, and that the minister himself would not run into difficulties.

Any draft law or decree on economic matters would be submitted by the minister who initiates the process to the *Economic Committee* via the Deputy Prime Minister for Economic Affairs. This committee was established in 1967, i.e. before the current presidential system was developed, as a policy-planning and steering body; it would pre-decide all economic policy matters of importance, study, among other things, the annual budget and public investment projects, and submit recommendations on both particular and general economic-policy matters to the Prime Minister. The Committee consists of the Deputy Prime Minister for Economic Affairs (Chairman), the ministers concerned with economic affairs, and a representative each of the Ba'th party Regional Command (RC) and the General Federation of Trade Unions (GFTU). Meeting twice weekly, the committee is in practice mainly occupied with executive procedures that finally will have to be decided upon by the Prime Minister. This includes public-sector appointments, price regulations, contracts and agreements or financial allocations for public-sector establishments.

The *prime minister* has the final say in most administrative matters. To some extent, how broad the margin for decision is that the Prime Minister leaves to the members of his cabinet depends on his personality. Mahmud al-Zu'bi, who has been serving as Prime Minister since 1987, is known to have taken over a lot of procedures which his predecessor had left for ministers or deputy ministers to decide. Under Zu'bi, for example, all decisions on tenders for the public sector and the administration have been routed through his office. Even without that, however, convention has it that the Prime Minister, in person, is overburdened with administrative procedures that need his approval and signature. More often than not, prime ministers themselves have become concerned with the technical or financial problems of a particular public-sector unit. They have to decide on matters such as exceptional import licences, the appointment or transfer of leading civil servants, as well as subordinate employees in any of the administrative units connected to the prime minister's office, or the establishment of mixed-sector companies and any private company set up under the 1991 investment law and approved by the Higher Council for Investments. Ministerial decrees not involving any changes of policy would pass through the prime minister's office, be approved or rejected and returned to the ministry in charge for publication or reconsideration. The Prime Minister, though formally invested with responsibility for such rather technical decisions, may in fact not take them on his own. While 'Abd al-Ra'uf al-Kasm, Syria's Prime Minister from 1980 to 1987, was known to handle in person the files that accumulated over the week, Zu'bi would deal with them over a meeting with 'Izz al-Din Nasir, trade-union boss and member of the Ba'th party RC, 'Ali Duba, director of military intelligence, and probably some other persons. Both – Zu'bi more than his predecessor, however – would in some cases ask for a presidential guideline, particularly where decisions, though formally under their own authority and non-political in their nature, could touch personal interests or seemed to be particularly "large". The President himself would thus be consulted on such technical matters as the decision to permit the import of reinforcement bars and micro-buses.[12]

In contrast to rather non-political routine matters, economic-policy executive decisions of some political relevance would pass through what is known as the Guidance Committee, before being decreed by the Prime Minister or the minister in charge. Such decisions might concern permission for traders to keep a particular percentage of their foreign-exchange earnings or to import on behalf of the public sector, the lifting of other public-sector monopolies, or the rearrangement of exchange rates.

The Guidance Committee, officially the Committee for the Guidance of Imports, Exports and Consumption, consists of the Prime Minister, his deputy for economic affairs, the ministers in charge of economic matters, two members of the party leadership, a GFTU representative and the presidents of the Damascus Chambers of Commerce and of Industry. The committee, as noted, was established in

1981 with the task of encouraging exports and designing more rationalized import policies. It meets more or less bi-monthly. Though formally the committee's decisions have to be countersigned and issued by the Prime Minister or the minister in charge, the committee is in fact the main decision-making body for issues and policies related to foreign trade. The scope of its work ranges from rather detailed, technical matters, such as allowing or banning the import of particular raw materials for the manufacturers of particular goods, to important economic-policy issues such as public-sector trade monopolies, policies regarding the control over private-sector export earnings, exchange-rates to be applied on various types of foreign-trade operations, and foreign-trade licensing. More general economic-policy questions may be discussed in the committee without being submitted to it for decision. That apart, given the Syrian economy's high dependence on foreign trade, the Guidance Committee can be said to be in charge of most of the important, and a substantial proportion of the conflictual, economic policy issues. At the same time, the committee is the first and only governmental decision-making body that, apart from trade-union and party representatives, includes representatives of the private sector. The debates within the committee are said to be open and, more often than not, controversial. It is a place for private-sector interests and demands to be officially and directly injected into the process of governmental policy formation, as well as a corporatist body where private-sector and union representatives can bargain for their demands with government, party, and each other. Not all private-sector proposals are approved, but they are listened to and thus become part of the government's policy debates.[13]

There are a couple of other permanent government committees and councils dealing with economic policy issues, each headed by the Prime Minister and, like the Guidance Committee, *de facto* decision-making bodies for their specific fields. These include the Higher Council for Agriculture, the main steering body for defining agricultural policies, annual agricultural plans, and governmental procurement prices; the Higher Council for Planning, responsible for long-term development plans; the Higher Council for Companies, dealing with the needs and works of the public-sector construction companies; the Higher Council for Investment, and others. The Peasant Union is represented on the Council for Agriculture, the GFTU on the one for Companies. In none of these councils are private-sector interests represented, and none of them plays as important a role for Syria's overall economic transition policies as the Guidance Committee. The Chambers had voiced their interest in sitting on the Investment Council, whose sole responsibility is to decide, as the highest authority in this process, on applications for the establishment of companies under the 1991 Investment Law; but their demand was rejected. Neither are unions or the party represented in the Investment Council.[14]

Involvement of Organized Interests: The Stories of Public-Sector Reform and the Equity Market

Apart from heading these permanent councils and committees, the Prime Minister may form limited-objective interministerial committees to prepare a particular law or reform project. Legally, it is the job of the State Planning Authority – the former Ministry of Planning[15] – to coordinate between ministries and establish interministerial committees; in practice, it is the Prime Minister who does this, and ministries will coordinate their affairs through the prime minister's office or, rarely, directly with each other. Project-oriented committees may include representatives from outside the administration, as happened in the case of two reform projects that were still in the making as this study was being written.

In 1992, the Prime Minister formed a ministerial Committee for the Development of the Adminstration of the National Economy to prepare an all-out reform of the public sector. Regarding their special stakes in the subject, the trade-union leadership was invited onto the committee which was headed by the Prime Minister himself. Co-operation between the government and the GFTU over matters of public-sector reform or, as some critics may say, non-reform, was not new, and discussions about a public-sector reform were almost as old as the public sector. The latest more ambitious move to get the ailing public sector back on its feet through a reform process was set off with the trade unions' 1987 conference on National Creativity and Self-Reliance, which had studied and discussed the public sector's performance and problems at considerable depth.[16] After this conference, the Prime Minister formed a committee under the chairmanship of the Deputy Prime Minister for Economic Affairs to follow up the conference's proposals. This committee formed a couple of sub-committees, which at first were composed of both trade-union and ministerial experts and trade-union executive members. At issue were the internal organization of the public sector, public-sector finances, pricing policies, and other questions. After a while, the chairs of these subcommittees were taken over by cabinet ministers. The committees met up to five or six times over a two-year period and were then dissolved.[17] Although they did not achieve any tangible results, they served both to underpin the trade-union leadership's demand to be consulted or have a decisive say in all matters concerning the public sector, and to bring trade-union interests into the governmental debate.

In 1989, the GFTU, in cooperation with the prime minister's office, organized a Symposium on the Improvement and Development of the Administration of the Public Economic Sector, once again developing a couple of proposals which, after being studied and adopted by the GFTU council, were submitted to the Prime Minister in 1990.[18] There they remained. The establishment in 1992 of the governmental Committee for the Development of the National Economy, following a decision of the Prime Minister, represented both a continuation of previous discussions and a more sincere effort to work out and, if possible, decide authoritatively on the principles of public-sector reform. Including both the Minister of Economy and trade-union representatives with, in this context, their quite different interests and conceptions, the committee was all but unanimous in its discussions. 'Imadi, without explicitly demanding it, had never ruled out privatizations. The privatization issue was off the table when the committee first met, but 'Imadi demanded in a report to the commitee a transformation of the public sector to a still state-owned, yet quasi-capitalist sector. This would consist of a number of juristically independent joint-stock companies whose shares would be held by the General Insurance company and a new type of holding company established from the General Organizations – at the time of writing the administrative bodies overseeing the activities of public-sector establishments in different industries. The public sector thus transformed would have no social or political functions; each individual establishment would manage its business according to purely commercial criteria; wages would be tied to profits and – implicitly – to losses; trade-union interference in management functions would cease; and labour laws would be reviewed.[19] This latter demand, if put into practice, would facilitate lay-offs. The trade-union representatives responded relatively sharply to 'Imadi's report, denouncing it as the minister's "personal view" and as representing "regrettably, the understandings which the IMF is propagating".[20] While also invoking the need to allow public-sector units more financial and administrative independence, the trade-union response insisted that the leading role of the public sector be preserved; it further insisted that the social and political function of the public sector be taken into account – not only its economic profits or losses – and that the public sector be granted similar privileges as private-sector companies set up under the provisions of the 1991 Investment Law. Furthermore, measures of any kind that might open the door for future privatization, including the establishment of holding companies as proposed by 'Imadi, should remain out of bounds. In addition, the state should return to comprehensive planning, setting guidelines not only for the public sector, but also for the private economy; it should also also resume planned consumer prices and a stricter control over the use of foreign exchange.[21] At the time of writing, the committee's work had yet to be finished; doubts that it would produce any substantial reform measures were in place. More important, in our context, is that by establishing this committee the government opened up a bargaining place. Committee discussions could provide the chance to bring the partly conflicting but, from the regime's perspective, equally legitimate interests represented by the Minister of Economy on the one hand and the trade-union leadership on the other, into line before a final governmental decision had to be taken, and could help to prevent conflictual issues from being carried out in public.

Another still pending project of some importance for Syria's economic reform, officially involving in its preparatory stage persons not in the administration or the political leadership, concerned the establishment of an equity market or stock exchange. As early as 1987, the Ministry of Economy had proposed to the Prime Minister that a committee be constituted to prepare the establishment of an institution where Syrian company shares could be traded. In a letter to the him, the Minister of Economy argued that such an institution was necessary in order to protect small shareholders who, without an official share market, could easily fall victim to dubious businessmen promising high interest to small investors. With the Prime Minister's agreement, a first government committee was set up, comprising officials of the prime minister's office, the Ministries of Economy, of Finance, and of Supply, and the Central Bank. This committee met a couple of times, inviting representatives of the Damascus Chamber of Commerce to some of the meetings, and worked out an initial draft law on the establishment of an Office for Share Circulation (Maktab tadawul al-ashum). The office was to be connected to the Chambers and organize the buying and selling of company shares. Things remained static until, in 1990, with a number of joint-stock companies active and the 1991 investment law in the making, the issue was once again brought to the table. The government then set up a second inter-ministerial committee, called the Committee for the Project of a Stock-Market Law. It consisted of a deputy minister of finance as chairperson, an advisor to the Prime Minister, and representatives as advisors of the Ministry of Economy and other ministries. Also officially included was a member of the Damascus Chamber of Commerce executive. The party, the unions and other sectors were not involved.

The committee's work began with the draft project prepared by the first committee. The majority of the committee members did not find the proposal far-reaching enough. 'Imadi's representative demanded that the committee consult his minister before any further action. With 'Imadi's go-ahead finally secured, a three-man subcommittee was formed of the representatives of the Ministry of Economy, the prime minister's office, and the Chambers of Commerce in order to work out a new proposal. This subcommittee studied the stock-exchange laws of Lebanon, Jordan, Oman, and the UAE, and on this basis put together a project which envisaged the establishment of what was called a Shares-and-Equity Market (*suq al-ashum wa-l-awraq al-maliya*), i.e. a full-scale bourse, in Damascus. By the autumn of 1991, the project had been submitted to the government.

'Imadi, however, had received signals from the President's office that the committee's draft was too far-reaching. He therefore commis-sioned officials from his own ministry to prepare another proposal. The ministry again consulted individual representatives of the cham-bers. Its new draft provided for the establishment of a Shares Market (*suq al-ashum*) that would be connected to the Ministry of Economy and deal only with company shares, not for instance with government bonds. Parallel to that, discussions were held in the Guidance Com-mittee and bilaterally between the Damascus Chamber of Commerce and the Ministry of Finance over some more technical, but never-theless important aspects of the project, namely the question as to whether shares or only the profits from share circulation should be taxed.

By mid-1992, two drafts for a stock-exchange or shares-office law were thus on the table. There was in fact a third draft which one of Syria's leading businessmen, after a private meeting with the Prime

Minister, had commissioned from one of his employees and then submitted to the Minister of Economy. Officials of the Ministry of Economy then discussed and revised their own project with the Ministry of Finance. The process, however, had lost momentum: at the time of writing the work of the committees had not been resumed, nor had any of the projects been passed on – as normally would be the case following the government committee stage – via the Economic Committee and the prime minister's office, to the Council of Ministers for final governmental decision.

Even though a final decision has yet to be taken, the story of the equity-market law is of particular interest. Never before under the Ba'th had the Damascus Chamber of Commerce or any other representative of organized business interests been invited to sit on an intra-governmental committee that would draft an important law and thus, officially, participate in the policy-formation process from an elementary stage.[22] This process, as it seems, was fairly open. No particular decision was determined from the beginning. Obviously, there was a green light from the Prime Minister, and probably from the President, to pursue the issue. Since there were joint-stock companies, some way had to be found to allow a public circulation of the shares. As a matter of fact, neither the business side nor the government were unanimous in their approach to the issue. Some of Syria's big businessmen had, initially at least, preferred to have people contact their companies directly if they wanted to purchase or sell any shares. The Minister of Economy, while in principle favouring the establishment of some equity market, was obviously interested to further the institutional interests of his own house and tie the project to the ministry rather than let it become an independent institution. Some cabinet members also feared that the establishment of a full-fledged bourse would in the end lead to the establishment of private-sector banks and thereby further erode state control over the economy. The issue no doubt had a high-policy dimension. Delay, therefore, was caused by the political leadership.

Party and President: The Leadership Level

Formally, the Prime Minister submits draft laws and projects needing cabinet approval to the Council of Ministers, once government committee work is done. Decisions in the Council are of a rather formal nature; the place for cabinet members to discuss and probably change a project would be the Economic Committee. The cabinet would not in any way block a proposal submitted by the Prime Minister for a final decision. Drafts are usually approved without lengthy debates and then officially submitted to the President.

Where issues considered "political" are at stake, however, both the President and the Ba'th party command, i.e., the political leadership level, are involved even before the government passes its final decision. Generally – as far as economic affairs are concerned – the Ba'th Party Regional Command (RC) regards itself responsible for the overall political line, not for executive decisions – except for administrative appointments; this is keeping with the constitutional notion according to which the Ba'th is the "leading party in society and state". It does, however, as noted, watch and to some extent control the performance of government, bureaucracy and public sector through its Regional Economic Office and the economic offices at party-branch level.

Though not formally an institution whose consent would be needed at a certain stage of governmental decision-making and legislative process, the RC is informed about government proceedings. The RC, as a body, does not deal with individual ministries directly[23] – neither do individual ministries submit proposals or drafts to the RC. The usual communication between the RC and the government is through the Prime Minister who himself is an RC member. In addition, there exists a sub-committee of the RC for coordination with the government consisting of the Prime Minister, Assistant Regional Secretary Sulayman Qaddah, trade-union boss 'Izz al-Din Nasir and one or two other RC members. This committee meets on request, daily if necessary. The RC meets weekly. President Asad as the party's secretary-general attends only rarely, scarcely once a month. His attendance would mean that high-policy issues were scheduled. He usually informs and consults the RC on these issues, and he listens to their views though it is he who finally decides.

All important economic issues and reform projects, such as Legislative Decree 10/1986 by which the agricultural mixed sector was introduced, and the 1991 tax law are brought to the knowledge of and discussed by the RC. Critical administrative measures may also be submitted to RC discussion. The question of subsidies on basic goods, for instance, is considered a critical one.[24]

As a rule, the RC takes no policy initiatives of its own. The President, of course, may do so, and he may involve the RC. This was the case with one of the most important single elements of Syria's second *infitah*, the 1991 investment law. By 1988, discussions had begun on practically all levels about how to attract more private investments beyond the limited scope of agriculture and tourism – where special laws provided incentives – and purely commercial or speculative ventures. Opening the space for private, perhaps even foreign, investments and encouraging and privileging investors was obviously a political issue that needed highest-level support to be tackled concretely. The President therefore, acting through the RC, formed a Committee for the Encouragement of Investments. It was chaired by the then head of the RC's Economic Office, Rashid Ikhtarini, and consisted also of Deputy Prime Minister for Economic Affairs Salim Yasin, 'Imadi, and four other cabinet ministers. The committee held meetings over a one-and-a-half year period, consulting the investment laws of Jordan, Egypt, Turkey, and the USSR, and preparing a first draft for a Syrian law. The draft went through the regular governmental decision-making process where it was reviewed and redrafted several times. The final draft was discussed in the RC before then officially being submitted to the President.

Not all members of the RC were happy with the investment law; nor were they all at ease with the general *infitah*-tendency that emerged in the second half of the 1980s. The RC has commented on certain reform projects; it may always propose changes, ask the Prime Minister to have things reconsidered, question certain government measures and thus cause some delay. However, government projects are not voted upon or blocked in the RC. It is highly unlikely in the first place that any substantial, issue-related conflict between the government and the RC would evolve. This is prevented by the personal interweaving of the two bodies and, even more so, by the fact that both are supposed to follow the President's directives.

In general, economic affairs are not among the *President*'s major concerns. Asad personally takes care of high policies, i.e. defence and internal-security policies, and foreign affairs. He also supervises information, and oil matters. General economic and development policies, as is clear from his speeches and conversations since he has been in power, are secondary issues supposed to serve his high-policy goals.[25] The President would personally deal with economic developments and affairs only inasmuch as they positively or negatively affect the pursuit of these goals, including, prominently, the stability of the regime. Development, growth, or the societal distribution of gains and losses, though important tenets of the regime's official rhetoric, are considered means rather than ends. This explains, as far as the President is concerned, his pragmatism or undoctrinaire approach to questions of economic policy, as well as accounting for some of the neglect by his regime of developmental issues.

Legislative and administrative initiatives that entail policy changes would, as mentioned, normally only be started with a go-ahead from the presidency. In some cases, as indicated, the President himself would initiate a particular policy-formation process. The presidency, i.e. the staff on the presidential office, monitors the process; however it does not usually intervene during the phase of ministerial and government work. Rarely would a law or decree that falls in the wider sphere of economic affairs actually be drafted, or redrafted, in the presidency.[26] Any final decision on politically important government measures would again need a green light from the presidency. Thereafter, a draft law would be formally approved by the Council of Ministers, then officially submitted to the President to be passed on to the parliament or be directly promulgated as a legislative decree.

The President himself would look into any political important draft no later than at this stage, and more probably before the final cabinet decision. Where he deemed it necessary, he would order further studies or consult individuals. Delay may be caused simply because of the President's occupation with high-policy issues. The President is also likely to deliberately slow down some critical reform measures brought on the table before, as Syrian administrators would say, the atmosphere has been prepared. In the case of the equity market, for instance, all the above apply. From 1991, the peace process occupied most of the President's energy; the government had not arrived at a clear opinion about the final form of the project; the topic had hardly been touched on by Syria's state-controlled media and, given the uneasiness of parts of the party and the bureaucracy with both economic liberalization and the peace process, there was no point in forcing them to swallow too many changes unprepared and at one time.

The President also becomes personally involved in executive matters which, although not entailing policy changes or general policy decisions, are critical inasmuch as they entail conflicts of interest between different parts of the regime, or between the government and parts of the regime's political support base. Obviously, presidential backing is needed where executive measures clash with deep-rooted individual interests of high-level military or mukhabarat personnel, as was the case with the government's decision, in the spring of 1993, to clamp down on cigarette smuggling and provide for a regulated import of cigarettes instead. Further, the President may personally become involved where a critical economic situation demands extremely fast action. This was the case, for instance, in the summer of 1993, when increasing electricity cuts – up to 20 hours a day in some towns and provinces – produced tangible public discontent and substantial difficulties for Syria's industrial sector. The shortage was obviously due not only to a low water level in Lake Asad, the reservoir feeding the Tabqa power station on the Euphrates, and to technical problems delaying the coming on stream of the Tishrin power plant near Damascus; it was also, and more importantly, due to a lack of long-term planning and concern regarding maintenance and the need for energy production to keep pace with population growth and industrial demand. As the crisis seemed to exceed proper bounds – complaints even being voiced in a meeting of the PNF leadership which Asad happened to attend – the President called, chaired and made public a meeting with high party and government officials, declared electricity a priority issue and stated, to the astonishment of his subjects, that to "obtain electrical energy is a citizen's right".[27] More substantial measures were then taken rather hastily. A crash programme to install new electricity-generating capacities was started and external financing secured within a couple of weeks.[28] The government also licensed the establishment of a mixed-sector company for electricity production, thereby for the first time since the Ba'thist takeover allowing the private sector to become active in this strategic industry, and lifting an important public-sector monopoly.[29] A sensitive political move like this, and a quick shift of priorities and budget allocations, could under no circumstances be executed without the President's clear support.

Decisions affecting the income or living standard of key groups are always considered quite critical and therefore often dealt with by the President. In 1991, for instance, the President reportedly ordered the government to cancel its decision to raise the customs dollar – the exchange rate according to which customs duties are levied on imports – from the low official to the realistic neighbouring countries' rate.[30] The measure would have entailed substantial price increases for imported goods and certainly further annoyed, in particular, parts of the urban middle classes with their largely westernized consumer habits.

Another case of personal presidential interference with a not really highly political, however conflictual, executive decision was the public-sector wage rise of 1991. The Ministry of Finance had proposed a 14 per cent increase; the cabinet, after protests from the trade unions and discussions in the Economic Committee, made it a 17 per cent increase instead. Asad, responding to trade-union complaints that even 17 per cent would fall short of covering the price rises of the two years from the last wage rise, decided that the increase be 25 per cent. At the same time, however, he personally told the trade-union leadership to stop pressing for additional demands, namely for the exemption from taxation of all income below minimum wage level.[31] Otherwise, he would only decree a 20 per cent wage rise.

At times, the President consults the *Progressive National Front* and thus includes it in the decision-making process. The front is informed about government plans and projects, usually by Vice-President Zuhayr Masharqa. The front leadership meets about once a month, the President as its chairman attends only when he wants to discuss, or to raise support for, particular high-policy issues. The front leadership discusses government policies, and it has discussed some of the economic reform projects controversially. No formal vote of approval, however, is needed from the PNF to pass a law or to pass it on from the cabinet, through the President, to parliament.

Legislative Participation

The role of the *parliament* or People's Council (*majlis al-sha'b*) has been somewhat enhanced since the parliamentary elections of 1990, though, as mentioned, it is still far from being a counterweight to the executive. The major feature distinguishing the parliament of 1990 from its predecessors was that about a third of its seats had been reserved for independent deputies, and that a considerable number of these independent deputies represented Syria's commercial class. The 1990 parliament was as docile as former parliaments in its relations with the President. However, a number of its members did try to extend parliament's room for manoeuvre vis-à-vis the government and the president of the chamber, 'Abd al-Qadir Qaddura. The latter is a core member of the Ba'th party RC who has functioned as the regime's supervisor of parliamentary affairs rather than as parliament's representative in the leadership. Attempts to widen parliamentary functions have been made particularly with regard to policy fields considered to be both less political and of specific importance for some of the more ambitious independent deputies, namely those for economic and social affairs.

Formally, draft laws are submitted to parliament by the President; parliament then discusses these drafts in its committees and, after that, in plenary session. There, any amendments the deputies would want to make to a bill would be discussed with the government. Debates, generally, are between individual deputies and cabinet ministers rather than between the deputies themselves, let alone parliamentary groups or factions. Officially, no factions exist; however there are loose circles around individual deputies in addition to the party groups – Ba'this, Communists and others – within the PNF. After a final parliamentary vote, a bill would be re-submitted to the President who would promulgate it, send it back to parliament with a demand for changes within one month, or veto it. Theoretically, parliament could overrule a presidential veto with a two-thirds majority; in practice, this has never happened. Once a law is promulgated, it falls within the responsibilities of the prime minister to issue whatever regulations and implementing statutes are considered necessary.

In addition to parliament's legislative functions, deputies can discuss government policies, demand explanations about certain problems or government activities, and raise issues. It has mainly been independent deputies who have in their interpellations and speeches raised a couple of issues and demanded policy changes that went beyond, or anticipated, the government's schedule at that time. Ihsan Sanqar, for instance, a Damscene businessman, who during the legislative period of 1990 became an unofficial spokesman of sorts for an equally unofficial group of independent deputies, demanded in the parliamentary debate on the 1993 budget the amendment of a couple of key laws, including Law No. 24 on currency smuggling, the agricultural-relations law, the rent law, the law on appropriation – a law entitling public institutions to appropriate, if against compensation, private land – and the labour law.[32]

In practice, the participation of parliament in the design of economic-policy and policy-reform elements has remained limited. No bills have, as yet, been introduced from within the parliament, and annual budgets – decisions about which are considered the traditional privilege of parliaments – have always been passed without change. Individual deputies or groups have more than once opposed or rejected a bill, but parliament has never done so in its – Ba'thist – majority.

Also, parliament has rarely amended draft laws. When it has done so, the government has given its consent to the move. Attempts to amend a law against the government's wishes are not supposed to happen, let alone to succeed.

A case in point was parliament's dealing with the 1991 tax law – basically a major tax reform according to which business taxes were substantially reduced. Even though the bill was in principle welcomed by deputies concerned with the issue, there was some criticism on the part of both independent, business-oriented and leftist, trade-unionist deputies. The former stressed the need to reduce taxes even more to encourage investments, instead of almost encouraging capital flight; the latter complained that wage-earners, in contrast to business people, were unfairly treated. Representatives of the two tendencies agreed during the committee discussions to amend the law so as to exempt from taxation the first 18,000 LS of both business profits and wage income.[33] In the committee, this amendment was passed with a two-thirds majority. In the plenary debate, however, the Minister of Finance told the deputies that this amendment would cost the treasury too much and was therefore unacceptable. Despite that, when the bill was put to a vote, the amended paragraph was approved of by a majority. Prime Minister Zu'bi protested, and Chamber President Qaddura adjourned the meeting pretending there had been no quorum. When parliament assembled again in the afternoon of the same day the vote was repeated, and again the amended paragraph was passed. Qaddura, however, claimed there had been a majority against. A large number of deputies protested, and Qaddura announced another vote, by call, at the same time calling on the discipline of the Ba'this by saying that the law had been prepared by the RC and that the President himself had participated in drafting it. Voting by call, thus, would make public who was disloyal to the President. At that stage, some 60 deputies, mainly independents, left the meeting in protest. Qaddura then put the entire bill in its original form to a vote and finally, against the votes of a couple of trade unionists, got the majority wanted, demonstrating through this episode the limitations of parliamentary participation – even in one of the less critical policy fields.

Presidential Hegemony and Bureaucratic Dictatorship

Given the authoritarian nature of the Syrian regime, it is not surprising to find that the President hegemonizes economic-policy decision-making. The President is the supreme arbitrator between legitimate but conflicting interests. He serves as decision-maker of last resort where subordinate policy-makers like the Prime Minister, despite their legal competences, do not want or dare to take certain decisions. The President's prior consent is sought to protect any reform initiative against potential opposition. Only his personal decision can, if so needed, suspend the restrictions of plans and budgets. He decides, in cases of doubt, whether the time is ripe for a particular reform element. And it is he, of course, who appoints those in charge of economic-policy decisions.

Asad's hegemony over economic-policy decisions, though, does not imply that he actually makes these policies, or commissions particular projects from the government, the party, or an individual minister. He may occasionally, as was the case with the 1991 investment law, initiate work on a project; but this is not the rule. The President's directives or guidelines (tawjihat), so frequently referred to in the official discourse of party, government, and media, are in no way clear instructions demanding this or that project or particular reform schedule. Rather, as noted, the President encourages or discourages his Prime Minister or the Minister of Economy to go ahead with a project or a proposed course of action. Economic-policy decisions certainly involve more actors than foreign affairs or security where the President, though assisted by a group of aides, can be regarded the sole decision-maker.

Parliament has a role to play in economic-policy making. In fact, as noted, Prime Minister Zu'bi, in a policy statement in 1991, defined the concern with economic questions as the prime function of the chamber.[34] Where actual policy decisions are at stake, however, this role is limited to consultation on request. As yet, the right to legislate is in practice understood as the right to discuss bills, to submit to the government proposals for their amendment, and to approve of them – but not the right to reject. As far as economic policies are concerned, the government and the regime leadership regard parliament as a body that represents legitimate interests and comprises some expertise; they would not allow it, however, to block any measures or to set the pace for economic reform.

The party leadership, as outlined, is involved in economic-policy decision-making, both through institutional arrangements such as its representation on the Economic Committee and the Guidance Committee, and the interweaving of personnel which allows for informal coordination rather than formalized government–leadership relations.

The leadership of the security establishment – military and mukhabarat – are consulted and informed on economic-policy matters by the Prime Minister. Individual high officers can further private interests – their own or those of their private-sector business partners – and reserve, as long as the President does not intervene, economic margins in which the state would not interfere. Cigarette importation represented such a margin for over a decade. As a body, however, the military establishment is not involved in economic-policy decisions nor, more precisely, in civilian economic policy-making. Military expenses, however they may influence the overall economic climate, are not considered economic matters but security affairs that have to be decided by the President. Significantly, the annual budget of the Ministry of Defence, in contrast to the budgets of other ministries, is entered into the general budget as a lump sum, i.e. it is not broken up into titles for different purposes or administrative divisions. The reduction of military expenditures since the mid-1980s has clearly been decided by the President himself. Open budget battles between civilian decision-makers and the military have not yet occurred.[35]

The trade-union leadership is officially represented on government committees as well as in the central leadership of the PNF which, however, has consultative functions at best. In addition, 'Izz al-Din Nasir is a member of the Ba'th party RC and a key figure in the coordination group around the Prime Minister. The business sector, represented by the Damascus Chambers, has been incorporated into governmental decision-making structures, and is listened to. Apart from this, individual businessmen are consulted by the President and, more often and occasionally over detailed questions, by the Prime Minister and by cabinet ministers. Both organized labour and business, as well as the Peasant Union in agricultural-policy questions,[36] may thus have an influence on economic-policy decisions, however, the government still decides how deeply and where to involve these organized interests.

If the President hegemonizes economic policy-making, the government dominates it. The centrality of the Prime Minister in the structural framework of economic-policy decisions is obvious, as is the preponderance of the government over parliament. In practice, the government, not the legislative body, makes the laws under which it acts. Many administrative decisions taken by the government without parliament being involved, and only occasionally involving the political leadership, are *de facto* substantial reform elements. Consider the importance for the process of economic transition of foreign-trade regulations, rules about the use of foreign-exchange, and provisions for investments. The government, with individual cabinet ministers playing a considerable role, prepares the agenda of economic reform. Although it needs the consent of the President, it is not the latter who sets that agenda, let alone the party RC, the legislative, or the representatives of labour and business. There is, therefore, in the field of economic-policy decisions a large element of what a Syrian economist has called a *de facto* dictatorship of the bureaucracy.[37]

3. The Style of Economic-Policy Formation

The style of Syria's economic policy-making could be characterized in a nutshell as gradualist, reactive, and personalized, with some corporatist, consultative elements. These combined features are inseparably related to Syria's authoritarian system whose prime decision-maker, as mentioned, considers economic questions of secondary importance, while national security and regime stability hold primacy.

Gradualism and Reactive Reform

Gradualism is probably the most apparent feature of Syria's economic-reform policies. The country's ongoing process of economic transition began in 1985, or even before, almost unnoticed, and far from being finished by 1994, appears to be very much a hesitant, step-by-step undertaking.[38] Observers may be tempted to equate the gradualism of economic reform with Asad's cautious yet persistent style in dealing with internal and regional high-policy issues, behind which both friends and foes have assumed long-term planning and strategy. Consider, for instance, Asad's gradual path to power before 1970, and his stubborn treatment of the Lebanese file.

Personal idiosyncrasies of authoritarian leaders can certainly be reflected, to some extent, in the style of economic policy-making.[39] It would be erroneous, though, to infer from what apparently is Asad's approach to high policy, the existence of an equally strategic and therefore gradualist approach to economic policies and economic reform by Syrian policy-makers. The economic-reform process in Syria has taken place by degrees; this gradualism may have saved the country's leadership some problems; and it has occasionally been declared a strategy in itself aimed at avoiding the harsh effects of adjustment policies.[40] Reforms, however, did not follow any comprehensive long-term plan or strategy of transition.[41]

Instead, the usual pattern in Syria's economic policy-making has been that the government would react to crises and try to cure phenomena that demanded immediate treatment. Treatment, accordingly, was sectoral rather than comprehensive. Consider the decision, in 1989, to allow private merchants to import scrap iron and waste paper for processing in the public-sector steel works of Hama and the Dayr al-Zur paper mill against payment in hard-currency cash or in materials. This decision was clearly aimed at treating a particular problem, not at gradually liberalizing foreign trade, let alone allowing the private sector a say over some important public-sector industries. Changes in the regulations regarding the percentage of hard-currency export earnings that exporters were allowed to keep for their imports, and the exchange-rate at which the rest would have to be sold to the state were frequently made; but these changes represent sectoral and partial responses to urgent needs and, in this case, private-sector complaints and demands, rather than a series of planned steps. Had there been any reform plan or strategy to follow, a law like Law No. 41 of December 1986, which imposed a ban on all private car dealing, even forbidding private car owners to sell their own vehicles to anyone outside their immediate family, would most probably not have been passed. The law represented an isolated and poorly studied response to a sectoral problem, namely speculation in automobiles which, because of an import ban, were a scarce commodity. Being impractical, the law had to be rescinded after a couple of months, causing considerable embarrassment to the government. And while this is an episode from the early years of Syria's second *infitah*, the hasty reactions in 1993 to the electricity crisis, which at that time was suddenly considered politically critical, particularly the lifting of the public-sector monopoly on energy production, showed that economic policy-formation had remained reactive and sectoral.

Most of these and other sectoral measures – not all, as the car-sales episode shows – have involved a relaxation of state control, the lifting of public-sector monopolies, or the granting of some privilege to the private sector or parts of it, and may therefore appear like a series of steps aimed at gradually establishing a more market-oriented economic system. They only appear so in hindsight, however. We can

assume that in 1983, when the government first allowed private manufacturers to keep a percentage of their export earnings for import
needs, it did not plan to gradually abandon foreign-exchange control.
And in 1986, when, under Legislative Decree No. 10, mixed-sector
agricompanies were permitted, the political leadership did not expect,
let alone plan, that a few years later it would extend this pattern to
industry, allow and encourage foreign industrial investment, and even
force strategic public-sector industries to withstand private-sector
competition.[42]

There is, of course, a sequential logic of certain reform elements
and Syrian policy-makers have been aware of this. Attempts to
encourage private exports, for instance, demand some relaxation of
foreign-exchange control; an investment law that encourages the
establishment of joint-stock companies demands some framework for
the organized circulation of shares and a development of the banking
system. Policy-makers and business representatives pushing for change
have frequently argued with the necessity of implementing a particular second measure in order to complement a preceding first one and
secure its success.[43] The logic of developing one step after another, as
well as the practice of studying particular laws and reform measures
of other countries, remained nevertheless sectoral and piecemeal.

As a rule, economic needs have forced the regime into its step-by-
step adjustment, not a strategic plan for change and certainly not the
ideology or economic convictions of the regime elite. Syria's economic situation was critical enough at some point, particularly in
1986/87, to make the regime leadership and the government, or parts
of it at least, recognize the need for more substantial policy changes.
At that time and later, individuals in the government and the leadership, notably Vice President 'Abd al-Halim Khaddam and Economy
Minister 'Imadi have commissioned or encouraged a couple of
consultants' reports on the Syrian economy.[44] These reports called
for more or less cautious steps towards a more market-oriented
economy. Private investments were to be encouraged; however a more
flexible and not necessarily dominant public sector was to remain.
These studies helped to set the agenda for reform steps insofar as
they provided theoretical support for those practitioners in the
political elite who considered a substantial *infitah*, not just ad-hoc
measures, necessary. But the studies were never officially adopted,
nor did they constitute a blueprint for Syria's reform process. Con-
trasting, among others, the Egyptian case, where the IMF determined

full transition to a free-market system as the expected outcome of a reform process – however gradual – with Chile under Pinochet where a domestic elite determined such a transition,[45] no such clear direction or reform goals has been defined in the Syrian context. Ultimately, Syria's gradual and sectoral reform measures did add up to a particular form of economic liberalization. The palpable failure of the country's state-run enterprises and the relative success of measures to encourage the private sector have thereby supported the arguments of those forces who pleaded for progressive *infitah* steps, i.e. the reform-minded elements in government and leadership and the private sector itself.

As far as ideology or macro-economic theories are concerned, the gradualist, sectoral, and reactive approach suited the predispositions of Syria's policy-makers fairly well. The President, giving only secondary importance to the economy and not having a clear understanding of economics either, has followed a rather pragmatic, undoctrinaire economic-policy line. His general attitude towards the private sector has always been positive, provided the representatives of this sector stuck to their business and did not oppose his regime. Asad would neither block nor further any reform project for ideological reasons. His main concerns, as mentioned, are of a different nature, namely whether economic policy would support or contravene his regime's high-policy goals. For that reason, Asad has never favoured abandoning unnecessarily any element of state control and the means of patronage such control implies, nor introducing or envisaging far-reaching changes that might be considered a challenge to parts of his political base.

Although the Ba'th, under Asad, has lost its ideological leadership, it has maintained a basically nationalistic and anti-capitalist stance, strongly opposed to any form of foreign influence, wary of giving way to those social forces that had been removed from power with the Ba'thist takeover, and as such suspicious of the whole liberalization business. Wariness of economic liberalization even without such an ideological tradition would not be surprising for a party the majority of whose civilian members are employed in the public sector and administration. At its last congress, in 1985, the party declared support for a policy that would encourage a "productive private sector", making it clear, however, that the private economy should remain subject to state planning, a politically defined system of investment licensing, and governmental supervision and control.[46] In the early

1990s, the party still had no business membership of any importance, and there were no official contacts between the party leadership and organized business. Private contacts, of course, though limited, do exist.

Rather than representing a binding guideline for government policies, the party line and, quite similarly, the trade-union discourse, express the views and feelings of a large part of the regime elite or state bourgeoisie. A considerable number of the younger members of this elite hold degrees from the former socialist countries; some of the older members who were trained in Western universities during the 1950s have equally been educated to scepticism about the market as a regulator of developing economies. Most members of this elite are party members, many owe their position to the Ba'thist revolution or their party connections. The majority of Syria's cabinet members, in Zu'bi's cabinet of 1992 for instance, and the party leadership, are professional politicos or bureaucrats whose careers have been restricted to the party bureaucracy, the public sector, public administration including security, and sometimes to the universities. Technocrats in the meaning of experts able to prove their abilities outside the structure of Syria's anything but merit-oriented party-bureaucracy complex are rare. Among the cabinet ministers with economic-policy portfolios, there are at best three: Muhammad al-'Imadi who for a couple of years was employed with the Arab Fund for Economic and Social Development in Kuwait; 'Abd al-Rahim Siba'i, Minister of State for Planning Affairs who, although a career bureaucrat in his own ministry, has at least two years' experience as a consultant with the same Kuwaiti Fund, and Oil Minister Nadir Nabulsi, a geologist whose experience in the Syrian oil industry dates back to the time before the Ba'th came to power.[47]

Ideological orientations and convictions, of course, are also subject to change and adjustment. Understanding and learning, the consideration of developments in other countries, sheer frustration, personal gain, the concern for one's own and one's family's social status and how to keep it in a changing socio-economic and perhaps political environment, as well as opportunism, all play a role. Most members of Syria's political elite have in this sense adjusted; they have accepted that economic policies must change and perhaps further change must be expected. There remains, however, a lot of uneasiness about the need to liberalize and "give way", and a residual fear that changes that are too far-reaching could ultimately extend to this elite's own positions, control, and patronage. Caution, they say, should therefore prevail, the atmosphere be prepared, and the methods of others not necessarily copied. More reform-oriented elements, like 'Imadi, are wary of developing any long-term reform strategies that could rouse the opposition of their more cautious colleagues, the party leadership, the unions, and sections of the military. Neither has organized business, as represented by the chambers, demanded at any time since the beginning of Syria's second *infitah* that a long-term comprehensive plan for economic transition be developed. This has been partly due to their caution against advancing too far and too fast beyond the official line of discourse, and partly to the fact that Syria's business community, especially its spokespersons, have not necessarily been in favour of introducing a fully-fledged market economy which would, among other things, remove protective measures for Syrian producers and endanger some people's *de facto* market monopolies.

Personalization and Controlled Debate

Despite the development of a complex institutional framework, economic policy-making in Syria has remained a highly personalized affair. This feature which clearly reflects the overall structure of Syria's authoritarian-structured political system applies to all levels of government and leadership. It is striking, for instance, that both in the presidency and in the prime minister's office, there exists no economic-policy planning team.

There is an economic office in the presidency, and there are a couple of economists in the rank of advisor (*mustashar*) in the prime minister's office.[48] The role of this advisory staff, however, has gradually decreased. In the first years of his rule, Asad still gave importance to the presidential economic office and its advice. On the staff were economists of some standing like Dr George Hauranieh, who in 1976 was promoted Minister of State for Planning Affairs, and Dr Sadiq al-Ayubi who became Minister of Finance. Over the years, Asad has increasingly refrained from using the expertise of the presidency. Positions in the economic office were left as spoils for well-connected individuals, qualification was no obstacle but less important, and the expertise of these persons was rarely sought. The President sought economic-policy advice from outside his own apparatus, asking different persons – including acting and former cabinet ministers and businessmen – for briefings or memoranda.

A similar development occurred in the prime minister's office, related here, however, to an exchange of persons at the top, not to one person's changing patterns in seeking consultation. Well through the 1970s, economic advisors in the prime minister's office were able to exercise influence on government decisions through their studies and advice. Their role has been circumscribed since 'Abd al-Ra'uf al-Kasm's assumption of office in 1980. Apparently not liking his economic experts seeking to interfere in decision-making, Kasm abolished what was called the Economic Studies Department in the prime minister's office. Formally maintaining their position as advisors to the prime minister, most of the economists remained virtually without function. Decisions that have to be made in the prime minister's office have since been taken by the prime minister in person whereby, as mentioned, Kasm's successor Zu'bi used to consult a number of high-ranking party and military leaders.

At the lower levels of Syria's highly centralized administrative structure, decisions are equally personalized. As noted above, governmental decisions are usually initiated by the minister as the highest-ranking official in the ministry concerned with the issue. Lower-level bureaucrats have systematically learned to refrain from taking initiatives or decisions on their own. Quite characteristically, for instance, the representative of the Minister of Economy in the governmental Committee for the Project of a Stock-Market Law insisted that his minister see the whole committee and give a go-ahead before he and his colleagues form a subcommittee to prepare a new draft law. Persons attempting to get things done in a ministry would, for the same reason, usually try to see the minister or request a mediator see him on their behalf. Many administrative decisions are therefore taken informally, in direct contact between public-sector directors, party-branch officials, trade-union functionaries, or businessmen and the minister in charge.

Although government ministers are considered high-ranking civil servants rather than political leaders, some of them can exercise considerable discretion, not only where purely technical matters are concerned. Since none of Asad's prime ministers has been an expert on economics, at least one of the key economic ministers – either the deputy prime minister for economic affairs, the minister for economy and foreign trade, or the finance minister – has usually enjoyed substantial influence over economic-policy decisions. 'Imadi, who became Minister of State for Planning Affairs in 1972 and has been Minister of Economy from 1975 to 1980 and again since 1985, has certainly more discretion over economic policies than Prime Minister Zu'bi. The President may delay the final decision on a particular reform project or make clear to the government that it refrains from a particular issue or project. But he has rarely reversed governmental economic-policy decisions. While an ambitious government minister, as mentioned, would usually seek a presidential green light before starting a reform initiative, the presidential go-ahead would then allow him a lot of room to manoeuvre.

Policy initiatives are usually pursued in a rather individualistic manner. Ministers rarely cooperate in preparing or pursuing particular projects, and there is no trace of a change team behind the economic reform process: no brain-storming or planning group that would link reform-minded members of the political elite with each other and with experts from the bureaucracy, deputies, independent consultants, private-sector representatives, or academics. Such contacts remain individual and informal. Any organized grouping of this sort, emerging from within the regime elite and pressing for reform, would, likely, be suspected of trying to become an independent power centre.

Nor is there a resistance team. Certainly, particular proposals from 'Imadi's side, such as to allow the privatization of some of the public sector, have met a largely successful resistance from the trade-union leadership and the public-sector bureaucracy, and a large part of the regime elite does not feel at ease with *infitah* and reform. There is, however, no organized grouping of reform resisters in government and party that would try to block or even derail the reform process which, after all, has the President's blessing in principle.

Generally, government ministers campaign for the corporate interests of their ministries rather than for policies, occasionally even publicly disagreeing. The Ministry of Industry, for instance, is in constant disagreement with the Ministry of Supply on the one hand, and with the Ministry of Agriculture on the other. While the Ministry of Supply is interested in keeping consumer prices low, the Ministry of Industry has an interest in product prices that make the public industrial sector more profitable.[49] And while the Ministry of Agriculture is interested in securing encouraging procurement prices for industrial crops, the Ministry of Industry insists that "peasants should not be supported at the expense of our companies".[50] As a rule, the Ministries of Finance, Supply, and Industry tend to be more economically conservative than the Ministry of Economy and Foreign Trade. While, for instance, the latter made it clear that it would favour a reduction of customs tariffs, the Ministry of Finance and the Central Bank, whose main concern is with securing the revenue needed to cover public expenses, have not been supportive of such a move.[51]

At leadership and government level, therefore, as far as economic policies are concerned, we find a rather narrow circle of core decision-makers, or members of the regime elite, with some notable variance in their views on economic policies, rather than different teams pushing for or against change. Basically, this core consists of the Ba'th party RC, the head of the military mukhabarat, and the cabinet members with economic portfolios. The President and Zu'bi follow a pragmatic line which allows for necessary adjustments without pushing for them; Khaddam and 'Imadi represent a more market-oriented tendency, Nasir, Ikhtarini, Qaddura and others a more statist one. These core decision-makers are all, to varying degrees, dependent on the President; they would not oppose what is obviously his will. In cases of conflict he is the supreme arbitrator. In the first place, however, conflictual decisions are avoided and consensual ones sought – among other things by pursuing reforms incrementally and seeking to apply hard choices only in doses. Apart from being considered detrimental to regime stability, open conflict and conflictual decisions within the regime elite would contradict the corporatist notion that the regime, and ideally the entire polity, constitute one more or less harmonious body. Notably, government and leadership decisions are practically never taken by majority vote.[52]

From below this core level, a number of representatives of what are regarded as legitimate interests are consulted on economic-policy questions – partly informally, partly through their incorporation into formal decision-making institutions. Aside from being consultant bodies, the Guidance Committee and, on a broader base, parliament, are places to raise issues and to articulate interests, and they offer some space for bargaining. For the most part, such bargaining occurs between the representatives of the respective organized interests – merchants, industrialists, public-sector labour, organized peasantry – and the government. Parliament and the Guidance Committee also constitute a channel for some direct, if government-mediated, bargaining between different interest groups. As yet, such elements of interest-group participation as bargaining and consultation have remained controlled; demands for a greater measure of representation and influence than the the regime is prepared to allow are easily checked. Consider the chambers' claim to be represented on the Investment Committee and the flawed attempt at amending the tax law in parliament.

Interest articulation is not restricted to discussions within official regime structures and more or less informal meetings between interest groups and government representatives. There is, as far as economic policies are at issue, some space for public policy debate, and this space, however controlled, is wider than it is for other political issues. The GFTU as well as, where agricultural questions are at stake, the Peasant Union as the regime's two most important popular organizations articulate their interests quite straightforwardly in their own media. Chambers do so with more restraint and less publicity; they do not have any mass media of their own. General trade union congresses are important events for the articulation of GFTU and public sector interests; they are widely publicized, usually opened by the President and attended by a number of high party officials and cabinet members. Conferences organized by the GFTU or individual industrial unions have occasionally become a place for intensive policy debate. The 1987 Conference on Self-Reliance and Creativity was an outstanding example in this respect. It brought together participants from the unions and other popular organizations, the government and the public sector, universities, and the private sector. Discussions were open and critical, apparently more so than planned by the organizers.

An important forum for the public economic-policy debate is the Economic Sciences Association. This is the only forum which is not linked to either the state, the party – which used to discuss economic policies when congresses were still held – or a popular organization. A voluntary society of economists, it organizes an annual series of public lectures on economic-policy issues, bringing together Syrian academics, government ministers, businesspeople, journalists, and an interested public. Papers given are for the most part policy-oriented, and sometimes critical and controversial. 'Imadi may use the Economic Sciences Association to publicly reveal his ideas on necessary policy steps, private-sector representatives to criticize exaggerated state control over the economy, and unabated Ba'thi etatists to demand more of it.[53] The lectures are the only forum in Syria where a minister is required to defend government policies publicly and before a critical audience. Such criticism is tolerated within bounds. During the 1986 season, a couple of lectures exceeded these limits by sharply attacking government policies. As a result, the annual lecture series was stopped for the following three years. In 1990 it started again, with a series of considerably softer lectures.[54]

Syria's state-controlled media also play some role in the policy debate. There has always been, particularly in Syria's three country-wide daily papers, a margin for critical investigations of and complaints against the performance of government and public sector. Media coverage of this kind has served both as an outlet for popular discontent and as an instrument to discover defects. For the most part, it has dealt with the implementation of policies and the critical evaluation of particular laws and decrees rather than discussing the overall tendency of the regime's economic policy. Only with the emergence of Syria's second *infitah* has the scope of policy debate in the press been widened, accompanied by a more friendly attitude towards private business. Not before the late 1980s did the term businessman (*rajul a'mal*) come into use in the Syrian press; before that it was not uncommon to speak of the parasitic bourgeoisie. Rarely were parts of the bourgeoisie referred to in a positive fashion. By 1988, however, Syria's newspapers had started to mention businessmen by name, in a positive context, by 1990 to interview them and occasionally publish their photographs. On 8 March 1993, Radio Damascus conducted a highly symbolic interview with Sa'ib Nahhas, one of Syria's three most prominent new-class tycoons, allowing him to speak for almost an hour of this 30th anniversary of the Ba'thist revolution about the private sector, its performance and its advantages. From the late 1980s also, the press started to discuss economic policies more generally, and to ask government ministers and academics as well as businessmen and independent deputies for their views, proposals and demands regarding economic policy. The debate thereby became increasingly controversial – or pluralistic. While a number of journalists continued to defend what they regarded as the public interest against private greed and sell-out, sometimes strongly criticizing the course of *infitah*,[55] others began to question established basics of Syria's economic policy and to discuss issues that obviously were not on the government's agenda at that time.[56] Some of these articles were inspired by individual ministers, deputies, or businessmen who began to use the press as a vehicle by which policy issues that went beyond the discourse of party and government could be launched.

Still, Syria's press is far from being free. Not only are there no independent mass media, the press is overseen by the Ministry of

Information which for its part, since information policies are part of the President's main concerns, is closely supervised by the presidency. The ministry determines the limits of criticism in the media, decides the content of press releases on parliamentary debates, and indicates to the press how far it can open up the discussion. Media discussions, no less than the other fields of public-policy debate, remain a controlled affair.

Style and Structure

It is evident from the above how much the style of economic policy-making in Syria – and, to a large extent, its outcome – is related to the authoritarian structure of the regime. Asad's hegemony over economic-policy decisions does not imply that he takes all decisions. The system leaves space for individual actors in the core elite, and the personality of these actors makes a difference. 'Imadi is certainly more assertive than his predecessor and later Deputy Prime Minister Salim Yasin, who would rather avoid taking any decisions, let alone try to set the agenda for policy reforms. Kasm, as noted, used to rely less on the advice of the small circle of top military and party bosses (at the same time avoiding personal involvement in all government decisions), while Zu'bi tends to involve this group when working through his files. However, all these persons – practically the full regime elite – owe their position and discretion to the President, not to the institution to which they belong: party, bureaucracy, even military – let alone parliament or electorate.

Accordingly, there is no change team. Government ministers or party executive members are individually dependent on the President; teams or blocs that could form the nucleus of an alternative power centre are not supposed to emerge. As a matter of fact, government ministers do not choose their own assistant or deputy ministers; confidence between the minister and his deputy is more often than not non-existent. Direct coordination between ministers is limited. As a rule, interministerial contacts have to be made through the prime minister's office since the – originally – main coordination body in the government, the Planning Authority, has lost most of its functions. Moreover, there is a general lack of critical and pro-active policy debate and discussion: the public-policy debate is restricted, government exercises a *de facto* control over parliament, and advisory bodies have been dismantled or do not play their role. At the same time –

with technical expertise held at bay and parliamentary or public control limited – the personalized structures of the regime allow vested interests, particularly for those crony capitalists who live off their privileged relations with high-ranking persons, to penetrate relatively easily into decision-making processes.

The lack of an independent base to lean on does not make members of the regime elite particularly daring in pushing for change or taking initiatives in the first place. Only a few cabinet ministers would endeavour to publicly campaign for a policy issue, thereby risking arousing the suspicion of colleagues, and eventually seek a presidential green light to launch a reform project. Since the general rule is that ministers follow and execute leadership directives rather than trying to force them, a cautious approach and a certain wariness of change is often more functional for one actor's personal career and ambitions than an assertive, independent and reform-oriented behaviour.

Given all this and the overcentralized bureaucracy with its personalized decision structure and discouragement of initiative at subordinate bureaucratic levels, incentives for pro-active decision-making and long-term planning are scarce. Indeed the system may increase negligence and inertia. As outlined above, Syria's electricity crisis, a clear result of lack of coordination and long-term planning, was allowed to smoulder unresolved until it suddenly became a political problem, forcing the President to intervene and to order hasty priority and policy rearrangements.

Another more political case in point was the striking absence of any organized attempt at evaluating the changing economic environment Syria was about to encounter as a result of the Middle East peace process. Even by the time of the May 1994 Israeli–Palestinian autonomy agreement, neither the government, the party, the universities or the chambers had commissioned any study on the economic repercussions of a regional peace for Syria, let alone planned economic responses to such new regional questions. Neither did state-employed Syrian academics participate in international workshops or study groups – regardless of whether or not there were Israeli participants – that attempted to develop scenarios for the region's economic future.[57]

This apparent inertia was due to authoritarian structures rather than lack of expertise or concern. Fear played a role: the objective fear that the Syrian economy would find it difficult to cope with the challenges of a regional economy of peace; the subjective fear that any merciless analysis of this situation could be considered defeatist; and, more importantly, the fear that touching upon the whole issue of peace and regional change before the actual signing of a Syrian–Israeli agreement would give the impression of trying to influence the country's foreign policy. The decision to undertake any such studies – for example on Israel's market power, Israeli–Syrian competition, the prospects of infrastructural integration, the role of an independent Palestinian economy – or actually to prepare a set of possible Syrian policy responses was considered a matter of high policy.[58] It was not an issue which, for instance, Syria's Central Bureau of Statistics – the government's only social science think-tank of sorts – could uni-laterally decide to work on, or for which the cabinet, let alone an individual minister, could commission a group of scholars or advisors. Also, in the press the prospects – or risks – of regional peace for Syria were not discussed. Independent research centres or think-tanks that could have worked on the topic were in any case non-existent.

Matters left for a top-level, i.e. presidential, decision could easily, as has been shown, remain undecided. The President could simply be overloaded, particularly when foreign-policy and security issues de-manded time and concern. Since the President considers economic-policy issues of secondary importance, they could either be delayed deliberately in order to avoid antagonizing parts of his political base, or simply left on the shelf until he was free. This applies to concrete reform projects such as the stock-market law as much as to pro-active economic-policy planning. Only where economic-policy questions tend to become critical, i.e. politically threatening – as was the case with the electricity situation in 1993 – would they be tackled energetically on the spot.

In sum, it seems that the authoritarian structure of the regime constitutes the main systemic constraint on economic policies that would be more effective, less reactive and, arguably, more rational and less biased towards a certain category of well-connected vested inter-ests. Syria, certainly, is not unique in this respect. To prioritize the avoidance of political crisis in the short run over long-term planning is not uncommon for political systems where regime stability and survival are the central motivation of economic policy,[59] nor is it un-common for analysis and expertise to be deliberately abandoned in order to avoid open conflict when criteria other than economic ration-ality determine economic-policy decisions.[60] While political-structural variables thus obviously influence the style and content of economic-policy reform, Syria's reform policies have on their part impacted on decision-making structures.

4. Conclusion: Economic Reform and Patterns of Incorporation

The institutional framework of economic decision-making in Syria – with a complex government structure, a parliament, and the PNF as a formalized body of coordination between the ruling party and its allies all in place – had been established by the mid-1970s. The notable exception was the Guidance Committee which was set up only in 1981. The establishment of this committee meant an important amendment to the structure since, for the first time, private-sector representatives were incorporated into governmental decision-making bodies. No further important structural changes to the institutional framework have come about since. However, the weight and role in economic policy-making of the different parts of the structure and of institutional actors have changed, particularly since the mid-1980s, i.e. along with the second *infitah*.

There are, so to speak, winners and losers. The main loser has been the party. The Ba'th, as outlined in Chapter IV, has gradually been deprived of its political and ideological leadership since the take-over of 1970. Its demobilization, however, began only in the second half of the 1980s, most clearly expressed through its failure – to date at least – to convene a Regional Congress after that of 1985. As far as economic policies are concerned, it was evident that the whole drive towards economic reform and liberalization went against the official party line as established at the 1985 congress. Only the RC, a hand-picked group of clients to the President, retained a say in economic policy formation. As a body, however, this say was limited to being allowed to discuss government policies.

Similarly, the PNF lost discretion over economic policy-making. The central leadership of the front was still informed about economic-policy changes, they were allowed to discuss such changes critically but not in any way to block them. Representatives of the smaller front parties murmured a lot about what, in particular, they regarded as the class-biased content of Syria's second *infitah*, having to realize, however, that from the late 1980s onwards their influence on economic-policy decisions was close to nil.[61] Decision-making concerning the direction of economic policy by-passed both the *jabha* (PNF) and the Ba'th party except for, in the latter case, a couple of individuals with leadership functions in the government.

Within the government itself with its dominant role for economic policy-making, some minor yet significant shifts took place. These included the loss of importance of the State Planning Authority or Ministry for Planning. Planning was not explicitly abandoned, and the Authority continued to work on five-year plans, regardless of whether or not they ever saw the light. The Minister of Planning Affairs also continued to sign development-loan agreements with foreign agencies. But the authority had lost its main function of co-ordinating between different portfolios, pre-deciding investment priorities and tenders, and thereby securing, or at least trying to do so, a harmonious development approach. Some of its functions were taken over by the Prime Minister, others by the Guidance Committee. In general, however, economic planning simply lost out in the course both of relatively decreasing public investment capacities and the move towards a more liberalized economy.

The cabinet as a whole has for most of the time under Ba'thist rule been ratifying economic-policy decisions rather than designing or determining them. Until the mid-1980s, the Economic Committee was the most important body for the discussion and formation of economic policies at government level. Along with the new *infitah*, however, and the obvious wish and need to consider private-sector interests and proposals more seriously before deciding on particular policy initiatives, the Economic Committee has gradually ceded its role to the Guidance Committee. This body has incrementally developed into something like a mini-cabinet for economic affairs, deciding on matters that relate to foreign trade, as well as discussing other important economic-policy issues.

Before 1990, parliament played little part in economic policy-making. Since the legislative elections of that year, its status has been enhanced. Still, as outlined, parliament has no power – power understood in the Weberian sense of having one's way even in face of opposition – but it has gained a real role in the economic decision-making process. It allows a widened representation of societal interests, opens space for interest articulation and for a broader policy debate, and offers an opportunity for consultation where the government deems that necessary. Doubtless, government and political leadership have taken the parliaments of 1990 and 1994 more seriously than previous chambers. Such new respect was due to the presence in parliament of a number of independent deputies: independent not only in the meaning of being elected from outside the PNF list, but also of not being economically dependent on their function in the party, the bureaucracy and public sector, a mass organization or the parliament itself. The opening of the parliament to include these independent elements – as well as the increasing importance of the Guidance Committee – can in fact be considered complementary to the economic *infitah*. It extends official legitimation to hitherto underrepresented, bourgeois interests by incorporating them into regime structures side by side with the party and those organized interests that form the traditional basis of the regime. Since the regime had to rely increasingly on the contribution of the private sector – for the generation of foreign exchange and jobs at least – an inclusion of some of its representatives was only functional.

Notably, the representation of bourgeois interests is broader – more diversified – in parliament, i.e. in the sphere of interest articulation and policy debate, than in the Guidance Committee, in the sphere of policy design, where private-sector representation is functionally connected to the presidents of the Damascus chambers. Since the government interferes with the composition of the board of the chambers, especially with the elections to the presidency of the prestigious Damascus Chamber of Commerce, it also controls who is to represent the interests of the bourgeoisie in government bodies. A similar feature applies to the representation of labour. Apart from a number of GFTU-executive members, a few independent trade unionists or former trade unionists have been elected into parliament. Where policies are actually designed, only representatives of the hand-picked leadership of the GFTU are allowed in. Corporatist representation remains controlled.

By giving the chambers a place in the decision-making structure, the corporatist elements of the system have been extended. Both the chambers and the trade unions – and, as has to be mentioned again even without further studying their case, the Peasant Union as far as agricultural policies are concerned – are regarded as bearing segmental, functional responsibilities for the whole and as such as representing legitimate interests.

Organized labour has been politically demobilized – not unlike the party. The trade unions, however, maintain an important systemic function, being regarded as legitimate representatives of bureaucratic and, above all, public-sector interests. This includes, as outlined, both the furtherance of the material concerns and well-being of those employed by the state, and their control. In this capacity, Syria's trade unions have not actually gained a veto power, but they could achieve something short of it, i.e. they are intensively consulted and real participants in all decisions that concern the public sector.

The chambers as representatives of the private sector are far from enjoying any veto power, but they have inceasingly been consulted on all matters that concern the private sector more than others. Through this consultation they have, since the general economic-policy climate has changed in their favour, considerable chances to influence decisions. Certainly, private-sector demands should not conflict with regime control, which is maintained among other means by the penalization of unauthorized currency transactions; nor should it conflict with some highly echeloned individual interests – as was the case with cigarette smuggling over a long time – or with the vested interests of key support groups of the regime. At first sight, this list of taboos may look fairly far-reaching; yet there is space for private-sector interests. Consider, for instance, the relations between labour and business. An important development accompanying the *infitah* of the 1980s was that the trade unions by and large came to refrain from aggressively defending the rights of those employed in the private sector, and especially to tolerate the *de facto* right of private employers whom they want to dismiss.[62]

Rather than struggling over wages or dismissals, let alone the general line of social and economic policies, trade unions and business have begun to mark out claims within the existing system. The unions no longer oppose the general drive towards a more liberalized economy, in particular the gradual expansion of scope for private-sector activities; but they remain wary of anything that could be considered private encroachment on the public sector. The chambers for their part have realized that they should avoid calling for any dismantling of the public sector or for privatization, and avoid also directly calling into question trade-union privileges.[63]

Still, public-sector interests and business – as represented by the unions and the chambers – are not equally incorporated into decision-making structures, nor have their respective spheres of influence and their functional position in the state been clearly delineated. A fully developed corporatist system has not yet emerged. In such a system a group of non-competitive associations regarded as representing important functional sectors of society would participate fully in policy formation and implementation. If the process of economic reform continues, however, Syria's political system may well further develop along a corporatist model.

Notes

1. Author's interviews, Damascus, 1987–94.
2. Cf. e.g. *MEED*, 24 February 1989, 11 August 1989, 23 February 1990, 27 September 1991; *al-Hayat*, 5 October 1993.
3. *al-Hayat*, 1 October 1993.
4. Cf. Tim Niblock, "International and Domestic Factors in the Economic Liberalization Process in Arab Countries".
5. Cf. *al-Hayat*, 6 October 1993.
6. The rehabilitation and extension of the sewage system of Syria's four biggest cities, for example, which initially the World Bank planned to finance, was later financed by the Kuwait-based Arab Fund for Economic and Social Development.
7. Occasional rumours about Saudi pressure for economic reform in Syria have so far not been substantiated. After the second Gulf War, it seemed for a while as if the Saudis and other GCC countries wanted to push for a greater measure of economic liberalization in both Syria and Egypt, who were supposed to become the main beneficiaries of a prospected GCC fund for countries that had supported Kuwait during the war. GCC officials announced that the IMF and the World Bank would be invited to participate in the management of that fund. Moreover, fund loans should primarily be extended to projects that had been approved by the IMF or World Bank (Cf. *al-Ahram*, 23 and 27 April 1991; *MEED*, 3 May 1991). It is worth noting, however, that the prospected fund has not come into existence in the three years following the war, and financial aid from GCC countries still flows without any IMF or World Bank interference to projects which the respective governments consider important.
8. Cf. UNDP/World Bank, *Syria: Issues and Options in the Energy Sector*; ESCWA, *Exports of Manufactures and Semi-Manufactures from the Syrian Arab Republic: Trends, Problems and Prospects. Performance of General Industrial Organizations in the Syrian Arab Republic*, July 1986.
9. Cf. Suman K. Bery, "Economic Policy Reform in Developing Countries", p 1129.
10. Reform, here, does not necessarily imply a move towards the better. Instead, reform is used interchangeably with policy change. Different reform options will not be discussed.
11. Cf. e.g. Muhammad al-'Imadi, "Siyasat al-tijara al-kharijiyya fi al-thamaniat wa-afaquha fi al-tisa'inat"; idem, "Adwa' 'ala ba'd awjah siyasatina

al-iqtisadiyya" (paper presented to the Seventh Economic Tuesday Symposium, Damascus 1992), p 43ff. 'Imadi's undated memorandum on Syria's banking sector was submitted in 1993.

12. This latter decision had to be taken after the implementation of the 1991 investment law. Petty details like this, if not otherwise indicated, stem from author's interviews in Syria, 1990–93.

13. Cf. Heydeman, "The Political Logic", p 37 (n 38); author's interviews.

14. The Council consists of the Prime Minister, the Deputy Prime Minister for Economic Affairs, seven cabinet ministers and the director of the Investment Bureau which functions as a general secretariat to the Council.

15. The Authority is still often referred to as the Ministry of Planning since it is headed by a cabinet minister, the Minister of State for Planning Affairs.

16. Cf. GFTU, *Mu'tamar al-ibda'*.

17. Cf. GFTU, *The 22nd Conference*, p 387; author's interviews.

18. Parallel to the GFTU, the Ba'th party leadership showed an interest in the question of public-sector reform. In March 1989, following a demand from the Ba'th party RC, the Economic Committee recommended that an interministerial expert committee chaired by the Minister of State for Planning Affairs be constituted and prepare a "comprehensive report about the situation of the public economic sector". The committee met during a period of about half a year and prepared a report which, however, was not implemented. Cf. GFTU, *22nd Conference*, p 385; Ahmad 'Abd al-Salam Dabas, "Dirasat al-lijan al-hukumiyya wa-l-munazzamat al-sha'abiyya tusiy bi-ihdath hay'a markaziyya li-l-tanmiya al-idariyya" [The Studies of the Government Committees and the Popular Organizations Recommend the Establishment of a Central Authority for Administrative Development], *al-Thawra*, 9 September 1993.

19. SAR, Ministry of Economy and Foreign Trade, *Taqrir hawl asalib tatwir al-qita' al-'amm.*

20. General Federation of Trade Unions, *Ba'd mulahazat awwaliyya 'an al-qita' al-'amm wa-l-mawqif minh wa-l-jadal al-da'ir hauwlah* [Some Preliminary Remarks on the Public Sector, the Position Toward it, and the Discussion About it] unpublished manuscript (June 1992), p 32.

21. Cf. ibid., pp 35ff.

22. The chambers are represented on some technical committees established by individual ministries. Also, since 1986, the chambers have been represented on sub-committees drafting parts of the never-published 1986–90 five-year plan.

23. This is not to say that heads of the RC's functional offices – for national security, peasants, higher education, etc. – may not interfere with the work of the ministries in their field, particularly where ministers are weak; nor does it exclude the interference in government work for the sake of illegal individual gains.

24. In 1989, the government proposed cutting bread subsidies by introduc-

ing a less subsidized "high-quality" bread and then gradually removing the normal-quality bread from the market. The RC demanded that this measure be followed by a public-sector pay rise. The pay rise came. It was, however, in the offing even without the RC's insistence.

25. Cf. above, Chapter II. Cf. also Seale, *Asad of Syria*, p 441.

26. An exceptional and in our context marginal case seems to have been Law No. 1/1985, the Unified Labour Law for Those Employed by the State. Reportedly, substantial parts of the law which practically transformed all persons employed with the public sector and the bureaucracy into quasi-civil servants were drafted in the presidency.

27. *al-Thawra*, 9 September 1993.

28. Cf. *MEED*, 8 October 1993.

29. Cf. *al-Hayat*, 30 September 1993; *The Middle East*, January 1994, p 32.

30. Cf. *al-Ba'th*, 30 October 1991. Only in 1993 was the customs dollar eventually raised to a medium rate, and this only for what were considered luxury imports (particularly automobiles).

31. This issue had emerged somewhat embarrassingly during parliamentary discussions about the 1991 business tax reform. See below.

32. Ihsan Sanqar, "Mudakhala hawl taqrir mashru' al-muwazana al-'amma" [Intervention on the Report on the Public Budget], mimeographed typescript, 3 May 1993, p 1.

33. On the discussion in parliament, cf. 'Ali 'Abud, "Mudakhalat hamma wa-ghanniyya hawl mashru' ta'dil al-nisab wa-l-shara'ih al-daribiyya" [Important and Rich Interventions about the Project for a Reform of Tax Classes and Rates], *al-Ba'th*, 9 July 1991; Na'um Ibrahim 'Abud, "al-Qanun al-'ashrun al-jadid" [The New Law No. 20], *al-Iqtisad*, 24 (August–September 1991) 331–332, pp 37–42.

34. Cf. *al-Thawra*, 1 January 1992.

35. Sadowski gives the impression of such battles actually being fought by 'Imadi and other civilian technocrats. Cf. his *Scuds or Butter*, pp 32ff. In my view, Sadowski overstates in this respect the energy and courage of civilian government ministers. They certainly lobby for their particular budgets. They would, however, not endanger their projects and positions by getting into open conflict with the military.

36. For a study of agricultural-policy making cf. in detail Hinnebusch, *Peasant*, pp 31–60.

37. The expression stems from 'Arif Dalila.

38. Cf. above, Chapter II, and Perthes, "Stages".

39. Cf. Laurence Whitehead, "Political Explanations of Macroeconomic Management: A Survey", *World Development*, 18 (1990) 8, pp 1133–1446 (pp 1142f). It is noteworthy, for instance, that Asad has relied on trusted persons for very long periods. This applies not only to his vice-president Khaddam and his defence minister Tlas, but to some members of the "economic team" too. Minister of Economy Muhammad al-'Imadi was first appointed to cabinet rank in 1972; Deputy Prime Minister for Economic Affairs Salim Yasin has

been a government minister since 1978. The longevity in office of individual ministers adds to the general impression of stability and cautious rather than volatile policy-making.

40. Cf. in this sense a statement in parliament by Deputy Prime Minister Salim Yasin as reported in *Tishrin*, 17 April 1994.

41. Syria's five-year development plans are long-term investment plans. As such they follow a certain economic philosophy. They do not, however, contain a policy programme or an outline of economic policies to be pursued within the five-year period. Even the investment part of the plans has been far from compulsory, and the five-year plans or their drafts have, since the 1980s, followed developments rather than planning them. The 1981–85 plan, as noted, was the last development plan to be officially issued.

42. "When Decree No. 10/1986 was discussed," the author was told by a member of the Ba'th party RC in 1992, "we did not allow a discussion of similar industrial investments."

43. Cf. 'Imadi, "Adwa' 'ala ba'd awjah"; see also the interview of Syrian businessman Sa'ib al-Nahhas, *al-Sharq al-awsat*, 12 January 1993.

44. Without mentioning the name of the author, one of these reports was leaked to and published in *al-Yaum al-sabi'*, 11 July 1988 to 10 August 1988. There were at least two additional reports at that time. One is: Nabil Sukr, *Nahwa iqtisad ishtiraki mutatawwir fi al-qutr al-'arabi al-suri*. Only a later study was published in Syria: Husayn Murhij al-'Ammash, *Tajawuz al-ma'ziq*.

45. On the Egyptian and Chilean cases cf., e.g., Dessouki, "Policy Making in Egypt"; Patricio Silva, "Technocrats and Politics in Chile" in *Journal of Latin American Studies*, 23 (May 1991), pp 385–410.

46. Cf. ASBP, *Eighth Regional Conference. Economic Report*, p 232 ("Recommendation No. 11"). I can therefore not agree to the thesis that the "trend toward liberalization dates from the January 1985 Regional Congress of the Ba'th Party," as is argued by Lawson, "External versus Internal Pressures", p 1.

47. As for the other "economy ministers" in Zu'bi's 1992 cabinet, Deputy Prime Minister for Economic Affairs Salim Yasin represents a storybook career of a Ba'thist academic. He has been a professor of economics, became a dean and a president of a university within six years of completing his Ph.D., and has been working as a government minister since 1976. Deputy Prime Minister for Services Rashid Ikhtarini is a politico and public-sector bureaucrat: he has served as director of the Aleppo tractor factory, as secretary of a party branch, and, since 1985, member of the Ba'th party RC. The Minister of Finance, Muhammad Khalid al-Mahayni, has served his way up through the ranks of the Finance Ministry. The Minister of Industry, Ahmad Nizam al-Din, is a public-sector bureaucrat; before becoming a minister he served as director of the Dayr al-Zur paper mill and later as director of the General Organization for Chemical Industries. The Minister of Transport, Mufid 'Abd al-Karim, is a Soviet-educated economics professor known for his mukhabarat connections rather than for his academic production. The Minister of Supply,

Nadim 'Akkash, is best characterized as a security technocrat, which is the usual qualification for this ministerial post. He obtained a law degree, has been a police officer and prior to his ministerial appointment a provincial governor. The Minister of Agriculture is a primary-school teacher with a party career, the Minister of Electricity an electrical engineer and a career bureaucrat in Syria's Electricity Company, the Minister of Irrigation a civil engineer and former director of a public-sector construction company. The main qualification of the Ministers of Communication and of Construction is their respective membership in one of the smaller PNF parties: The Ministry of Communication is treated as a fiefdom of the Communist Party, the Ministry of Construction as that of the Arab Socialist Union.

48. The number of staff in the prime minister's office and in the presidency is treated as a secret and not published. Reportedly, not more than three or four economists staff the economic office in the presidency while a considerably higher number are employed by the prime minister's office.

49. Cf. Hamash, *al-tanmiya al-iqtisadiyya*, pp 150f.

50. Cf. the lecture by Minister of Industry Nizam al-Din, "Waqi' al-sina'at al-suriyya wa-afaq tatawwuriha".

51. Cf. *al-Hayat*, 17 November 1993.

52. In the discourse of the regime, as noted, consensual decisions are usually referred to as "democratic"; "democracy" often simply meaning consensualism.

53. Cf. Muhammad al-'Imadi, "siyasat al-tijara"; Ratib al-Shallah, "Ara' fi al-tijara al-kharijiyya"; Mufid 'Abd al-Karim, "Dawr al-qita'at al-iqtisadiyya al-'amm wa-l-khass wa-l-mushtarak fi al-tijara al-kharijiyya al-suriyya", all in: Economic Sciences Association, *Sixth Economic Tuesday Symposium* 1990/91; Muhammad al-'Imadi, "Adwa' 'ala ba'd awjah siyasatina al-iqtisadiyya", in: *Seventh Economic Tuesday Symposium* 1992/93.

54. Compare the two lecture volumes: Economic Sciences Association, *Fifth Economic Tuesday Symposium 1986*; and idem: *Sixth Economic Tuesday Symposium 1990/91*.

55. Cf. e.g. Basam Ja'ara, "al-Tasdir" [Export], *al-Thawra*, 12 August 1992; Fahd Diab, "Mashari' al-istithmar" [Investment Projects], *al-Thawra*, 16 August 1992.

56. Cf., for instance, Riyad Darwish, "al-Suq al-hurra wa-ra'i matruh li-l-nuqash" [The Free Market: An Opinion up for Discussion], *al-Thawra*, 15 April 1988; Ahmad Mardini, "3 Ara' fi qanun tashji' al-istithmar" [Three Opinions on the Law to Encourage Investments], *Tishrin*, 9 December 1991; 'Ali 'Abud, "Qawanin ghayr haditha" [Unmodern Laws], *al-Ba'th*, 20 April 1992; Ahmad Mardini, "Hal yumkin ihdath jama'a mushtaraka?" [Could a Mixed-Sector University be Established?], *Tishrin*, 22 July 1992.

57. This did not prevent a few more or less secretive meetings of Israeli and Syrian academics.

58. Occasionally, Syrian officials have justified the absence of such peace-environment studies in Syria and of Syrian participants in international study groups on the matter with reference to Syria's politically motivated non-

participation in the multilateral groups of the Middle East peace talks. They argued that the approach of planning the region's post-peace economic future was similar to the approach of the multilaterals. It has to be noted, however, that in Lebanon, which equally boycotted the multilaterals, early efforts have been undertaken to analyse the economic risks and prospects of the peace process for the country, and the issue was also publicly debated.

59. Cf. Ravi Gulhati, "Who Makes Economic Policy in Africa and How?", *World Development*, p 1152.

60. Cf. Joel D. Aberach/Bert A. Rockman, "On the Rise, Transformation, and Decline of Analysis in the US Government", *Governance*, 2 (1989) 3, pp 293–314 (pp 294f).

61. "*De facto* the work of the *jabha* is frozen," the author was told by a member of the PNF central leadership in 1993. In a contribution to *al-Hayat*, 4 June 1993, Yusuf Faisal, head of one of Syria's two official communist parties, declared that the PNF had discussed some economic issues, but not all of them, and not constantly so.

62. Law No. 49/1962 is still in force. It prevents dismissals unless a special dismissal committee, consisting of chamber and union representatives and chaired by a civil servant, gives its approval. Mixed-sector companies, however, have been exempted from the provisions of the law, and dismissal committees have, since the late 1980s, increasingly come to look at cases from an employer's perspective. Employers therefore no longer find it particularly difficult to reach dismissals by agreement.

63. In 1990/91, the circular of the Damascus Chamber of Commerce published a couple of articles that implicitly demanded a circumscription of the role of the public sector and privatization (for instance: Muhammad Riyad al-Abrash, "al-Takhsis marra ukhra" [Privatization, Once Again], *al-Nashra al-iqtisadiyya* (1990), No. 4, pp 50–62; and "Iqtisad al-suq. al-Itar al-iqtisadi al-jadid li-l-'amal al-'arabi al-mushtarak" [Market Economy: The New Economic Frame of Arab Common Action], *ibid.* (1991), No. 3, pp 50–53). In the latter article, the author and editor of the circular also argued that after the world-wide victory of capitalism the role of the trade unions in developing countries which until now had followed a socialist development orientation would have to be reduced. The GFTU leadership reacted sharply, threatening to make the issue a public conflict. The chamber responded by dismissing the editor of their organ, implicitly conceding that they had exceeded their limits and encroached on the union's patch.

CHAPTER SIX

Conclusion: Authoritarian Adjustment and the Prospects of Political Development

Given that the present Syrian regime has been in power for more than two decades, and that it is very much under the control of one person, it makes sense to ask what will happen when eventually it comes to an end with the death of its leader. While a couple of authors claim to know almost for certain that Asad's death will trigger chaos, bloody sectarian strife or even civil war, I do not hold such a scenario to be the most likely one. The possibility that a new system will evolve smoothly from the structures that have taken shape since 1970 cannot be excluded. The question will be discussed briefly later in this chapter; but it cannot, at present, be answered. Based on the analysis of the economic, social, and political structures and developments which I have tried to provide above, the main purpose of this chapter is to ask about the development prospects of the present system; these prospects will themselves most probably affect coming events, including the question of transition and succession.

1. Adjustment and Control

Syria's economic reform, within the limits in which it has taken place, was precipitated by a severe economic crisis, mainly, as outlined, a foreign-exchange crisis, which reflected the structural inability of the statist economy to generate domestically the resources needed for further capital accumulation and imports. Economic crises may directly threaten the political stability of a country or even lead to a change of regime; and the economic problems faced by Syria from the mid-1980s in particular no doubt affected regime legitimacy. Economic reform, however, to the extent that it may help to get the state's resource balance straight, is itself a politically risky affair. While probably realizing "that the state has overreached its capacity to manage economic growth", incumbent elites are also likely to "fear that retreat in the economic sphere may lead to the erosion of political controls".[1] In a case like the Syrian where absolute primacy has been given to national and regime security, the recognition of the particular risks that economic liberalization may entail will corroborate the inclination of the regime to steer such a process according to its own schedule; or, if there exists no such schedule or plan in the first place, to at least maintain control over the process. This accounts to a large extent for the appearances of half-heartedness or (in friendlier) terms, caution with which reforms have been pursued in Syria.

In its attempts to keep the country's resources and the reform process as such under control, the regime has sought primarily to avoid any external interference in its policy-making. Syria's unwillingness to cooperate with the World Bank or other Western lenders on their terms has cost it some credit that otherwise might have flowed from these sources. Syria's government has also renounced the opportunity to blame the economic hardships borne by the lower strata of society in particular on the World Bank or IMF. At the same time, however, it has avoided political risks which other Third World regimes have fallen victim to. Reform programmes that have been pursued under the auspices of the IMF or other Western institutions have often deprived the regimes in question of their control over international aid and other rent flows, thereby curtailing their patronage, and causing their destabilization.[2] By maintaining control over economic adjustment, and introducing reform measures selectively, Syria's leadership has been able to maintain its patronage basis in the bureaucracy and public sector and extend it, rather than lose it, in the private sector.

Furthermore, by not allowing external actors any influence over its economic policies, the regime has been able to bolster its national credentials. This has been not so much among the broader public who are uninformed about Syria's debts and its negotiations with international financial institutions, but, rather, among the medium and upper echelons of the bureaucracy, party functionaries, parliamentarians and trade unionists. The deep-rooted Arab nationalist and

anti-imperialist convictions of this latter group has made them suspicious of any political business with the West and often of the whole
economic reform course. These same quarters, which have formed an
important part of the regime base, would not oppose Syria's seeking
regional political rents. Aid from the Gulf states, whether for arms
purchases or for development projects, was to boost Syria's strength
and progress; the respective donors did not interfere with the way in
which their money was spent, and most of it was in grants.

Certainly, both Syria's development achievements and the results
of its reform policies have been suboptimal. By means of Arab aid, oil
income, and international credit, Syria was enabled in the 1970s to
embark on an ambitious development strategy that centred on state-
led import-substituting industrialization, neglected agriculture, and
encouraged private commerce and trade more than manufacturing. To
a large extent, this strategy caused the imbalances that became apparent during the crisis of the 1980s. The performance of the public-
sector industrial base was dismal; instead of becoming the main source
of capital accumulation, it drained the foreign-exchange budget. Agricultural plans and pricing policies offered few incentives for peasants.
Many small producers, particularly land-reform beneficiaries, were
practically forced to give up agriculture if they wanted to make a
living; and the country's dependence on food imports increased. Mis-
allocations of resources that were due to poor planning and a measure
of gigantomania were compounded by clientelism and corruption, and
by an authoritarian structure that disencouraged initiative in the
bureaucracy and public sector and drove intellectual and entrepreneurial capacities out of the country. In short, Syria's development
potentials were not fully realized; achievements and progress, which
no doubt were made, lagged behind the country's potential.[3]

Even though the improvement of Syria's overall economic indicators from the late 1980s was largely a matter of increased oil
revenues and new aid flows from, especially, the Arab Gulf countries,
the crisis-born economic reform policies which the government pursued from about 1985 have borne fruit. Agriculture and private industry were successfully encouraged to increase their production,
investment, and exports; the country's balance-of-trade situation improved considerably; and budget deficits, as a percentage of the domestic product, were reduced. The most urgent and difficult economic
problem for the future is the creation of jobs for a still rapidly growing population. Most probably, more internal resources could have

been generated and geared towards productive investments if Syria's private industrial sector had been encouraged as much and as early as private commerce and trade. Productive investments would also have benefited if the government's opening towards private business had not been restricted, by and large, to deregulative measures, tax holidays, and exemptions from customs duties, but had included the introduction of government accountability, the establishment of an independent judiciary, and, generally, a greater measure of rule-of-law. Such political liberalization measures, however, would directly have affected the power of the regime. A certain loss of state control over production, consumption, and foreign trade, as liberalization measures entailed, was acceptable; inroads into the political control system were not.

In view of other countries' experiences, one should not expect economic-policy decisions to be necessarily economically rational. Not only do humans not always act rationally; more important, different rationalities are often at play, and the economically optimal allocation of resources may simply not be the main criterion for a given regime to give primacy to in its policy choices. Regime survival, especially, may have much higher priority.[4] In this sense, Syria's economic reform process, and its scope, sequencing, and course, have been very much a regime affair that followed a rationality of regime maintenance and stability more than pure economic or developmental rationalities. This is not to say that the government had a plan of how to sequence reform and adjustment. Rather, as has been shown, ad-hocism ruled. While lacking a plan of its own, however, the regime did not allow any other party – external or domestic – to set the pace of the process or determine its schedule.

Socially, Syria's economic reform and adjustment were anything but neutral. The dramatic deterioration of public-sector wages and salaries, which lost about half their real value over the 1980s, and the increase of conspicuous wealth in the hands of society's upper strata, underlined the fact that the losses of economic reform and liberalization were socialized while their gains had been privatized. Social inequalities and contradictions became more distinct; the growth of public social services did not hold pace with the growth of the population; and the cap on state employment closed one of the main channels for upward mobility which the Ba'th had opened from 1963 for climbers from the lower rural and urban strata. What was not allowed to happen, however, was an absolute impoverishment of state employees, a privatization of more than some marginal public-sector establishments, or a public-sector reform that would have involved large-scale lay-offs. Limits to structural adjustment were set where it could have entailed political destabilization. Notably, Syria has been spared any "bread" or "adjustment revolts" such as experienced by comparable countries like Tunisia or Egypt.

The lower echelons of the bureaucracy as well as the younger generation of the middle bureaucracy, public-sector employees, small and landless peasants, and the members of the marginalized urban strata all, in general, found themselves at the losing end of Syria's economic reform process; the bourgeoisie and particularly its commercial element were the main winners. In class terms, therefore, one might characterize Syria's reform path as expressing and serving, primarily, the interests of the dominant social alliance; a coalition, that is, of the state bourgeoisie, the new and parts of the old commercial bourgeoisie and – as a junior partner of sorts – the wealthier part of the independent peasantry. This alliance has no doubt been strengthened in the course of Syria's second *infitah*.[5] As noted above, only a very few of the children of Syria's state bourgeoisie and top bureaucracy chose a military or civil service career, and some members of these strata have begun to arrange for individual change-overs into the private sector. Partly at least, the alliance of the political, bureaucratic and military elite with parts of the private bourgeoisie could thus be succeeded by amalgamation.

Syria's bourgeoisie, in general, and that part of it in particular which openly allied itself with the men in power has profited, but it has not, through its alliance, gained a share of political control, nor is it likely to do so under the present regime. Rather, this alliance has followed a pattern according to which, in the words of Ghassan Salamé, bourgeoisies leave politics to their masters who secure the stability these bourgeoisies need to enrich themselves.[6] The chambers as the official representatives of Syria's business community would not even, as one member of the Damascus Chamber of Commerce executive sarcastically noted, submit a memorandum to the Prime Minister unless asked for it.[7] Until the late 1980s, indeed, the business community showed conspicuous restraint in publicly coming up with demands of their own for economic-policy changes. From the beginning of the 1990s, business representatives have voiced reform wishes more clearly, particularly so in parliament. They have not tried, however, to organize and exert pressure on the government in order to make it speed up economic reform or follow a particular policy direction. A substantial part of Syria's private sector was not eager, in the first place, to accelerate liberalization and reform measures and thereby risk monopolies and other selectively granted privileges, nor to dry up lucrative black markets and expose domestic industry to full competition.

Moreover, Syria's business community is not a particularly strong actor. Given that the state is more in need of private-sector resource generation than it was, it might be presumed that the bourgeoisie has acquired substantial bargaining power. Also, the public image of the private sector has been considerably enhanced in the course of Syria's second *infitah*. As noted, business representatives can now make their economic-policy suggestions known via the state-controlled media; and parliament members from the business class have been asked to speak at party rallies more than once since the elections of 1990. Image, however, should not be confused with strength. A close look at the Syrian private sector reveals that, as a whole, it is still politically weak. It is highly fragmented, both economically because of its overwhelmingly petty-bourgeois and small-scale structure, and as a sociopolitical force.

There exists, as yet, no single private industrial or trading establishment whose collapse or closure could cause any considerable damage to the national economy or create insoluble social problems – none of the kind, at least, which the bankruptcy of any of the larger public-sector establishments would entail. A handful of entrepreneurs, those commanding Syria's few big-business companies, have certainly acquired considerable bargaining power regarding their own business and their particular industries. This has enabled them to put through exemptions from certain rules and to have preferential access to public resources. These tycoons, however, do represent themselves more than the private sector. Inasmuch as they owe their position to an interventionist state and to regime patronage, they have only limited interest in furthering change. They have repeatedly proved, with other parts of the Syrian bourgeoisie, that they are likely to respond positively to the regime's selective policies. They will, that is, choose individual and group advantages rather than gamble for collective gains.

Individually, the majority of Syria's businessmen are still subject to the constant threat of being prosecuted for one of the economic offences and crimes most of them have been committing, particularly

illegal currency transactions. Currency black-marketeering, as a matter
of fact, has for the most part been tolerated, if not silently consented
to, by the government. Doing what legally remains an offence, however, weakens the position of private businessmen and is likely to
make them refrain from pressing political demands.

Organizationally, as outlined, Syria's business community enjoys
more independence than other societal groups. The chambers, as its
acknowledged interest organization, are not financially dependent on
the state as most of the popular organizations are, and their executives are comparatively freely elected from their membership. The
business community is represented, via the chambers and by independent deputies, in parliament and in governmental committees; and
it is listened to and consulted. Some government ministers, particularly the Minister of Economy, have long displayed an openly
friendly attitude towards the private sector and share most of its
views on current economic policies. It is not unlikely that an individual, well-connected businessman will take over the Ministry of
Economy at some stage. Such a direct representation of private-sector
interests in the cabinet would fit the logic of a gradual expansion of
corporatism. As yet, however, quite different from countries such as
Egypt or Tunisia, no entrepreneur has been appointed to a government position, no businessman is openly figuring as a presidential
advisor, and neither the Ba'th party nor the other front parties have
any business membership worth mentioning. The actual leverage of
the business community is limited. This is particularly apparent where
questions are at stake which, from a regime perspective, may concern
social control or otherwise be of political relevance. Notably, the
chambers have failed, to date, to reach an abolition of the notori-
ously harsh and practically unfeasible law on currency smuggling.[8]
They may publicly ask that "the private sector be allowed to give its
opinion" if an amendment of the law is prepared.[9] The regime, however, has left no doubt that this particular matter or other comparable issues will be discussed and decided upon according to its own
priorities and agenda.

At the same time, while the regime has not been forced by external
actors or by domestic, private-sector interests to stick to a particular
adjustment schedule or speed up its reforms, there has been remarkably little resistance on the part of the party or the bureaucracy to the
reforms so far enacted. Syria is not unique in this respect; resistance
to reform and adjustment is in fact often more feeble than one would

expect.[10] The would-be defenders of the old arrangements, namely, in the Syrian case, the party and trade-union leadership, have lost credibility; and the losers of economic reform, particularly public-sector employees and graduates who no longer find employment with the state, tend to seek individual solutions. Moreover, as outlined, party and trade unions have been emasculated and depoliticized and cannot be expected to actively oppose government policies. Among leading bureaucrats and public-sector managers, there are quite a few enlightened technocrats who are receptive to change and reform – particularly to a cautious reform course such as the one the government has been pursuing. Others have in time feathered their nests, and still others seek personal alternatives with the private sector. Given the authoritarian structure of the bureaucracy, the emergence of a resistance team which, in an organized way, would try to further its own alternative policy projects is practically out of the question. By the same token, as noted, a governmental change team that would actively push for reform has not come into being.

2. Economic Liberalization and Political Change

With Syria's economic reform in progress, the question is on the table whether and how such reform measures will also entail political structural changes. It is convenient to assume – and international development agencies have, by the 1990s, made it a basic tenet of their often wishful thinking – that economic and political liberalization are mutually interdependent or even twin processes.[11] Reality, unfortunately, does not always support this assumption. Even though the nature of a political system certainly influences the patterns of development in the country in question, comparative evidence suggests that a direct and clear relationship between economic liberalization or a more economically rational allocation of resources on the one hand, and political liberalization or democratization on the other, does not exist.[12] Some authoritarian regimes, most prominently Korea, Taiwan, and, with qualifications, Chile, have proved successful economic reformers, while others – Algeria, for instance – failed to adjust, and ran their countries into unmanageable crises and turmoil. In some democratic or democratizing countries, such as Turkey before 1980, necessary adjustment was blocked, and democracy thereby endangered; in others, such as Peru, adjustment programmes have led to destabilization and a return to authoritarian rule; while in still other, more promising cases – take such different countries as Hungary, Argentina, or Zambia – democratization and economic liberalization went together. There is little doubt, though, that the emergence of a more complex and pluralistic economic system necessitates some form of parallel political adjustment. What is particularly needed for a "liberalizing" authoritarian regime in order to counter the political risks which economic reform involves, is an appropriate form of participation and representation that secures the political incorporation of relevant societal groups and channels their conflicts.[13] Such an overhaul of patterns of representation and participation as well as, for that matter, frequent elections, must not be confused with democratization.

The political risks of liberalization have not been lost on Syria's rulers. To avoid these risks, the regime has sought more inclusive institutional arrangements other than open political competition, namely an expansion of the corporatist elements of the system. Authoritarian corporatism, as outlined, allows the selective incorporation into consultative and decision-making structures of societal elements from outside the regime's traditional social and political bases. Hitherto under-represented groups and interests can thereby be adequately represented and participate in particular policy fields without actually bidding for, or achieving, political power. Ideally at least, conflicts of interest between different groups will be dealt with inside the institutional frame, arbitrated by the regime leadership as the brain of the body politic, and thus remain under control. As the representation of group interests is through co-optation from above rather than democratic election, the regime remains capable of excluding those who might not accept the rules of the game. Syria's parliamentary reform, so to speak, of 1990, particularly the broader representation of interests which it involved, indicated the form and limits of political adjustment which the regime deemed necessary.

It is not unusual that Syrian officials and propagandists refer to the country's political system as democratic – skipping the prefix "popular" which previously indicated necessary qualifications, but underlining that Syrian democracy is different from that of other, particularly Western, countries.[14] In the broader Arab world and its political discourse, "democracy" is more and more operationalized according to the liberal concept; as a system of governance, that is, whose attributes are human rights, free political organization, government accountability, and the principle of change of government through periodic elections.[15] As this is obviously not what the Syrian regime intends to implement, the more cautious term "pluralism" (*ta'addudiyya*) has increasingly come into use in Syria's official rhetoric. The self-characterization of the Syrian regime as pluralistic expresses, however euphemistic it still is, some conceptual change. While it is anything but a promise of democratization, it is an implicit acknowledgement that conflicts of legitimate interests exist and are bound to grow in an increasingly complex socio-economic system. Asad himself, in a speech to trade unionists, acknowledged that there was a direct link between economic and political pluralism.[16] The so-called pluralistic project of the Syrian regime, as has been shown, demands a selective incorporation of certain economic and social interests that are indispensable for the generation of resources. The private sector has increasingly, over Syria's second *infitah*, become one of these indispensable sectors: it generates surplus and foreign exchange; it relieves the state of responsibilities which the latter previously had assumed but was unable to sufficiently fulfil, particularly employment and supply; and it provides opportunities for parts of the regime elite to transform some of its wealth into capital. A stronger incorporation of other societal segments, such as urban intellectuals, rural notables, and men of religion, may also be advisable, mainly for political reasons, to substitute for the loss of allegiance on the part of the losers of economic adjustment. Any more far-reaching structural change of the system, however, has not been on the agenda of the regime's leadership. Pluralization has not been intended to lead to a gradual loss of power, but rather to consolidate, re-invigorate and probably to rationalize the control and legitimacy of the regime.[17]

The attempt to open up economically without an earnest political liberalization can well be manageable as long as some rent inflows – foreign, particularly Arab aid, and oil revenues – continue to support the budget and regime autonomy, and the private sector makes use of the generally more friendly investment and business climate which the government has created. In the long run it may have its limitations. Authoritarian structures do not as such set limits to economic growth, but they form a rather unfavourable condition for the development of human capital and creative, innovative forces.[18] The conspicuous lack, by 1993/94, of attempts, on the part of Syrian universities, the chambers, or the government, to develop scenarios for the economic repercussions on Syria of a regional peace, has shown shortcomings in this respect. If Syria wants to compete – rather than simply form a reservoir of cheap labour and agricultural products – in the new Middle Eastern economy that is going to emerge, human capital development and the stimulation of innovative capacities will become particularly important. From a regime perspective, such long-term socio-economic considerations are of rather secondary importance. The regime's prime concern has been, and is, with the economic and political problems of the day,[19] and, above all other things, with the maintenance of stability and control.

As it seems unlikely that the Syrian regime itself, out of an understanding of long-term necessities, or because of external pressure, would change its course and start to implement political reforms of more than a limited nature, one might ask whether there are social actors that have more far-reaching projects and are able and prepared to push them forward. Generally in the Arab world, hopes have been raised that socio-structural change and the inability of authoritarian regimes to solve their countries' social and economic problems will strengthen civil society, and that the forces of civil society will in turn press for democracy.[20]

In Syria, one should not for the time being be over-optimistic. The bourgeoisie, as has been seen, is too weak to push through its economic-policy objectives, and it is therefore hardly imaginable that it would be able to enforce on the regime a schedule for democratic change. Moreover, it seems as if the bourgeoisie had no such democratic agenda in the first place. Parts of the business class are doubtless interested in political liberalization, particularly in increased government accountability, transparency of decisions and deals, and an implementation of rule-of-law. Others, notably those who have well-established relations with the regime elite and, as a rule, happen to be the main winners of the transformation process that has so far taken place, certainly do not want to risk their gains through democratic reform. Democratization would be likely to strengthen demands for a more equitable distribution of the costs and for a taxation of the profits of economic transformation. Private-sector pressure for more substantial political change, for more, that is, than a gradual expansion of corporatist mechanisms, has therefore been and will probably remain very limited.

There are other societal segments whose interest in political liberalization and democratization is stronger. Both independent professionals and state-employed educated salary-earners – professors and planners as well as technicians and teachers, and even some higher-ranking bureaucrats – can be said to harbour, in their majority, a strong wish for an expansion of political breathing space. In their ranks, the socio-cultural effects of authoritarianism are also most clearly felt: the emigration of technical and intellectual capacities, the promotion of party loyalists into academic positions and, in due course, the deterioration of higher education, etc. Regardless of whether the democratic aspirations of the educated middle classes are stable, or whether they could easily be traded off for material benefits, this stratum will, on the whole, be supportive of a political opening. It is not, however, in a state to push for or to prepare it. It is fragmented and dependent, and it has little organizational power. Those professional unions which, in 1980, tried to challenge the regime on issues of human rights and civil liberties were crushed as independent forces and have not yet recovered. The trial, in 1992, of the members of a barely established human rights group who, among other things, had dared to question the 99.9 per cent result of the presidential referendum of 1991, was a clear warning that people had better not try to establish any liberal, regime-critical associations. It is highly indicative for the scope allowed to civil society in Syria that the number of social, cultural, scientific, educational, religious, and charity organizations permitted, being extremely low from the beginning, has actually been decreasing since 1980 – from the time, that is, when the government broke the back of the professional organizations.[21] Neither is there a dissident technocracy,[22] specialists and academics grouped around independent research institutes or other institutions, who would prepare proposals and plans ready for submission and implementation once the current regime gives way. No independent social science or economic research establishments exist in the first place – except for a couple of consulting bureaux called institutes, which university professors and former or active civil servants have set up in the wake of the 1991 investment law.[23]

Generally, the state has penetrated deeply Syria's civil society. The legal political spectrum, as outlined, is limited to the Progressive National Front; and the parties of the front, while securing themselves a place in the system, have lost their independence and, to a large extent, their legitimacy by their subjection to the leadership of the Ba'th and the President. Popular organizations, as the trade-union example has shown, have become strictly regime-controlled corporations. Parts of the trade-union membership, including not a few of the middle- and lower-level functionaries, are certainly interested in political opening and change. Their main concern at present, however, is rather defensive: namely the protection, as far as possible, of those employed in public administration and the public sector against the risks of economic restructuring. The masses (in the Ba'th's own jargon), that is the majority of the people, are rather politically indifferent and lethargic. They try to make their living as public employees, small peasants, wage-labourers, casual workers, or self-employed vendors of marginal products and services, and to cope with the difficulties of reduced real wages, housing problems, and questions about the education, employment and marriage of their children. It is the everyday economic problems that keep them going, not politics.[24] For the majority, to quote a Damascene notable, "the party and the government are like the Qasiun [the mountain over-looking Damascus]: You may like it or not like it; it's still there."

Thus, by a combination of political incapacitation and de-politicization, open repression, and selective incorporation, the regime has managed to keep the civil-society threat at bay. There is occasional grumbling, even from within the party, the government, the popular organizations, the parties of the front, or parliament. Parts of the traditional regime base are disappointed with the regime's socio-economic policy course and, particularly since the beginning of the Iraq–Kuwait crisis of 1990, its foreign-policy orientation. Some of its allies from the business class have expected more and faster change. However, as long as the security architecture holds, alternative power centres cannot emerge, clientelism continues to fragment key societal groups, discontent remains unorganized, and social demands can be dealt with selectively; the ability of the regime to act, by and large, on its own preferences is not in question.

3. Domestic Control and Regional Role

Since Asad's takeover, as we have seen, Syria has developed into a strong security state. The regime is firmly in control of society and, quite importantly, of its own apparatuses and the informal clientelist networks it has established or allowed to emerge. In the official reading of Syria's rulers, regime stability and political control, and, implicitly, the measure of repression that goes with it, constitute an indispensible element of national security. The "domestic front" has to be stable and firm to avert inroads from the enemy and be prepared for external confrontations; opponents of the regime or, what practically is the official synonym, "the revolution", play the game of the external enemy.[25]

Syria, not only in the rhetoric of the regime, sees itself surrounded by multiple threats; and this perception of its security environment is not totally unwarranted. Western forces have, in the past, more than once exploited Syria's internal frictions and destabilized the country in the pursuit of their regional designs.[26] Syria's relations with its two larger neighbours, Iraq and Turkey, have been conflictual and occasionally tense for a long time. The possibility of a disintegration of Lebanon which, for many years, could not be excluded, has always been perceived as an immediate security threat to Syria. Above all, of course, Syria has been in a state of war with Israel for more than 45 years, Syrian territory has been occupied since 1967, and Syrian fears of Israel, its military strength, regional ambitions and the possibility that it might drag Syria into another unwanted war, are real.[27] While Syria could arguably have secured internal stability and maintained its territorial integrity – as far as it actually has been able to do so – even without authoritarian rule, there is no doubt that the development of Syria's domestic stability and regional stance have been mutually enforcing.

Without the ambitious and ruthless leadership of Hafiz al-Asad, the stability of his regime, and the emergence of a comparatively strong state, Syria would not have been able to develop in the 1970s and 1980s into the regional power which it now is – endowed with a regional influence which, as Drysdale and Hinnebush have noted, is in fact out of proportion to the country's size, population, and economic resources.[28] At the time this study was written, Syria had successfully coped with the breakdown of its main international ally, the USSR. It had acquired a strong and more or less internationally accepted influence over Lebanon – and it gradually anchored this influence in a political basis so as to enable it to survive a later military withdrawal. Together with Egypt, Syria had become the main regional partner of the Gulf monarchies and thereby strengthened its position in the inter-Arab context. Moreover it was playing a pivotal role in the Middle East peace process as the strongest adversary of Israel and the one Arab state without whose consent a stable regional peace would not be won. After a period of tension in the second half of the 1980s, Syria had also, by and large, re-ordered its relations with the West. Western governments showed no deeper interest in furthering political liberalization in Syria. Their main concern, instead, was with the existence in Syria of a government which, at the end of the day, would be able to compromise, to make peace, and to keep it. There was little doubt that Asad, particularly because of his hold over society, was the leader who could deliver Syria and guarantee its commitment to a negotiated solution.

Domestically, Syria's regional stance serves as a main source of legitimacy. It has been essential for the regime, particularly since it rules in the name of Ba'thist Arab nationalism, to demonstrate its adherence to what can be considered a national myth: namely, the conviction that Syria is the heartland of Arabism and the most ardent defender of Arab and especially Palestinian rights. After decades of fruitless confrontation and sufficient proof that strategic parity with Israel will remain out of Syria's reach, the majority of the Syrian public can be assumed to support a peaceful termination of the Arab–Israeli conflict – on condition, however, that the solution to be reached can be regarded as "just". It would be difficult, even for Asad's strong regime, to settle for less, bilaterally, than a return of Syrian sovereignty over the occupied Golan heights and a full – if probably phased – withdrawal of Israel's troops. It would also be difficult for the regime to make peace with Israel if an acceptable solution for the Palestinians and an Israeli withdrawal from southern Lebanon was not achieved or scheduled.[29]

Syria's posture as a "credible" enemy to Israel is not only of ideological and legitimatory importance. It has also been, as shown, a crucial element of the country's political economy. Only by means of its constant and demonstrative mobilization of society, the maintenance of a huge army, and the allocation of enormous resources to the military could Syria secure the strategic rent which it has collected from the wealthier Arab states, from the USSR, and, for a couple of years, from Iran. Arab, Soviet, and Iranian aid which Syria received because of its strategic importance and its stance as a confrontation state would not, or would only partly, have been assigned to it otherwise. This aid not only financed most of Syria's arms imports. It also enabled the government to pursue the ambitious industrialization and infrastructural development programme of the 1970s, to cover trade and budget deficits, to allow – till the end of that decade – for generally rising living standards, and even thereafter for the rapid growth of the mostly state-employed salaried middle class, and for the distribution of a range of subsidies and privileges to various societal segments. The decrease of this rent inflow, at the end of the 1980s, uncovered much of the structural deficits of Syria's economy and development model, and added to the need for economic reform and the state's surrendering of some economic levers to the private sector. Conversely, Syria's taking sides with the anti-Iraq alliance during the second Gulf War and the formation, after that war, of the Damascus Declaration group of the six Gulf monarchies, Egypt, and Syria, helped to reopen the Gulf Arab aid source for Syria and to reduce economic pressure.

Syria's military build-up and mobilization, its investment, so to speak, in military strength, is no longer intended to lead to or involve Syria in another war with Israel following the Syrian–Israeli disengagement agreement of 1974. Rather, from that time, and irrespective of occasional political-military brinkmanship, the Syrian leadership has sought to avoid military confrontation with Israel. The *de facto* no-peace-no-war situation that has prevailed, with notable interruptions, between Israel and Syria from 1974 to date, has in fact served Syrian regime interests best. It provided a legitimatory background at home and among the Arab public, secured strategic rents and Syria's regional and international weight, and did not – as outright war would have done – endanger the material benefits which the country could draw from its strategic position, or the army itself. Israel's 1982 invasion of Lebanon and its blow to the Syrian forces had clearly shown that Syria could not risk a full-scale confrontation with Israel. Another defeat, especially if it involved further territorial losses, would seriously weaken the regime and might even bring it down – if with some time lag, as was the case in 1967. When the Syrian leadership agreed to participate in the US-sponsored Madrid peace process in 1991, it knew that one of the alternatives to an eventual peaceful settlement – renewed war – would be disastrous. Furthermore, given that the world's leading powers had lost their own interest in the maintenance of tension in the Middle East after the end of the Cold War, the other alternative to a settlement, namely the continuation of the no-war-no-peace situation, would be increasingly difficult to sell.

Syria has been prepared to negotiate, on the grounds of Security Council resolutions 242 and 338 – that is, on the basis of the land-for-peace principle – since its acceptance of these resolutions in 1974; and it is today prepared to make peace with Israel. However, Syria's main objective is, as yet, the avoidance of war; and Asad and his men have been in no hurry to sign a peace treaty. Syria needs time to prepare for full peace and for the new economic, technological, intellectual, and political challenges that come with it. The regime may well be able to secure a continued inflow of political or strategic rent – particularly by furthering its cooperation with the Gulf monarchies. At best, however, such aid is likely to stagnate, rather than increase.

In the long run, comprehensive regional peace will be in the interests of all Middle Eastern countries. In the short run, however, it is anything but certain that there will be a substantial peace dividend for Syria. Israel's highly productive economy is considered a threat by Syrian policy-makers and entrepreneurs alike. Syria could gain a reasonable share of the Palestinian market; at the same time, however, there is going to be Israeli competition to Syrian fruit, vegetable and manufactured goods exports to the Gulf, and there will be Israeli–Syrian competition in other important sectors too, namely transport and ports. International capital-seeking investment opportunities is in short supply, and there are in the Middle East more interesting locations than Syria for foreign investment.

Furthermore, regional peace will not immediately translate into a drive towards disarmament and military budget cuts, and thereby release resources for development purposes. As mutual suspicions and fears are likely to persist for some time, all regional parties will remain on their guard and, with the notable exception of Jordan and the Palestinian entity, maintain a high level of armament for the foreseeable future. Moreover, Syria's armed forces, by all international standards and comparisons, are in urgent need of modernization. Not only does most of the hardware used by Syria's ground forces represent the technology of the 1960s and 1970s, much of the material has also been cannibalized, and most of Syria's air force has been practically grounded for lack of spare parts. Peace, from a Syrian military perspective, will therefore primarily be an opportunity to spend on the rehabilitation of the armed forces.[30]

At the same time, peace is likely to alter domestic variables inside Syria. As the external confrontation is going to lose importance, it will be increasingly difficult to justify the maintenance of Syria's extensive armed forces, the privileging of the military, and the militarization of public life. Notably, by the time this study was finalized, many Syrians were expecting a political rather than an economic peace dividend, hoping that peace would bring about a reduction of the security apparatus and its political power, a restoration of respect for the law, and an increase of government accountability and public space.[31] Such hopes may, for the short-term future at least, exceed reality. Syria's military should not be expected to give up its strong position once the state of war between Israel and Syria is terminated. For reasons mentioned above, military budgets will probably remain fairly high, and there are strong arguments against a reduction of the numerical strength of the armed forces, which cheaply contain a substantial number of Syria's otherwise unemployed youth. Most likely, Syria's army and security apparatus will remain a strong corporate actor that will ward off attempts to reduce, beyond certain limits, its privileges; and it will maintain a veto power, at least for some time, over Syria's political future. The popular mood, nevertheless, the expectations of declining military and security influence, reflect an actual delegitimation of the security state, whose era may well come to an end in the somewhat longer run.

4. Asad – and after?

As long as Asad remains at the helm we may, as noted, expect a further expansion of corporatist structures and a continuation of piecemeal reforms that remain short of threatening regime control. In a post-Asad Syria, the hold of the state over society is likely to weaken. For one, as outlined, external rents – both political rents and oil revenues – will most probably, under favourable conditions, remain stagnant; i.e. they will decline relative to the size of the population and to other economic indicators. A relatively reduced rent income will force the state to lean more heavily on society and private-sector resource generation. Second, two essential elements for the emergence of strong states, namely a serious external threat and skilful leadership,[32] will probably be lacking. The main external threat to Syria, that of Israel, will be reduced, so it seems, with the progress of regional pacification. As regards leadership, it is highly unlikely that whoever follows Asad in power will prove – and from the beginning – of similar cunning. This weakening of state power will almost certainly open the space for society. Most probably, political conflicts, class conflicts and other conflicts of interest would then be more openly debated, negotiated, and settled; the political leadership would no longer decide alone what the legitimate interests of various societal groups and segments are; new parties could come into being, and the

PNF could fall apart. Such a development may be understood as a loss of internal stability, but also as the return of politics.[33]

Instability, in this sense, would in the first place break up the ossified structures of a regime that has entrenched itself in power for more than two decades and, to an extent, paralysed societal energies. This is not, of course, what the regime plans. From the late 1980s, it tried to prepare for the perpetuation of these structures beyond the eventual death of the President and to build up Basil, his eldest son, as a dynastic successor. Though he was never officially named as successor, Basil was trained to fit into his father's shoes, and much propagandistic energy was spent on making him appear a proper heir apparent. He was one of the few among the sons of the regime elite who had a military career; and he was made a member of the General Staff and head of a brigade of the Republican Guard. In the years before his fatal car crash in 1994, he had reportedly even become the *de facto* commander of this praetorian guard, overseeing its modernization and building the base of his personal support within its officer corps and ranks, or at least sharing the command with its official commander, his uncle 'Adnan Makhluf. In addition, Basil had built his own network in the security apparatus, particularly relying on younger officers who like him had an academic degree; he had established personal relations with the younger generation of Lebanon's political leaders, and he had been entrusted with security tasks that created a positive image – such as the participation in crack-downs on smuggling from, and hashish-growing in, Lebanon. Posters of Basil could be seen increasingly on military cars and other places, mostly, but not always, together with posters of his father. While it is difficult to be certain whether an attempt to impose Basil could have succeeded – despite opposition from some of the regime's more senior barons and professional army cadres, the country's republican traditions, anti-Alawi feelings, and the hopes for a return to civilian rule – Basil was, from a regime perspective, not the worst choice. Unlike most of the offspring of the top members of the regime, he was not known for corruption and public misbehaviour. He was young and could be imaged as representing the aspirations of Syria's overwhelmingly young majority. And he was, other than the generation of officers from peasant families that took power in the 1960s, very much a Damascene, brought up, educated and networked in the capital, a facet which many conservative Damascenes overtly appreciated. He had, in fact, gained a certain popularity that by far exceeded the

Alawi community. By not having any function in the Ba'th party, he
also underlined his father's non-ideological approach, further demon-
strated the marginalization of the party as a policy-making force, and
distanced himself from economic mismanagement, pre-modern rhetoric, and the arrogance of functionaries which could all be connected
to the party. Following Basil's death, clear attempts were made by the
regime's propaganda machine not only to transfigure and idealize Basil
as the embodiment of all the good qualities of Arab youth, but also to
put the President's second son, Bashar, in Basil's place, entrusting
him with the same positions that his brother had occupied. To date,
it seems highly unlikely that such dynastic strategies could succeed.
The loyalties that bind secondary regime strongmen to Asad are neither simply transferable to a son who has not proved his political
skills, nor do they as such constitute a basis for the control of the
corporate agencies of power, let alone of society.

The end of the Asad era, however, need not, as some pessimists in
things Syrian as well as some Syrian regime loyalists claim, lead to
the breakdown of the state and public order. The civil war scenario,
forecasting chaos, more or less bloody sectarian strife, and probably
even Syria's disintegration for the time after Asad's eventual departure,[34] is but one likely scenario; and it does not seem to me the most
likely one. While the regime and its leadership certainly lack legitimacy, the legitimacy of the state is not in doubt. Other than in the
early 1960s – when Arab nationalism was stronger, when important
segments of the political scene still worked for, at least, a reunification
of Syria with Egypt, and when the country was less regionally integrated than today – people from all parts of Syria have come to
regard Damascus as their legitimate capital and to accept the Syrian
state as the proper frame for national politics – Greater-Syria or pan-
Arab visions, and regional ties and animosities notwithstanding. The
existence and extensive utilization of primordial loyalties has not
prevented the development of a strong sense of Syrian identity; and
almost all societal groups – including the bourgeoisie and the military
who will both have a say in determining Syria's political future – are
interested in maintaining the state, its stability, and if possible its
regional role. The unrest, or close-to-civil-war situation of 1979–82
was an experience which few would like to repeat. Different from the
1960s too, there is no longer a highly politicized officer corps with a
socio-political mission that would want to topple existing socio-
economic structures. There is a professional military and security

apparatus today with entrenched corporate interests. And despite the putschist tradition of the Syrian army, it does not have a tradition of falling apart and allowing different units to fight each other. Rather, if a post-Asad civilian government proves incapable, in the eyes of the military, of doing its job, one could expect military leaders to agree between themselves as to who is to take control.

Moreover, the system that has emerged since the 1970s in Syria is not built on military force, patronage, confessional ties, corruption and other rather uncivil means of control alone. The institutions of a modern state, as outlined, have actually been established, although, under the system of authoritarian rule which they have so far been furnishing, they do not play their role. Regarding the general interest in the maintenance of stability and in a smooth transition, there is a chance, therefore, that these institutions – parliament, government, the judiciary – may develop and play their role more fully. Constitutionally, the death of a president does not leave a vacuum; there would be a vice-president, at present 'Abd al-Halim Khaddam as the first of Asad's three deputies, to act as an interim head-of-state. One should not preclude that in order to prevent chaos and destruction, Syria's military and security strongmen – much like their Egyptian counterparts after the assassination of Sadat – could respect constitutional rules. It is likely that they would do so on certain conditions; these might be, in particular, that parliament only nominate a presidential candidate whom the military supports, that military budgets not be cut overproportionally and a modernization of the armed forces be allowed, and that, analogous to several Latin American cases, the security apparatus be indemnified against any prosecution for crimes and offences committed during the Asad years.

While a military coup, as mentioned, cannot be ruled out, any successor regime, if civilian with military backing, or military, will for reasons mentioned above almost certainly be less personalized, less strong, and probably more inclined to accept the competition of market forces as well as ideas and, to some extent at least, political groups and parties. Regional states such as Tunisia and Egypt could serve as examples for Syria's post-Asad political development. Still far from democratic, they are politically more open and economically more liberal, allow a considerable amount of freedom of the press, a relatively independent judiciary and a high measure of legal stability and rule-of-law. Economic liberalization, it seems, does not as such demand or entail more substantial political changes.[35] Democracy and human rights are not necessarily the attributes of a liberalized economy. In a more open political environment, demands for their realization are likely to grow, irrespective of whether or not they will also enhance economic growth and flexibility. They constitute independent political options, whose value, in their absence, an increasing number of Syrians have learned to appreciate.

Notes

1. Alan Richards/John Waterbury, *A Political Economy*.
2. Cf. Stefan Mair, "Klientelismus als Demokratiehemmnis in Afrika".
3. For a broader discussion, from a development perspective, of Syria's socio-economic policies and their results, cf. Perthes, *Staat und Gesellschaft*.
4. Cf. e.g. Gulhati, "Who Makes Economic Policy?"
5. Cf. more detailed Perthes, "Syria's Upper Class."
6. Cf. Ghassan Salamé, *al-Mujtama' wa-l-dawla fi al-mashriq al-'arabi*, p 206.
7. Author's interview, Damascus 1993.
8. Legislative Decree No. 24/1986.
9. Cf. the interview with Ratib Shallah, President of the Damascus Chamber of Commerce, *al-Hayat*, 4 October 1993.
10. Cf. John Waterbury, "The Heart of the Matter? Public Enterprise and the Adjustment Process".
11. Cf. e.g. Stephan Haggard/Robert R. Kaufman, "Economic Adjustment and the Prospects for Democracy", ibid., pp 331f.
12. Cf. e.g. Lothar Brock, "Lateinamerikanisierung des Ostens? Zur Wechselwirkung zwischen Demokratisierung und wirtschaftlicher Transformation", in idem and Ingomar Hauchler (eds), *Entwicklung in Mittel- und Osteuropa. Über Chancen und Risiken der Transformation* (Bonn: Stiftung Entwicklung und Frieden, 1993); Michael Th. Greven, "Ist die Demokratie modern? Zur Rationalitätskrise der politischen Gesellschaft", *Politische Vierteljahresschrift*, Vol 34 (1993), pp 399–413. For a discussion of the rather weak link between economic liberalization and democratization in Arab countries cf. David Pool, "The Links between Economic and Political Liberalization", in Tim Niblock and Emma Murphy (eds), *Economic and Political Liberalization in the Middle East* (London/New York: British Academy Press, 1993); Perthes, "Private Sector, Economic Liberalization".
13. Cf. Alan Richards, "Economic Imperatives and Political Systems", *Middle East Journal*, Vol 47 (1993), pp 217–227; Haggard/Kaufman, "Economic Adjustment", p 324.
14. Cf. Asad's speech of 12 March 1992, *al-Ba'th*, 13 March 1992. The attempts of some regime loyalists to prove that Syria, after all, is a democratic country, may come across with a measure of unintended irony. Iliyas Najmah,

for instance, a university professor and parliamentary deputy, explained in an interview with the Syrian daily *Tishrin* (21 April 1992): "To the extent that they [the West] have a democracy and a system of government that suits the structure of man [in their countries], we have our democracy and regime which correspond to our ambitions and to our mental, historical, cultural and religious structure."

15. Cf. among others Wahid 'Abd al-Majid, "al-Dimuqratiyya fi al-watan al-'arabi" [Democracy in the Arab Homeland], *al-Mustaqbal al-'arabi*, Vol 13 (August 1990), No. 138, pp 80–94; Muhammad 'Abid al-Jabiri, "Ishkaliyat al-dimuqratiyya wa-l-mujtama' al-madani fi al-watan al-'arabi" [The Problematique of Democracy and Civil Society in the Arab Homeland], *al-Mustaqbal al-'arabi*, Vol 15 (January 1993), No. 167, pp 4–15.

16. Cf. SWP ME/1566, 17 December 1992.

17. In the spring of 1994, Asad explained to a visitor that he wanted Syria to follow the Chinese model of liberalization. To the extent that this means gradualism and the maintenance of elements of an interventionist state, it also means, and probably primarily so, that any political liberalization should remain limited.

18. Cf. e.g. Rizkallah Hilan, "The Effects on Economic Development".

19. Ad-hocism, muddling-through, and lack of pro-active planning are in no way a specifically Syrian phenomenon. They represent an understandable and, under the premises of regime legitimacy and stability, even a justifiable policy style. "Don't ask how we'll solve our problems tomorrow," an economic-policy administrator told the author in an interview. "The people want the government to solve the current problems."

20. Cf. *al-Mujtama' al-madani fi al-watan al-'arabi wa-dawruh fi tahqiq al-dimuqratiyya* [Civil Society in the Arab Homeland and its Role in Achieving Democracy] (Beirut: Center for Arab Unity Studies, 1992); al-Jabiri, "ishkaliat al-dimuqratiyya"; August Richard Norton, "The Future of Civil Society in the Middle East", *Middle East Journal*, Vol 47 (1993), pp 205–216.

21. In 1980, 650 of these organizations were registered. By 1992, their number had dropped to 504. Cf. *Statistical Abstracts 1981*, p 476, *1993*, p 413.

22. The term is borrowed from Silva, "Technocrats and Politics". Silva outlines the extremely important role of independent technocratic elites for the transition to democratic government in the case of Chile.

23. Investment Law No. 10/1991 demands that investors who apply for a licence under the favourable provisions of that law forward a feasibility study with their application. To produce such studies, in a way that convinces the members of the Higher Council for Investments, seems to be one of the main services which these institutes provide – in addition to more subtle advice and connections for newcomers on the Syrian market who want to deal with the bureaucracy.

24. Occasional conflicts arise nonetheless, even violently, between the authorities and groups of citizens. It is notable, however, that such conflicts,

for the last decade or so, have usually been over local matters, did not become national issues, and were easily subdued.

25. The theme is recurrent in many of Asad's speeches, media commentaries, and other official statements. An interesting example is Asad's speech to the Revolutionary Youth Organization of 8 March 1990, *Tishrin*, 9 March 1990.

26. Although this was predominantly a feature of the 1950s, memories and fears of external conspiracies against Syria have remained vivid. The best account of the events of that time remains Seale's *The Struggle for Syria*.

27. Cf. Drysdale/Hinnebush, *Syria*; Perthes, "Syrien".

28. Drysdale/Hinnebusch, *Syria*, p 62.

29. Cf. ibid., pp 200ff; Volker Perthes, "Incremental Change in Syria", *Current History*, Vol 92 (1993), pp 23–26, 144 (erratum); Muslih, "The Golan: Israel, Syria, and Strategic Considerations".

30. Cf. Volker Perthes, "From War Dividend to Peace Dividend? Syrian Options in a New Regional Environment", paper prepared for the symposium on "The Middle Eastern Economy in a Prospect of Peace", Strasbourg, 29–30 June 1994.

31. This view is well expressed in Hilan, "The Effects on Economic Development".

32. Cf. Migdal, *Strong Societies*, pp 273ff.

33. Cf. Eberhard Kienle, "The Return of Politics".

34. Cf. in particular Pipes, "Syrie: L'après-Assad".

35. Cf. Perthes, "Private Sector, Economic Liberalization".

Bibliography

'Abd al-Fadil, Mahmud, *al-Tashkilat al-ijtima'iyya wa-l-takwinat al-tabaqiyya fi al-watan al-'arabi. Dirasa tahliliyya li-ahamm al-tatawwurat wa-l-ittijahat khilal al-fatra 1945–1985* [Social Formations and Class Structures in the Arab Homeland. An Analysis of the Most Important Developments and Tendencies 1945–1985] (Beirut: Center for Arab Unity Studies, 1988)

'Abd al-Karim, Mufid, "Dawr al-qita'at al-iqtisadiyya al-'amm wa-l-khass wa-l-mushtarak fi al-tijara al-kharijiyya al-suriyya" [The Role of the Public, Private and Mixed Economic Sectors for Syrian Foreign Trade], in Economic Sciences Association of the SAR, *Sixth Economic Tuesday Symposium, On Development and Foreign Trade, Damascus, 8 May 1990 – 12 March 1991* (Damascus, n.d. [1991])

'Abd al-Majid, Wahid, "al-Dimuqratiyya fi al-watan al-'arabi" [Democracy in the Arab Homeland], *al-Mustaqbal al-'arabi*, Vol 13 (August 1990), No. 138, pp 80–94

Aberach, Joel D./Rockman, Bert A., "On the Rise, Transformation and Decline of Analysis in the US Government", *Governance*, Vol 2 (1989) 3, pp 293–314

al-Abrash, Muhammad Riyadh, "al-Takhsis marra ukhra" [Privatization, Once Again], *al-Nashra al-iqtisadiyya* (1990), No. 4, pp 50–62

———— "Iqtisad al-suq. al-Itar al-iqtisadi al-jadid li-l-'amal al-'arabi al-mushtarak" [Market Economy: The New Economic Frame of Arab Common Action], *al-Nashra al-iqtisadiyya* (1991), No. 3, pp 50–53

———— "al-Tanmiya al-iqtisadiyya al-'arabiyya 1985–1990. Sanawat al-'auda min al-istratijiya ila al-la istratijiya" [Arab Economic Development 1985–1990. The Years of Return from Strategy to Non-Strategy], *al-Nashra al-iqtisadiyya*, (1993), No. 1, pp 40–45

Abu 'Amud, Muhammad Sa'd, "Sana' al-qarar al-siyasi fi al-huqba al-sadatiyya" [Political Decision-Making in the Sadat Era], in *al-Mustaqbal al-'arabi*, Vol 11 (June 1988), No. 112, pp 112–128

Abu Diah, Sa'd, *'Amaliyyat ittikhadh al-qarar fi siyasat al-urdunn al-kharijiyya* [The Decision-Making Process in Jordanian Foreign Policy] (Beirut: Center for Arab Unity Studies, 1990)

Abu Jaber, Kamal, *The Arab Ba'th Socialist Party: History, Ideology, and Organization* (Syracuse: Syracuse University Press, 1966)

Abu Khalil, Asad, "Syria and the Arab–Israeli Conflict", *Current History*, Vol 93 (1994), pp 83–86

Abu Sha'ar, Laila, "al-Mara'a wa-l-tanmiya fi 'aqd al-mar'a al-dawli" [Woman and Development in the International Decade of Women], in General Union of Women (ed), *al-Mar'a al-'arabiyya al-suriyya fi 'aqd al-mar'a al-dawli 1975–1985* [The Syrian-Arab Woman in the International Decade of Women] (Damascus: General Union of Women, 1987)

'Abud, Na'um Ibrahim, "al-Qanun al-'ashrun al-jadid" [The New Law No. 20], *al-Iqtisad*, Vol 24 (August–September 1991) 331–332, pp 37–42

'Abud, Samu'il, "Ikhtilal tawazzu' al-tanmiya makaniyan wa-dawr al-takhtit al-iqlimi fi i'adat tawazuniha fi al-qutr al-'arabi al-suri" [Regional Imbalances of Development and the Role of Regional Planning for its Rebalancing in the Syrian Arab Region] (mimeographed paper, Training Course for Planning Cadres, 30 November – 12 December 1991, Planning Institute for Social Development, Damascus)

Aleman, Ulrich von/Heinze, Rolf G., "Kooperativer Staat und Korporatismus", in Ulrich von Aleman (ed), *Neokorporatismus* (Frankfurt/New York: Campus, 1981)

al-Akhras, Muhammad Sufuh, *Tarkib al-'a'ila al-'arabiyya wa-waza'ifuha. dirasa li-waqi' al-'a'ila fi suriya* [The Composition of the Arab Family and its Functions. Field Study on the Situation of the Family in Syria] (Damascus: Ministry of Culture, 2nd revised ed., 1980)

'Ali, Ibrahim, "al-'Alaqa al-mutabadila bayn tauzi' al-sukkan wa-l-tanmiya fi al-qutr al-'arabi al-suri" [The Mutual Relationship between the Distribution of the Population and Development in the Syrian Arab Region], in SAR, CBS and United Nations Fund for Population Activities, *al-Nadwa al-dawliyya hawl al-sukkan wa-l-tanmiya wa-ahammiyat al-raqm al-ihsa'i, Homs, 25–27 October 1983* [International Symposium on Population, Development and the Importance of Statistics, Homs, 25–27 October 1983] (Damascus: CBS, 1983)

'Alush, Khalid, "Dawr al-mar'a fi al-nishat al-iqtisadi: waqi'uhu wa tatawwuratuh" [The Role of Women in Economic Activity: Situation and Development] (unpublished paper presented to the SAR, CBS and ESCWA Regional Symposium on the 1984 Labour Force Study in the SAR, Damascus, 1–3 November 1986)

al-'Ammash, Husayn Murhij, *Tajawuz al-ma'ziq. Muntaliqat al-islah al-iqtisadi fi suriya* [Overcoming the Dilemma. Points of Departure for Economic Reform in Syria] (Damascus: Tlass, 1992)

Arab Socialist Ba'th Party (ASBP), National Command, *Ba'd al-muntaliqat al-nazariyya allati aqarraha al-mu'tamar al-qawmi al-sadis fi tishrin al-awwal 1963* [Some Theoretical Principles as Approved by the Sixth National Conference in October 1963] (Damascus: ASBP, 5th ed., 1978)

────── *Nidal hizb al-ba'th al-'arabi al-ishtiraki* [The Struggle of the Arab Socialist Ba'th Party] (Damascus, 1978)

────── Regional Command, *Reports and Decisions of the Fifth Extraordinary Regional Conference convened in Damascus, 30 May – 13 June* (Damascus, 1974)

────── *Reports and Decisions of the Sixth Regional Conference convened in Damascus, 5 – 15 April 1975, Economic Report* (Damascus, 1976)

────── *Reports and Decisions of the Seventh Regional Conference convened in Damascus, 22 December 1979 – 6 January 1980, Economic Report* (Damascus, 1980)

────── *Reports and Decisions of the Seventh Regional Conference convened in Damascus, 22 December 1979 – 6 January 1980, Organizational Report* (Damascus, 1980)

────── *Reports and Decisions of the Eighth Regional Conference convened in Damascus, 5–20 January 1985, Economic Report* (Damascus, 1985)

────── *Reports and Decisions of the Eighth Regional Conference convened in Damascus, 5–20 January 1985, Organizational Report* (Damascus, 1985)

Avi-Ran, Reuven, *The Syrian Involvement in Lebanon since 1975* (Boulder: Westview, 1991)

Bahout, Joseph, *Les Entrepreneurs Syriens. Économie, affaires et politique* (Les Cahiers du Cermoc, No. 7, 1994)

Bakdash, Khalid, *al-Taqrir al-siyasi ila al-mu'tamar al-sadis li-l-hizb al-shuyu'i al-suri awasit tamuz 1986* [The Political Report to the Sixth Conference of the SCP, mid-July 1986] (n.p., n.d.)

Barakat, Halim, *The Arab World. Society, Culture and State* (Berkeley: California University Press, 1993)

al-Barazi, Tammam, "Syrian Corruption", *The New Statesman*, 5 September 1980

Batatu, Hanna, *The Old Social Classes and the Revolutionary Movements of Iraq. A Study of Iraq's Old Landed and Commercial Classes and of its Communists, Ba'thists, and Free Officers* (Princeton: Princeton University Press, 1978)

────── "Some Observations on the Social Roots of Syria's Ruling, Military Group and the Causes for its Dominance", *Middle East Journal*, Vol 35 (1981), pp 331–344

────── "Syria's Muslim Brethren", *MERIP-Reports*, Vol 12 (November–December 1982), No. 110, pp 12–20

────── *The Egyptian, Syrian and Iraqi Revolutions. Some Observations on Their Underlying Causes and Social Character* (Inaugural Lecture, Georgetown University, Center for Contemporary Arab Studies), (Washington: CCAS, 1983)

Beblawi, Hazem, "The Rentier State in The Arab World", in Giacomo Luciani (ed), *The Arab State* (Berkeley: University of California Press, 1990)

Bery, Suman K., "Economic Policy Reform in Developing Countries: The Role and Management of Political Factors", *World Development*, Vol 18 (1990) 8, pp 1123–1131

Bianchi, Robert, *Unruly Corporatism. Associational Life in Twentieth-Century Egypt* (New York/Oxford: Oxford University Press, 1989)

Bitterlin, Lucien, *Hafez el-Asad. Le parcours d'un combattant* (Paris: Éditions du Jaguar, 1986)

Brock, Lothar, "Lateinamerikanisierung des Ostens? Zur Wechselwirkung zwischen Demokratisierung wirtschaftlicher Transformation", in idem and Ingomar Hauchler (eds), *Entwicklung in Mittel- und Osteuropa. Über Chancen und Risiken der Transformation* (Bonn: Stiftung Entwicklung und Frieden, 1993)

Chatelus, Michel, "La croissance économique: mutation des structures et dynamisme du déséquilibre", in André Raymond (ed), *La Syrie d'aujourd'hui* (Paris: CNRS, 1980)

Clawson, Patrick, *Unaffordable Ambitions: Syria's Military Build-Up and Economic Crisis* (Washington D.C.: The Washington Institute for Near East Policy, 1989)

Cobban, Helena, *The Superpowers and the Syrian-Israeli Conflict. Beyond Crisis Management?* (New York: Praeger, 1991)

Czichowski, Frank, "'Ich und meine Vettern gegen die Welt...'. Migration, 'Wastah', Verteilungskoalitionen und gesellschaftliche Stabilität in Jordanien", *Orient*, Vol 29 (1988), pp 561–578

Dalila, 'Arif, "Tajribat suriya ma' al-qita'ayn al-'amm wa-l-khass wa-mustaqbal al-tajriba" [Syria's Experiment with the Public and the Private Sectors and the Future of this Experiment], in *al-Qita' al-'amm wa-l-qita' al-khass fi al-watan al-'arabi* [The Public and the Private Sector in the Arab Home-land] (Beirut: Center for Arab Unity Studies, 1990)

——— "al-Qita' al-'amm fi suriya. al-Waqi' wa-l-afaq" [The Public Sector in Syria. Situation and Perspectives], in Economic Sciences Association, *Seventh Economic Tuesday Symposioum, Issues of the Syrian Economy, Damascus 28 April 1992 – 27 April 1993* (Damascus, n.d. [1993])

Damascus Chamber of Commerce, *al-Taqrir al-sanawi 1990* [Annual Report 1990] (Damascus: The Chamber 1991)

Darwish, 'Isa, *al-Sina'a wa-l-taqa fi al-jumhuriyya al-'arabiyya al-suriyya* [In-dustry and Energy in the Syrian Arab Republic] (Damascus: Ministry of Culture, 1983)

Dessouki, Ali E. Hillal, "Policy Making in Egypt: A Case Study of the Open Door Economic Policy", *Social Problems*, Vol 28 (April 1981), pp 410–416

Drysdale, Alasdair, "The Syrian Political Elite, 1966–1976: A Spatial and Social Analysis", *Middle Eastern Studies*, Vol 17 (1981), pp 3–30

——— "The Asad Regime and its Troubles", *MERIP-Reports*, Vol 12 (November–December 1982), No. 110, pp 3–11

―――― "The Succession Question in Syria", *Middle East Journal*, Vol 39 (1985), pp 246–257

―――― /Hinnebusch, Raymond, *Syria and the Middle East Peace Process* (New York: Council on Foreign Relations Press, 1991)

Economic Sciences Association, *Fifth Economic Tuesday Symposium on Economic Development in the Syrian Arab Region, Damascus, 14 January – 29 April 1986* (Damascus, n.d. [1986])

―――― *Sixth Economic Tuesday Symposium, On Development and Foreign Trade, Damascus, 8 May 1990 – 12 March 1991* (Damascus, n.d. [1991])

―――― *Seventh Economic Tuesday Symposioum, Issues of the Syrian Economy, Damascus, 28 April 1992 – 27 April 1993* (Damascus, n.d. [1993])

―――― *Eighth Economic Tuesday Symposium, Syrian Industry: Situation and Perspectives; Damascus, 4 May – 30 November 1993* (Damascus, n.d. [1993])

Economic and Social Commission for Western Asia (ESCWA), *Exports of Manufactures and Semi-Manufactures from the Syrian Arab Republic: Trends, Problems and Prospects. Performance of General Industrial Organizations in the Syrian Arab Republic*, July 1986

Economist Intelligence Unit (EIU), *Country Report Syria*, 1/1993 (London: The Economist Intelligence Unit, 1993)

―――― *Syria: Country Profile 1993/94* (London: The Economist Intelligence Unit, 1993

Elsenhans, Hartmut, "Dependencia, Unterentwicklung und Staat in der Dritten Welt", *Politische Vierteljahresschrift*, Vol 27 (1986), pp 133–158

―――― *Abhängiger Kapitalismus oder bürokratische Entwicklungsgesellschaft: Versuch über den Staat in der Dritten Welt* (Frankfurt a. M./New York: Campus, 2nd ed., 1984)

Escher, Anton, *Sozialgeographische Aspekte raumprägender Entwicklungsprozesse in Berggebieten der Arabischen Republik Syrien* (Erlangen: Fränkische Geographische Gesellschaft, 1991)

Evron, Yair, *War and Intervention in Lebanon. The Israeli-Syrian Deterrence Dialogue* (London/Sydney: Croom Helm, 1987)

Faksh, Mahmud A., "The Alawi Community of Syria: A New Dominant Political Force", *Middle Eastern Studies*, Vol 20 (1984), pp 133–153

―――― "The Military and Politics in Syria: The Search for Stability", *Journal of South Asian and Middle Eastern Studies*, Vol 8 (1985), pp 3–21

Farsoun, Samih K./Hajjar, Lisa, "The Contemporary Sociology of the Middle East: An Assessment", in Hisham Sharabi (ed), *Theory, Politics and the Arab World. Critical Responses* (New York/London: Routledge, 1990)

Filonik, A., *Su'ubat al-zira'a al-suriyya al-haditha* [Problems of the Modern Syrian Agriculture] (Damascus: Dar al-Jumhuriyya, 1987)

General Federation of Peasants (Peasant Union), *The Sixth Conference of the Peasants, Damascus, 8 March 1986* (Damascus, 1986)

General Federation of Trade Unions in the Syrian Arab Republic (GFTU), *Proceedings and Decisions of the 17th Conference of the GFTU in the Syrian Arab Region, Damascus, 20–23 September 1972* (Damascus, n.d.)

—— *Proceedings, Decisions and Recommendations of the 18th Conference of the GFTU in the Syrian Arab Region, Damascus, 21–24 September 1974* (Damascus, n.d.)

—— *Marahil sarayan ahkam qanun al-ta'minat al-ijtima'iyya wa-ta'dilatih* [The Phases of Implementation of the Social Security Law and its Amendments] (Damascus: GFTU, 1974)

—— *Proceedings and Decisions of the 19th Conference of the GFTU in the Syrian Arab Region, Damascus, 15–19 November 1978* (Damascus, n.d.)

—— *The 21st Conference of the General Federation of Trade Unions in the Syrian Arab Republic, Damascus, 16 – 20 November 1986. Economic Report*

—— *The 21st Conference of the General Federation of Trade Unions in the Syrian Arab Republic, Damascus, 16 – 20 November 1986. General Report*

—— *al-Khidmat al-ijtima'iyya al-'umaliyya. Suwwar wa-arqam* [Workers' Social Services. Pictures and Figures] (Damascus: GFTU, 1986)

—— *Mu'tamar al-ibda' al-watani wa-l-i'timad 'ala al-dhat* [Conference on National Creativity and Self-Reliance], *Damascus, 21–24 November 1987, General Report*

—— *The 22nd Conference of the General Federation of Trade Unions in the Syrian Arab Republic, Damascus, 7–11 December 1992. General Report*

Greven, Michael Th., "Ist die Demokratie modern? Zur Rationalitätskrise der politischen Gesellschaft", *Politische Vierteljahresschrift*, Vol 34 (1993), pp 399–413

Gulhati, Ravi, "Who Makes Economic Policy in Africa and How?", *World Development*, Vol 18 (1990) 8, pp 1147–1161

Halpern, Manfred, *The Politics of Social Change in the Middle East and North Africa* (Princeton: Princeton University Press, 1963)

al-Hamash, Munir, *Tatawwur al-iqtisad al-suri al-hadith* [The Development of the Modern Syrian Economy] (Damascus: Dar al-Jalil, 1983)

—— (ed), *al-Istithmar fi suriya. As'ila wa-ajwiba* [Investment in Syria. Questions and Answers] (Damascus: al-Ahali, 1992)

—— *al-Tanmiya al-sina'iyya fi suriya wa-afaq tajdidiha* [Industrial Development in Syria and the Perspectives of its Renewal] (Damascus: Dar al-Jalil, 1992)

Hanf, Theodor, Koexistenz im Krieg: *Staatszerfall und Entstehen einer Nation im Libanon* (Baden-Baden: Nomos, 1990)

Hanna, 'Abdallah, *al-Haraka al-'ummaliyya fi suriya wa-Lubnan 1900–1945* [The Labour Movement in Syria and Lebanon 1900–1945] (Damascus: Dar Dimashq, 1973)

Hannoyer, Jean and Seurat, Michel, *État et secteur public industriel en Syrie* (Beirut: CERMOC, 1979)

Hasan, Ibrahim, "La Syrie de la guerre civile", *Peuples méditerranéens*, Vol 12 (July–September 1980), pp 91–107

Henle, Hans, *Der neue Nahe Osten* (Frankfurt a. M.: Suhrkamp, 2nd revised ed., 1972)

Heydemann, Steven, "The Political Logic of Economic Rationality: Selective

Stabilization in Syria", in Henri J. Barkey (ed), *The Politics of Economic Change in the Middle East* (New York, St. Martin's Press: 1992)

Hilan, Rizkallah, "The Effects on Economic Development in Syria of a Just and Long-Lasting Peace", in Stanley Fisher, Dani Rodrick and Elias Tuma (eds), *The Economics of Middle East Peace. Views from the Region* (Cambridge, Ma/London: MIT Press, 1993)

―――― (Rizqallah), *al-Thaqafa wa-l-tanmiya al-iqtisadiyya fi suriya wa-l-buldan al-mukhallafa* [Culture and Economic Developments in Syria and the Countries Left Behind] (Damascus: Dar Maysalun, 1981)

Hinnebusch, Raymond A., "State Formation in a Fragmented Society", *Arab Studies Quarterly*, Vol 4 (1982), pp 177–197

―――― "Revisionist Dreams, Realist Strategies: The Foreign Policy of Syria", in Bahgat Korany and Ali E. Hillal Dessouki (eds), *The Foreign Policies of Arab States* (Boulder/Cairo: Westview/AUC Press, 1984)

―――― "Syria", in Shireen Hunter (ed), *The Politics of Islamic Revivalism* (Bloomington: Indiana University Press, 1988)

―――― *Peasant and Bureaucracy in Ba'thist Syria. The Political Development of Rural Development* (Boulder: Westview, 1989)

―――― *Authoritarian Power and State Formation in Ba'thist Syria. Army, Party and Peasant* (Boulder: Westview 1990)

―― "State and Civil Society in Syria", *Middle East Journal*, Vol 47 (1993), pp 243–257

Hopfinger, Hans, "Kapitalistisches Agro-Business in einem sozialistischen Land. Syrien versucht neue Wege in der Landwirtschaft", *Die Erde*, Vol 121 (1990), pp 157–176

―――― *Öffentliche und private Landwirtschaft in Syrien. Eine wirtschafts- und sozialgeographische Untersuchung im Nordwesten und Norden des Landes* (Erlangen: Fränkische Geographische Gesellschaft, 1991)

―――― "Problems of Privatization and Economic Liberalization in Syria's Agricultural Sector" (paper presented to the Conference on Privatization and Economic Liberalization in Socialist Countries of the Arab World, Banz Castle, 23–26 February 1994)

Hosry, Mohamed, *Sozialökonomische Auswirkungen der Agrarreform in Syrien* (Saarbrücken/Fort Lauderdale: Breitenbach, 1981)

Husseini, Amal, *Profile of Women in Agriculture and Rural Development in the Syrian Arab Republic* (Damascus, unpublished, 1979)

Ibrahim, Sa'd al-Din et al., *Kaifa yusna' al-qarar fi al-watan al-'arabi* [How are Decisions Produced in the Arab Homeland?] (Beirut: Center for Arab Unity Studies, 1985)

al-'Imadi, Muhammad, "Siyasat al-tijara al-kharijiyya fi al-thamaniat wa-afaquha fi al-tisa'inat" [Foreign Trade Policies in the 1980s and their Perspectives in the 1990s], in Economic Sciences Association of the SAR, *Sixth Economic Tuesday Symposium, On Development and Foreign Trade, Damascus, 8 May 1990 – 12 March 1991* (Damascus, n.d. [1991])

―――― "'Adwa' 'ala ba'd awjah siyasatina al-iqtisadiyya" [Spotlights on Some

Aspects of Our Economic Policies] (paper presented to the Seventh Economic Tuesday Symposium, Issues on the Syrian Economy, Damascus, April 1992 – April 1993)

International Institute for Strategic Studies (IISS), *The Military Balance* (London: Brassey's, various years)

International Monetary Fund (IMF) (ed), *Balance of Payment Statistics* (Washington, D.C.: The Fund, various issues)

——— *Government Finance Statistics Yearbook* (Washington D.C., various issues)

Isbar, Amin, *Tatawwur al-nuzum al-siyasiyya wa-l-dusturiyya fi suriya, 1946–1973* [The Development of the Political and Constitutional Systems in Syria] (Beirut: Dar al-Nahar, 1979)

al-Jabiri, Muhammad 'Abid, "Ishkaliyat al-dimuqratiyya wa-l-mujtama' al-madani fi al-watan al-'arabi" [The Problematique of Democracy and Civil Society in the Arab Homeland], *al-Mustaqbal al-'arabi*, Vol 15 (January 1993), No. 167, pp 4–15

Ja'far, Qasim Muhammad, *Suriya wa-l-ittihad al-sufiyati* [Syria and the Soviet Union] (London: Riad El-Rayyes, 1987)

al-Ja'fari, Bashar, *al-Siyasa al-kharijiyya al-suriyya* [Syrian Foreign Policy] (Damascus: Tlass, 1987)

Janhani, al-Habib, "al-Sahwa al-islamiyya fi bilad al-sham: mithal suriya" [The Islamic awakening in the Bild al-Sham: The Example of Syria], *al-Harakat al-islamiyya al-mu'asirra fi al-watan al-'arabi* [Contemporary Islamic Movements in the Arab Homeland] (Beirut: Center for Arab Unity Studies, 2nd ed., 1989 [1987])

al-Jarjur, Taufiq, *al-Hijra min al-rif ila al-mudun fi al-qutr al-'arabi al-suri* [Rural–Urban Migration in the Syrian Arab Region] (Damascus: Ministry of Culture, 1980)

al-Jundi, Sami, *Attahaddi … wa-attahim* [I confront … and accuse] (Beirut: Fu'ad Karam, n.d.)

Kaffa, Muhammad, *Tahawwulat al-iqtisad al-zira'i fi suriya* [The Changes of the Agricultural Economy In Syria] (Damascus: Dar al-Shabiba, n.d.)

Kanovsky, Eliayahu, "What's behind Syria's Current Economic Problems?", *Middle East Contemporary Survey 1983–1984*, Vol 8 (1986), pp 280–345

Kaplan, Robert, D., "Syria – Identity Crisis", *The Atlantic*, Vol 271 (February 1993), pp 22–27

Karsh, Efraim, *The Soviet Union and Syria. The Asad Years* (London: Routledge, 1988)

Kessler, Martha Neff, *Syria: Fragile Mosaic of Power* (Washington D.C.: National Defense University Press, 1987)

Khafaji, 'Isam, *al-Dawla wa-l-tatawwur al-ra'asmali fi al-'iraq 1968–1978* [The State and Capitalist Development in Iraq, 1968–1978] (Cairo: Dar al-Mustaqbal al-'arabi, 1983)

al-Khattib, 'Abd al-Muhaimin, *al-Sina'a wa-tatawwuruha fi suriya* [Industry and its Development in Syria] (Damascus: author's edition, 1979)

Khayr, Sufuh, *Suriya. Dirasa fi al-bina' al-hadari wa-l-kiyan al-iqtisadi* [Syria: A Study of its Culture Structure and Economic Nature] (Damascus: Ministry of Culture, 1985)

Khayyir, 'Abd al-Rahman, *'Aqidatuna wa-waqi'na: nahnu al-muslimin al-ja'fariyin al-'alawiyin* [Our Faith and Our Situation: We, the Alawi Ja'farite Muslims] (Damascus: Kutub dhat fa'ida, 1991)

—— *Naqd wa-taqriz kitab tarikh al-'alawiyin* [A Critique and an Appraisal of the Book: The History of the Alawis] (Damascus: Kutub dhat fa'ida, 1992)

—— *Risala tabhath fi masa'il muhimma hawl al-madhhab al-ja'fari al-'alawi* [A Letter Studying Important Questions regarding the Ja'farite Alawi School] (Damascus: Dar Sa'd al-Din, 1993)

Khuri, 'Isam, "Rabt al-tijara al-kharijiyya bi-mutatalibat al-tanmiya, al-waqi' wa-l-imkaniyat", in Economic Sciences Association, *Sixth Economic Tuesday Symposium, On Development and Foreign Trade, Damascus, 8 May 1990 – 12 March 1991* (Damascus, n.d. [1991])

Kienle, Eberhard, *Ba'th versus Ba'th. The Conflict between Syria and Iraq, 1968–1989* (London: I.B.Tauris, 1990)

—— "Entre jama'a et classe. Le pouvoir politique en Syrie contemporaine", *Revue du Monde Musulman et de la Méditerranée*, Vol 59–60 (1991), No. 1–2, pp 211–239

—— (ed), *Contemporary Syria: Economic Liberalization between Cold War and Cold Peace* (London: British Academic Press, 1994)

—— "The Return of Politics? Scenarios for Syrian's Second *Intifah*", in Eberhard Kienle (ed), *Contemporary Syria: Liberalization between Cold War and Cold Peace* (London: British Academic Press, 1994)

Kiwan, Fadia, *La tradition des coups d'État et la pérennisation d'une dictature* (Doctorial Thesis, Université de Paris 1, 1984)

Krämer, Gudrun, *Arabismus und Nationalstaatlichkeit: Syrien als Nahöstliche Regionalmacht* (Ebenhausen: Stiftung Wissenschaft und Politik, 1987)

Lawson, Fred H., "Social Bases for the Hamah Revolt", *MERIP-Reports*, Vol 12 (November–December 1982), No. 110, pp 24–28

—— "Comment le régime du président el-Assad s'emploie à remodeler l'économie syrienne", *Le Monde Diplomatique*, January 1984

—— "Libéralisation économique en Syrie et en Irak", *Maghreb-Machrek*, No. 128 (April–June 1990), pp 27–52

—— "External versus Internal Pressures for Liberalization in Syria and Iraq", *Journal of Arab Affairs*, Vol 11 (1992), No. 1, pp 1–33

Le Gac, Daniel, *La Syrie du général Assad* (Bruxelles: Editions Complexe, 1991)

Leca, Jean, "Social Structure and Political Stability: Comparative Evidence from the Algerian, Syrian and Iraqi Cases", in Giacomo Luciano (ed), *The Arab State* (Berkeley: University of California Press, 1990)

Little, Douglas, "Cold War and Covert Action. The United States and Syria, 1945–1958", *Middle East Journal*, Vol 44 (1990), pp 51–75

Lobmeyer, Hans Günter, *Islamismus und sozialer Konflikt in Syrien* (Ethnizität und Gesellschaft, Occasional Papers No. 26) (Berlin: Das Arabische Buch, 1990)

───── "Islamic Ideology and Secular Discourse. The Islamists of Syria", *Orient*, Vol 32 (1991), pp 395–418

Longuenesse, Elisabeth, "Reflexions de methode pour l'étude de la classe ouvrière dans la pays arabe", (paper presented to the symposium on "Les origines et la formation de la classe ouvrière dans la pays arabe", Algiers, December 1978)

───── "The Class Nature of the State in Syria. Contribution to an Analysis", *MERIP-Reports*, Vol 4 (May 1979), No. 77, pp 3–11

───── "L'industrialisation et sa signification sociale", in André Raymond, *La Syrie d'aujourd'hui* (Paris: CNRS, 1980)

───── "Structure de la main d'œuvre industrielle et rapports de production en Syrie", (conference paper presented to the "Colloque sur l'Origine et l'Évolution de la Classe Ouvrière dans le Monde Arabe", Algiers, 23–26 February 1981)

───── "The Syrian Working Class Today", *MERIP-Reports*, Vol 15 (July–August 1985), No. 134, pp 17–24

───── "État et syndicalisme en Syrie. Discours et pratiques", *Sou'al*, No. 8, February 1988, pp 97–130

Ma'oz, Moshe/Yaniv, Avner (eds), *Syria under Assad: Domestic Constraints and Regional Risks* (London/Sydney: Croom Helm, 1986)

Ma'oz, Moshe, *Asad. The Sphinx of Damascus: A Political Biography* (New York: Weidenfeld & Nicolson, 1988)

───── "Syrian-Israeli Relations and the Middle East Peace Process", *The Jerusalem Journal of International Relations*, Vol 14 (September 1992), pp 1–21

Mahr, Horst, *Die Baath-Partei. Portrait einer panarabischen Bewegung* (Munich/Vienna: Olzog Verlag, 1971)

Mair, Stefan, "Klientelismus als Demokratiehemmnis in Afrika", *Europa-Archiv*, Vol 49 (25 April 1994), No. 8, pp 231–238

Mayer, Thomas, "The Islamic Opposition in Syria 1961–1982", *Orient*, Vol 24 (1983), pp 589–609

Mayntz, Renate, "Problemverarbeitung durch das politisch-administrative System: Zum Stand der Forschung", in Joachim-Jens Hesse (ed), *Politikwissenschaft als Verwaltungswissenschaft* (*Politische Vierteljahresschrift*, special issue, No. 13) (Opladen: Westdeutscher Verlag, 1982), p 75

McLaurin, R. D./Peretz, Don/Snider, Lewis W., *Middle East Foreign Policy. Issues and Processes* (New York: Praeger, 1982)

Metral, Françoise; "Le monde rural syrien à l'ère des réformes", in André Raymond, *La Syrie d'aujourd'hui* (Paris: CNRS, 1980)

───── "State and Peasants in Syria: a Local View of a Government Irrigation Project", in Nicholas S. Hopkins and Saad Eddin Ibrahim (eds), *Arab Society. Social Science Perspectives* (Cairo: AUC, 1985)

Meyer, Günter, *Ländliche Lebens- und Wirtschaftsformen Syriens im Wandel.*

Sozialgeographische Studien zur Entwicklung im bäuerlichen und nomadischen Lebensraum (Erlangen: Fränkische Geographische Gesellschaft, 1984)

Middle East Watch Committee (ed), *Syria Unmasked. The Suppression of Human Rights by the Regime* (New Haven: Yale University Press, 1991)

Migdal, Joel, *Strong Societies and Weak States. State-Society Relations and State Capabilities in the Third World* (Princeton: Princeton University Press, 1988)

Miqdad, Qasim, "Tatawwur al-qita' al-khidmi fi al-iqtisad al-suri" [The Development of the Service Sector in the Syrian Economy], in Economic Sciences Association, *Fifth Economic Tuesday Symposium on Economic Development in the Syrian Arab Region, Damascus, 14 January – 29 April 1986* (Damascus, n.d. [1986])

Mitwalli, Hisham, *Abhath fi al-iqtisad al-suri wa-l-'arabi* [Studies on the Syrian and the Arab Economy] (Damascus: Ministry of Culture, 1974)

Murish, Yusuf, *al-Jabha al-wataniyya al-taqaddumiyya wa-l-ta'addudiyya fi al-qutr al-'arabi al-suri* [The Progressive National Front and Political Pluralism in the Syrian Arab Region] (Damascus: Dar al-Na'ama, 1993)

Muslih, Muhammad, "The Golan: Israel, Syria, and Strategic Considerations", *Middle East Journal*, Vol 47 (1993), pp 611–632

Najmah, Iliyas, "al-Mas'ala al-iqtisadiyya fi al-qutr al-'arabi al-suri" [The Economic Question in the Syrian Arab Republic], Economic Sciences Association, *Fifth Economic Tuesday Symposium on Economic Development in the Syrian Arab Region, Damascus, 14 January – 29 April 1986* (Damascus, n.d. [1986])

al-Naqib, Khaldun Hasan, *al-Dawla al-tasallutiyya fi al-mashriq al-'arabi al-mu'asir. Dirasa bina'iyya muqarina* [The Authoritarian State in the Contemporary Arab East. A Strucutural and Comparative Study] (Beirut: Center for Arab Unity Studies, 1991)

Niblock, Tim, "International and Domestic Factors in the Economic Liberalization Process in Arab Countries", in Tim Niblock and Emma Murphy (eds), *Economic and Political Liberalization in the Middle East* (London/New York: British Academic Press, 1993)

——— /Emma Murphy (eds), *Economic and Political Liberalization in the Middle East* (London/New York: British Academic Press, 1993)

Nizam al-Din, Ahmad, "Waqi' al-sina'at al-suriyya wa-afaq tatawwuriha" [The Situation of Syrian Industries and the Perspectives of their Development], in Economic Sciences Association, *Eighth Economic Tuesday Symposium, Syrian Industry: Situation and Perspectives, Damascus 4 May – 30 November 1993* (Damascus, n.d. [1993])

Norton, August Richard, "The Future of Civil Society in the Middle East", *Middle East Journal*, Vol 47 (1993), pp 205–216

OECD Development Assistance Committee (ed), *Development Co-operation* (Paris: OECD, various issues)

Perthes, Volker, *Staat und Gesellschaft in Syrien, 1970–1989* (Hamburg: Deutsches Orient-Institut, 1990)

——— "Einige kritische Bemerkungen zum Minderheitenparadigma in der

Syrienforschung", *Orient*, Vol 31 (1990), pp 571–582

———— "A Look at Syria's Upper Class: The Bourgeoisie and the Ba'th", *Middle East Report*, Vol 21 (May–June 1991), No. 170, pp 31–37

———— "Syria's Parliamentary Elections. Remodeling Asad's Political Base", *Middle East Report*, Vol 22 (January/February 1992), No. 174, pp 15–18

———— "The Syrian Economy in the 1980's", *Middle East Journal*, Vol 46 (1992), pp 37–58

———— "The Syrian Private Industrial and Commercial Sectors and the State", *International Journal of Middle East Studies*, Vol 24 (1992), pp 207–230

———— "Incremental Change in Syria", *Current History*, Vol 92 (1993), pp 23–26, 144

———— "Syrien", in Veronika Büttner and Joachim Krause, *Die Rüstung der Dritten Welt nach dem Ende des Ost–West–Konflikts* (Baden-Baden: Nomos, 1995)

———— "The Private Sector, Economic Liberalization and the Prospects of Democratization: The Case of Syria and Some other Arab Countries", in Ghassan Salamé (ed), *Democracies without Democrats* (London: I.B.Tauris, 1994)

———— "From War Dividend to Peace Dividend? Syrian Options in a New Regional Environment" (paper prepared for the symposium on "The Middle Eastern Economy in a Prospect of Peace", Strasbourg, 29–30 June 1994)

———— "Stages of Economic and Political Liberalization in Syria", in Eberhard Kienle (ed), *Contemporary Syria: Liberalization between Cold War and Cold Peace* (London: British Academic Press, 1994)

Petran, Tabitha, *Syria* (London: Ernest Benn, 1972)

Petzold, Siegfried, *Staatsmacht und Demokratie in der Syrischen Arabischen Republik* (Berlin: Staatsverlag der DDR, 1975)

Picard, Elizabeth, "Syria Returns to Democracy: the May 1973 Legislative Elections", in Guy Hermet et al. (eds), *Elections without Choice* (London: Macmillan, 1978)

———— "Clans militaires et pouvoir ba'thiste en Syrie", *Orient*, Vol 20 (1979), pp 49–62

———— "La Syrie de 1946 à 1979", in André Raymond (ed), *La Syrie d'aujourd'hui* (Paris: CNRS, 1980)

———— "Y a-t-il un problème communautaire en Syrie?", *Maghreb-Machrek* (January–February–March 1980), No. 87, pp 7–21

———— "Could Salvation Come From Syria", in Nadim Shehadi and Bridget Harney (eds), *Politics and the Economy in Lebanon* (Oxford/London: Centre for Lebanese Studies/SOAS, 1989)

———— "Arab Military in Politics: From Revolutionary Plot to Authoritarian Regime", in Giacomo Luciani, *The Arab State* (Berkeley: University of California Press, 1990)

———— "Critique de l'usage du concept d'éthnicité dans l'analyse des processus politiques dans le monde arabe", *Études politiques du monde arabe*.

Dossiers du CEDEJ (Cairo, CEDEJ, 1991)

Pipes, Daniel, "The Alawi Capture of Power in Syria", *Middle Eastern Studies*, Vol 25 (1985), pp 429–450

—— *Greater Syria. The History of an Ambition* (New York/Oxford: Oxford University Press, 1990)

—— *Damascus Courts the West: Syrian Politics 1989–1991* (Washington D.C.: The Washington Institute for Near East Policy, 1991)

—— "Syrie: L'après-Assad", *Politique internationale*, No. 59 (Spring 1993), pp 97–110

Piro, Timothy J., "Privatization in Jordan: The Political Economy of Public Sector Reform", (paper submitted to the 26th Annual Middle East Studies Association Conference of North America, Portland, 28–31 October 1992)

Pool, David, "The Links between Economic and Political Liberalization", in Tim Niblock and Emma Murphy (eds), *Economic and Political Liberalization in the Middle East* (London/New York: British Academic Press, 1993)

Qandil, Amani, *Sina'at al-siyasa al-iqtisadiyya fi misr, 1974–1981* [The Making of Economic Policy in Egypt, 1974–1981] (Cairo: Mu'assasat al-Ahram, 1979)

Qudsi, Safwan, *al-Batal wa-l-tarikh. Qira'a fi fikr Hafiz al-Asad al-siyasi* [The Hero and History. A Reading of the Political Thought of Hafiz al-Asad] (Damascus: Tlass, 1984)

Rabinovich, Itamar, *Syria under the Ba'th 1963–66. The Army-Party Symbiosis* (Jerusalem: Israel University Press, 1972)

Rabo, Annika, *Change on the Euphrates. Villagers, Townsmen and Employees in Northeast Syria* (Stockholm: University of Stockholm, 1986)

Ramet, Pedro, *The Soviet-Syrian Relationship since 1955. A Troubled Alliance* (Boulder: Westview, 1990)

Raymond, André, *La Syrie d'aujourd'hui* (Paris: CNRS, 1980)

al-Razzaz, Munif, "al-Tajriba al-murra" [The Bitter Experience], in: idem, *al-A'mal al-fikriyya wa-l-siyasiyya* [Theoretical and Political Works] (Amman, 1986)

Reed, Stanley F., "Dateline Syria: Fin de Régime?", *Foreign Policy*, No. 39 (Summer 1980), pp 176–190

Richards, Alan, "Economic Imperatives and Political Systems", *Middle East Journal*, Vol 47 (1993), pp 217–227

—— /Waterbury, John, *A Political Economy of the Middle East. State, Class, and Economic Development* (Boulder: Westview, 1990)

Roberts, David, *The Ba'th and the Creation of Modern Syria* (New York: St. Martin's Press, 1987)

Sadiq, Mahmud, *Hiwar hawl suriya* [Discussion about Syria] (London: Dar al-'Ukaz, 1993)

Sadowski, Yahya M., "Cadres, Guns and Money. The Eighth Regional Congress of the Syrian Ba'th", *MERIP-Reports*, Vol 15 (July–August 1985), No. 134, pp 3–8

—— "Patronage and the Ba'th: Corruption and Control in Contemporary

Syria", *Arab Studies Quarterly*, Vol 9 (1987), pp 442–461
——— "Ba'thist Ethics and the Spirit of State Capitalism: Patronage and the Party in Contemporary Syria", in Peter J. Chelkowski and Robert J. Pranger (eds), *Ideology and Power in the Middle East. Studies in the Honor of George Lenczowski* (Durham/London: Praeger, 1988)
——— *Political Vegetables? Businessman and Bureaucrat in the Development of Egyptian Agriculture* (Washington D.C.: Brookings, 1991)
——— *Scuds or Butter. The Political Economy of Arms Control in the Middle East* (Washington, D.C.: Brookings, 1993)
Salamé, Ghassan, *al-Mujtama' wa-l-dawla fi al-mashriq al-'arabi* [State and Society in the Arab East] (Beirut: Center for Arab Unity Studies, 1987)
Salih, Amani 'Abd al-Rahman, "Usul al-nukhba al-siyasiyya al-misriyya fi al-saba'inat: al-nash'a wa-l-tatawwur" [The Roots of the Egyptian Political Elite in the 1970s: Origins and Development], *al-Fikr al-istratiji al-'arabi*, Vol 26, October 1988, pp 9–50
Saqr, Aziz, *Dirasat ishtirakiyya fi al-dimanat al-ijtima'iyya wa-l-tijariyya* [Socialist Studies on Social and Commercial Insurance] (Damascus: Dar al-Jumhuriyya, 1982)
Schäbler, Birgit, " 'Der Drusenaufstand' in Syrien. Zum Verhältnis von Ethnizität und sozialer Bewegung", *Blätter des iz3w*, No. 195 (February 1994), pp 37–41
Schahbandar, Mohammed Adnan, *Probleme der Entwicklung, des Status und der Perspektive der nationalisierten Industriebetriebe als Bestandteil des Planungs- und Leitungssystems der SAR* (Doctoral Thesis, Hochschule für Ökonomie, Berlin, 1969)
Sheffler, Thomas, *Ethnisch-religiöse Konflikte und gesellschaftliche Integration im Vorderen und Mittleren Orient* (Berlin: Das Arabische Buch, 1985)
Seale, Patrick, *The Struggle for Syria. A Study of Post-War Arab Politics* (New Haven/London: Yale University Press, 2nd ed. 1987)
——— *Asad of Syria: The Struggle for the Middle East* (London: I.B.Tauris, 1988)
Seurat, Michel, "Les populations, l'État et la société", in André Raymond, *La Syrie d'aujourd'hui* (Paris: CNRS, 1980)
——— *L'État de barbarie* (Paris: Éditions du Seuil, 1989)
Shallah, Badr al-Din, *al-Tarikh wa-l-dhikra, qissat jahd wa'umr* [History and Remembrance. A Story of Effort and Life] (Damascus: author's edition, 1990)
al-Shallah, Ratib, "Ara' fi al-tijara al-kharijiyya" [Opinions on Foreign Trade], in Economic Sciences Association of the SAR, *Sixth Economic Tuesday Symposium, On Development and Foreign Trade, Damascus, 8 May – 12 March 1991* (Damascus, n.d. [1991])
Siba'i, Badr al-Din, *Adwa' 'ala al-rasmal al-ajnabi fi suriya, 1850–1958* [Spotlights on Foreign Capital in Syria] (Damascus: Dar al-Jamahir, 1968)
——— *al-Marhala al-intiqaliyya fi suriya. 'Ahd al-wahda 1958–1961* [The Transition Phase in Syria. The Union Period 1958–1961] (Beirut: Dar Ibn

Khaldun, 1975)

Silva, Patricio, "Technocrats and Politics in Chile: From the Chicago Boys to the CIEPLAN Monks", *Journal of Latin American Studies*, Vol 23 (May 1991), pp 385–410

Skripkin, A., "The CIS-Syria: Direct Links between Enterprises Needed", *Asia and Africa Today*, 1992, No. 3, pp 45–46

Springborg, Robert, *Mubarak's Egypt. Fragmentation of the Political Order* (Boulder: Westview, 1989)

Stockholm International Peace Research Institute (SIPRI) (ed), *SIPRI Yearbook. World Armaments and Disarmaments* (Oxford: Oxford University Press, various issues)

Sukr, Nabil, *Nahwa iqtisad ishtiraki mutatawwir fi al-qutr al-'arabi al-suri* [Towards a Developed Socialist Economy in the Syrian Arab Region] (mimeographed, 1988)

Sullivan, Dennis, "The Political Economy of Reform in Egypt", *International Journal of Middle East Studies*, Vol 22 (1990), pp 317–334

Suwaydan, Ahmad, *Ma'ziq al-'amal al-niqabi fi suriya* [The Dilemma of Trade Union Work in Syria] (Beirut: Dar al-Haqa'iq, 1980)

Syrian Arab Republic (SAR), Central Bureau of Statistics (CBS), *Statistical Abstracts* (Damascus, annually, various issues)

——— *1970–1971 Agricultural Census Data. First Stage – Basic Data in the Syrian Arab Republic* (Damascus: CBS, 1972)

——— *Population Census in the Syrian Arab Republic 1970* (Damascus, n.d. [1976])

——— *Dirasa 'amma 'an qita' al-sina'a wa-l-mu'ashirat al-ra'siyya, 1971– 1975* [General Study on the Industrial Sector and the Main Indicators 1971–1975] (mimeograph, October 1977)

——— *Nata'ij hasr al-munsha'at al-iqtisadiyya fi al-qutr al-'arabi al-suri li-'am 1981* [Results of the 1981 Survey of Economic Establishments in the Syrian Arab Region] (Damascus: CBS, September 1985, unpublished)

——— *1981 Agricultural Census Data* (Damascus: CBS, 1986)

——— *Nata'ij al-ta'adad al-'amm li-l-masakin 1981* [Results of the 1981 Housing Census] (Damascus, 1986)

——— *Nata'ij bahtay al-istiqsa' al-sina'i li-l-qita' al-khass li-'amay 1989–1990* [Results of the Studies of the Investigation of the Private-Sector Industry Survey for Years 1989 and 1990] (unpublished mimeograph, June 1992]

——— /United Nations Fund for Population Activities, *al-Nadwa al-dawliyya hawl al-sukkan wa-l-tanmiya wa-ahamiyyat al-raqm al-ihsa'i, Homs, 25–27 October 1983* [International Symposium on Population, Development and the Importance of Statistics, Homs, 25–27 October 1983] (Damascus: CBS, 1983)

——— Ministry of Agriculture and Agrarian Reform, *The Annual Statistical Abstract* (Damascus, n.d., various issues)

——— Ministry of Economy and Foreign Trade (MEFT), *Taqrir hawl asalib tatwir al-qita' al-'amm* [Report on the Methods of Developing the Public

Sector] (unpublished typescript, n.d. [1992])

—————— Ministry of Information (ed), *al-Qarrarat al-ishtirakiyya fi suriya* [The Socialist Decrees in Syria] (Damascus, n.d. [1965])

—————— *Suriya al-thawra fi 'amiha al-sadis* [Revolutionary Syria in its Sixth Year] (Damascus, 1969)

—————— *Suriya al-thawra fi 'amiha al-rabi' 'ashar* [Revolutionary Syria in its 14th Year] (Damascus, 1977)

—————— Ministry of Planning (ed), *al-Ittijahat al-asasiyya fi al-khitta al-khamsiyya al-thaniyya li-l-tanmiya al-iqtisadiyya wal-l-ijtima'iyya 1966–1970* [The Basic Tendencies of the Second Five Years Plan for Social and Economic Development 1966–1970] (Damascus, 1966)

—————— State Planning Authority, *Taqrir taqwim al-khitta al-khamsiyya al-khamisa, 1981–1985, qita' al-sina'at al-tahwiliyya* [Report on the Evaluation of the Fifth Five Year Plan 1981–1985. Converting Industries' Sector] (Damascus, unpublished, 1986)

—————— *Mudhakkira hawl: al-takhtit li-l-tanmiya al-iqtisadiyya wa-l-ijtima'iyya fi al-jumhuriyya al-'arabiyya al-suriyya* [Memorandum: Planning for Social and Economic Development in the Syrian Arab Republic] (unpublished mimeograph, 1987)

Syrian Communist Party (SCP), *Documents of the Third Conference of the SCP* (n.p., n.d.)

—————— *The Fifth Conference of the SCP, May 1980. Documents and Decisions* (Damascus, n.d.)

—————— *Conference Documents from the Sixth Conference of the SCP, mid-July 1986. Economic Report* (Damascus, n.d.)

—————— *Hawl ba'd al-tatawwurat wa-l-tadabir al-iqtisadiyya fi suriya* [Regarding Some Economic Developments and Measures] (Damascus: SCP, December 1988)

Thomas, Jens, "Zur Staats- und Gesellschaftsstruktur Syriens", *Blätter für deutsche und internationale Politik*, Vol 19 (May 1974), pp 461–470

Traboulsi, Fawaz, "Confessional Lines", *Middle East Report*, Vol 20 (January/February 1990), No. 162, pp 9–10

UNDP/World Bank, *Syria: Issues and Options in the Energy Sector. Report of the Joint UNDP/World Bank Energy Sector Assessment Program*, May 1986

U.S. Arms Control and Disarmament Agency (ACDA) (ed), *World Military Expenditures and Arms Transfers* (Washington, D.C.: various issues)

Van Dam, Nikolaos, "Sectarian and Regional Factionalism in the Syrian Political Elite", *Middle East Journal*, Vol 32 (1979), pp 191–209

—————— *The Struggle for Power in Syria. Sectarianism, Regionalism and Tribalism in Politics, 1961–1978* (London: Croom Helm, 1979)

—————— "Middle Eastern Political Clichés: 'Takriti' and 'Sunni Rule' in Iraq; 'Alawi Rule' in Syria. A Critical Appraisal", *Orient*, Vol 21 (1980), pp 42–57

Van den Boogaerde, Pierre, *Financial Assistance from Arab Countries and Arab Regional Institutions* (Washington D.C.: IMF, 1991)

Waterbury, John, *The Egypt of Nasser and Sadat. The Political Economy of Two Regimes* (Princeton: Princeton University Press, 1983)

———— "Twilight of the State Bourgeoisie?", *International Journal of Middle East Studies*, Vol 23 (1991), pp 1–17

———— "The Heart of the Matter? Public Enterprise and the Adjustment Process", in Stephen Haggard and Robert R. Kaufman (eds), *The Politics of Economic Adjustment. International Constraints, Distributive Conflicts, and the State* (Princeton: Princeton University Press, 1992)

Weinberger, Naomi Joy, *Syrian Intervention in Lebanon: The 1975–76 Civil War* (New York/Oxford: Oxford University Press, 1986)

Whitehead, Laurence, "Political Explanations of Macroeconomic Management: A Survey", *World Development*, Vol 18 (1990) 8, pp 1133–1446

Wirth, Eugen, *Syrien. Eine geographische Landeskunde* (Darmstadt: Wissenschaftliche Buchgesellschaft, 1971)

World Bank, *World Development Report 1992* and *1993* (New York: Oxford University Press)

Yasin, Bu ʻAli, "Mauqiʻ al-tabaqa al-ʻamila fi al-mujtamaʻ al-suri" [The Position of the Working Class in Syrian Society], *Dirasat ʻarabiyya*, Vol 7 (October 1971), No. 12, pp 7–29

———— *Hikayat al-ard wa -l-fallah al-suri 1858–1979* [History of the Land and the Syrian Peasant, 1858–1979] (Beirut, 1979)

———— *al-Sulta al-ʻummaliyya ʻala wasaʼil al-intaj fi al-tatbiq al-suri wa-l-nazariyya al-ishtirakiyya* [Workers' Power over the Means of Production in the Syrian Practice and in Socialist Theory] (Beirut: Dar al-Haqaʼiq, 1979)

———— "Adwa' ʻala al-hayat al-thaqafiyya li- tabaqa al-ʻamila al-suriyya" [Spotlights on the Cultural Life of the Syrian Working Class], *Dirasat ʻarabiyya*, January 1980

———— "ʻAlaqat al-intaj fi al-rif al-suri baʻd tanfidh al-islah al-ziraʻi" [Production Relations in the Syrian Countryside after the Implementation of the Land Reform], in Economic Sciences Association of the SAR (ed), *Fifth Economic Tuesday Symposium on Economic Development in the Syrian Arab Region, Damascus, 14 January – 29 April 1986* (Damascus, n.d.)

Zakariyya, Khudr, "al-Muʼashshirat al-iqtisadiyya al-ijtimaʻiyya fi al-watan al-ʻarabi wa-madlulatuha al-mustaqbaliyya li-ʻamaliyyat al-tanmiya" [The Socio-Economic Indicators in the Arab Homeland and their Future Relevance for the Development Process], *Dirasat ʻarabiyya*, Vol 19 (April 1983), No. 6, pp 69–91

———— *al-Tarkib al-ijtimaʻi li-l-buldan al-namiya* [The Social Structure of Developing Countries] (Damascus: University of Damascus, 1986)

———— *al-Hijra al-dakhiliyya fi suriya – Nushuʼuha wa-tatawwuruha* [Internal Migration in Syria. Its Origins and Development] (Tunis: League of Arab States, n.d. [1988])

Index